Colonial Identity in the Atlantic World, 1500-1800

Colonial Identity in the Atlantic World,

❧ 1500-1800 *Edited by*

Nicholas Canny and Anthony Pagden

PRINCETON UNIVERSITY PRESS

Copyright © 1987 by Princeton University Press

Published by Princeton University Press, 41 William Street, Princeton,
New Jersey 08540
In the United Kingdom: Princeton University Press, Chichester, West Sussex

Library of Congress Cataloging-in-Publication Data

Colonial identity in the Atlantic world, 1500 1800
    Chiefly revised versions of essays presented at a seminar held in 1982 at the Institute for
Advanced Study, Princeton, N.J.
    Includes index.
    Contents: Introduction: colonial identity in the Atlantic world / John H. Elliott—The
formation of a colonial identity in Brazil / Stuart B. Schwartz—Identity formation in Spanish America / Anthony Pagden-[etc.]
        1. America—History—To 1810— Congresses. 2. Europe—Colonies—America—Con-
gresses. 3. Ireland—Civilization—Congresses. I. Canny, Nicholas P. II. Pagden, Anthony.
III. Institute for Advanced Study (Princeton, N.J.)

E18.82.C64   1987   909'.09812   87-2241
ISBN 0-691-05372-3 (alk. paper)
ISBN 0-691-00840-X (pbk.)

First Princeton Paperback printing, 1989

Publication of this book has been aided by a grant from the
Paul Mellon Fund of Princeton University Press

This book has been composed in Linotron Goudy

Princeton University Press books are printed on acid-free paper
and meet the guidelines for permanence and durability of the
Committee on Production Guidelines for Book Longevity of
the Council on Library Resources

Printed in the United States of America by Princeton Academic Press

10   9   8   7   6   5   4   3

to The Institute for Advanced Study

❧ Contents

๛ Acknowledgments

EARLIER versions of most of these essays were commissioned for a seminar held in 1982 at the Institute for Advanced Study. When it was mentioned at the seminar that Jack Greene was working on problems in relation to colonial West Indian society similar to the ones that were under discussion, it seemed appropriate that he should contribute to the volume. We are grateful to him for having agreed to do so and to John H. Elliott for setting the individual pieces in a broader context. The concluding remarks are of course our own, but they as well as some of the other essays in this book have benefited greatly from the comments of the two readers appointed by Princeton University Press. The views expressed in these essays were also sharpened by the criticisms and observations of the other participants in the Princeton seminar: Clifford Geertz, Albert Hirschman, John Murrin, P. E. Russell, and Kevin Sharpe. While acknowledging the help of all these individuals, we owe a special debt to Albert Hirschman, who has discussed the form and purpose of this volume with us at several stages in its development and whose habitual clarity has often made it possible for us to see what we were trying to achieve. We would also like to thank those officers of the Princeton University Press, in particular Joanna Hitchcock, who have encouraged and advised us from the beginning. The fluency of the volume has been greatly enhanced by the expert editing of Elizabeth Gretz.

Both we ourselves as editors of the collection and the other contributors are deeply indebted to the Andrew W. Mellon Foundation for the financial assistance that made its realization possible. Over the years 1979–1982 the Mellon Foundation gave a generous grant to the Institute for Advanced Study for a program to be operated jointly by the Schools of Historical Studies and Social Science. The theme of this three-year seminar was "self-perception, mutual perception, and historical development," and although neither of us was a formal participant, we were both Members in the School of Historical Studies in 1979–1980 and found in the theme of self-perception an idea that could be fruitfully used in our own work on colonization in Ireland and Mexico. It was out of this that the volume was born.

This acknowledgment will reveal our even greater debt to the Institute for Advanced Study. It was when we were both members there that the book was conceived; it is to the Director and Members of the Institute that we have been, in so many ways, most consistently indebted, and it is to them, as a token of our gratitude and affection, that this book is dedicated.

N.C.
A.P.

∾ Contributors

Nicholas Canny is Professor of Modern History in the National University of Ireland at University College, Galway.

John H. Elliott is Professor in the School of Historical Studies at the Institute for Advanced Study, Princeton.

Jack P. Greene is Andrew W. Mellon Professor in the Humanities at the Johns Hopkins University.

Anthony Pagden is Fellow of King's College and Lecturer in History at the University of Cambridge.

Gilles Paquet is Dean of the Faculty of Administration, University of Ottawa.

Stuart B. Schwartz is Professor of History at the University of Minnesota.

Jean-Pierre Wallot is Federal Archivist of Canada.

Michael Zuckerman is Professor of History at the University of Pennsylvania.

Colonial Identity in the Atlantic World, 1500-1800

1 ❧ Introduction: Colonial Identity in the Atlantic World

John H. Elliott

THIS VOLUME of essays represents a pioneer attempt to explore on a comparative basis a notional entity—the Atlantic colonial world. Whether the Atlantic colonial societies of the sixteenth, seventeenth, and eighteenth centuries can be successfully treated as joint members of an Atlantic community, with important common characteristics, rather than as individual entities with their own distinctive natures and problems, is for readers to judge for themselves. The general practice has been to discuss them in isolation, partly because of the immensity of the task involved in mastering vast quantities of information in a variety of languages and partly because the contrasts, for example, between the experience and the practices of French settlers in Canada and Portuguese settlers in Brazil appear so striking as to make any attempt to treat them in unison a nugatory exercise.

Historical compartmentalization, however, has its disadvantages. Intensity of research, whether on the Caribbean colonies, colonial Mexico, or British North America, has inevitably led to a narrowing of focus. Regions have been broken up into subregions and colonial empires have been fragmented into a congeries of individual historical units, leaving a great divide even between specialists working on the same empire. Historians of Peru sometimes find themselves barely within hailing distance of those of Mexico, and to historians of New England those of the Chesapeake may seem equally remote. The editors of this volume, one of them concerned with British overseas expansion and the other with Spanish, found in the course of discussions during a year spent at the Institute for Advanced Study that, in spite of the marked differences between the two colonizing powers, the settler communities which they established had a number of characteristics and problems in common. As a result of their discussions the editors felt that it might be of value to include other historians of the Atlantic colonial world in their debate, if only to determine whether the things that united them might not be as important as those that divided them. This volume is the outcome of their initiative.

The "Atlantic colonial world" of the sixteenth and seventeenth centu-

I SHOULD like to express my gratitude to Professor Stephen Innes of the University of Virginia for his discussion of the essays and an early draft of this introduction with me and for his valuable counsel and bibliographical guidance.

ries rightly conjures up visions of the New World of America, with its indigenous Indian populations. The inclusion of Ireland in this volume may therefore at first sight seem surprising. The crossing to Ireland may have been unpleasant, but the rigors of the voyage were hardly comparable to those involved in crossing "that frightful ocean"[1]—an experience that etched itself deep into the consciousness of generations of European migrants. Nor did the native Irish, however alien to the English settlers, have much in common with the American Indians. Or so at least one might imagine. But Nicholas Canny has sought to show in a number of publications how the colonization of Ireland was almost a laboratory experiment for the colonization of North America, and how the settlers saw it as their mission to introduce civility to an indigenous Irish population which in their eyes was as barbarous and unchristian as any in the Americas.[2] Ireland, as one of Europe's first overseas conquests and areas of settlement, would therefore seem to play an integral part in the Atlantic colonial story.

If one innovative feature of this book is its attempt to portray the Atlantic colonial world from Ireland to Brazil as a relatively homogenous unit, moving in common response to common requirements and pressures, another is the grand theme to which the contributors have addressed themselves. This volume is not just a reworking of the story of European transatlantic conquest and colonization, approached this time from a comparative standpoint. It is focused specifically on a great but neglected issue—the question of the formation of distinctive colonial identities. Much has been written on the consolidation and growth of colonial societies, and much, too, on the winds of change that began to blow through the Americas during the eighteenth century, reaching gale force in British North America in the 1770s and in Iberian America a generation later. The painful process of emancipation from the mother country has often been charted in meticulous detail, and its origins traced far back into the history of colonial society and the colonial mentality. But the essays here suggest that this teleological approach runs the risk of simplifying a frequently complex process of metropolitan-colonial dialectic, which by no means moves through logical stages to a preordained dénouement. In some instances the formation of a sense of identity may well precede independence, but in others, like Canada, the search for identity may follow rather

---

[1] Eliza Pinckney, quoted by Zuckerman, below.
[2] See especially N. P. Canny, *The Elizabethan Conquest of Ireland: A Pattern Established, 1565–1576* (Hassocks, Sussex, and New York, 1976), and his "The Permissive Frontier: The Problem of Social Control in English Settlements in Ireland and Virginia, 1550–1650," in *The Westward Enterprise: English Activities in Ireland, the Atlantic and America, 1480–1650*, ed. K. R. Andrews, N. P. Canny, and P.E.H. Hair (Liverpool, 1978), ch. 2.

than precede effective emancipation. In the effort to break loose from the constrictions of an approach that makes independence the end of the colonial story, the contributors were asked to consider the question of identity—of self-definition and self-image in their societies—as a subject of study in its own right, rather than as one necessarily tied to the more conventional history of the achievement of political independence.

What was it that encouraged these transplanted European communities to begin to think of themselves as in some ways distinct and separate from the mother country? Why did some colonies have more success than others in establishing a separate identity for themselves, and what held them back for so long from going one stage further and achieving both psychological and political emancipation? These are the central questions posed by this volume, and as readers will quickly appreciate for themselves, they raise some fascinating but complex problems of comparative history. At first sight, the sheer variety of the colonies under discussion may seem to make comparison almost worthless. The settlers came from mother countries that by the sixteenth century were already sharply differentiated in their legal and administrative systems and their institutional structures and that soon would be differentiated by religion as well. Great changes also occurred in both Europe and America in the century between the arrival of the first Spaniards on the American mainland and the settlement of the first English in the Chesapeake and New England. Not only were there major intellectual and religious upheavals in Europe itself during that intervening century, but the pioneering experiences of Spaniards and Portuguese in their New World settlements, especially in their dealings with the indigenous population, were bound to have an impact on the assumptions and expectations of colonists from other countries arriving in the New World two or three generations later. By the seventeenth century the New World conjured up visions in the European consciousness of gold and silver in abundance and of native Indian peoples lacking the rudiments of civility. These visions consciously or unconsciously shaped the attitudes and reactions of seventeenth-century colonists, differentiating them from the first generation of European arrivals, whose expectations of the New World had been formed exclusively in Europe.

There were enormous variations, too, in the types of emigrants and in the ideal societies which they envisioned. Many of them, whether from England or the Iberian peninsula, originally came with no intention of permanent settlement, planning to return home in due course with the riches they had won in the Indies. The presence of this restless element in Virginia or Mexico or Barbados clearly made it more difficult for the new overseas societies to strike roots and establish their own identities. But even

5

those emigrants who settled and stayed held widely differing views about the kind of society in which they wished to live. The sharpest of these differences were not necessarily those deriving from differences of nationality, important as these were. A Spanish hidalgo in Mexico and an English gentleman in Virginia may well have had more in common with each other than with merchant and artisan settlers from their own native countries when it came to envisaging the form of community they wished to establish. The essays below suggest the existence of divisions in the attitudes of settlers that transcend the conventional boundaries of nationality. Stuart Schwartz, for instance, writes that "in social or religious terms Brazil was created to reproduce Portugal, not to transform or transcend it," and he contrasts this ambition with the attempt of the Puritans of New England and the Quakers of Pennsylvania to escape from the corruption of the society they had left behind and to build their "city on the hill." But he also shows how two groups in Brazil, the Jesuits and the New Christians, did indeed dream of creating new and distinctive societies in the New World environment. The same holds true of colonial Mexico, where "the conquistador ambition to create a society of orders in all formal respects like that of Spain," as Anthony Pagden notes, coexisted with the ideal of missionaries who arrived with millenarian hopes of establishing in the New World a society purified of the vices of the Old. This Iberian version of the city on the hill brings the Franciscans of Mexico and the Jesuits of Brazil closer in some respects to the Puritans of New England than the Puritans found themselves to their own kith and kin in the Chesapeake colonies, discussed by Michael Zuckerman, or to the Barbados settlers, described by Jack Greene.

Further variations were introduced by the vast differences in the kinds of environment that were settled. The French trapper communities in Canada, described by Gilles Paquet and Jean-Pierre Wallot, were worlds away from the plantation societies of Barbados and Brazil. Yet in all the societies under discussion we can see similar processes at work. The new communities gradually take on a local coloring in response to their new environment—a local coloring that begins to set them apart from their country of origin. Paquet and Wallot write that in Canada, for instance, by the late seventeenth century the colonists, "both through their contacts with and their borrowings from Indian customs and through an effective shaking off of the constraints of the metropolitan plan, had managed to create new social types." Similarly, on the Amazonian rivers, the Brazilian colonists "adopted Indian forest crafts, foods, material culture, and customs," and spoke the local Indian language, Tupí, as Schwartz notes. The character of the environment, as determined by climate, ecology, and the presence or absence of large indigenous populations, was critical in creating patterns of settlement and behavior that again transcended national characteristics and produced colonial communities, like the plantation settlements in Barbados, Virginia, or in parts of Spanish America, which in several respects had more in common with each other than with the mother country or with communities of similar nationality in other parts of the Atlantic colonial world.

All these variations—some of them the result of differences of European background, and others of wide local and regional disparities in the areas of settlement—would seem at first sight to preclude any serious attempt to trace a collective process of self-definition among the Atlantic colonial communities. But there are certain overriding constants in the process of Atlantic migration and settlement. There was, first, the fact of the sea crossing itself, creating a sense of physical and even psychological separation from the mother country that made the New Englanders, for example, see the transatlantic voyage as "the decisive divide of their lives," as Zuckerman terms it. There was, too, the fact of confrontation on arrival with indigenous populations, densely settled in Mexico and Peru, less so in North America by the time of the arrival of the British (thanks in particular to the northward advance of the diseases brought from Europe by the Spaniards), but none the less menacing in their strangeness even where their actual behavior proved to be mild. All the migrants therefore found themselves confronted by essentially similar challenges. They had to work out a relationship, whether in Ireland, the Caribbean, or on the American mainland, with peoples who had come there long before them. Except where the newcomers extinguished the native populations, this involved attempting to subjugate, Christianize, and "civilize" them. At the same time the colonists had to work out their relationship to the land itself, to an essentially alien environment, with its own flora and fauna and its own potential, or lack of it, for development along preconceived European lines. In the Caribbean, Virginia, and Brazil, where native labor was insufficient to achieve the kind of development they had in mind, this involved importing African slaves, whose increasingly obvious presence in colonial communities would itself raise new and difficult problems of self-image and identity. Finally, as the new communities consolidated themselves, drawing on new waves of immigrants from the mother country and at the same time replicating themselves with children who knew no mother country but the one in which they were born, they were all faced with the same problem of attempting to establish a satisfactory relationship with a metropolis to which they owed allegiance and to which they were bound by a multiplicity of institutional, economic, and psychological ties.

Starting from these common experiences of migration and settlement, the contributors have very different stories to tell. But amidst all the variety, there appear to be a number of recurring characteristics which make it possible to determine at least some of the elements that either encouraged or militated against the achievement of a sense of identity in colonial societies. Yet it is important to be aware of the limitations inherent in any such inquiry. The very concept of "identity" in a colonial society is itself fraught with ambiguity. Whose identity is at issue, and what determines it? The authors of these essays are overwhelmingly concerned with the development of a self-image among colonial elites. Only Schwartz, in his examination of colonial Brazil, hints at the fact that another and very different story remains to be written—that of the development of a sense of identity among the less privileged groups in colonial society. Much energy, as he points out, has been invested in literary analysis, in the search for "nativist, localist, and ultimately nationalist sentiments among the educated poets, chroniclers, and epistolaries." But there is good reason to suspect that "a feeling of distinctiveness, a lack of identification with Europe, and a profound realization of the colonial reality existed precociously among the *mestiço* and mulatto population." The problem is to find the evidence that will allow us to examine the process of self-definition among the underprivileged in the same kind of detail as is likely to prove possible for the colonial elites.

There is also a danger of assuming that self-definition constitutes a linear process, whereby newborn societies progress by predetermined stages from a condition of total dependence on the mother country to a physical and psychological maturity that ends with full emancipation. Paquet and Wallot specifically reject this linear model as a device for the interpretation of Canadian history, and other contributors are at pains to emphasize the way in which the corporate sense of self in their colonial societies changes in response to changing internal and external circumstances. "No collective identity," writes Greene, "is static, and an analysis of its changing content reveals, perhaps as well as can the study of any other single phenomenon, the character of a given colony's responses to the successive social, economic, cultural, and political transformations it underwent." The sense of identity, as he insists, was both "place-specific and time-specific." Much also depended on which society was being used at any given moment as the yardstick against which a colonial community was defining itself. It was possible, for instance, for the dominant groups in a colony to assume a proud stance in relation to the mother country, while identifying themselves closely with it when faced either by external dangers or by perceived threats from other racial or national groups within the borders of their own communities. Canny, for example, shows how the New English in Ireland, who had been busily forging an Irish identity for themselves, hastily reverted to their British identity when unexpectedly confronted in 1641 by the Gaelic and Old English rebellion.

The problem, therefore, may be as much one of keeping track of shifting identities as of following the development of one specific sense of identity through time. These colonial societies, like all societies, were in constant process of defining and redefining themselves. But, as settlements and colonies that owed their existence to a distant mother country, they all found themselves trapped in the dilemma of discovering themselves to be at once the same, and yet not the same, as the country of their origin. The dilemma was made all the more acute by the fact, which emerges so clearly from all these essays, that without exception their countries of origin held them in low regard. Metropolitan contempt for provincial cousins seems to have known no bounds. To peninsular Spaniards the creole population of Mexico was as fickle and irrational as the Indian population among which it had settled. To the British, Bermuda was a "hideous and hated place," Barbados a "dunghill," and New England a "colluvies of wild opinionists." "He who knows Portugal and experiences Brazil," wrote an eighteenth-century Portuguese Jesuit quoted by Schwartz, "can surely say that he has fallen from heaven to hell."

The continuous bombardment of calumny to which settler communities were subjected gave them an early and powerful incentive to develop a more favorable image of themselves, if only in self-defense. Where the settlers lived in the midst of an allegedly "barbaric" native population, as in Ireland or Mexico, this meant in the first instance differentiating themselves from these alien peoples to whose characteristics they were assumed by misguided Europeans to have fallen victim, as if slothfulness, mendacity, and barbarism were some kind of contagious disease. But what elements could they draw upon to disabuse their malicious or uninformed critics and refurbish their image in a way that would allow them to hold their heads high in the world? Greene identifies four ingredients that went into the formation of a collective self-image—the sense of place, the identification of goals, the insistence on standards, and the sense of history. These would seem to be no less valid for the other communities under discussion, although the mixture of ingredients and the quantities available are different in each.

The sense of place—the realization that their newly adopted land, though initially strange, had distinctive beauties of its own—clearly played an important part in developing a local patriotism that was essential to the formation of a collective self-image. But in one of the paradoxes that runs through the whole history of metropolitan-colonial relationships, the colonists, even while coming to appreciate the qualities that made their environment unique, devoted a great deal of time and energy to making it resemble as closely as possible the environment they had left behind. In his book *Changes in the Land*, William Cronon has emphasized the importance of the settlers' perception of the landscape in determining the fate of the new colonies.[3] The perception of the North American landscape by the seventeenth-century immigrants, based as it was on Old World assumptions and expectations, was profoundly different from that of its native Indian inhabitants, and English perceptions were to have a drastic impact on the land's subsequent appearance, as it was put to new uses to satisfy new requirements and aspirations. To perceive a landscape was to endow it in the mind's eye with a distinctive shape and purpose, suggesting what it might become if put to "proper" use. This meant, for example, constructing English-style country houses in English-style parks. The contributors to this volume have little opportunity to do more than touch on the neglected question of colonial architecture, which vividly epitomizes the dilemma of communities caught between their desire to ape metropolitan fashions in order to show themselves the equals of their countrymen at home, and the need to construct buildings that would enable them to live in some comfort in what was often a very different climate from that of the mother country. The demands of gentility made them yet another cultural province of a distant European metropolis, but at the same time this did not preclude the growth within a transatlantic cultural system of a local vernacular, borrowing where necessary from the high culture, but firmly rooted in local customs and needs.[4]

Transformation of the landscape by the construction of European-style cities and houses constitutes a striking example of the way in which one of the ingredients in the formation of a corporate sense of identity—a sense of place—could be affected by another, the identification of specific goals. In 1705 a first-generation Virginian, Robert Beverley, described the Virginian landscape as one that was richly endowed but still deficient in many of the characteristics of an idealized English countryside. Some twenty years later there were encouraging signs of "improvements" that were steadily narrowing the gap between the ideal and the actual.[5] One of the most striking features of these colonial societies is the frequency of their resort to the lan-

[3] New York, 1983.

[4] See the suggestive essay by Richard L. Bushman, "American High-Style and Vernacular Cultures," in *Colonial British America*, ed. Jack P. Greene and J. R. Pole (Baltimore and London, 1984).

[5] See Rhys Isaac, *The Transformation of Virgina, 1740–1790* (Chapel Hill, 1982), pp. 13–17.

10

guage of improvement. Canny notes that in Ireland the earl of Cork insisted that his new tenants improve the land, while woods were cut down to develop the iron industry. "The language of improvement," writes Jack Greene, "was ubiquitous in the early-modern British world." But it was by no means restricted to that world. Francisco López de Gómara, in his *History of the Indies*, published in 1552, writes approvingly of the extent to which Hispaniola and New Spain had been "improved" by the Spanish settlers, and one of those same settlers, Gonzalo Fernández de Oviedo, recounts proudly how "we found no sugar mills when we arrived in these Indies, and all these we have built with our own hands and industry in so short a time."[6]

There was good reason for this insistence on improvement. On the one hand, it countered the prevailing assumption in the mother country that all colonists were endemically idle. On the other, it helped to legitimate their enterprise in their own eyes and also—or so they hoped—in those of their fellow countrymen. It provided them with a sense of purpose and helped to place them in a divine order of things, which was perceived in essentially developmental terms. Canny writes that the New English in Ireland cited the "material benefits that would derive from the implementation of the proposed conquest and colonization of Ireland as evidence of its godly purpose." It also, no doubt, helped to assuage feelings of guilt about their treatment of the native population. The sense of being engaged in a civilizing mission, whether in Ireland, Virginia, or Mexico, was a potent element in creating a corporate sense of identity among settler societies which found themselves consistently misunderstood and abused by their European critics.

A society like that of colonial Massachusetts, with its very specific collective goals and its exalted sense of its unique place in the divine plan, had no reason to suffer from that nagging consciousness of inferiority to the mother country that afflicted the white populations of Virginia, Barbados, or Mexico. New England's crisis of identity seems to have come when the second and third generation of colonists measured themselves not against the standards of the mother country but against those of their own founding fathers and found themselves sadly wanting.[7] For them, the development of a collective historical consciousness led to a disturbing process of self-questioning and self-doubt. But elsewhere in the Atlantic colonial world it would appear to have had a positive effect in helping to promote a more confident self-image. In colonial Mexico, as Anthony Pagden shows, a collective historical consciousness could be built up over the generations on

[6] See J. H. Elliott, *The Old World and the New* (Cambridge, 1970), p. 78.
[7] Perry Miller, *Errand into the Wilderness* (Cambridge, Mass., 1956), ch. 1.

the basis of the heroic feats of the conquerors and first settlers, the Christianization and civilization of the indigenous population, and the development of the land. By the late seventeenth century, as Siguenza y Góngora's triumphal arch of 1681 vividly illustrates, the creoles felt confident enough to be able to incorporate their former Aztec adversaries, suitably mythologized, into their national pantheon. This was a luxury that their Peruvian kinsmen, more troubled by the potential for rebellion of their Indian population, felt less able to afford.

If the creoles of Mexico were unique in their ability to incorporate the figure of the heroic Indian into their historical self-image, the development of a historical consciousness, however partial and restricted, made it possible for colonial communities undergoing the process of transformation from societies of immigrants to societies of natives to reassess their situation in relation to mother countries which by turns neglected and exploited them. But the essays below raise interesting questions about why some of these societies were more successful than others in forging a sense of historical self-awareness. To what extent, for example, did the absence of a printing press in Brazil hold up the process of identity formation? How much did the absence of universities in Brazil or the West Indies, and their consequent continuing dependence on the home country for higher education, reduce those societies' chances of establishing a firm sense of their own identities in comparison with Mexico or New England, which had their own universities?

The usefulness of a volume devoted to the history of a number of different societies lies precisely in the possibilities it offers for raising questions of this kind—questions that may well not emerge when only one society is under consideration. It is for this reason that comparative studies have an outstanding part to play in stimulating new historical inquiry and research. Any conscientious reader of this book is likely to come away from it not only with new information but also new ideas and questions, including questions about metropolitan attitudes as well as colonial reactions. The contributors have barely touched on the differences in the imperial policies adopted by England, Spain, Portugal, and France and the way in which these may have assisted or impeded the process of identity formation in the colonies. Nor have they considered the effect of warfare between the European powers on the transatlantic societies. Problems of imperial defense, which required increasingly heavy fiscal and military contributions, did much to promote the sense of a distinctive identity in British and Spanish America alike.[8]

[8] On this point in relation to the British North American colonies, see John M. Murrin, "Political Development," in Greene and Pole, *Colonial British America*, pp. 446–47.

The very absence of discussion of major issues like these is an indication of the pioneering quality of these essays. All too often where they fall silent it is because the research has never been done. But they perform the great service of bringing on to center stage the fascinating question of self-image in the infinitely complicated history of the triangular relationship of mother country, colonists, and subject populations during the age of Atlantic colonization and settlement. In this period, "holding on" and "breaking away" were for a long time half-options in which profit and loss, hope and disillusionment, interest and risk endlessly counterbalanced each other in uneasy equilibrium. In some of these societies there were conspiracies and rebellions—however unsuccessful—against the dominance of the mother country. In others there were not. "Breaking away" had first to be thought before it could happen, and the unthinkable would not have become thinkable without a prior process of self-definition. It is this process of self-definition, sometimes advancing, sometimes regressing, but never static, that the contributors have sought to analyze.

2 ～ The Formation of a Colonial Identity in Brazil

Stuart B. Schwartz

IN 1830, during the considerable political turmoil that preceded the abdication of Brazil's first independent monarch, Dom Pedro I, a political broadsheet appeared on the streets of Santo Amaro, Bahia, calling for the emperor's resignation and appealing for the accession of his young son, Prince Dom Pedro, whom it called "cabra como nós" (colored like us). The meaning here was that the young heir-apparent was Brazilian-born while his father was European and still associated with the old colonial ties, but the word *cabra* in Brazil was in reality a term of racial description, referring to one of the intermediate racial categories resulting from miscegenation. Little blue-eyed, blond-haired Pedro was no cabra in the usual sense, but the fact that such a word might be used as a designation of his nationality signified a transformation in the perception and discourse of national sentiments in Brazil.[1] The use of such a term to describe the monarch certainly did not portend the crumbling of the color bar or the hierarchy of racial status, but the identification of the nation with such formerly despised elements as the mixed-bloods or more commonly with a romanticized version of the Indian was an important sea change of self-perception.

In the case of Portuguese America, we must view the creation of a distinct colonial identity not only within the context of the changing economic conditions and opportunities of the colonial compact but also as an extension of the attitudes associated with a multiracial slave-based society. How Brazilians were seen and how they saw themselves in relationship to each other profoundly influenced how they viewed their relationship to the metropolis.

The question of national consciousness or self-awareness in the American colonies has too often been treated in isolation from the social and political context within the colony. The matter of colonial distinctiveness is essentially one of collective mentality, but the evidence used to perceive the commonly shared ideals and perceptions of the *vox populi* is, in Brazil at least, generally limited to the production of a tiny group of literati, all of

THE AUTHOR wishes to thank Professor Dauril Alden for providing copies of unpublished documents and Professors Russell Menard and Richard Graham for helpful criticism.

[1] Arquivo Público da Bahia (Salvador) [hereafter APB], Presidencia da provincia 1.425 (22 October 1830).

whom belonged to the colonial aristocracy, the bureaucracy, or the clergy. A great deal of "chronicler combing" has characterized Brazilian literary analysis, as critics search for nativist, localist, and ultimately nationalist sentiments among the educated poets, chroniclers, and epistolaries. One suspects, however, that a feeling of distinctiveness, a lack of identification with Europe, and a profound realization of the colonial reality existed precociously among the *mestiço* and mulatto populations. They, unlike the colonial elite that was composed of immigrants and the white American-born children of European parents, had no particular attachment to Portugal, nor did they feel the pull of sentiments in conflicting directions. The European deprecation of things American and especially of mixed-bloods from the early sixteenth century was not ignored by the nonwhite Brazilians. The problem for the historian, however, is to isolate and recapture these sentiments in an essentially inchoate and illiterate populace. In the search for colonial consciousness the issue of class or social hierarchy cannot be ignored; I wish at the outset to make clear the sense of incompleteness and loss that this limitation creates.

The Portuguese colonial enterprise in America began, it would seem, by accident when in 1500 an expedition, organized to continue the seaborne contact established with India by Vasco da Gama two years before, made an unexpected landfall on Brazil's tropical shore en route to Asia. For the first thirty years Brazil was very much a colonial afterthought, coming far behind the spices and riches of the Orient in Portuguese calculations. An attempt to shift the burden of colonization and settlement to private initiative through royal concessions had only limited success and by 1549, when a rudimentary royal government was established in the colony, it was still a secondary concern of the crown. With the growth of a sugar industry and the subjugation or elimination of the coastal Indian populations by warfare, disease, and missionary effort, the colony began to take form and to increase in importance. From about 1570 to 1670 Brazil was the world's leading exporter of sugar and, as the spice trade to India was beset by shipwrecks, foreign competition, and other difficulties, Brazil began to figure prominently as Portugal's essential colony in economic terms, if not in prestige.

During the mid-seventeenth century, while Brazil enjoyed a position as Europe's major supplier of sugar, political events dragged the colony into the vortex of European rivalries. The union of Spain and Portugal (1580–1640) made Brazil a prime target for Habsburg enemies. The Dutch, cut off from their traditional trade with the Portuguese, attacked and captured a large portion of northeastern Brazil, the major area of sugar production. Portugal's separation from Spain in 1640 led to a peace treaty with the

Dutch, but the Portuguese living in Dutch Brazil, restive under Protestant rule and heavily in debt to the Dutch West India Company, rose in revolt in 1645. After nine years of guerrilla campaigns the Dutch were expelled; the fact that Portugal was officially at peace with the Hollanders led to a view of this victory as essentially one of the colonials. Since that time Brazilians have seen the Dutch war as the beginnings of their nationality.

The colony entered into a period of hard times after 1670. Foreign competition in tropical crops and a general crisis in the Atlantic economy caused considerable economic dislocation, but the discovery of gold in the interior seemed to provide a panacea. A rush to the mines began about 1695 as whites, slaves, and a new wave of Portuguese immigrants flooded the gold washings. Brazil became, in the words of the Portuguese monarch, his "milch cow"; governmental control over the colony was tightened in order to protect the newly valuable asset. The production of gold crested in the 1760s and then began to decline, leaving in its wake, however, a distinctive cultural and intellectual tradition in Minas Gerais, the center of the mining activity.

Declining gold revenues, increasing governmental deficits, costly international conflicts, and low prices for Brazilian agricultural commodities in Atlantic markets created a situation by the mid-eighteenth century that called for drastic remedies. The architect of the reforms, the marquis of Pombal (1750–1777), launched a series of programs designed to strengthen the Portuguese empire; Brazil, by this time clearly the keystone of that structure, figured prominently in his plans. Monopoly companies aimed at regional development in the colony were created, new products were sponsored, new taxes were introduced, and efforts were made to foment trade. Active and forceful royal officials arrived in Brazil to carry out the policies of Pombal's version of enlightened despotism. Social and political reforms accompanied alterations in commerce and economy. Pombal expelled the Jesuits from the Portuguese empire in 1759. Educational reforms were instituted in Portugal and Brazil and a secularization of the Indian population was attempted.

Many of the marquis' reforms were ill-conceived and others bore little fruit before he fell from power in 1777, but in the following two decades changing market conditions created a powerful stimulus for a dramatic rise in Brazilian exports—sugar, tobacco, cotton, hides, indigo, and cacao. To some extent Pombal's programs had laid the basis on which this late colonial boom could take place. It did so, nevertheless, by the use of traditional methods and techniques and without any great transformation of the social organization of the colony. Slavery was intensified, with the level of slave imports increasing by two-thirds in the period between 1780–1785 and

1801–1805, the plantation system expanded into new areas, and the colonial elite was not displaced from a limited role in government or from their position of social dominance.

Brazil's burgeoning economy at the close of the eighteenth century altered the nature of Portugal's place in the Atlantic world. Portugal's former deficitary trade relationship with Great Britain and France was reversed so that by 1791 the balance shifted in Portugal's favor, largely on the basis of Brazilian products. But this in turn created a trade imbalance between Portugal and its own colony, which now acquired large amounts of manufactured goods directly from British "smugglers."[2] Currency flowed from the metropolis to the colony and the colonial relationship was inverted. Brazilians began to agitate for political and economic changes, including free trade and a lessening of metropolitan control, and a few colonials were swept up in the winds of revolutionary political change abroad in the 1780s and 1790s. Matters in Brazil might have followed the course of events in Spanish America had not Napoleon's army driven the Portuguese court to seek refuge in Brazil under the protection of British guns. Instead, from the arrival of the court in 1808 to its return in 1822, Brazilians sought to have Brazil become the metropolis rather than to break away from it. Their inability to do so and Portugal's attempt to return to the colonial status quo eventually brought the political rupture in 1822, but with a son of the Portuguese king on the throne as an independent monarch in Brazil.

The Colonists and the Colony

At its origins Brazil was modeled on Portugal's other overseas possessions. During the first thirty years when contact was intermittent and essentially carried out by private contractors, the model seems to have been the *feitorias* or trading stations of the West African coast, but with the creation of donatarial captaincies in the 1530s, a shift toward a plan for colonization somewhat akin to Portugal's previous experience in Madeira can be seen.[3] Unlike uninhabited Madeira or the Azores, the Portuguese encountered in Brazil a previously unknown "savage," non-Christian people, and the crown by the mid-sixteenth century pointed to its responsibilities as a bearer of the cross as the reason for its conquest in Brazil. The missionary effort from this point forward always stood alongside economic motives in Portuguese considerations or justifications of their presence in Brazil.

[2] Fernando A. Novais, *Portugal e Brasil na crise do antigo sistema colonial (1777–1808)* (São Paulo, 1979) and José Jobson de A. Arruda, *O Brasil no comercio colonial* (São Paulo, 1980) are two fundamental monographs on the changing relationship between Brazil and Portugal in this period.
[3] Harold B. Johnson, "The Donatary Captaincy in Perspective: Portuguese Backgrounds to the Settlement of Brazil," *Hispanic American Historical Review* 52, 2 (May 1972):203–214.

In social or religious terms Brazil was created to reproduce Portugal, not to transform or transcend it. There was no attempt there to create a "city on the hill," as the Puritans would do in New England, or a Quaker commonwealth, as in Pennsylvania. Instead, traditional forms of governance and settlement, modified to the new reality, were implanted in the colony.[4] Catholicism and Portuguese law provided uniformities in each of the settlements and the donatarial captaincies and land grants (*sesmarias*) provided the means by which a reproduction of Portuguese seigneurialism could be created.

Only for two groups, unlikely companions, did Brazil present a canvas on which they hoped to paint a new society. The Jesuits, caught up in the first rush of missionary fervor in the sixteenth century, saw in the new land and its thousands of unconverted inhabitants a chance to create a great Christian mission state.[5] The early Jesuit letters make it clear that they saw Brazil as their enterprise, a position that came increasingly into conflict with that of the colonists. Similarly, for the forced converts from Judaism, the so-called New Christians, Brazil presented a place to create a refuge, freer of the threats and constraints under which they lived in Europe. New Christians and Jesuits became the most ardent propagandizers for the new land.[6] The majority of the colonists, however, saw in Brazil opportunities to achieve wealth and thus to live according to the "law of nobility," without recourse to trade, craft, manual labor, or base occupation. Brazil was, to them, a place to rise within the traditional social order. Their mobility was made possible by the existence of an indigenous population and later by imported Africans, who provided the labor upon which society was constructed. While edenic images and motivations were always present, they tended to become subordinated to traditional goals and patterns of social organization.

In the action of colonial formation there are two related but somewhat

[4] Cf. Jack P. Greene, "Search for Identity: An Interpretation of the Meaning of Selected Patterns of Social Response in Eighteenth-Century America," *Journal of Social History* 3, 3 (Spring 1970):189–219. There is a copious literature on the formation of Brazilian national character. Some important examples are Gilberto Freyre, *Casa grande e Senzala* (Rio de Janeiro, 1933); Sérgio Buarque de Holanda, *Raices do Brasil* (Rio de Janeiro, 1936); José Honório Rodrigues, *Aspirações nacionais* (São Paulo, 1963).

[5] The classic work on the Jesuits is Serafim Leite, *História da Companhia de Jesus no Brasil*, 10 vols. (Lisbon, 1938–50), but on this issue the now overlooked work by Robert Ricard is informative. See Robert Ricard, "Les Jesuites au Bresil pedant la seconde moitc su xvi siècle (1549–1597)," *Revue d'histoire des missions* 3 (September 1937):321–66, 4 (December 1937):435–70.

[6] Arnold Wiznitzer, *The Jews of Colonial Brazil* (New York, 1960). Cf. Sérgio Buaruqe de Holanda, *Visão do paraiso* (Rio de Janeiro, 1959). See also José Gonsalves Salvador, *Cristãos-novos, Jesuitas e inquisição* (São Paulo, 1969).

19

distinct processes that call for examination. The first is the growth of a colonial identity, that is, the definition of the colonists as somehow different from their metropolitan compatriots—a transition from immigrant to native. The second is a recognition of this distinctiveness as transcending localism to the point that separateness from the mother country becomes a viable intellectual (and ultimately, political) position. This second position logically but not necessarily flows from the first.

For about a century and a half (1500–c. 1660) the colonists in Brazil were predominantly European-born and strongly identified themselves with Portugal. Father Manuel da Nóbrega complained in 1549 that Brazil needed farmers who would settle and remain, instead of officials who only wished to pocket their salaries. "They do not love the land," he said, "and all their affection is for Portugal."[7] Similar criticism was made in the early seventeenth century. Ambrósio Fernandes Brandão cited five types of colonists, all of whom were more interested in personal profit than in developing the colony, and of them the sailors, merchants, and planters all wished to return to Portugal.[8] The first thing the colonists taught their pet parrots was "parrot royale, back to Portugal," and if goods and chattels could be similarly taught to speak, they, too, would have learned the phrase, said Brazil's first historian in 1627.[9]

The Portuguese emigration to overseas conquests and colonies began in the fifteenth century. By 1534 the poet Garcia de Resende could muse that so many people had left for Brazil and the Atlantic islands and the flow of African slaves to Portugal was so great that the nation was becoming black. Despite some poetic license, Resende's observation underlined the fact that Portugal had a relatively small population of about one million in this period, and the outflow of about 3,500 immigrants a year was perceptible. The Portuguese historian Magalhães Godinho estimates that between 1500 and 1580 some 280,000 people emigrated from Portugal and another 300,000 in the following sixty years. By 1760 between a million and a million and a half people had emigrated, a rate of departure of 2.5 to 3 persons per 1,000 during the period. This tide of emigration to India, East and West Africa, and the Atlantic islands as well as Brazil is all the more impressive given the fact that Portugal's population during this whole period never exceeded three million souls.[10]

---

[7] Serafim Leite, ed., *Cartas do Brasil e mais escritos do P. Manuel da Nóbrega* (Coimbra, 1965), p. 114.

[8] José Antônio Gonçalves de Mello, ed., *Diálogos das grandezas do Brasil*, 2d ed. (Recife, 1966), pp. 9–11.

[9] Frei Vicente do Salvador, *História do Brasil 1500–1627*, 5th ed. (São Paulo, 1965), ch. 2, pp. 58–59.

[10] Vitorino Magalhães Godinho, "L'emigration portugaise (xv⁰–xx siècles): Une constante structurale et les réponses aux changements du monde," *Revista de história económica e social* 1 (January–June 1978):5–32. See also Joel Serrão, *Emigração portuguesa* (Lisbon, 1971).

In its first century Brazil was not particularly favored as a place for emigration, nor were those who went there held in much regard. "God save me and free me from Brazil," says a character in one of Gil Vicente's plays, dated 1518.[11] The land of dyewood, parrots, and cannibal Indians seemed to hold little attraction in comparison with the spices and riches of India and the attention of the Portuguese was riveted on the latter, as the works of João de Barros, Camões, and Diogo de Couto attest. In Brazil, the Portuguese tried by means of grants to minor nobles (*capitanias*) to shift the burden of colonization to private initiative. In addition, convicts and penal exiles were sent to colonize the tropical coast. The first royal governor, Thomé de Sousa, brought four hundred of these *degredados* to Bahia in 1549 and others arrived regularly in the sixteenth century. Debtors, petty criminals, and crypto-Jews were all among the penal exiles and from time to time the crown dispatched small numbers of "honorable" orphan girls to make up the deficit of marriageable European women.[12] Degredados were not universally welcomed. Duarte Coelho, donatary of Pernambuco, refused to accept them and called them worse than the plague.[13] A royal judge complained that there were so few colonists with the minimal social standing needed for holding public office that he had seen municipal officials who had lost their ears for some crime in Portugal.[14] The seventeenth-century Portuguese soldier-author, Luís Mendes de Vasconcellos, wrote that "Brazil was populated by penal exiles, people taken from the kingdom to its advantage." This opinion, which generations of Brazilian historians have subsequently combated, underlined the low esteem in which Brazil and its inhabitants were generally held.[15]

Brazil was a place for convicts, but also a place to become rich. Even a penal exile like João Pais Barreto in Pernambuco could own plantations and many Indian slaves, and settlers with four or six Indian slaves could live comfortably and slowly enrich themselves.[16] The poor emigrants who arrived, according to the chronicler Magalhães de Gandavo, were helped by those already established and no "poor man went begging from door to door as in Portugal."[17] The colonists wished to re-create Portugal but their pur-

[11] *Auto da Barca do Purgatório* (1518) in Gil Vicente, *Obras completas* (Lisbon, 1961), 2:99.

[12] Tales de Azevedo, *Povoamento da cidade do Salvador* (Salvador, 1969), pp. 104–105.

[13] José Antônio Gonçalves de Mello and Cleonir Xavier de Albuquerque, eds., *Cartas de Duarte Coelho e El Rei* (Recife, 1967), pp. 42–43.

[14] See the discussion of Pero Borges' letter in Stuart Schwartz, *Sovereignty and Society in Colonial Brazil* (Berkeley, 1973), pp. 29–30.

[15] Luís Mendes de Vasconcellos, *Do sitio de Lisboa*, 3d ed. (Lisbon, 1803).

[16] On Barreto see *Cartas de Duarte Coelho*, p. 26; Pero Magalhães de Gandavo, *História da provincia de Santa Cruz* (São Paulo, 1964), p. 34.

[17] Gandavo, *História*, p. 34.

suit of wealth had its disadvantages, for it upset the metropolitan social hierarchies of status, race, and wealth. The settlers of Brazil, said Gandavo, "shed their humble manners that they were forced to use by poverty and necessity in Portugal; and their *mestiço* sons shed their red skins like snakes and used the most honorific titles in everything."[18] The linking of sexual promiscuity, mixture of the races, and an unbridled quest for wealth seems to have characterized opinions about the early colonists. "This people of Brazil," said Father Manuel da Nóbrega, "gives consideration to nothing but sugar mills and property although it be with the perdition of all the world's souls."[19] By the 1580s the planters of Pernambuco were described as living like counts, in a life of largesse, extravagance, and ostentation. There was "more vanity in Pernambuco than in Lisbon."[20] These were classic descriptions of a nouveau-riche society.

There are no adequate demographic statistics from Brazil's first century that permit an examination of the composition of the population, but the records of the two inquisitorial investigations of 1591–1593 and 1618 reveal the names and social characteristics of 3,426 individuals who appeared as accused, accusers, and witnesses before the tribunal.[21] Although the Inquisition's concern with crypto-Judaism makes its records unrepresentative of the colony's population, they do provide some idea of the ratio of native-born inhabitants among the residents in northeastern Brazil. First, about 10 percent of all persons mentioned had lived in Brazil at some time but had then returned to Portugal; if the mestiços, slaves, and Indians are excluded, that ratio rises to about 25 percent. Even after one hundred years of Portuguese control, movement back from the colony was still important. About one-half of all those who are mentioned in the two inquests were born in Portugal (42 percent), the Atlantic islands of Madeira and the Azores (9 percent), or Portuguese Africa (1 percent). Even if we include all those for whom no place of birth can be established with the Brazilian-born, that total is still less than 50 percent. These imperfect figures indicate that as late as the seventeenth century the white population of the colony was predominantly European by birth. As might be expected, this popula-

---

[18] As cited in John Hemming, *Red Gold: The Destruction of the Brazilian Indians, 1500–1760* (Cambridge, 1978), p. 77.

[19] Leite, *Cartas Nóbrega*, p. 346.

[20] Fernão Cardim, *Tratados da terra e gente do Brasil* (São Paulo, 1978), pp. 201–202.

[21] Tarcizio do Rêgo Quirino, *Os habitantes do Brasil no fim do século xvi* (Recife, 1966) is an early study based only on the 1591–1593 visit. Rêgo Quirino discusses the unrepresentative nature of the sample as a measure of the colony's whole population. A large sample but less fully analyzed is found in Sonia A. Siqueira, "A inquisição portuguesa e a sociedade colonial," 2 vols. (thesis of Livre-Docênica, São Paulo, 1972), 1:132–60. Unfortunately, much of this material does not appear in her book of the same title (São Paulo, 1978).

tion was also predominantly male and over half of them were bachelors or widowers.

The impression given by these numbers is of a colonial population still heavily European in origin and closely tied to the metropolis. Although the population of mixed or African origin increased during the seventeenth century, the close tie to Portugal remained strong. Not only was Brazil still essentially a plantation colony economically oriented toward export and dependent on Europe for most manufactured goods, its colonial elite was constantly penetrated and rejuvenated by arrivals of young men from the metropolis. In Bahia as late as the period 1680 to 1720, about one-third of the planters (senhores de engenho) were themselves immigrants and another 20 percent were the sons of immigrants.[22] The Brazilian planter class was not a closed, self-perpetuating aristocracy and seems always to have been particularly open to Portuguese merchants, who then either bought sugar works or made marriages with colonial women that eventually resulted in landed property. There was by the end of the seventeenth century a colonial aristocracy made up of fourth- and fifth-generation colonials, but there was little to distinguish them from the sons of immigrants in terms of prestige, success, and selection for local offices.[23] Eighteenth-century genealogies confirm the fact that many of the dominant families of the northeast originated with immigrants who arrived in the mid- or late 1660s, a century and a half or more after the foundation of the colony.[24]

Merchants, as we might expect, were predominantly European-born. A sample drawn in the 1680–1725 period showed that of 132 merchants resident in Bahia, 87 percent were born in continental Portugal or the Atlantic islands; only 6 percent were Brazilian-born. Whereas in the eighteenth century the landowning elites became increasingly colonial in origin, the merchant class remained essentially European to such an extent that the term commerciante and mescate (peddlar) became virtually synonymous with Portuguese. Merchants, even those who married and settled in Brazil, tended to prefer other immigrants or European relatives as agents, representatives, and partners. A common pattern seems to have been for an immigrant merchant to marry in Brazil and direct his sons into sugar planting or the professions but invite a nephew or cousin from Portugal to assume

[22] Rae Jean Flory, "Bahian Society in the Mid-Colonial Period: The Sugar Planters, Tobacco Growers, Merchants, and Artisans of Salvador and the Reconcavo, 1680–1725" (Ph.D. diss., University of Texas, 1978), pp. 101–104.

[23] Ibid.

[24] For example, Father Antônio de S. Maria Jaboatão, "Catálogo genealógico das principaes famílias (1768)," Revista do Instituto Histórico e Geográfico Brasileiro 52 (1889):5–484; Pedro Taques de Almeida Pães Leme, Nobiliarquia paulistana histórica e genealógica, 3 vols., 5th ed. (São Paulo, 1980).

the direction of the business.[25] Even at the close of the colonial era the merchant community was overwhelmingly Peninsula-born. Of 180 merchants registered in Salvador in the period 1790 to 1807, 78 percent were Portuguese by birth.[26]

Most of the immigrants who arrived were not merchants but threadbare bachelors, landing on the docks with a "few dirty bags and lice," in the pungent image of the Bahian poet Gregório de Mattos. "The Portuguese overtaken by any misfortune emigrates thither," said another observer in 1645, and during the hard years of the 1670s in Portugal every ship deposited a few dozen peasants on the shore of Bahia, according to an eyewitness.[27] As in most migrations, regional and local ties were maintained. Overpopulated northern Portugal provided the majority of the immigrants. In Pernambuco those from Viana do Castelo predominated and Bahia was referred to as a colony of Minho.[28] What attracted them were the obvious opportunities for social mobility made possible by slavery. A popular folk song in Portugal said, "God take you to Pernambuco and return you with such riches that even the King of Denmark could not equal your successes."[29]

Colonists, royal officials, travelers, and residents perceived Brazil within the same mental framework that Europeans generally developed to accommodate the New World. In this the Portuguese seem little different from other Europeans.[30] In the earliest reports there is a strain of wonder, enthusiasm, and excitement. The strange flora, the exotic animals and geography, and most of all, the indigenous inhabitants elicited vivid descriptions like that found in the letter of Pero Vaz de Caminha.[31] Others

[25] Flory, "Bahian Society," pp. 217–81. See also David G. Smith, "The Mercantile Class of Portugal and Brazil in the Seventeenth Century: A Socio-Economic Study of the Merchants of Lisbon and Bahia, 1620–1690" (Ph.D. diss., University of Texas, 1975).

[26] Catherine Lugar, "The Merchant Community of Salvador, Bahia, 1780–1830" (Ph.D. diss., State University of New York, Stony Brook, 1980), pp. 53–56.

[27] Statement of Gaspar Dias Ferreira (1645) cited in Charles Boxer, The Golden Age of Brazil (Berkeley, 1964).

[28] Father Fernão Cardim witnessed in Pernambuco the marriage of a local belle to a man from Viana, "the principal persons of the land" (Tratados da terra e gente do Brasil [São Paulo, 1978], p. 30); on Bahia see Orlando Ribeiro, Aspectos e problemas da expensão portuguesa (Lisbon, 1965), p. 111.

[29] Reproduced in Joel Serrão, ed., Testemunhas sobre a emigração portuguesa: Antologia (Lisbon, 1976), pp. 60–61.

[30] Cf. John H. Elliott, The Old World and the New (Cambridge, 1970); Michael T. Ryan, "Assimilating New Worlds in the Sixteenth and Seventeenth Centuries," Comparative Studies in Society and History 23, 4 (October 1981):519–38; Regina Maria Paulino de Melo e Cruz, "O Brasil visto pela cultura francesa do século xviii" (Licenciate thesis, University of Lisbon, 1964).

[31] The best edition in English is William B. Greenlee, ed., The Voyage of Pedro Alvares Cabral to Brazil and India (London, 1938).

followed along this path. In addition, another line of argument developed that saw Brazil as an "earthly paradise" in a literal sense. Not only do we find authors like the Francisan Frei Vicente do Salvador, who believed that in the future Brazil would be a great country, but quite early the Jesuits promoted the new land as an extraordinary place. Said one Jesuit in 1560, "if there is a paradise here on earth, it is, I would say, this Brazil"; he then proceeded to compare the climate, food, and animals favorably with Portugal and even suggested that Brazilian water was superior to Portuguese wine. Among the Jesuits this theme continued. The work of Father Simão de Vasconcelos, *Crônica da Compania de Jesús do Estado do Brasil* (1663), contained a long section in defense of Brazil, once again emphasizing its paradisical aspects.[32] Along with the Jesuits, the other group that saw Brazil as a great country of the future and for their enterprise in the present were the New Christians. Their writings are filled with an admiration of this land that seemed to them so far from the control of the ecclesiastical and royal officers. A New Christian in 1632 in Bahia stated that "those who live in the kingdom are mad not to live here in Brazil where they can be at their ease."[33]

Such euphoria was matched on the negative side by the many Europeans who found Brazil to be a dirty, uncouth, and unpleasant place, lacking in social and cultural amenities and severely handicapped by its large black and mulatto population. Jesuit brother Ignácio Brandão wrote in Bahia in 1746 that "he who knows Portugal and experiences Brazil can surely say that he has fallen from heaven to hell and if God takes accounts of this land, I believe it will be a perpetual hell."[34] High-ranking colonial administrators in particular found Brazil an unpleasant exile and the Brazilians to have many deficiencies. The count of Sabugosa complained in 1734 that "the crime of falsehood is so common that I am persuaded that here it is held as a virtue."[35] The marquis of Lavradio, viceroy of Brazil in the 1770s, found the colony boring, lacking in culture and comforts, and its people slothful, careless, and prone to excessive vanity. He also detested the colored population, an attitude shared by others.[36] For some, like the pro-

---

[32] Padre Rui Pereira to Fathers and Brothers in Portugal (15 September 1560), in Serafim Leite, ed., *Monumenta Brasiliae*, 5 vols. (Rome, 1956–68), 3:296–97; Simão de Vasconcelos, *Crônica da Companhia de Jesus*, 2 vols., 3d ed. (Petropolis, 1977). Cf. Cornelius Jaenen, "Conceptual Frameworks for French Views of America and Amerindians," *French Colonial Studies* 2 (1978):1–22.

[33] Anita Novinsky, "Nota sobre a Inquisição na Bahia (um relatório de 1632)," *Revista de história* 36, 74 (1968):417–23.

[34] Arquivo Nacional da Torre do Tombo (Lisbon) [hereafter ANTT], Cartório dos Jesuítas, maço 70, n. 119.

[35] Sabugosa to Martinho de Mendonça (Bahia, 22 December 1734), ANTT, Ms. do Brasil 7.

[36] Marques de Lavradio, *Cartas da Bahia* (Rio de Janeiro, 1972).

foundly racist governor of Minas Gerais, Dom Lourenço de Almeida, the problem with Brazil was its unruly population, especially the mulattoes. Dom Lourenço felt that even a gallows at every crossroad could not bring order to such a place.[37] Such attitudes seem to have been common in Portugal, where in 1777 William Dalrymple witnessed a theatrical farce ridiculing the manners and habits of the Brazilians, to the guffaws of a Lisbon audience.[38] By that time, however, the Brazilians had developed their own negative view of the Portuguese.

The Colonists and the Indians

The presence of large numbers of Indians and later of Africans provided the settlers not only with the labor necessary to live in the colony but also with a sense of self-identification that reinforced the ties to Europe. Despite a certain early fascination with the Indians, the favorable evaluations provided by the Jesuits, and a "noble savage" concept that developed most fully in the eighteenth century, European colonists in early Brazil in general regarded the Indians as incorrigible, primitives lacking in every aspect of civilization.[39] The fact that Indians had "no law, no king, and no faith" was proof of their deficiencies and the colonists never seemed to tire of calling them *bugres* (buggers) and pointing to the common practice of cannibalism among them. The last two charges were particularly important because under the crown's prohibition against Indian slavery first issued in 1570, such crimes against nature were considered justification for enslavement.

As elsewhere in the Americas, in Brazil the Indians provided an example of what the colonists were not and what they should not be.[40] Indian barbarism and paganism were continually contrasted to Portuguese civility and Catholicism. Indian undependability, profligacy, and seeming disregard for profit, surplus, or savings were used to prove their irrationality. "Even in their sustenance they will not save for tomorrow that which is in excess today," said a governor in 1610.[41] Two hundred years later, the colonists had still not changed their opinion. A complaint against the Indians in 1806 argued that "the natural character of the Indians eludes all philosophy; they

[37] ANTT, Ms. do Brasil 27 (Villa Rica, 20 April 1722).

[38] Dauril Alden, *Royal Government in Colonial Brazil* (Berkeley, 1968), p. 482.

[39] Hemming, *Red Gold*, has a good general summary. The extensive historiography on European attitudes and perceptions of Indians that exists for British North America has no parallel in Brazil. Cf. H. C. Porter, *The Inconstant Savage* (London, 1979).

[40] Greene, "Search for Identity," pp. 207–208.

[41] Governor Diogo de Meneses to crown (1 September 1610), ANTT, *Fragmentos, caixa* 1, n. 6. I have discussed this problem more fully in Stuart B. Schwartz, "Indian Labor and New World Plantations: European Demands and Indian Responses in Northeastern Brazil," *American Historical Review* 83, 1 (February 1978):43–79.

26

have no ambition, they do not value property, and of the most precious property of Brazil, slaves, there is no memory that an Indian has owned one."[42] Indian political economy and attitudes toward production and consumption, like cannibalism, were the proofs of barbarism that distinguished the Indian from rational men.

The colonists thus had a standard by which they could measure themselves. Social distinctions of noble and commoner were transferred from Portugal, but in the colony, especially on the frontiers, these tended to be leveled and replaced by a hierarchy based on race and European culture, in which the Indian and later the African provided the basepoint against which status was judged. Campaigns against the Indians, the wresting of the land from them, and its domestication became the colonists' principal claim for reward and compensation. In 1753 Bahian planters petitioned the crown that "the Brazilian subjects—if not themselves, then at least their ancestors—are those who at the cost of their blood and fortune conquered Brazil from the savage Indian and made it beneficial to the crown, and even today continue to settle in the face of savage power for the greater benefit of the Portuguese scepter."[43] It was not only in the military struggle against the Indians but in the political conflict with the Jesuits over control of Indian labor that colonists defined themselves and took their first concerted actions. Colonist civil disturbances and riots over Indian control in Bahia (1610), São Paulo and Rio de Janeiro (1640), and São Luiz (1661) are clear examples of the political significance of the Indian question.

Despite the almost universal colonist deprecation of Indians and Indian culture (a position sometimes shared by the Jesuits as well), sexual and cultural contact between the Europeans and Indians was continual. Even before immigrants began to arrive in any numbers, castaways and voluntary exiles like the famous Diogo Alvares, Caramurú had begun to father a mixed-blood mestiço, or *mameluco*, population. This process took place all along the coast. In Pernambuco the fortunate marriage of the lord proprietor's brother-in-law to an Indian woman in 1540s had beneficial political consequences. In Bahia, early settlement was aided by the mameluco sons of Caramurú. The result of this process was the creation of a distinctly "Brazilian" population whose status complicated the social organization of the colony. Indian-white unions and offspring among even the wealthiest families led to a general suspicion of all colonial-born Portuguese as possible mixed-bloods and heightened sensitivity of the colonial elite to such attitudes. Persons of mixed origin (mamelucos, mulattoes) were not admitted

---

[42] Arquivo Histórico Ultramarino (Lisbon) [hereafter AHU], Rio Grande do Norte, *papéis avulsos, caixa* 6 (3 September 1806).

[43] AHU, Bahia, *papéis avulsos, caixa* 63 (1753), 1st series, uncatalogued.

to the religious orders in the colony and were sometimes specifically excluded from municipal office or from certain voluntary associations. A 1726 law prohibited mulattoes and whites married to them from serving as town councilmen, and in regions where Indian-white contact was heavy similar attitudes developed toward mamelucos.[44] It was argued in Rio Grande do Norte in the 1730s, for example, that mixed-bloods were by their quality and inclination to unruliness unfit for public office, and in Ceará mamelucos were simply called "the worst caste of people in all Brazil."[45]

By drawing the line ever more sharply between the whites and the mixed-bloods, the colonial whites sought to define themselves. The questionable social origins of many immigrants and the frequency of marriages or sexual liaisons between the early settlers and the Indians led to an intense sensitivity by colonials to hierarchies based on criteria of color and an acute desire for the insignia of nobility and gentle birth. Grants of nobility, knighthoods, pensions, memberships in the military orders, and entails were symbols of nobility (*fidalguia*) sought continually by the colonials. As early as 1591 a royal investigator suggested that the inhabitants of Brazil were well provided with money but lacking in honors and that these could be used to gain their support in military ventures. Others with projects for exploration also asked for the right to distribute such honors as a means of securing volunteers.[46] But the Portuguese crown was very stingy in this regard. Few entails were created and habits in the military orders were never issued in great numbers.[47] Moreover, unlike Spanish America, the crown created no titled nobility in Brazil prior to 1808.

[44] *Provisão* (27 January 1726) registered by the Relação of Bahia in Biblioteca Geral da Universidade de Coimbra [hereafter BGUC], Codice 711, f. 130. See also A.J.R. Russell-Wood, "Class, Creed and Colour in Colonial Bahia: A Study in Prejudice," *Race* 9, 2 (October 1967):133–57; Charles Boxer, *Race Relations in the Portuguese Colonial Empire* (Oxford, 1963), pp. 86–130.

[45] AHU, Rio Grande do Norte, *papéis avulsos*, *caixa* 3 (24 March 1734); Ceará, *caixa* 1 (1724). Even suspicion of such a background would call a man's qualification for office into question. In Cachoeira, Bahia, Antônio Pereira Porto was accused of being unworthy of office because "the quality of his blood" was unknown (Arquivo Publico Municipal Cachoeira (Bahia), 1-1-36, f. 82, *vereação* [26 June 1748]).

[46] "abastados em riquezas e faltos de merces e honras . . . ," Domingos Abreu e Brito, *Um inquerito a vida administrativa e económica de Angola e do Brasil*, ed. Alfredo de Albuquerque Felner (Coimbra, 1931), p. 9. Gabriel Soares de Sousa and former Governor Francisco de Sousa both sought the right to distribute habits in the military orders as part of their request for royal support in discovering mines in the late sixteenth century. See my discussion of their projects in *Sovereignty and Society*, pp. 123–27, and the sources cited therein, especially Archivo General de Simancas, Secretarias provinciales 1466, fs. 284–325.

[47] There is no adequate study of entails (*morgados*) in Brazil. A beginning is Vera Lucia Vilhena de Marques, "O morgado de Marapicu" (M.A. thesis, University of São Paulo, 1977). Of 105 petitions submitted by veterans of the campaigns against the Dutch in Brazil, only 48 received permission to enter the Order of Christ. See Evaldo Cabral de Mello, *Olinda restaurada* (São Paulo, 1975), p. 133.

Lacking these external proofs of gentility, the colonists sought to demonstrate their nobility by a seigneurial life style, including a landed estate, numerous slaves and retainers, liberality, patriarchal attitudes, and personal justice. In the famous words of Antonil: "To be a plantation master [*senhor de engenho*] is a title that many aspire to because it means to be served, obeyed, and respected by many. . . . To be a *senhor de engenho* is considered in Brazil like having a title among the nobles of Portugal."[48] Eventually, other substitutes for noble status, like commissions in the militia, filled the void, but as late as the 1790s immigrants and natives in the colony still lusted for titles, honors, and the other symbols of nobility. At exactly the time that traditional concepts of noble status were under attack in Portugal itself during the eighteenth century, the colonial aristocrats increasingly sought ways of acquiring noble rank for themselves, a status they felt equal to their position in the colony's society.[49]

Insecure about their origins and lacking the patina provided by the emblems of noble birth, the Brazilian elite created in the eighteenth century a well-developed genre of genealogical history to compensate for social deficiency. Authors like Antônio Borges da Fonseca in Pernambuco traced the major families of their region, extolling their virtues and qualities. Great planter lineages became "noble by antiquity," meaning the longer they had been in Brazil, the more the common birth of the line's founder could be overlooked. Any association with a noble house in Portugal was used to give an impression of nobility without actually saying so, and when all else failed families were called at least honorable, or free of stain. Indians in the family tree, when they could not be overlooked, were noted but with a justification that these "alliances of the soil" were common among the best families and in Brazil caused no loss of the respect with which these houses were held.[50] Indian women became "princesses" and nobility was thus gained. The genealogical histories of Borges de Fonseca (Pernambuco), Jaboatão (Bahia), and Paes Leme (São Paulo) symbolized a codification of colonial elite society and of its aspirations.[51] Despite the fact that late colonial critics ridiculed phony genealogies, purchased honors, and inflated self-opinions, the Brazilian aristocracy was creating a self-justifica-

[48] André João Antonil, *Cultura e opulência do Brasil por suas drogas e minas*, ed. Andrée Mansuy (Paris, 1965), p. 84.

[49] Manoel da Silveira Cardozo, "The Modernization of Portugal and the Independence of Brazil," in *From Colony to Nation*, ed. A.J.R. Russell-Wood (Baltimore, 1975), pp. 185–210.

[50] Antônio José Victoriano Borges da Fonseca, "*Nobiliarchia pernambucana*," in *Anais da Biblioteca Nacional do Rio de Janeiro* [hereafter ABNRJ] 47 (1925); 48 (1926). For the statement on Indian marriages, see 47:462.

[51] Antônio Candido, "Literature and the Rise of Brazilian National Identity," *Luso-Brazilian Review* 5, 1 (June 1968):36–37.

tion that surmounted its deficiencies according to European standards, and this was in itself a process of liberation.[52]

Colonies and Indians

It is useful here to draw a distinction between the various regions of Brazil in terms of their level of miscegenation, settlement, and integration into the Portuguese commercial system. Along the coast from Pernambuco to Rio de Janeiro, where the sugar plantation economy was created in the sixteenth century, the European population was relatively dense, the institutions of government were well established, and the social and cultural norms of Portugal were more or less implanted. In the interior, as one moved away from the coast, this was much less the case except in Minas Gerais, which after a short raucous gold rush became by 1730 a close approximation of coastal society, with heavy European immigration, an urban network, and an active and sometimes oppressive royal government. At the northern and southern extremes of Portuguese America, in the Amazon basin and in the southern temperate area centered on modern São Paulo, a different situation obtained.[53] These regions were until the late eighteenth century less directly tied to the export economy and the flow of immigrants from Europe, especially of women, was slight. Not many African slaves arrived in these areas, because there were few who could afford to import them and little for them to do profitably. Government in these regions was tenuous and the colonists always displayed a staunch independence from royal control, especially over the issues of Indians, slavery, and labor use.

In both São Paulo and the state of Maranhão e Pará the levels of miscegenation and of Indian cultural impact on the colony were greater than in the plantation zones. With a small European population and constant contact with the Indians, mamelucos in the first generations held a somewhat different position in these peripheral regions. Often they were accepted as Portuguese and, in truth, there was little to distinguish them from the colonists. On the Amazonian rivers and in São Paulo, the colonists adopted Indian forest crafts, foods, material culture, and customs. Tupí, the predominant Indian language, was more widely spoken than Portuguese in these regions, even by the colonists, and it was only after a law of 1727 prohibiting it and the expulsion in 1759 of the Jesuits who had fostered its use that Tupí began to disappear as the common language of daily life.[54]

[52] Luís dos Santos Vilhena, A Bahia no século xviii, 3 vols. (Salvador, 1969), 1:51–52.
[53] See James Lockhart and Stuart B. Schwartz, Early Latin America: A Short History of Colonial Spanish America and Brazil (Cambridge, 1983), ch. 9, "The Fringes," pp. 253–304.
[54] Fernando de Azevedo, Brazilian Culture (New York, 1950), pp. 193–228. On Indian culture in Brazil see also Sérgio Buarque de Holanda, Caminhos e fronteiras (Rio de Janeiro, 1957).

The considerable biological, social, and cultural intimacy of Indians and Europeans on the plateau of São Paulo and in the Amazon basin did not elicit higher colonist opinions of the Indians in these regions. The capture and enslavement of Indians were major activities in both places, justified by the same desire to bring the heathen to human society and the light of God, and the colonists, disregarding their family origins, were no less quick to clearly mark themselves off from the Indian.

But, despite the pretensions of the colonists on the peripheries of Portuguese America, especially of the Paulistas, they were viewed by the inhabitants of the coastal areas with suspicion and distrust. The forest skills, guerrilla tactics, and valor of settlers in the peripheries were highly prized and were put to use by the colonial government to fight still unreduced tribes and to explore for mineral wealth, but they were generally viewed as troublesome and reckless, little better than the Indians they captured and to whom they were related. The truculent independence of both São Paulo and the state of Maranhão caused both to be called the "La Rochelles" of Brazil in the 1660s, and more than one governor accused them of obeying no law, justice, or holy commandment. On their part, a spirit of independence and arrogant pride developed. When the Paulistas discovered gold in the area of Minas Gerais in the 1690s, they tended to view the washings as theirs alone and sorely resented the flood of immigrants who rushed in. The resulting civil war of the Emboabas (tenderfeet) in 1710 demonstrated the depth of their pride and their localism. It was not a war between Paulistas and Portuguese, but between the southern backwoodsmen and everyone else, including other colonials.

Until the middle of the eighteenth century Portuguese America can be seen as three distinct colonies: a core area of coastal plantations and then later a mining zone beyond the coastal range; the southern periphery centered on the temperate plateau of São Paulo; and the northern region of the Amazon basin, created in fact as the separate state of Maranhão in 1621.

The peripheries lacked a major export and tended to have meager populations. Even in 1672 the Maranhão had only eight hundred Portuguese inhabitants. The first generation of colonists in these areas were relatively humble and mostly male. European society and institutional structures were truncated, fragmented, and less differentiated than in the colonial centers. Physically isolated and poor, these regions were not well integrated into the colonial commercial system and royal control in them was tenuous at best. Missionary orders played a crucial role in these regions long after their activity in the plantation zones had diminished, and secular society remained highly militarized. In these peripheral regions the colonists continued to live among, like, and off the Indians that surrounded them. In

many ways the peripheries resembled the plantation zones in the first stage
of colonization: Belem on the Amazon in 1680 was like Salvador in 1600,
but the lag was structural rather than chronological. As São Paulo was increasingly pulled into the mining economy after 1700 and Maranhão became an exporter of cacao and cotton in the eighteenth century, they more
and more came to resemble the coastal plantation zones socially and culturally as well as economically.

I would suggest that the localism, independence, isolation, and "Indi-
anness" of the peripheral colonies were the earliest manifestations of a distinct colonial mentality. Those regions most isolated and poor elicited the
least royal interest or control and generated the most intense realizations of
separateness on the part of the colonials. The lower the level of capital accumulation, the looser the tie to the metropolis and the more independent
the colony. But these regions, being the least developed and lacking, or almost lacking, basic European-style institutions, tended to express their distinctiveness in action rather than in thought, and in them we must seek
popular expressions of *mentalité* rather than an intellectual discourse on
their sentiments. Instead, it is in the core plantation and mining zones,
where capital accumulation was the greatest and the forms of Europe the
fullest, that a traceable tradition of colonial distinctiveness or self-awareness ultimately emerges, although belatedly, and eventually grows into a
proto-nationalism. In the core areas, however, these sentiments were
muted by the form and organization of royal government and the integration of the colonial elite within the imperial structure.

The Colonists and the Empire

The political organization of the Brazilian colony and the manner in
which the colonists viewed it influenced their perceptions of themselves
and the colony. The Portuguese imperial structure, of which Brazil was to
become the most important part by 1640, was based on the underlying principles of colonial fragmentation and imperial centralization. The latter
principle also informed the educational system and the circulation of royal
servants within the bureaucracy. In the sixteenth and seventeenth centuries the governors-general who sat at Bahia often found their powers in the
colony circumscribed by geography, imperial design, and subordinate resistance. The far north, the state of Maranhão, was an independent colony
(1621–1777) with even its episcopal diocese suffragan in Lisbon rather
than in Salvador. Isolated, distant, and closer to Lisbon than to Bahia in
terms of sailing time, Maranhão was in effect a separate colony. The crown
twice tried to separate the region from Rio de Janeiro southward (1572–
1578, 1608–1612) and though these experiments failed, governors in Bahia

often had little control over the southern region and its people. Moreover, when the governor-generalship was created in 1549, the preexisting system of proprietary captaincies was not abolished. Thus governors-general sometimes faced defiance to their authority from the lords proprietors, especially in Pernambuco. Subordinate royal governors in the Brazilian captaincies also resisted the colony's central authority. Between 1670 and 1720 the crown in fact increased the powers of the subordinate governors, elevating their title to that of governor and captain-general and allowing them to correspond directly with Lisbon and to receive royal orders that did not pass through the office of the senior crown officer (called viceroy after 1720).[55]

The decentralization of colonial government tended to make each captaincy more dependent on Lisbon. This situation forestalled the integration of the colony as a whole or the development of colony-wide movements or actions. Municipal councils existed at the local level, but there was no estates general or assembly where all were represented and no Brazilian representation in the Portuguese Cortes, itself a moribund institution by the late seventeenth century. A brief junta of town council representatives held in 1710 in Minas Gerais on a tax issue was later manipulated by the crown to give an impression of consent. However, by the 1730s the government was strong enough to suppress this kind of representation. Governor Martinho de Mendonça put it simply when he said, "No government, no matter how dependent it may be on the vote and consent of the people, cedes the right to vote on public matters to colonies and conquests. . . ."[56] The colonists were not permitted to develop representative institutions other than the municipal councils, and individual colonists like subordinate officials were encouraged to correspond directly with royal councils in Portugal. This policy served to stimulate localism in the colony but to diffuse broader sentiments that might be expressed as a colonial or Brazilian opposition to the metropolis.

Nothing was done to give a sense of unity or real political cohesion to Portuguese America. The powers of the viceroy were limited, no archbishopric existed until 1676, there was no standing army, and only the judiciary was centralized under the High Court of Appeals that sat in Salvador. Local institutions were invariably modeled on Portuguese precedents, although their content did sometimes reflect local realities. Brazil by the mid-sev-

---

[55] Alden, *Royal Government*, pp. 491–93; Mitchell Gurfield, "Class Structure and Political Power in Colonial Brazil: An Interpretive Essay in Historical Sociology" (Ph.D. diss., New School of Social Research, 1975), makes a contradictory argument, claiming that centralization demonstrated weakness and that this led to a maintenance of the system for three hundred years.
[56] Donald Ramos, "A Social History of Ouro Preto: Stresses of Dynamic Urbanization in Colonial Brazil, 1695–1726" (Ph.D. diss., University of Florida, 1972).

enteenth century had become the most important colony of the empire and by the 1730s its gold had made it the "milch-cow" of Portugal, but at no time were separate administrative bodies created in the metropolis to administer it. Instead, it continued, along with India, Angola, Macao, and Timor, among others, to be controlled by the Colonial Council, the Board of Conscience, and other such imperial institutions. Frei Vicente do Salvador probably expressed the sentiments of other Brazilians when he chided the king for taking the title lord of Guinea, but not including Brazil in his official honorary form of address. He felt that the kings knew only how to collect Brazil's taxes and income and otherwise paid it no regard.[57]

The integrated nature of the Portuguese empire was reflected in the selection of royal officers and the patterns of placement and promotion. Natives of the metropolis and the colonies were used in every level of government, keeping in mind always the restrictions placed on New Christians, mulattoes, moors, blacks, and other "infected races." Sons of the Brazilian elite served in lesser and higher offices in Portugal and Brazil and in other colonies, and in this way the bureaucracy of the empire was integrated into a single system that in theory at least did not exclude the sons of Portuguese America.[58] Having said this, it is fair to note that there were considerable limitations on this situation, especially in terms of service in Brazil. One of the basic tenets of the Portuguese bureaucracy was that men should not serve in high office where they might be influenced by personal considerations. Thus, the tendency was always to appoint men to serve outside their home area. None of the viceroys or governors-general of Brazil was Brazilian-born, and only a few of the bishops were. Among the governors and captains-general a few more native sons could be found, but by far the vast majority of those who served in high office in Brazil were Europeans by birth. The myriad of minor nonprofessional offices in the colony were generally held by local incumbents.

The professional judiciary, which also served in administrative capacities, had the strictest code against home service, but even in it the law was bent and Brazilians served in the High Court of Bahia, the chancery of the colony. Colonials appointed to judicial office in Brazil did cause problems, but when the crown sought to prohibit Brazilians from holding these offices in Brazil, there rose a great cry against such discrimination. The elite of the colony hoped to enroll its sons in law courses at the University of Coimbra and then have them follow a career of royal service. The colonial aristocracy found that even those magistrates and civil or military officers who

[57] Frei Vicente do Salvador, *História do Brasil*, ch. 2, pp. 58–59.
[58] Schwartz, *Sovereignty and Society*, pp. 314–56.

were not born in the colony could be "Brazilianized" by marriage, association, money, and kinship. Although government in the colony was often corrupt, ineffective, and sometimes oppressive, it was rarely seen as a tool of foreign domination. From the viewpoint of Lisbon, this was a most positive result of the imperial structure's operation.

At issue here is what royal government provided and what the colonials expected from it. The growth of the Portuguese state and its judicial bureaucracy represented the triumph of Roman law, especially of lex or public law, which regulated the relationship of the subject to the state. The legal system and the polity provided a framework for control of property, commerce, and the distribution and control of labor. These were essential functions needed by the colonists for the operation and maintenance of the colonial economy and the society based upon it. In Brazil, a colony erected on slave labor, one is struck by the lack of royal legislation that stood between the master and the slave. For moral, theological, and economic reasons Indian enslavement had provided a thorny issue but a modus vivendi between crown and colonists was eventually worked out. On black slavery there was little done. Other than a decade of crown interest in ameliorating slave conditions (1690–1700), royal government essentially let the planters and miners have their way without interference. Municipal councils, dominated by local elites, were far more active than the crown in settling the standards for slavery.

The value of Brazil as a colony during its first two centuries depended on the inputs of private individuals who provided the capital to set up plantations. The crown gave planters free reign in determining the social hierarchy, provided them advantages to ensure their successful operation, and simply taxed their production. Tax exemptions were used to stimulate the building of new sugar mills; a general exemption from foreclosures was given to mill owners and cane growers in Bahia in 1663 and then later expanded to cover other regions. The state provided the political context in which the dominant groups were able to achieve their goals, and as long as the crown allowed them to order and control the colony's productive forces, the colonists were willing to forebear the minor irritations of colonial government. The period after 1690 saw both a notable increase in royal control exercised over local government in the colony and a growth in power, or at least a growth in the ability of the mercantile class to express its interests. The following decades were not particularly good ones for the sugar economy and the combination of hard times, increased royal control, and the rise of a more powerful or at least more influential commercial class, most of whom were Portuguese by birth, contributed to a sense of dissatisfaction and sensitivity on the part of the Brazilian elite. The tensions gen-

35

erated by this situation were muted, however, by another aspect of the empire's operation.

In no areas was the integrated centralism of Brazil and the metropolis clearer than in the matter of education. The first schools in the colony were created by the Jesuits and by 1572 a course in philosophy was offered in the Jesuit College of Bahia. Eventually similar studies were created at Rio de Janeiro, Olinda, Recife, São Paulo, and São Luiz. The sons of the colonial elite could pursue an education in Brazil, but only up to a certain point. No advanced studies were available in the colony and any student seeking a higher degree in medicine, theology, arts, or canon or civil law was required to obtain them at the faculty at Evora or at Coimbra, the one true university of the empire. There was a continual flow of Brazilian-born youth back to Portugal for this end, especially to obtain degrees in canon or civil law preparatory to entry into the royal administrative-judicial bureaucracy.[59]

By the mid-seventeenth century the colonials wished to break the dependence on Coimbra by replicating the metropolitan situation. In 1663 the municipal council of Salvador petitioned to have the local Jesuit college elevated to the status of a university equivalent to that of Evora and, in a later request, to that of Coimbra.[60] The Overseas Council, on advice from the University of Coimbra, refused to comply, ostensibly because of Coimbra's desire for exclusivity but most likely because the centralized system of higher education served the political purposes of the crown. The only concession made to the residents of Brazil was to grant one year of credit toward a Coimbra degree to those who had completed the Jesuit course in Brazil. The crown did insist, however, that despite the objections of white Brazilians, persons of color could not be excluded from the Jesuit College of Salvador just as they could not suffer such disabilities at Coimbra. In fact, persons of mixed origin were few in any Portuguese school of higher learning and they did suffer discrimination in this regard.[61]

The result of Portugal's educational policy was to reinforce the intellectual dependence of the colony on the mother country and to socialize the

---

[59] Fernando de Azevedo, *Brazilian Culture*, pp. 325–64, is a good general survey of colonial education. On the late colonial era see Maria Beatriz Nisza da Silva, *Cultura no Brasil colonia* (Petropolis, 1981), pp. 68–143.

[60] The incident is summarized in Leite, *História*, 7:190–98.

[61] AHU, Bahia, *papéis avulsos, caixa* 16 (30 January 1689). The Jesuits argued that there were many *pardos* (mixed-bloods) who sought admission and they set a bad example to the whites, but the council felt that such efforts to "better their fortune of their color by studious effort" should set a good example. The Jesuits then argued that if their college were private, it could exclude the mulattoes, and if it were public, it should be allowed to grant them degrees. The request was denied.

colonials in political as well as intellectual terms. As early as 1575 Brazilian-born Portuguese were studying at Coimbra, and in the eighteenth century some 1,875 Brazilian colonials passed through the halls of Coimbra. This process contributed to an intellectual bond between Brazil and Portugal that did not begin to diminish until the nineteenth century, and in this regard the policy had its desired effects.[62] It is virtually impossible to conceive of a Brazilian educated elite without Coimbra or a colonial intellectual life uninfluenced by contact with Portugal.

Brazilian students far from home sensed a certain commonality and took pride in their accomplishments while at Coimbra. One wrote home in the 1690s that "if in matters of intellect the sons of Brazil do not exceed those of Portugal, at least they are their equals."[63] Such statements not only indicate Brazilian pride but also suggest that some questioning of Brazilian capabilities may have been common in Portugal. This kind of depreciation of colonial abilities heightened Brazilian sensibilities and the recognition of their common origins as colonials. As early as 1718 Brazilian students at Coimbra sponsored a mass in honor of Nossa Senhora do Desterro as a collective symbol of their solidarity. The policy of educational limitation and centralization did have its desired effects of socializing the colonials into accepted modes of thought, but by the end of the eighteenth century the unexpected result of stimulating a "colonial consciousness" could also be noted. In the closing years of the eighteenth century and beginning of the nineteenth, when the crown sought to isolate Brazil from the contagion of "French ideas," Brazilian students in Portugal and the few who traveled to Montpellier and other foreign universities served as vectors by which these ideas did enter the colony.[64]

The Pombaline reforms of the mid-eighteenth century disrupted education in Brazil but also eventually set it upon a new course. The expulsion of the Jesuits in 1757 left their seventeen colleges and seminaries in Brazil empty, and only slowly did other institutions and courses of study develop

[62] Manuel Xavier de Vasconcelos Pedrosa, "Letrados do século xviii," *Anais do Congresso commorativo do bicentenário da transférência da sede do govêrno do Brasil* [hereafter ACCBTSGB], 4 vols. (Rio de Janeiro, 1967), 4:257–318; José Murilo de Carvalho, "Political Elites and State Building: The Case of Nineteenth-Century Brazil," *Comparative Studies in Society and History* 24, 3 (July 1983):378–99.

[63] A.J.R. Russell-Wood, "Preconditions and Participants of the Independence Movement in Portuguese America," in his edited volume *From Colony to Nation*, p. 33. Russell-Wood's observation is based on the correspondence of Antônio Alvares Pereira, who studied at Coimbra in the 1690s. Probably like many of the colonials at Coimbra he suffered most from the cold and the lack of slaves. See A.J.R. Russell-Wood, "Educação universitária no Imperio portugûes: Relato de um caso Luso-Brasileiro do século dezasete," *Studia* 36 (July 1973):7–38.

[64] José Ferreira Carrato, *Igreja illuminismo e escolas mineiras coloniais* (São Paulo, 1968), emphasizes the impact of Coimbra on Brazilian political thought.

to fill the gap. Pombal's subsequent reform of the University of Coimbra, with his emphasis on new methods of study and on mathematics and natural science, also influenced the generation of Brazilian students at the end of the colonial era, the very generation that would participate in the movement for independence.[65]

The educational backwardness of the Brazilian colony symbolized a wider and more profound intellectual dependency manifested in many ways. Unlike Spanish America, no printing press operated in Brazil during the first three centuries of the colonial era, and only with the arrival of the Portuguese court in 1808 did a royal press begin to function. Any writing about Brazil or by native-born Brazilians thus had to be published in Portugal under the watchful eye of the crown and the Inquisition. It is difficult to gauge the effect of this situation on indigenous intellectual life, but it should be noted that many of the most admired poets and prose authors of colonial Brazil, like the historian Frei Vicente do Salvador, the essayist Ambrósio Fernandes Brandão, or the poet Gregório de Mattos, were unpublished in their own lifetime or, in fact, during the colonial era, and were only resurrected by Brazilian scholars in the nineteenth century.

I would argue that until 1700 and probably well beyond that date that there was essentially no separate Brazilian literature and that this, too, was a result of the centralization of political and economic life in the empire. Brazilian intellectuals moved within the orbit of the mother country, usually knew it personally, and viewed themselves as part of a broader, more inclusive tradition. Authors were either Portuguese by birth or were educated there, and they generally wrote for a Portuguese-reading public primarily in the metropolis. The two great figures of seventeenth-century Brazilian literature demonstrate the integration of colony and metropolis. The satirical poet Gregório de Mattos e Guerra was born in Brazil, educated at Coimbra, returned to Brazil, and was eventually exiled to Angola. The great Jesuit essayist and pulpit preacher Antônio Vieira was born in Portugal, raised in Brazil, returned to Europe, traveled to the Maranhão as a missionary, went back to Europe, and eventually died in Brazil. The empire of Portuguese thought was an integrated whole, and though Brazilian themes and a certain pride in local things can be seen in Brazilian authors, such bairrismo (localism) can be found in Iberian authors writing in the same period from a provincial rather than a colonial perspective.

In quantitative terms the literary production of Brazil prior to 1750 is small. All the genre of the period—histories, honorific and satiric poetry, promotional literature, moral and religious tracts, sermons, and descrip-

[65] Azevedo, *Brazilian Culture*, pp. 360–63.

tions of pious and public events—were created, but this production tended to be fragmentary and dispersed with no universities to serve as focal points for intellectual interchange and activity. The ephemeral literary societies of the eighteenth century (whose membership was mostly Portuguese) never really provided an adequate substitute. The intellectual production of the colony seems meager unless we keep in mind the size of the literate population and the integration of the colony within the broader intellectual community of the empire.

Sons of the Soil

In both intellectual and economic terms, the decades between 1660 and 1700 witnessed an increasing growth in Brazilian self-sufficiency and identity. The war against the Dutch (1645–1654) had reunified the colony under Portuguese control, but the major role in the fighting taken on by the colonists had led to an increased sense of worth and a new pride in colonial accomplishments. By the 1660s and 1670s colonials increasingly sought to replicate metropolitan institutions or to free themselves from cultural dependence on them. An archepiscopal see was created in 1676, giving the colony a certain religious independence. In 1677, after many petitions, a convent for women was created, thus freeing the elite from the expense of sending their daughters back to Portugal. The attempt to create a Brazilian university failed as we have seen, but the colonials were successful in having the highest levels of the judicial bureaucracy opened to them. These changes not only symbolized a growing maturity of the colony but also were due to Portugal's distraction with other matters. The War of Restoration against Spain (1640–1668) demanded Portugal's attention, and its resources were severely strained in this period. Foreign wars, a palace revolt, and declining colonial revenues perhaps contributed to a loosening of royal control in Brazil.

The formation of colonial identity in Brazil was infused with ambiguities. Nativist sentiments and a growing sense of distinctiveness developed alongside the continuing tradition of loyalty as subjects of the Portuguese crown, who thereby felt themselves deserving of favor and reward. In 1653 Frei Mateus de São Francisco petitioned in the name of the State of Brazil that, because of the love its inhabitants had for their land and because of their services in the war in Pernambuco, they be allowed to send representatives to the Portuguese Cortes (parliament).[66] The persistence of these two tendencies side by side complicates the problem of establishing a chronology of the process. Furthermore, the multiethnic and multiracial com-

[66] AHU, Bahia, *papéis avulsos*, caixa 4 (25 August 1653).

position of Brazilian society both impelled and restrained its inhabitants in their quest for identity, creating other contradictions and ambiguities.

The process is easiest to trace among the Brazilian whites, who during the second half of the seventeenth century began to make overt distinctions between themselves and immigrant Portuguese. Within the context of Baroque literary style and themes, authors like Manoel Botelho de Oliveira composed poetry eulogizing local glories. More to the point, Gregório de Mattos e Guerra commented critically on the arriving immigrants, or reinóis, and used the new term mazombo to describe native-born Brazilians. Mattos, a Coimbra-trained lawyer and son of a Bahian planter, also expressed the attitudes of the Brazilian-born whites in his ridicule of the mulattoes and blacks around him. Although the process has never been carefully traced, there was a hardening of the racially based attitudes of hierarchy as the native-born colonists began to assume the role of nobility and to differentiate themselves from the rest of the population.

These pretensions brought the Brazilian planters increasingly into conflict with the predominantly European-born mercantile community in the colony. The hostility between the native-born agrarian elite and the metropolitan-born commercial bourgeoisie became apparent. In 1707 the merchants of Rio de Janeiro complained that they were being excluded from local government: their wealth allowed them to live like nobles, and therefore entitled them to office. In 1718, a royal order forced equality in municipal councils in Minas Gerais between Brazilians and Europeans. In Pernambuco, despite royal ordinances of 1654 and 1705 that promised to provide honors and positions to natives, reinóis countinued to be appointed. The planters, by this time referring to themselves as "nobles of the land," objected to this situation and the hostility between the two groups expressed itself in a rivalry between the capital of Olinda and the growing merchant center at Recife. The attempts of the "nobles" to limit Recife's growth ultimately failed after a brief civil war (1710–1711). It was a struggle between two groups who had created mythic claims to social dominance in the colony: the planters, whose pretensions rested on noble actions in the use of arms and their role as landowners, and the merchants, most of whom were plebeian in origin but had the wealth to justify their ascendancy.[67]

Some authors have seen the growing tension between Brazilians and Portuguese in this period as essentially the rise of a commercial class challenging the power of the colonial landed elite. Although this element was involved in the competition, it does not satisfactorily explain the dimensions

---

[67] José Antônio Gonçalves de Mello, "Nobres e mascates na câmara do Recife," Revista do Instituto Arqueológico, Histórico e Geográfico Pernambucano 53 (1981):113–262.

and depth of colonial feelings.[68] There were strange manifestations in unexpected places. In 1733 a mysterious young man supported by a priest of disreputable fame wandered around the interior of Alagoas and Pernambuco calling himself the Prince of Brazil and attracting to his cause blacks, mulattoes, and mamelucos. More frightening from the government's viewpoint was the adherence to his cause by wealthy landowners, who in turn received noble titles as counts and marquises. Once captured, the strange youth was held in secret and intensively questioned about his origins and possible foreign contacts. The fact that he had won supporters in the interior, especially among the landed elite, gave the officers of the crown further reason to view the Brazilians with some suspicion.[69]

Curiously, the segment of society in which the rivalry between Brazilians and Portuguese emerged most openly and quite early was within the religious orders. The closed atmosphere of the orders, less subject to royal control than the diocesan clergy, magnified the hostility between colonials and metropolitans.

The underlying distrust of Brazil and the Brazilians shared by many Portuguese institutions and officers was made clear in the "First Constitutions of the Order of St. Benedict in Brazil," prepared in the Monastery of Pombeiro, Portugal, in August 1596. To begin with, it was believed that "because the land was weak and the food of less sustenance," a different and less rigorous order of fasting and abstinence was prescribed for Brazil than existed in Portugal.[70] Moreover, right at the outset the order prohibited mestiços from entering the religious life. Only persons of "noble" birth or those from whom benefit could be expected to result were to be admitted, which apparently by definition excluded persons of mixed blood.

The distrust of Brazil and its people became even more apparent in a subsequent set of laws added to the Benedictine code in 1600 and 1602. In 1600 the council of the order ordered that "because of the humor of the people of Brazil and to maintain the gravity of the habit of the Order," Benedictines could only go about the cities and towns in pairs.[71] The sign of Venus was simply too strong in the tropical skies. When in 1602 a proposal was made to admit Brazilians to the order, it was strongly voted down.[72] At

[68] Caio Prado, Jr., História económica do Brasil, 10th ed. (São Paulo, 1967), pp. 79–122; Evolução política do Brasil e outros estudos (São Paulo, 1957), pp. 35–54.

[69] I have never seen any other reference to this strange movement. The relevant correspondence is found in APB, Ordens régias 29, n. 141, 148; APB, Cartas do governo 153, 10v, 11–12, all of which date from 1733 and 1734. On a parallel Mexican case, see Jacques LaFaye, Quetzalcóatl et Guadalupe (Paris, 1974).

[70] "Primeiras constituições da Ordem de São Bento no Brasil," Mosteiro de São Bento (Salvador) [hereafter MSSB] pasta 28 (26 August 1596), 12, 21.

[71] MSSB, Leis acresentadas na Junta do Pombeiro (12 January 1600).

[72] MSSB, Leis acresentadas (20 August 1602).

this time "Brazilian" probably meant Indian or mestiço, but over time those Portuguese of American birth who eventually entered the Benedictine order also felt themselves deprecated and ignored.

Like the Brazilians in the other orders, the native-born Benedictines counted the numbers and saw that they were disadvantaged. Of 287 monks who died in the Monastery of Salvador, only 114 (38 percent) were Brazilian-born.[73] In 1738 the Brazilians voiced their frustration in a long letter, claiming that in 157 years there had been forty-five Provincials elected in Brazil, but only six of them had been Brazilian-born. It was, claimed the Brazilians, "as if it were enough to have been born in Brazil to cause a degeneration as rational persons, Christians, Portuguese and most loyal vassals of His Majesty."[74]

In the dispute of equality between American and European religious, the Benedictines were not alone in Brazil. The same issues had also been raised among the Jesuits over "indigenous vocations," as early as the 1650s. There seems to have been a strongly racial overtone to the original reluctance to admit Brazilians into the Company of Jesus, but by the late seventeenth century the objections had been codified in such a way as to imply the inferiority of all American-born. A debilitating climate, the lack of proper upbringing in which Brazilian children were never chastized properly and thus did not adapt well to religious discipline, the low social origins of many Brazilian candidates, the Brazilian prejudice against work, the unstable personality of mestiços, and the fact that even the whites imbibed their first milk from the breast of blacks and mulattoes with all the defects that it carried were all used as arguments against the entrance of Brazilians into the Jesuit order.[75]

In the face of these attitudes, those who favored the colonials pointed out the discrimination against them. Father Antônio Vieira pointed out in 1688 that of the thirty-three Provincials and Visitors of the order in Brazil from 1549 to that date, only three had been Brazilian-born. Although the Portuguese-born Vieira argued that place of birth had not played a role in the order's membership and administration, his own figures demonstrated that while 310 Brazilians had been admitted in the province, the number of those born in Portugal or the Portuguese Atlantic islands was 538. Moreover, almost a third of the Brazilians were ultimately rejected; the rate for

[73] MSSB pasta 28, "Monges que fallecerão neste Most.° de São Bento (1591–1815)."

[74] Padres gerais de São Bento to King (22 February 1738), AHU, Bahia, *papéis avulsos, caixa* 14.

[75] Eduardo Hoornaert et al., *História da igreja no Brasil* (Petropolis, 1977), pp. 206–209; Leite, *História*, 7:233–35.

Portuguese was just over a quarter.[76] Still, the Jesuits seemed to have coped with the problem of factions relatively successfully, something that could not be said of the other orders in the colony.

The rivalry between Europeans and Americans in the Franciscan order has been documented in Spanish America and a similar situation existed in Brazil. When the competition began is unknown, but the creation of independent Franciscan provinces in Brazil (Santo Antônio in Bahia, 1584; Conceição in Rio de Janeiro, 1657) may have lain at the root. In any case, by the eighteenth century factions had developed—the *filhos da fora*, or Portuguese, and the *filhos da terra*, or sons of the soil—both of which jealously sought positions of authority within the order. As a result of their squabbling, Pope Innocent XIII issued a bull in 1721 requiring the admission of equal numbers of Europeans and Brazilians in the order and a second brief instituting the *alternativa*, or alternation in the senior offices, followed in 1723.[77] This official solution only regularized the divisions within the order, and by 1735 both parties had agents in Portugal to represent their interests. The potential for conflict remained just below the surface. When the alternativa was broken in 1779, the Portuguese complained against the *paixão patricia* (nativist passion) of the Brazilians and the fact that despite their various defects, including that of birth, 173 Brazilians was now in the province compared to only 105 Portuguese.

In origins these rivalries were localist. Frei Antônio da Encarnação noted that factions of Bahians and Pernambucans as well as of Americans and Europeans existed within the Franciscan order. Suggestions, in fact, for a *tripartiva* or three-way alternation between Europeans, Bahians, and Pernambucans in the Franciscan monastery of Salvador was ultimately rejected as discriminatory to the Portuguese, who would receive senior posts only every third turn instead of every second one.[78] These native-born/foreign-born divisions seemed to transcend traditional localism by the eighteenth century. The Carmelites of Rio de Janeiro, despite an alternativa, were divided into two parties moved by "blind passion." The Sons of Rio and the Sons of Outside were two armed factions virtually at war; at one point the

---

[76] "Notícias e reparos sobre a Provincia do Brasil," Archivum Romanum Societatis Iesu (Rome) [hereafter ARSI], Bras. 3 (II). Vieira later penned a further comment of the problem of factions in "Brasiliensis factionis, et adversus visitatio coniurationis brevis noticia," ARSI, Bras. 3 (II), dated Bahia, 14 July 1691.

[77] AHU, Bahia, *papéis avulsos*, n. 17,437, Rio de Janeiro (1780); Ildefonso Silveira, "Partidarismo nacionalista nos claustros franciscanos no século xviii," ACCBTSGB, 3:123–46.

[78] ". . . nação e filiação não he o mesmo," Fray Antonio de Encarnação (c. 1781); AHU, Bahia, *papéis avulsos*, n. 17,437. On Spanish America see Antonine Tibesar, "The Alternativa: A Study in Spanish-Creole Relations in Seventeenth Century Peru," *The Americas* 11 (1955):229–83.

43

civil governor had to surround the Carmelite house in Rio de Janeiro in order to free the leader of one faction who was being kept under arrest.[79] In the barefoot Carmelite establishment of Olinda, founded in 1686, the problem was solved by admitting no Brazilians at all—to the dismay of the local residents.[80]

With rare exceptions none of the Brazilian religious houses opened their membership to persons of Indian, black, or mixed origins unless these were obscure or quite distant in time. Discrimination against Brazilian-born whites in admission and even more so in promotion was usual, but by the mid-eighteenth century a feeling of self-conscious identity had led the Brazilians to form parties to defend and promote their interests so successfully that it was the Portuguese-born who now complained of discrimination and partisan passions.

By the close of the century the animosity between Portuguese and Brazilians was intense. An anonymous report of 1790 written by a Portuguese in Rio de Janeiro demonstrates the bitterness and the way in which Brazilians had come to see themselves. The report accused the Brazilians of being lazy, proud, indebted, and vain, and all of them living in the "madness" of thinking themselves *fidalgos* (noblemen). At the same time they looked down on every Portuguese as a peddlar and on the metropolis. These "Americans" held an excessive view of the greatness of their homeland and believed that everything in Europe would be poverty-stricken were it not for the wealth of Brazil. The Brazilians were not to be trusted; their hatred for the Portuguese and Portugal was profound and their self-pride and exaltation of Brazil too great, said our anonymous informant. How matters had changed from the sixteenth century.[81]

Brazilian self-esteem and hostility to European-born Portuguese certainly existed by the late eighteenth century. Were such sentiments enough to generate a movement for independence, one might have occurred much sooner in Portuguese America. To understand why it did not, we must finally examine the economic and social context in which these attitudes developed and the limitations that this context placed upon them.

Colonial Persistence

By the close of the seventeenth century, colonialist self-identity had begun to emerge in both religious and secular society. The process was inten-

---

[79] Father Inocéncio do Desterro Barros do Conselho Ultramarino, Rio de Janeiro (15 November 1783); also see AHU, Rio de Janeiro, *papéis avulsos*, 1st series, uncatalogued (24 May 1768).

[80] C. R. Boxer, The Portuguese Seaborne Empire (London, 1969), pp. 260–62.

[81] Letter to Martinho de Mello e Castro from "Amador Patricio de Portugal," AHU, Rio de Janeiro, *papéis avulsos* (4 March 1790).

sified and redirected in the period after 1700. The discovery of gold (c. 1695) transformed Brazilian society in many ways and altered the relationship of the colony to Portugal. Levels of Portuguese immigration soared and led eventually to a restrictive law in 1720. With mineral wealth available, the crown's former policy of relatively loose administration changed to one of direct control. In the mining zones ambitious governors created new administrative structures under close government surveillance. Dragoons were stationed near the mines, a mint was established in 1725, and a variety of oppressive taxes were imposed. Frightened of the threat to the mines posed by foreign invasion and distressed by contraband, the Portuguese crown sought ways to isolate the colony even more directly under royal control. The absolutist policies of Dom João V (1706–1750), which included heavy taxation and government monopolies on basic commodities, elicited negative responses from the colonists, on whose backs these policies fell most heavily. When gold production began to decline in the decade of the 1760s, the crown sought even more stringent means of eliminating illegal trade and ensuring treasury receipts.

The policies of the marquis of Pombal were designed to strengthen the empire's economy and lessen Portugal's dependence on England. Brazil figured as the centerpiece of these reforms, but the introduction of state-sponsored monopoly companies, boards of agricultural inspection, local finance commissions, and new taxes upset the established interests in the colony and drew heated complaints from the "Portuguese American vassals" of the crown. Pombal had not sought to attack established interests in the colony and, in fact, he tried to protect those that might contribute to his ultimate goals. Colonial complaints in the face of the Pombaline reforms were thus muted by the facts that the Brazilian oligarchy was not excluded from office and the new organs of government allowed for the participation of colonials.

The essential social contract of Brazil and the role of the oligarchy within it was not upset by the Pombaline reforms. The expansion of plantation crops was accompanied by increased levels of slave importation and there was no tampering with the basic institution of slavery within the colony. Although Pombal abolished the distinction between New Christians and Old Christians and tried to foment miscegenation by removing restrictions on mestiços, the social hierarchy of Brazil remained unchanged. The population, however, was expanding and by 1780 had reached about 1,500,000, of which over one-third were slaves and slightly under one-third were free persons of color. The size and composition of the population were elements that influenced the reaction of the oligarchy to Portugal's programs in the colony.

Despite Pombal's program, the results of his efforts were not immediately positive. Throughout this period Brazil faced an economic depression, brought on by declining gold production and low prices for its agricultural products, that no fiscal measures could remedy. Brazilian exports in 1776 were only 40 percent of their value in 1760. But Pombal had laid the foundation of reform. After 1780 the economy expanded as revolutionary upheavals in the Atlantic world created new patterns of supply and demand for tropical products. These events also provided a stimulus to intellectual ferment in Brazil and new models to be followed or avoided.

That ferment had, in fact, accompanied much of the political and economic change of eighteenth-century Brazil. Literary societies, most of them short-lived and usually composed of priests and European-born bureaucrats but including some Brazilians, sprang up in Salvador and Rio de Janeiro and in less organized forms in other cities.[82] Influenced by European thought in general and by Portuguese trends in particular, these academies reflected on the situation and history of the colony as well as on broad questions of morality, taste, style, and even science. These were certainly not revolutionary or radical groups in intent or membership (most were patronized by the senior royal officials in their area), but questions on the present and past of the colony were addressed directly in a coherent fashion for the first time in their meetings. While the academies praised and honored the classes of their members, they also gave considerable attention to the natural phenomena of America, "the fourth and greater part of the World, the best, most opulent, and most fertile region."[83]

One aspect of this activity that merits special attention is the creation of a colonial history. Frei Vicente do Salvador had written a history in Brazil in 1627, but it had never been published. Other works describing particular events had appeared in the seventeenth century, particularly in relation to the Luso-Dutch War, but the first published history of the colony by a Brazilian appeared in 1730. Sebastião da Rocha Pitta was a Bahian sugar planter who, as a member of the Academy of the Esquecidos at Bahia in 1724, had taken on the task of writing a history of the colony. Much has been made of Rocha Pitta and his work as an early manifestation of Brazilian nationalism, but this has been overstated. As a corresponding member of the Lisbon Academy of History (established in 1720), his work was probably stimulated as much by its activity as by Brazilian developments. His choice of title—*The History of Portuguese America*—also reflects his orien-

---

[82] E. Bradford Burns, "The Intellectuals as Agents of Change and the Independence of Brazil, 1724–1822," in *From Colony to Nation*, ed. Russell-Wood, pp. 211–46; José Aderaldo Castello, *O movimento academista no Brasil*, 3 vols. in 14 (São Paulo, 1969–78).

[83] "Dissertacões acadêmicas e históricas," in Castello, *O movimento*, 1, r.5, 167.

tation.[84] Still, like many of the works of the academies, his history eulogizes Brazil and his appendix listing the names of Brazilians who had achieved high office in the empire demonstrates not only pride but also a desire to affirm the positive qualities of his fellow colonials. Such an attitude seems almost defensive and suggests that prejudices against the Brazilians were deeply felt. With virtually no concern for the Indians or blacks of the colony except as dangers to be overcome, Rocha Pitta defended the talents and "nobility" of the class to which he belonged.

As we have seen, these concerns also characterized the works of the genealogists of the eighteenth century, but some changes were beginning to appear by the 1750s. Written in 1757, the work of Domingos de Loreto Couto, the strange one-time Franciscan, later Benedictine, was never published. Its purpose, however, was explicitly to refute the "errors and calumnies" written about Brazil and its inhabitants. His work, essentially a catalog of his fellow Pernambucans who had excelled in virtue, arms, and letters, was not limited to the oligarchy; separate chapters were given to Indians, blacks, and women. A second volume to honor the natives of the other provinces of Brazil was planned. His defense of the Indians demonstrated an incipient awareness of the symbolic relationship between the colony and the Indian and was one of the first attempts to link an intellectual defense of the latter with the identity of the former.[85] This tendency found increasing expression in epic poems of the 1780s that celebrated the "noble savage" in the early history of the colony.[86] The captaincies where these poems and histories were written had few Indians by the late eighteenth century and were predominantly populated by slaves and free people of color. It was easier to see the disappearing Indian as a symbol of nationality than to recognize the nationality of the majority of the population. With few exceptions, blacks rarely appear in the poetry and prose of the late colonial period.[87]

The first real stirrings of Brazilian independence came in Minas Gerais in 1788, when a group of lawyers, poets, clerics, military men, and local oligarchs, moved by the example of the United States and smarting under the

---

[84] Sebastião da Rocha Pitta, *História da America Portugeza*, 2d ed. (Lisbon, 1880). See Manoel Cardozo, "Azeredo Coutinho and the Intellectual Ferment of His Times," in *Conflict and Continuity in Brazilian Society*, ed. Henry Keith and S. F. Edwards (Columbia, 1969), pp. 72–103.

[85] Domingos de Loreto Couto, *Desagravos do Brasil e glorias de Pernambuco* in ABNRJ 24 (1902); 25 (1903). The best study of Loreto Couto is José Antônio Gonçalves de Mello, *Estudos pernambucanos* (Recife, 1960), pp. 139–68.

[86] Claude Hulet, "The Noble Savage in Caramuru," in *Homage to Irving A. Leonard*, ed. Raquel Chang-Rodriquez and Donald A. Yates (Lansing, 1977), pp. 123–30; Silvio Romero, *História da literatura brasileira*, 7 vols., 6th ed. (Rio de Janeiro, 1960), 2:404–425.

[87] Raymond Sayers, *The Negro in Brazilian Literature* (New York, 1956), pp. 58–64.

threat of back taxes, conspired to declare independence from Portugal. An Indian breaking the chains of bondage with the inscription "Libertas quae sera tamen" (roughly, "Liberty at last!") was the preferred banner of the conspirators. On the question of slavery, however, the plotters faltered. In a province in which half the inhabitants were slaves, their choices seemed limited. Their proposal to free Brazilian-born slaves while leaving Africans in bondage revealed the class and racial restrictions on their plans.

Such a proposal, freeing the children while leaving the parents in bondage, demonstrated a misreading of slave reaction, but it was not as shortsighted as it might first appear. The Brazilian slave system had generated or fostered strong feelings of distinctiveness among segments of the slave and free colored population. "Tribal" rivalries existed among the various African peoples enslaved in Brazil, a situation stimulated to some extent by intentional policies that permitted the maintenance of dances and other African cultural traditions. Both slaves and masters recognized an even more profound division between the *crioulos* (blacks) and mulattoes born in Brazil and those born in Africa. Deep feelings of self-identification had developed among the Brazilian-born slaves, who were favored by the slave system. They had higher rates of manumission, received privileged or skilled occupations, and were generally held to be more trustworthy. In the colony, religious sodalities, voluntary associations, and militia units were organized by color, ethnic origin, and place of birth among the slave and freed population.

The depth to which the feelings of distinctiveness among the Brazilian-born people of color had reached can be seen in an incident in 1755. In that year the black militia regiment of Bahia complained that African freedmen were being appointed to posts of command, against the usual practice in Pernambuco and Bahia. The crioulo supplicants claimed that the Africans were suspect in their faith and orthodoxy and were capital enemies of the whites, against whom they often plotted rebellion.[88] The crioulos, however, were loyal servants of the crown who had proven their value on many occasions. This crioulo petition was contradicted by the governor, who pointed out that the exclusion of Africans was not due to any royal order but rather to the practice of the regiment. Although many of the whites found the pretensions and vanity of the crioulos and especially of the mulattoes a matter of concern, there was, in fact, a recognition that in comparison to the foreign Africans, the Brazilian-born population at least shared some of the attitudes and loyalties of the colonials. Perhaps this rec-

[88] The incident can be traced in APB, Ordens regias 54 (30 January 1754); AHU, Bahia, *papéis avulsos, caixa* 66 (8 December 1756); AHU, Bahia, *maço* 18 (11 May 1756).

ognition lay behind the thinking of the Minas conspirators. Creole self-awareness and white sensitivity to African foreignness was intensified in the last decade of the eighteenth century, as the colony's economic expansion brought the slave trade to new heights.

The Minas conspiracy of 1788 failed. Although the elite continued to feel disadvantaged, desired more commercial freedom, and responded to the events of Paris, their peculiar situation as a colonial elite moderated the nature and intensity of their desire to break the colonial compact. Black and mulatto freedmen were less constrained and they came increasingly to define themselves as Brazilians. The slogans of Paris had other meanings for them. The truly revolutionary movement of mulattoes that failed in Bahia in 1798 bared the essential problem of moving from feelings of colonial identity to collective actions for political independence. After suppressing the movement, the governor of Bahia wrote to the crown that there was no need for concern because the upper classes had not joined in. "That which is always most dreaded in colonies," he said, "is the slaves on account of their condition, and because they compose the greatest number of the inhabitants. It is therefore not natural for men employed and established in goods and property to join a conspiracy which would result in awful consequences to themselves."[89]

The contradictions inherent in a segmented society like Brazil were to some extent intensified during the last three decades of the colonial era. The Haitian revolution of 1791 presented to white Brazilians the specter of an inverted social order in which slavery was smashed by its victims. It was an image that made them wary of political change.

The arrival of the Portuguese court at Rio de Janeiro in 1808 created a new situation that intensified the existing contradictory tendencies. Brazilians expressed a new pride as their homeland became the center of the empire and acquired the institutions of self-government, but at the same time the influx of Portuguese courtiers intensified the longstanding dislike of the continental Portuguese. The court in Rio de Janeiro divided into Lisbonian and Brazilian factions.[90] Radical republicans and humanitarians emerged who wished to abolish the slave trade, reduce the abuses of the institution itself, and even to abolish it altogether. Defenders of the rights of the free colored population emerged. The Bahian Cipriano José Barata de Almeida pleaded their cause at the Portuguese Cortes, calling them "Portuguese cit-

---

[89] Kenneth Maxwell, *Conflicts and Conspiracies: Portugal and Brazil* (Cambridge, 1973). See also Luís Henrique Dias Tavares, *História da sedição intentada na Bahia em 1798* (São Paulo, 1975).

[90] John Luccock, *Notes on Rio de Janeiro and the Southern Part of Brazil* (London, 1820), pp. 99–100.

izens" and stating that "whatever their color, whatever their status, they were born in Brazil."[91] But such progressive ideas were easier to express than to enact.

The class and racial divisions within Brazilian society and fear of the *canalha* (mob), especially the great sea of mixed-bloods and slaves, ultimately placed severe restrictions on the actions and thoughts of the Brazilian oligarchy. Despite their growing hostility toward Portugal, they were willing to compromise to maintain their society and they did so until 1821. Not surprisingly, the authors of the Brazilian romantic movement of the nineteenth century chose the Indian as theme and symbol of the new nation. The slave and the mulatto are in the main absent from Brazilian literature until the 1850s. The patriot who posted the seditious broadsheet in Santo Amaro in 1830 had come to see his nation identified with the people of color, the mixed-bloods, the cabras.[92] How he came to this view we do not know and of his own color we can only speculate. But there may be an unwritten history of colonial identity that at present cannot be reconstructed. It is one no less valid than that we have traced.

[91] Burns, "Intellectuals as Agents," p. 240.

[92] Thomas Flory, "Race and Social Control in Independent Brazil," *Journal of Latin American Studies* 9, 2 (November 1977):199–224.

3 ❧ Identity Formation in Spanish America

Anthony Pagden

SELF-IDENTITY in the Spanish American world developed in different ways, in different periods, and in response to different contingencies throughout the various colonies. The native-born (*criollo*) elite in Mexico and Peru, with whom this essay will be primarily concerned, had already acquired by the middle of the seventeenth century a clear sense of belonging to a culture that in many, if not yet all, respects was independent of the "mother country." In most other areas, economically more dependent upon the metropolis, such self-awareness came much later. Nor, until long after independence (and perhaps not even then), was the process ever completed. Mexicans who were proud of their Mexicanness might, nevertheless, urge their countrymen, as did the "Señor Diarista" of the *Diario de Mexico* in 1805, to "raise [their] speech to the standard of the mother country."[1]

By the end of the eighteenth century, however, most of the inhabitants of the Spanish American mainland were conscious that they belonged to communities that, though they still shared a common language, a common religion, and much else in addition with Spain, were no longer Spanish. "The New World," wrote the Jesuit Juan Pablo Viscardo in 1791, "is our *patria*, its history is our history."[2] It was a sentiment expressed in different ways by his near contemporaries Francisco Clavigero, Juan Ignacio Molina, and Andrés Cavo, all of whom attempted to rewrite the history of their own regions as the histories of separate and culturally independent "nations." Their historical vision was, in most cases, informed by a specific political ideology, but it was not as tendentious as it might appear. Some sense of belonging to a society (if not yet to a culture) rooted in the land of America and thus, in some as yet imprecise sense, other than the society they had left behind, is to be found even among the original conquistadores. Although a large number of these early settlers came to America in the hope of being able to return to Spain rich and ennobled, many more, in particular after the conquest of Mexico in 1521–1522 and of Peru ten years later,

[1] Quoted in Shirley Brice Heath, *Telling Tongues: Language Policy in Mexico, Colony to Nation* (New York and London, 1972), p. 55.

[2] Juan Pablo Viscardo, *Carta derijida [sic] a los Españoles Americanos por uno de sus compatriotas* (London, 1801), p. 2.

51

recognized that the full extent of their ambitions could only be realized in the fluid social environment of a new world.

The conquistadores and "first settlers" (*primeros pobladores*) were men with archaic ideals and archaic ambitions. Some were, and many more claimed to be, hidalgos, the impoverished members of the lesser fighting nobility, a class whose aspirations were to linger on well into the seventeenth century but whose political power and social usefulness had been on the wane since the mid-fifteenth century. Hernán Cortés, true to the aspirations of the world in which he had been reared, saw himself as the feudal vassal of a medieval monarch and the instrument, as he never tired of repeating, of a God-directed enterprise. "New Spain" was to be no mere province, much less a colony. It was to be a kingdom within the world empire of Charles V. "The things of this land," he told Charles, even before the conquest had begun, "are so many and of such a kind that one might call oneself emperor of this kingdom with no less glory than that of Germany which Your Majesty already possesses."[3] New Spain was to be a Germany overseas, with the emperor as its sovereign lord and Hernán Cortés as its governor and de facto ruler. The whole history of the conquest of Mexico was conceived as a *translatio imperii* from the old world to the new. It was the secular equivalent of the Franciscans' dream of a new apostolic Church, to replace and surpass in piety that which had been lost to Luther.

These new men had come to New Spain to act out the role of the great magnates of the Old Spain. Like nearly all the colonists in the Atlantic world, they had come to found a new society where their otherwise hopeless social ambitions might be fulfilled. Like the settlements of the English in Ireland or America, or the Portuguese in Brazil, this new society was intended to be a faithful image of the one that had been left behind. Unlike either the English or the Portuguese (or, indeed, the French), however, the Spanish settlers possessed a distinctive set of political aspirations. These—of which Cortés's *Cartas de relación* are the most articulate expression—were grounded on a loose and imperfect understanding of medieval contractualism. By the terms of the covenant between the king and his noble vassals, military service was to be rewarded by political concessions. Feudal jurisdiction in Spanish America came in the form of the *encomienda* in New Spain or the *mita* in Peru, a grant of Indians made to an individual conquistador for the duration of his lifetime only. The Indians paid the *encomendero* tribute and worked for him in return for an exiguous and frequently nonexistent wage. They were not, in law at least, slaves, but the fact that

[3] Hernán Cortés, *Letters from Mexico*, ed. and trans. Anthony Pagden (New Haven and London, 1986), p. 48.

the encomienda was not an hereditary institution also made them imperfect feudal vassals. For the encomendero only the conversion of his grant into a perpetual institution would provide the necessary conditions—seigneurial control over "his" Indians, the right of continuity within the same family—of the noble status he had come to America to acquire. Not surprisingly, the encomenderos' constant demands for a perpetual encomienda became a source of bitter conflict with a crown that had no wish to see the establishment in America of a social class it was doing its best to suppress at home. But the loyalty of the encomenderos and their willingness to provide the military assistance on which, in the early years, the colony's defense and continuing expansion depended could only be purchased with feudal grants. Only when the encomienda had been made perpetual, Philip II was told by a commission of 1556, would the loyalty of the criollos be assured, "for as they are feudatories they will thus quench the fires of rebellion . . . which until now has not been the case, rather some of them have taken some pleasure in these disturbances because they are not holders of perpetual *encomiendas*."[4]

Like the English emigrants to North America, these men too had come, as Michael Zuckerman writes below, "in willful rejection of the Old World and its emerging modes." Because of this they already possessed some degree of political self-awareness. Like the Cid in the "land of the Moors," the conquistadores considered themselves to be the founders of a new kingdom that would be a fief of the Spanish crown but in all important respects a self-governing polity.[5] Those who, on their arrival in America, had masses said for the soul of the Cid were stating quite clearly that in this land, among the heathen God had given them to conquer, they were to be their own masters. Like the Cid they had endured a long and dangerous journey to a land inhabited by alien and hostile peoples; and although, unlike the Cid, they had gone of their own free will, it was not difficult later for them to see themselves in the role of "good" vassals ill-treated by a misguided lord.

These conquistadores knew that if the noble vassals of the king were denied the rewards that were theirs by natural right, they were entitled to resist. As the officers of the *audiencia* (the royal court) of Mexico pointed out as late as 1598, a failure on the part of the crown to observe the terms of

---

[4] *Parecer acerca de la perpetuydad delas encomiendas de indios delos Reynos del Piru que hizieron los tres comissarios iuezes que el dicho Reyno embio al Rey Don Felipe II nuestro señor por el año 56* (Lima, 1556[?]), f. 4v.

[5] See Stuart B. Schwartz, "New World Nobility: Social Aspirations and Mobility in the Conquest and Colonization of Spanish America," in *Social Groups and Religious Ideas in the Sixteenth Century*, ed. Miriam Usher Chrisman and Otto Grundler (Kalamazoo, 1978), pp. 23–37 at p. 35.

the feudal contract might lead to open rebellion. "Honorable men," they wrote, "who by chance see themselves, their encomiendas exhausted, [reduced] to great poverty while others who arrived yesterday grow wealthy in the land their forefathers helped to win, taking due account of the value of their services, these men, who are unused to suffering ills, may join up with mulattoes, blacks, and other perfidious peoples and attempt some uprising. And although it seems that we need not fear this in our day, yet it would be wise to take precautions against what might occur in the future."[6]

The kind of uprising these officials had in mind would not take place for another two hundred years. But the history of the Spanish dependencies in America was marked from the beginning by always unsuccessful, often ludicrous attempts by overambitious men, deprived of what they regarded as their rights as vassals, to create independent states for themselves. Cortés himself had been suspected of plotting rebellion. His own lieutenant, Cristóbal de Olid, had attempted to carve out an independent principality in the jungles of Honduras. The image of men such as these became in time the substance of a conquistador myth, in the name of which so many later, less intrepid criollos were to make their own claims to independence.

The most important of these uprisings was the abortive attempt in 1565–1568 by a small group of men acting in the name and probably under the guidance of the conqueror's son, Martín Cortés, second Marqués del Valle, to seize control of Mexico. His "conspiracy," the so-called *conjuración del marqués*, like so many subsequent revolts, was sparked by rumors that the crown intended to suppress the encomienda. The revolt was a failure, but a highly significant failure that for the crown marked forever the descendants of the old conquistadores as a social group that could not be trusted.

Although the planned uprising never took place, it was preceded by an event that demonstrated quite starkly, in dramatic and ritual language, the criollos' vision of themselves and of their relationship with the land they inhabited. One night two prominent members of the conquistador elite, Gil Gonzalez de Avila and his brother Alonso, staged a procession through the streets of Mexico City. Dressed as Mexican chieftains they marched to Cortés's house, followed by a group of masked retainers garbed as Indian warriors. Cortés opened the gates of his house to them and the brothers handed him a crown of flowers bearing the inscription, "do not fear to fall for by this act you shall rise higher." Cortés accepted the crown and withdrew. The "Indians" then dispersed. To the royal judges (*oidores*) the meanings of both the charade and the inscription on Cortés's crown were

[6] *Parecer* of the *audiencia* of Mexico, May 1598 in *Epistolario de Nueva Espana, 1505–1818* [hereafter ENE], ed. Francisco Paso y Troncoso, 16 vols. (Mexico City, 1939–42), 13:244.

clear enough. The Avila brothers had been reenacting the submission of Moctezuma to Cortés's father. "The entire *fiesta*," commented the judges, "was meant to indicate that the Marqués was to be king of this land."[7]

This ritual also spelt out in unequivocal terms the true relationship, as they understood it, between the conquistador aristocracy and the land of Mexico. Cortés had received the old Aztec Empire from the hands of its last legitimate ruler. In Cortés's imaginative account of the event, Moctezuma had surrendered his domain "to dispose of as you choose."[8] This donation had been received in the name of the emperor, but the emperor's heir, by attempting to suppress the encomienda, had become a tyrant and had thus forfeited his claims upon his subjects' loyalty. Cortés's son would now become the true ruler of the land that his father had won. Neither Cortés's own followers nor the oidores had forgotten how the conqueror, on his return from Honduras in 1526, had staged a spontaneous demonstration of the loyalty and love he inspired in the Indian masses as a means to suppress the audiencia, which had seized control of Mexico in his absence.[9] Whereas the father had still been able to call upon real Indians, the son was limited to white men in disguise; but whether in reality or in dramatic reenactment, it was clear to all involved that in the eyes of the conquerors and their offspring, if nowhere else, participation in the conquest, whether direct or indirect, conferred a legitimate right to independent political action. It was the conquest, the blood that the conquistadores had spilt on the soil of Mexico, that bound them inextricably to a land that, as one of their number had told the king in 1548, "is not only for those already born, but also for those yet to be born, not only for Spaniards, but also for the natives . . . not for ten or twenty years but forever."[10]

The revolutionaries, the court claimed, had planned to crown Martín Cortés king because, as one friar put it, "this land cannot be at peace until it has its own king and natural lord."[11] They had also planned to obliterate all memory of their history as the subjects of the Castilian crown. After killing all the king's men, "they intended," said one witness, "to make a great fire in the plaza of all the papers and writings which were in the archives and offices so that there should remain no written memory of the name of the king of Castile; and once this was done they would crown the aforesaid marquis king by reason of the authority which belonged to them by just

---

[7] The records of the trial are printed in Manuel Orozco y Berra, *Noticia histórica de la conjuración del Marqués del Valle: Años 1565–1568* (Mexico City, 1853), pp. 59–60.

[8] Cortés, *Letters*, p. 86.

[9] Ibid., p. 433.

[10] "Carta al rey de Jerónimo López quejandose de que cumplen con el las mercedes que le estaban hechas . . . ," Mexico, January 1548, ENE, 6:71.

[11] Orozco y Berra, *Noticia histórica*, p. 74.

right, and they would remove the tyrannies which the king [of Castile] had worked in this land."[12]

The *conjuración* was both the first and the last significant attempt by the conquistador elite to create an independent Mexican kingdom. It also signaled the final demise of their political influence. After the collapse of the revolt, the execution of the Avila brothers, and the expulsion of Cortés from Mexico, the conquistadores went into rapid decline. As encomiendas fell vacant, they reverted to the crown. By the end of the century, there were very few families who had the means to sustain the illusion that they formed part of a feudal fighting nobility. The Indians themselves, decimated by disease and ill-treatment, had shrunk to a fraction of their pre-Conquest numbers and could no longer supply either the tribute or the labor required to support the encomenderos in an appropriate style of life. By the beginning of the seventeenth century the old elite of conquest had been reduced, with a few exceptions, to a small and largely impoverished group. By 1604, according to Baltasar Dorantes de Carranza, son of one of the companions of Alvar Núñez Cabeza de Vaca and the criollo elite's most impassioned champion, the descendants of some 1,326 conquistadores now numbered 109 sons, 65 sons-in-law, 475 grandsons, and 85 great-grandsons, a total of 733;[13] many of these were the offspring of the once despised "new" conquerors whom Cortés had claimed to trust even less than he did the Indians, men who were often, in practice, former vagrants sent off to settle some distant province.[14]

But if the conquistadores' traditional means of support and effective political influence had been all but eroded, the social attitudes and expectations of the majority of the group remained constant. The criollos, even in the mid-seventeenth century when many of them were in fact the descendants of later settlers who had had no share in the conquest and had made their money out of trade rather then men, still regarded themselves as predominantly a landed aristocracy. "The Spaniards," wrote Juan Ortíz de Cervantes, procurator-general of Peru in 1619, "from the able and the rich to the humble and the poor all hold themselves to be lords and will not serve."[15] Many of these men took to vagabondage rather than engage in the "vile" occupations that would have deprived them of the hidalgo status

---

[12] Ibid., p. 201.

[13] Baltasar Dorantes de Carranza, *Sumaria relación de las cosas de la Nueva España*, ed. José María de Agreda y Sánchez (Mexico City, 1902), p. 234.

[14] See C. E. Marshall, "The birth of the mestizo in New Spain," *Hispanic American Historical Review* 43 (1963):161–84.

[15] Juan Ortíz de Cervantes, *Memorial que presenta a Su Majestad . . . sobre pedir remedio del daño y diminucion de los indios y propone ser medio eficaz la perpetuydad de encomiendas* (Mexico City, 1619), f. 1r.

Charles V had conferred upon them and thus finally compel them to abandon the American dream they had come so far to realize. The sight of destitute Spaniards traveling the roads of Mexico with two or three Indian mistresses in tow had become a common one as early as 1529.[16] Others sought socially uncontaminating employments in the church and supplemented their meager incomes by crime. Criminals in Mexico were, complained the viceroy Juan de Ortega Montañéz in 1697, "as many as the heads of the Hydra."[17] The image that most Peninsular Spaniards came to form of the colonists, despite the latter's insistent pretentions to nobility, was little different from Josiah Child's description, cited by Jack Greene below, of the Virginians and Barbadians as "a Sort of loose vagrant People, vicious and destitute of Means to live at Home." The royal officers were, or so they imagined, threatened simultaneously from three directions: from the Indian and half-caste masses, from over-mighty criollo patricians, and from what another viceroy, the duke of Linares, called "the pusillanimous but evil-intentioned plebe."[18]

The old Spanish settlers and their progeny, with their aspirations to nobility and their willingness to turn to crime as well as to rebellion to defend their claims, soon came to be regarded by the crown as little different in temperament and no more reliable than the Indians. "I have known many of them," wrote the viceroy Martín Enríquez, in 1580, "whom I would not trust in the discharge of any office. Let the services of their fathers be rewarded by other means."[19] The entire population of the American colonies soon came to acquire in the minds of many peninsular Spaniards a single, if varied, character. By the early eighteenth century the white settlers, the Indians, the several types of half-breeds, known as *castas*, and even the blacks seemed to be part of a single community fired by one ambition. "From the lowest Indian," wrote the duke of Linares, "to the most exalted gentleman, their ambition is to live in absolute liberty, believing that merely by saying that they recognize the king as sovereign, they have performed their duty as vassals."[20] The criollos' identity, their pride in all that separated them from the Old World Spaniard, the *gachupín*, was in part a necessary response to the persistent hostility and undisguised contempt on the part of the metropolitan authorities.

[16] N. F. Martín, *Los vagabundos en la Nueva España, siglo XVI* (Mexico City, 1957), pp. 23–38.

[17] "Informe del Exmo. Señor Dn. Juan de Ortega Montañéz arçobispo, Virrey que fue de este Nueva España, quando le entrego el gobierno al Exmo. Sr. Dr. Joseph Sarmiento Valladares, conde de Moctezuma," British Library [hereafter BL], Add. Ms. 28,204, f. 4v.

[18] *Instrucciones que los virreyes de Nueva España dejaron a sus sucesores*, 2 vols., Biblioteca histórica de la Iberia, vols. 12–14 (Mexico City, 1873), 1:248–49.

[19] Ibid., p. 5.

[20] Ibid., p. 246.

Because the criollos saw themselves, at least during the sixteenth century, as primarily a feudal aristocracy living by tribute and arms, their culture drew its coherence and its appeal from an attachment to the land. "Every day," wrote Dorantes de Carranza, "the monarchy of the Indies was settled with more and more Spaniards, both with those who were born and reared here, the descendants of the conquerors and first settlers, as with those who, with the passage of the years, after the discovery and conquest have come and been naturalized here, marrying and setting down roots, and spreading their lineages, families, and descendants through the breadth of such far-flung provinces."[21] This sense of belonging was strengthened by what the criollos came to see as the crown's rejection of both their claims and their merits. "Two things I perceive," wrote the conquistador Jerónimo López to the king in 1548, "are held in low esteem, the first is those who won the land and the other those who work and cultivate it."[22] For men like López the natural social order was being undermined from above. A feudal landed society was being replaced by one of merchants and miners, by men engaged in "vile" occupations. "Now the season has arrived," wrote Dorantes de Carranza, "when deceit and lies, when idleness and the distrust of one's neighbor are held in high esteem, when it is possible to build great estates by selling wine or spices or cloth or old iron."[23] As the old values, the older understanding of what being noble was collapsed, so the social world of manners and customs collapsed too. For Dorantes America had become a world turned upside down, "a support for fools, a brothel for the good, a madhouse for the sane, the end and destruction of nobility, the suppression of virtue, confusion of the wise and the discrete, a delirium and a fantasy for the simple-minded." It had become a world where not only did the vile grow rich and the noble poor, but where all the natural distinctions between men had dissolved into what Dorantes described with horror as "equality of treatment."[24] Like the savage Indian tribes, the Chichimeca and the Otomi, who did not discriminate between high-born and low or indeed much between men and women, white society in America had become "unnatural," a place wholly without a proper social order. What Dorantes viewed with such distaste was, of course, precisely the socially fluid, socially mobile community that had permitted his own ancestors to rise from low peasant or artisan origins to become petty feudal seigneurs.

II

The conquistador ambition to create a society of orders in all formal respects like that of Spain demanded that they close the doors of the colony

---

[21] Dorantes de Carranza, *Sumaria relación*, p. 105.
[22] ENE, 6:69.
[23] Dorantes de Carranza, *Sumaria relación*, p. 113.
[24] Ibid.

as soon as a sufficient number of their own kind had entered.[25] But the doors, of course, remained open to a succession of immigrants whom the old elite saw as a threat to their livelihood, their status, and the credibility of the image of the society to which they wished to belong. At first the threat had come from the crown's officials and the new conquistadores, later it came from the new settlers, and finally from the peninsular Spaniards, the gachupines, the men who had gone to America in the hope of growing rich from mining or trade. The last group was the most persistently hated of all, because its members had no stake in the land. Many had no intention of settling and their presence, "constantly sighing for their *patria*,"[26] was an ever-present reminder to the criollos of how different from the peninsular Spaniards they themselves had become. These differences became apparent within a single generation, so that families often found themselves divided, the distinction between criollo and gachupín merging with more traditional conflicts between parents and their children. "There is no family of a man married in Spain . . . ," wrote Juan de Savaeta, a fiscal officer from Lima in 1681, "which does not find itself involved in a civil war, for even the children and the women condemn the Spanish nation at all hours of the day."[27]

To this gachupín royal official it seemed that the criollos had seized political and military control of the colonies. To the criollos it seemed rather that America had become, as Dorantes phrased it, a "mother of foreigners, succor of outsiders and delinquents, common *patria* of the unnatural, a sweet kiss of peace to the newly arrived."[28]

The self-image that this passage proclaims, predicated upon an identification with the land, a fear and hatred of "foreigners," and an insistence upon the enduring worth of the old aristocratic values by which the first conquistadores had lived or had claimed to live, persisted until independence. But it underwent certain changes. One such change was the understanding of what constituted fitting employment. The first generation of settlers, Cortés's men and some of their sons, had lived off men and land. The only offices they had aspired to were those on the *cabildos*, the city councils, posts that were traditionally held by the lesser aristocracy in Spain. These men possessed, or so they imagined, the traditional feudal

---

[25] Ortíz de Cervantes argued that the creation of a perpetual encomienda would have exactly this effect and would thus put an end to "all the novelties in this land" (*Memorial*, f. 4r).

[26] This complaint appears in almost every criollo petition to the crown. See, e.g., Juan Ortíz de Cervantes, *Información en favor del derecho que tiene los nacidos en las Indias a ser preferidos en las prelacías, dignidades, canonigías y otros beneficios ecclesiásticos y oficios seculares en ellas* (Madrid, 1619), ff. 7–8.

[27] Quoted by Alfredo Torero, *El quecha y la historia social andina* (Lima, 1974), p. 201.

[28] Dorantes de Carranza, *Sumaria relación*, pp. 113–14.

right of *consilium*—even though, as Bernardo de Vargas Machuca noted in 1599, "princes prefer to be served rather than advised"[29]—as well as the duty to provide *auxilium*; but they made little effort to seek employment in the king's government. The criollo's usefulness as a military aristocracy had, however, ceased by the second generation. Even if as late as the 1590s Juan de Cervantes, an archdeacon of Mexico cathedral, felt able to boast that "although they live in great poverty the defense of this kingdom consists in the knights and noblemen who are descended from the first conquerors,"[30] the militia had in fact become in Dorantes's words, "more like a troop of children playing scrimmage" than an army.[31]

Faced with a decline in their traditional means of support, a withering-away of their social role, and with it, their social status, the more adaptable of the settlers soon came to seek a place for themselves in the new nobility of service. Repeated claims by the viceroys that although they had searched they could find no criollos suitable to fill even the relatively lowly post of *corregidor*[32] is evidence that as early as the 1530s many of the conquistadores and their descendants were coming to see themselves as potential royal officers. By the middle of the seventeenth century they had come to view the holding of royal offices and ecclesiastical benefices as an inalienable right conferred, once again, by their ties with the land. All ecclesiastical benefices, argued Luís de Betancurt y Figueroa in 1634, should by right go to the Indians as the oldest inhabitants of the country; but, as they are "and always will be" incapable of holding any office, the right passed to the "Spanish commonwealth of the Indies," who "with the love of children and the experience of natives" are the only persons fully qualified to fill the major posts in the administration.[33] Such claims were upheld in theory, though less often in practice by the great law code of 1681, *Recopilación de leyes de los Reynos de las Indias*, which required that the sons of conquerors and "those who were born in these provinces" should be preferred, "because it is our wish that their sons and natives should be employed and the services of their ancestors rewarded."[34]

The criollos' arguments, on the basis of which they made appeal to this legislation, underwent a dramatic change. Place of birth, not conquest,

---

[29] Bernardo de Vargas Machuca, *Milicia y descripcion de las Indias* (Madrid, 1599), p. 123v.
[30] ENE, 12:75.
[31] Dorantes de Carranza, *Sumaria relación*, p. 115.
[32] The *audiencia* of Mexico to the Empress, Mexico, March 1531, ENE, 3:231.
[33] Luís de Betancurt y Figueroa, *Memorial i información por las iglesias metropolitanas i catedrales de las Indias sobre que sean proveidas sus prelacías en los naturales y capitulares dellas* (Madrid, 1643), f. 12.
[34] *Recopilación de leyes de los Reynos de las Indias*, 4 vols., (Madrid, 1681), vol. 1, p. 4, lib. 3, tit. ii, ley xiv.

now conferred membership in a community that possessed a virtual right of self-government. "The first consideration," wrote Ortíz de Cervantes in 1619, "which is of divine law, is that offices shall all be held by members of one nation, land, or lineage."[35] Such claims were to be repeated again and again. Antonio de Ahumada, a lawyer (*abogado*) of the audiencia of Mexico in 1725, complained that there were Peninsular Spaniards who believed that the criollos should not be given royal posts because, as descendants of the conquistadores, "they must have the wish to return to their old authority and customs." Ahumada rejected the idea but not the image of the conquistador. The accusation was unjust, he argued, not because the Spaniards' view of the conquerors was false, but because the criollos were not, in fact, their descendants; instead they were "the descendants of those who came to settle the land after those provinces had been won, and of those who came, or come, here with employment or have married, or marry here with the daughters of Spaniards."[36] For Ahumada, as for Ortíz de Cervantes before him, the claim to the right of office was founded upon an association not with the conquest but with settlement and service. The language of this claim was also very different from the one that had been employed by men like Dorantes, for it appealed to a concept that could have had no meaning for an older generation, that of citizenship. The demands of Ahumada and Ortíz de Cervantes were grounded not upon the *act* of conquest, the seizure of the land of Mexico from those, some of whose territorial rights the criollos had at least implicitly come to recognize, but upon what the poet Francisco de Terrazas called "the golden age"—"that holy age"[37] of the *rule* of the conquistadores and of their descendants. The possession of honors, argued Ahumada, is "the consequence of birth." As such it was grounded not only in the law of nations but also in natural law. It was a right that all citizens enjoyed as crucial to their existence as citizens, to their participation in the community, a participation that constituted their "reputation."[38] The shift of the basis of the appeal is significant. The criollo of the eighteenth century, though still grounding his claims to possess both independent political rights and an identity separate from the peninsular Spaniards in his associations with the origins of the colony, was now, in keeping with a general eighteenth-century distrust of heroism, appealing to

[35] Ortíz de Cervantes, *Información*, f. 3.

[36] Antonio de Ahumada, *Representación política-legal, que haze a nuestro señor soberano Don Phelipe Quinto . . . para que se sirva de declarar, no tienen los Españoles Americanos obice para obtener los empleos políticos y militares de la América, y deven ser preferidos en todos, assi eccelesiásticos como seculares* (Madrid, 1725), f. 20.

[37] Quoted by Dorantes de Carranza, *Sumaria relación*, p. 20. This and the other fragments that Dorantes reproduces are all that remains of Terrazas's great verse hymn to America.

[38] Ahumada, *Representación política-legal*, f. 5.

a genealogy based upon a history of service and development rather than one of arms and bloodshed.

Ahumada was also appealing to a political reality, for by the mid-seventeenth century the criollos had, in fact, come to occupy many of the key positions in the royal administration. When Martín Cortés rebelled in 1565 it was the judges of the audiencia who represented the "tyranny" of the king and who had been marked for execution. When in 1624 the criollos rose against the attempted reforms of the viceroy—the marqués de Gelves—in what was to be the most serious revolt of the seventeenth century and the only one to bring down the central administration, they were led by members of the same audiencia.[39]

The Bourbon reforms of the eighteenth century, however, attempted once again to restrict office to peninsular Spaniards by making it mandatory for all royal officials to have attended one of the Castilian universities, the *colegios mayores*.[40] For a group that had enjoyed a considerable degree of self-determination for nearly a century, this move was seen as a direct challenge to their status and position. If the criollo elite was to be denied its fundamental rights, then its all-important reputation would be imperiled. "The most politic nations of the world," who, Ahumada professed to believe, would be unable to imagine Philip V capable of an unjust act, would look upon the criollos as unworthy. "In what, Sire," he went on to ask, "have we erred that we should be marked in this way?"[41] Since, at least in their own opinion, criollos were in no obvious sense inferior to peninsular Spaniards, and since divine, natural, and positive law all demanded that native sons be favored over foreigners, the crown's refusal to so favor them constituted a clear violation of their natural rights.

Ahumada's *Representación política*, the famous *Representación* of the Ayuntamiento (town council) of Mexico City of 1771, the work of a lawyer named José González de Castañeda,[42] and the demands of the *comuneros* of New Granada in 1781 all set out with pedantic precision the argument that by denying the criollo right of office, the crown was violating the law of nature. Like their contemporaries in British North America, the criollos insisted that it was the crown, not they, who had transgressed what they saw as the ancient laws and privileges of the realm. The northern colonists couched their protests in a language of liberties and natural rights. For the

---

[39] J. I. Israel, *Race, Class and Politics in Colonial Mexico, 1610–70* (Oxford, 1975), pp. 136–60, provides the best account of the Gelves revolt.

[40] Mark A. Burkholder and D. S. Chandler, *From Impotence to Authority: The Spanish Crown and the American Audiencias, 1687–1808* (Columbia, Mo., and London, 1977), pp. 7–8.

[41] Ahumada, *Representación política-legal*, f. 4v.

[42] David Brading, *Los orígenes del nacionalismo mexicano* (Mexico City, 1973), p. 30.

Spanish liberty implied only license; but the language of the natural law offered to men who had been educated on the writings of Suárez and Molina very much the same general conclusions as a reading of Locke, Coke, and Magna Carta offered John Adams and James Otis. For all these colonists their monarch had transformed himself into a tyrant and by so doing had freed his subjects from any further obligation to obey his laws.

Denial of natural rights and, with it, the Castilian government's persistent attempt to impose upon the criollos a greater political and financial commitment to the crown, had created a state of almost constant rebellion during the seventeenth century.[43] But all these uprisings had been short-lived and devoid of any political cohesion. The men who had grown up after the failure of Martín Cortés's bid for independence had contented themselves with demanding their rights within the terms established by the monarchy itself. Like their counterparts among the lesser nobility in Europe, the focus of their anger had not been, as it had for Cortés, the king but the king's officers. During the revolt against the marqués de Gelves no attempt was made to create an independent state nor was the possibility ever discussed. There were some like the oidor Pedro de Vergara Gravina, who is said to have declared "that if his Majesty does not remove this government and office, he would remove the kingdom from obedience [to the monarch]."[44] But they were few. Most of the rebels' hostility was reserved for the person of Gelves himself, and the language of their battle cry—"long live the king, down with bad government"[45]—was typical of contemporary European revolts.

The political image of both Mexico and Peru to which all these revolts made tacit appeal was that of a quasi-autonomous "kingdom" within a larger cluster of kingdoms—what is referred to as "Greater Spain," *magnae hispaniae*—under a single sovereign.[46] Each part of this cluster was deemed to possess its own identity, its own native nobility, and its own government. All parts owed allegiance to the sovereign, but all were self-governing commonwealths with their own customs and culture, their own customary laws and *fueros*. Mexico and Peru were considered by their inhabitants to be no different from the Netherlands, Aragon, or Naples. They were not colonies—indeed the word is never used of any of the Amer-

---

[43] For a list of these uprisings, see Augustín Cue Canovas, *Historia social y ecónomica de Mexico (1521–1854)* (Mexico City, 1972), pp. 183–87.

[44] "Acusacion fecha y puesta al licenciado Pedro de Vergara Gravina, oydor de la Real Audiencia de Mexico, por el licenciado Matias de Palacios fiscal de la visita General de la Nueva España, año de 1626," BL Add. Ms. 13,975, ff. 270–275 at f. 270v.

[45] *Documentos para la historia de Mexico*, 2d series (Mexico 1855), 1:92.

[46] See, e.g., the comments of Francisco Cervantes de Salazar, *Mexico en 1554 y túmulo imperial*, ed. E. O'Gorman (Mexico City, 1963), p. 66.

ican possessions—they were kingdoms, which each should be governed as if it were the king's only realm. This view had been presented by Francisco Falcón before the Second Council of Lima as early as 1567 as the official description of the American colonies' relationship with the crown.[47] But the idea was set out most clearly by Juan de Solórzano Pereyra, oidor of the audiencia of Lima from 1609 to 1627, who, though a gachupín himself, had great understanding of and sympathy with the criollo cause. In his *Política Indiana* of 1648 he argued that it was of little real consequence that "all these kingdoms are now united and today constitute a single monarchy," for "the most certain thing is that, also in this case, the kingdoms have to be ruled and governed as if the king who holds them all were only the king of each one of them."[48] Though the language of its formal address and many of the terms of the laws of 1681 suggested that it acknowledged the claims implicit in Solorzano's contention, the crown never made any attempt to define clearly the true status of any of its dependencies. The fact that America had been incorporated into the crown of Castile as early as 1523 excluded the possibility (as Solorzano pointed out) that New Spain might enjoy the same legal status as Aragon, Navarre, Naples, or Milan. From immediately after the conquest until independence, however, the criollos persisted in assuming that their relationship with the mother country was founded upon a contract by which they enjoyed equal standing with all the other "kingdoms" of the empire.

Ahumada represented this conviction by a complex metaphor of marriage. The vassals of each kingdom are, he argued, like the sons of different marriages. "The Americans who are Your Majesty's sons by a second wife, which is America, should not be deprived of those goods which are their birthright from their mother; nor should those there [i.e. in Spain] who are the sons of the first marriage be given those things which by all rights belong to the offspring of the second marriage."[49] And this suggestion, despite the image of a bigamous monarch that it conjures up, was thought sufficiently compelling by the members of the Ayuntamiento of Mexico City for them to repeat it in a simplified form in the *Representación* of 1771.[50]

[47] Quoted by Mario Góngora, *Studies in the Colonial History of Spanish America* (Cambridge, 1975), p. 80.

[48] Juan de Solórzano Pereyra, *Política indiana*, 5 vols., Biblioteca de autores españoles, vols. 252–56 (Madrid, 1972), vol. 3, bk. 4, cap. xix, 37.

[49] Ahumada, *Representación política-legal*, f. 10v.

[50] "Representación que hizo la ciudad de Mexico al rey D. Carlos III en 1771 sobre que los *criollos* deben ser preferidos a los europeos en la distribución de beneficios y empleos de estos reinos," printed in *Colección de documentos para la historia de la guerra de la independencia de Mexico de 1808 a 1821*, ed. J. E. Hernández y Dávalos (Mexico City, 1877), 1:427–55 at p. 437.

In terms of "each realm by itself," it became possible to mobilize ancient Castilian legislation in defense of the criollos' claims, for if New Spain and Peru were true kingdoms, they had to be guided by the same legislative principles (if not the same laws) as Castile. As the *Representación* pointed out, not only had the *Recopilación* restricted office, and hence political power, to native sons, but a decree that the Cortes of Madrid had presented to Henry III in 1396 had established the principle, respected in the reconquered areas of southern Spain, that all important offices should be inalienable.[51] Of course, the Ayuntamiento admitted that it was not possible to regard peninsular Spaniards as foreigners in the same way that Englishmen or Dutchmen were foreigners. But since, in the view of the Ayuntamiento, citizenship was conferred as much by place of birth as by blood, the Spaniards were foreign in the sense that they possessed none of "the love that men have for the soil on which they were born, and the indifference to all others." The Spaniards, claimed the *Representación*, "have their fathers, their brothers and all that is capable of drawing the inclinations of a man in the old not the new Spain, for when a man exiles himself to such a distance to fulfill an employment, he does not change his nature."[52]

This was a clear and emphatic rejection of Charles III's desperate move to assert the Spanishness of a group that had long since lost any sense of identity with their "mother country" and of his attempt to create in America "a single nation" of criollos and *peninsulares* by making it possible at least in theory for criollos to pursue a public career in Spain.[53] The criollos only sought control of their own affairs and political authority in the land that they had regarded for at least two hundred years as their "mother country." They wanted no part of the government of Spain nor showed any special desire to be closer to the person of their king so that he might be able, as Charles claimed, "to ensure himself of their merits."[54] "We renounce," declared Juan Pablo Viscardo in 1791, "the ridiculous system of *union and equality.*"[55]

III

In the background of this battle of claims lay the realities and, perhaps more important, the myths of societies that were divided not merely into criollos and gachupines but also into whites and Indians, mestizos and mu-

---

[51] "Representación," p. 429, and see R. Konetzke, "La condición legal de los *criollos* y las causas de la independencia," *Estudios americanos* 11 (1950):31–54.

[52] "Representación," p. 430.

[53] Konetzke, "La condición legal de los *criollos*," p. 46.

[54] Charles IV in the preamble to the statutes of the *Real colegio de nobles americanos* founded in Granada in 1792, quoted by Konetzke, "La condición legal de los criollos," p. 50.

[55] Viscardo, *Carta*, p. 2.

lattoes, *pardos* and blacks. The first conquerors, as we have seen, claimed to be the feudal lords of the subordinate Amerindian population. Since the encomienda and the *mita* were grants of people, not land, Indians were the measure of the encomendero's wealth, which is why the settlers resisted so fiercely the idea, championed by both the crown and the mendicant orders, of a separate Indian "republic." Although this would not have deprived the settlers of their labor force, it would have eliminated their political authority and hence their political status, by placing the Indians under crown and ecclesiastical control.[56]

As the Indian population declined and the criollos slowly began to diversify their activities, however, there developed in the Spanish mind a clear distinction between the living Indian and his ancestors. Like the old conquistadores themselves, the Inca and the ancient Mexica—or the "Aztecs," as they became known during the eighteenth century[57]—with whom they had fought their legendary battles became rapidly mythologized. In this the Spanish relationship with the indigenous populations was quite unlike that of any of the other European settlers. None of the Brazilian or North American tribes showed any signs of possessing or of ever having possessed a culture that their conquerors could recognize as "civilized." The freedom-loving Indian might one day become a symbol of a free America, but the symbolism was not grounded in the sense of the possible existence of a historical association between the white man and the red. It was, as Michael Zuckerman says, the mere appropriation of attributes that the colonists "had long dared contemplate from afar, under cover of contempt." For the Spaniards, however, the existence of a "heroic" Indian past was crucial to the military imagery that made up so large a part of the criollos' vision of their own history as a self-aware people.

The degree of mythologization, however, and the role played by these mythic Indians in the criollos' consciousness of that history differed greatly between Mexico and Peru. In Peru the Indian population was far more numerous and more densely concentrated than it was in Mexico. Peruvian Indian revolts, although before the Tupac Amaru uprising of 1780–1783 they presented very little real threat to the viceregal government, were nonetheless a regular event. The Mexica, on the other hand, crushed by conquest and decimated by disease, had with one notable exception remained quiescent since the late sixteenth century. What few serious uprisings there were took place in the still "unpacified" areas among such "barbarous" tribes as the Chichimeca and the Otomi. Whereas the Mexican criollo

---

[56] Charles Gibson, *The Aztecs under Spanish Rule* (Stanford and Oxford, 1964), pp. 81–97.
[57] See R. Barlow, "Some Remarks on the Term 'Aztec Empire,'" *The Americas* 1 (1945):345–49.

could therefore reflect in relative safety upon the glories of the Aztec past, Peruvian whites were more apprehensive about the possibilities of awakening old loyalties and ancient ambitions among their subject peoples.

For the criollos of Mexico, however, the Indians, both ancient and modern, were perhaps the most important single element in the criollo interpretation of the history of "New Spain" and thus in the creation of their own national identity. Whether the Indians were, as they had been for Cortés, feudal vassals or, as they would be for Hidalgo and Morelos, the soldiers of a revolutionary army and the beneficiaries of a new revolutionary society, they were crucial to the sense that the criollos of New Spain had of what it meant to be a "Mexican." Cortés had portrayed the Mexica as a warrior race of great technical achievements, a worthy foil for his ultimately superior military and diplomatic skills. His images of the city of Tenochtitlan and detailed descriptions of Moctezuma's "court" are in large measure borrowed from accounts of Moorish Granada; Moctezuma and the other Mexica "princes" conform to an image of "barbarian" kings from the Great Khan to the Ottoman Sultan. The overbearing ambitions of men like Cortés and the Pizarro brothers, who were highly sensitive to the belief that the greatness of a man is to be measured by the quality of the things he can command, required the subjugation not of a race of inferior barbarians but of a people whose rule would redound to their conqueror's own glory. These Indians were men with whom Cortés spoke as equals and with whose daughters his followers (if not he himself) were prepared to marry and raise legitimate children. Marriage into the Indian "nobility" was at first seen to constitute a social advancement for some of the socially lower—and also for some of the not so low—members of Cortés's and Pizarro's armies. At least one family, the Toledo, even after it had become prosperous and returned to Spain, was happy to append the name "Moctezuma" to its own. These associations gave such families claims to political power that would otherwise have been denied them. Isabel Toledo Moctezuma, self-styled "Empress of Mexico," was still making claims for compensation, which seem to have been heard if not fulfilled, as late as the seventeenth century.[58] Association through marriage with Indian "kings" might also be used to confer legitimation on acts of rebellion. In 1546, for instance, Francisco Pizarro's brother Gonzalo, in revolt against the Castilian crown, spoke of marrying an Inca princess and thereby legitimatizing his wish to be crowned king of Peru.[59]

The idea that the Indians were noble barbarians like the Moors or the

[58] These are collected in Archivo General de Indias, Patronato 184, Ramo 26.
[59] G. V. Scammell, The World Encompassed (London and New York, 1981), p. 316.

Turks, together with the idea that Indian blood might confer some degree of nobility upon a plebeian Spaniard did not, however, last long. Although some of Cortés's and Pizarro's men had been proud to marry into the ancient Indian aristocracy, they were not keen to associate themselves with their successors, the *curacas* and *caciques*, who were little more than tribute collectors for the encomenderos. Intermarriage of course continued and was encouraged by the crown as preferable to concubinage. But in fact most Spaniards were more willing to marry white prostitutes than Indians.[60]

The cultural image of the noble Indian, together with the notion that noble Indian blood might confer noble status was revived during the eighteenth century, however, as part of a complex reworking of the early history of the conquest. "There are many [Americans]," declared the *Representación* of 1771, "who can trace their origins to the highest nobility in Spain. There are others, no less commendable by their origins, who carry in their veins the Royal Blood of America."[61] The criollos, it continued, had been accused by the peninsular Spaniards of being half-breeds (mestizos). But because the term mestizo suggested racial inferiority, it could not be applied to those who had married into the Indian nobility. They, in some unspecified sense, were pure. Yet too close an association with Indian blood, however noble, might imply an uncomfortably close link with living Indians; the *Representación* went on to point out that after so many generations the Indian strain in those whose ancestors had mixed their blood with "the royal families of the nation" was now so weak that they had all become "pure" Spaniards.[62] The criollos wished to assume a direct link through kin with an ancient Indian past that would provide them with an independent historical identity; at the same time they needed to avoid, in a society so obsessed with racial purity, any suggestion that this association might have contaminated their blood. This undertaking proved ultimately to be a ludicrous one, but it illustrates all too well the impossibility of any attempt to separate entirely the myth of the "Aztec" past from the living realities of the "Indian" present. The task was made even more perilous and uncertain by the fact that José González de Castañeda and those like him were living in a society that had since the middle of the sixteenth century been not biracial but multiracial.

The introduction of large numbers of black slaves and their subsequent interbreeding with both whites and Indians had produced a wide diversity of racial mixtures, generally known by the term *castas*. Eighteenth-century observers, overtaken by the contemporary passion for classification, listed,

---

[60] Magnus Mörner, *Race Mixture in the History of Latin American* (Boston, 1967), p. 26.
[61] "Representación," p. 442.
[62] Ibid., p. 441.

described, and even painted pictures of some sixteen different racial variations.[63] For most official purposes, however, society was divided into Spaniards, castas of every kind, blacks, and Indians. In law the social hierarchy
ran from white at the top to mulatto (half-white, half-black) at the bottom.
The pure Indian came after the mestizo and the black had no place on the
social map at all. In practice, however, it was the Indian who occupied the
lowest position, lower, as one observer noted with indignation, "even than
Blacks"[64] who, according to Hernán Carrillo Altamiro, mistreated them,
"making foul use of their women."[65] The existence of this racial pyramid,
and of the Indian's position at the very base of it, had the effect of both
reenforcing and unsettling the whites' view of themselves and of their relationship with the conquered and enslaved races over whom they ruled.
Within such a society, whiteness was frequently considered to be sufficient
for one to claim membership in the elite. "There is no Spaniard," observed
Juan Ortíz de Cervantes in 1619, "who does not wish to treat the Indians
imperiously, although the Spaniard may be low-[born], the Indian a chieftain, a curaca or an *alcalde* [mayor]."[66] But it was also a society that tolerated
a large degree of racial mobility, and this made it difficult for the criollos to
make any unassailable claims to purity of blood (*limpieza de sangre*). Until
the latter part of the sixteenth century, mestizos born in wedlock had been
categorized as Spaniards; by a decree of 1533, even those mestizo children
living in Indian communities were ordered to be housed in Spanish towns
and provided with a Spanish education.[67] By the beginning of the eighteenth century, there were few criollo families who were entirely without
Indian blood. As one observer noted in 1792, any attempt to distinguish
between pure whites and the whiter of the castas would be to "expose the
dark stains erased by time in many prominent families." In Tepetlaztoc, he
said, "you will find a town full of Spaniards," no matter how dark or tawny
they might appear.[68] The claims of near-white pardos (persons of mulatto

[63] Perhaps the best example of the genre is Pedro Alonso O'Crovley's "Idea compendiosa
del Reyno de la Nueva España" [1774], Biblioteca Nacional, Madrid, Ms. 4532; see also Mörner, *Race Mixture*, pp. 58–59.

[64] Angel Rosenblatt, *La población indígena y mestizage en América* (Buenos Aires, 1954),
2:165.

[65] *El doctor Hernán Carillo Altamirano vezino y natural de la ciudad de Mexico en la Nueva España, abogado de la real audiencia y protector de los indios de aquel reyno dize* . . . (Mexico?, n.d.),
p. 8. See also the (untitled) protest from an Indian chieftain ("cacique") to the king in 1630,
that everyone, "from the priests and the *corregidores* to the vilest negro and mestizo beats [the
Indians] and mistreats them (BL Add. Ms. 13,976, ff. 356–57v, at f. 357).

[66] Ortíz de Cervantes, *Memorial*, f. 13v.

[67] Jose Ma. Ots Capdequi, *El estado español en las Indias* (Buenos Aires and Mexico City,
1952), pp. 125–26.

[68] Quoted by G. Aguirre Beltrán, *La población negra de Mexico: estudio etnohistórico* (Mexico
City, 1972), p. 270. What all groups wished to avoid was being classified as either pardos or

and white origin) and mestizos to white status was tacitly accepted by both the lay and ecclesiastical authorities. There are instances in many parish records of the classifier *pardo* having been erased and replaced by the term *español*. And, as the viceroy, the marqués of Mancera, told his successor in 1673, behavior counted for as much as color provided that the shades were not too marked. "The mestizos," he wrote, "pride themselves on having our blood, and on some occasions have demonstrated that they know how to comply with such obligations."[69]

Such racial fluidity seriously undermined the criollo sense of being a closed white elite and consequently made the notion of interbreeding with Indians, however noble, very unattractive. The Americans, as they soon came to call themselves, were to have a culture that was "Mexican" or "Peruvian"-Spanish in customs and rooted in an understanding of a mythical Indian past. But it was to be white, español, by blood.[70]

IV

The desirability of a relationship between the conqueror and the conquered based upon kin did not survive Cortés's own lifetime. But it dominated much of the writings of the mestizo elite during the first half of the sixteenth century. Men like Fernando Alva Ixtlilxochitl, descendant on his mother's side from the "kings" of Texcoco who, after some forceful persuasion, had assisted Cortés in the conquest of Tenochtitlan; the Tlaxcalan Diego Muñoz Camargo; and, the most enduring of them all, Garcilaso de la Vega, "El Inca," son of a Spanish father and an Inca "princess," all attempted to articulate their divided heritage and their divided loyalties by writing histories that would establish for themselves and those like them a legitimate place in the conquerors' society. For all of them the true American society was to be a mestizo one, a hybrid culture mixing Spanish laws and the Christian religion with Indian customs. Without Texcocan or (more plausibly) Tlaxcalan support, argued Ixtlilxochitl and Muñoz Camargo, Cortés's armies would have been driven back into the sea. The conquest had been a joint venture with the Indians taking the major role. "The first Spaniards who came to these parts," wrote Ixtlilxochitl, "achieved little and came off badly." It was the actions of his ancestors that alone had made the conquest possible; it was they who had "led the dance and ran the

Indians, both of which were tributary groups. See John K. Chance, *Race and Class in Colonial Oaxaca* (Stanford, 1978), p. 178.

[69] *Instrucciones que los vireyes de Nueva España dejaron a sus sucesores*, 1:104–105.

[70] Fray Francisco de Ajofrín, an eighteenth-century traveler in Mexico noted that "they call all white men Spaniards," regardless of nationality. *Diario del viaje que por ordén de la sagrada congregación de propaganda fide hizo a la América septentrional en el siglo XVIII*, ed. Vicente Castañeda y Alcover, 2 vols. (Madrid, 1958–59), 1:66.

first risks."[71] Ixtlilxochitl's *Sumaria relación* and Muñoz Camargo's *Historia de Tlaxcala*, like Garcilaso's monumental *Comentarios reales de los Incas*, are in part a plea for the recognition of services rendered.[72] But they are a plea made on behalf of an entire race. In Ixtlilxochitl's claims that the Texcocans were the true instruments of conquest, in Garcilaso's careful reordering of the chronology of the Inca past to present the coming of the Spaniards as a quasi-divine act, prepared (as Rome had prepared for the coming of Christ) by an empire that had brought political cohesion, organized religion, and a single language to a heterogeneous group of societies, there is a demand that the historical role of the Indian peoples in the formation of a new Christian and multiracial society be granted its true significance. But the ambitions of Garcilaso and Ixtlilxochitl were doomed to extinction along with the conquistador hopes for a native nobility of service. Within a few years of the conquest the mestizos, far from being the bearers of a new mixed culture, had become a despised breed, contemptuous of their own Indian origins and rejected by a white elite that had come to fear racial contamination too much to wish to acknowledge direct association with them. By the middle of the sixteenth century the image of the Indian had become sharply divided: on the one hand was the living reality, the poor oppressed white man's beast of burden, and on the other, now infinitely remote, were the figures from a mythic past.

One of the earliest and most influential attempts by a criollo intellectual to exploit this division between mythic Indian past and real Indian present was made by the seventeenth-century Mexican scholar and royal cosmographer, Carlos de Sigüenza y Góngora (1645–1700). His works varied from a study of comets to a celebration of the Hospital of the Immaculate Conception in Mexico City, each part of an attempt to articulate a wide-ranging description, which is at the same time a defense, of what he referred to as "the *criollo* nation."[73] Like all colonies, however, the members of this nation could make only very restricted use of political arguments from tradition or example, because the only traditions and examples available to them were European ones. They had, therefore, either to insist on their Europeanness, like the English in America, the Caribbean, or Ireland, or to limit themselves to arguments from principle. But the Mexican and to a lesser degree the Peruvian *criollos* had, or so it seemed to Sigüenza y Gón-

---

[71] *Obras históricas de Don Fernando Alva de Ixtlilxochitl*, ed. Alfredo Chavero, 2 vols. (Mexico City, 1891), 1:389.

[72] This is made explicit by Ixtlilxochitl, *Obras*, 1:434.

[73] Carlos de Sigüenza y Góngora, *Theatro de virtudes políticas que constituyen a un príncipe, advertidas en los monarchas antiguos del Mexico imperio*, in *Obras*, ed. Francisco Pérez Salazar (Mexico City, 1928), pp. 1–148 at pp. 33–34.

gora, an advantage over the northern colonists, because they could appropriate a truly "national" political tradition whose sources were to be found not only in the "heroic piety" of the conquerors[74] but more specifically in the civic achievements of the civilization they had overthrown. In the ancient Mexica past, he argued, the criollo community possessed its own classical antiquity, inferior in many respects but no less fantastic nor any less instructive in the examples it could provide than that of Greece and Rome. The Mexica, although "buried in a distant darkness" because of their barbarity, had nonetheless possessed "politic schools in their antiquity."[75]

Sigüenza y Góngora's attempts to substitute Mexica models for Greco-Roman ones was carried out most strikingly in the program for a triumphal arch erected in 1681 to welcome the viceroy, the count of Paredes. Sigüenza y Góngora was not the first person in Mexico to employ a public monument as the vehicle for a political statement. Francisco Cervantes de Salazar, who although he was himself a gachupín soon became a cultural spokesman for the elite of the colony as professor of rhetoric at the newly created University of Mexico, had in 1554 composed a program for a ceremonial catafalque for Charles V. This had combined scenes depicting the deeds of Cortés with more traditional classical iconography. One of these showed Cortés in the act of grounding his ships, symbolizing the distance that had thereafter separated New from Old Spain. But there was nothing particularly original in Cervantes's tomb. Sigüenza y Góngora's arch, on the other hand, was, and loudly proclaimed itself to be, a radical departure from tradition. He published an account and an explanation of the program for this work with the title *Theatro de virtudes políticas* (The theater of political virtues). It is a treatise combining a number of apparently contradictory political arguments in a manner that suggests conceptual confusion rather than any attempt at a synthesis. The technique of deploying lengthy quotations to illustrate every point, however trivial, also demonstrates the criollo intellectual's overriding need to prove the breadth of his knowledge of European political literature to an audience ever ready to dismiss his efforts as those of an ignorant backwoodsman. But even through the dead weight of so much accumulated learning the message of the *Theater* is clear: for the criollos the "Mexican empire" is their classical heritage, one in whose civic virtues white Mexicans can share because they, like the "ancient monarchs" of the old empire, had been born in the land of Mexico.

---

[74] Carlos de Sigüenza y Góngora, *Piedad heroyca de Don Fernando Cortés*, ed. Jaime Delgado (Mexico City, 1962).

[75] Carlos de Sigüenza y Góngora, *Triumpho parthenico que en gloria de Maria Santissima immaculadamente concebida, celebro la pontificia, Imperial y Regia Academia Mexicana* (Mexico City, 1683), f. 4.

Furthermore, not only is Mexica history potentially as instructive as the history of the ancient world, it is also a part, albeit a remote part, of that history. Such an apparently improbable association between the Old World and the New is characteristic of the extensive contemporary attempt to account for the origin of the Indian tribes (where did they originally come from? how did they get there and when?) in a way that would both establish them as true sons of Adam and yield some causal explanation of their cultural behavior. Sigüenza y Góngora's explanation for the origin of the "Mexicans" is grounded in an attempt to establish a link between the Mexica, the ancient Greeks, and the sons of Noah by means of an interpretation of the name "Neptune."[76] In common with most seventeenth-century mythologizers, Sigüenza y Góngora regarded all myths as garbled versions of real historical events. Beneath the fabulous guise of a marine deity it was possible to discover a real historical figure, "Nephtuim," the son of Misraim, son of Shem, who was the true "progenitor of this New World."[77] This piece of reasoning provided the Indians with an impeccable Old World pedigree and made them the heirs to the myths and hence to the symbolic history of the ancient Greeks. It also did something else. According to Sigüenza y Góngora, Neptune was the historical person whose return the Indians had been expecting in the guise of their creator-deity Quetzalcoatl.[78] In making this claim, his intention (also based upon a false etymology) was to exploit another popular myth, the by then widely accepted story that Moctezuma had donated his empire to Cortés in the belief that he was Quetzalcoatl. If Neptune and Quetzalcoatl were in fact the same historical person, it might be possible to argue (though Sigüenza y Góngora does no more than suggest) that there was a sense in which the Spaniards had become, by the terms of Moctezuma's "donation," the true heirs of "Nepthuim." This elaborate edifice of analogy and allusion thus not only linked the Indians with the old world of the Greeks and Hebrews (and even, at a later point, with the Egyptians)[79] but also presented the Spanish conquerors as their natural rulers, reenforcing Sigüenza y Góngora's own claims that the criollo descendants of the conquerors were the beneficiaries of a Mexican ancient history.

[76] Sigüenza y Góngora, *Theatro de virtudes políticas*, p. 23.

[77] Ibid., pp. 18–19.

[78] Ibid., p. 30. Fray Servando Teresa de Mier attempted a similar reevaluation of the Mexica past by arguing that the Indians had had a full understanding of the theological principles of Christianity, a claim that had the effect of denying to the Spaniards the responsibility for the conversion of Mexico. His creation of an ancient genealogy for the Indians was, however, part of an attempt, to which he dedicated much of his life, to prove that Quetzalcoatl was in fact St. Thomas the Apostle. See his "Manifesto apologético" in *Escritos inéditos*, ed. J. M. Miguel Verges and Hugo Díaz Thomé (Mexico City, 1944), pp. 136–41.

[79] Sigüenza y Góngora, *Theatro de virtudes políticas*, p. 34.

Having made this leap from ancient Greece to ancient Mexico, the way was now open for a program in which figures from "Mexican" history could be used to represent civic and intellectual virtues in place of the traditional classical deities. Sigüenza y Góngora's purpose was clear and explicit. "It has been," he wrote, "the common style of the American [by which he meant *criollo*] mind to beautify the majority of their *triumphal arches* that they erect to welcome princes with mythological ideas and fabulous lies." This method he now rejects, because "who would be so unmindful of his *patria* as to require fabulous deeds to represent its achievements."[80] "In the *Mexican* emperors," he went on, "who really lived in this most celebrated empire of *America*, I discovered without difficulty what others had sought in *fables*." The *Theatro de virtudes políticas* is an elaborate exegesis on the proper contemporary significance of each of these figures, with the purpose of establishing indigenous models for civic virtue. "It would be to harass the *patria*," he wrote, "to turn to foreign heroes from whom the Romans learned the exercise of virtue, . . . when there is an abundance of precepts for political action even among those peoples who are taken to be barbarians."[81]

The actual message each scene on the arch proclaims is not so alarming as this general thesis might suggest. The vehicle for the expression of these Roman virtues may be the chieftains of old Mexico, but the virtues remain Roman. "Acampich" (Acamapichtli), the Mexica "king" who led his peoples out of slavery, appears in the guise of hope.[82] But it would be unwise to make too much of this. Sigüenza y Góngora had no wish to see an independent Mexico and no sense of belonging to a captive race. His writings are nevertheless the product of a society clearly troubled by the need to define and to find some means of representing its relationship both with the lands it occupied with which it had no immediate cultural connections, and with a "mother country" that as a source of cultural and political inspiration was rapidly losing its importance. Sigüenza y Góngora's Indian figures and his spurious genealogies were part of a new and still unstable political language that sought to exploit an indigenous history in the same way that the history of classical Europe had been exploited by the political theorists with whose works the Mexican scholar was, or at least claimed to be, so familiar. This led him to a preoccupation with the stuff of that past, the buildings, the writings, the artifacts, and the art, and also led to a greater concern with the criollo role in the wider world as the guardians of what he had come to see as a criollo heritage. How foreigners must despise the Mex-

[80] Ibid., p. 16.
[81] Ibid., pp. 17–18.
[82] Ibid., pp. 75–78.

ican nation, he complained, when the task of collecting American material had fallen to an Englishman, Samuel Purchas, who in his work had "compiled all that the finest lover of our *patria* could have expressed."[83]

Sigüenza y Góngora's use of the Mexica past did not, however, attempt to solve the problem of how to reconcile that past with the brute facts of the Indian present. For him, as for most other criollos, that problem remained insuperable. But it could not be ignored for long. In 1692 he was a witness, albeit from a safe distance, of an Indian uprising that caused widespread damage to Mexico City and that was clearly directed against all Spaniards, gachupín and criollo alike. Thereafter, and without a word, his own great endeavor to save the history of the Mexica from destruction, his collection of codices and artifacts and his entire "Indian Museum," were all abandoned.[84]

Their culture destroyed by the conquerors, both lay and ecclesiastical, and their identity all but erased by Spanish efforts to "civilize" them, the living Indians were ill-suited to play the role of the heirs to the "Aztec Empire." Few criollos before the beginning of the eighteenth century seem to have attributed this to the impact of the conquest. Most assumed that the Indians' "idleness and viciousness," their reluctance to adopt Spanish ways, their obvious distaste for Christian theology (if not for Christian ritual), their drunkenness, and their refusal to accept European economic norms were all to be attributed to their innate disposition. It was only in the eighteenth century, when a more dispassionate assessment of the conquest's impact on indigenous cultures became possible, that criollos began to point to the behavior of the conquistadores and their descendants as an explanation for the startling differences between the modern Indian and the image of the ancient one.

"It is uncertain," wrote Pedro Alonso O'Crovley, a Franciscan of Irish origin with a passionate interest in ethnography, "whether their great meekness and humility derives from a natural disposition or the miserable condition in which they live."[85] The great Jesuit historian of the eighteenth century, Francisco Clavigero, entertained no such doubts. His *Storia antica del Messico*—"the history of Mexico by a Mexican"—written from exile in Bologna and printed in 1770 was intended, in part at least, to demonstrate that the Indians were as innately gifted as any white.[86] What now

---

[83] Ibid., p. 34.

[84] Sigüenza y Góngora left an account of the event in *Alboroto y motín del 8 de junio 1692*, ed. Irving A. Leonard (Mexico City, 1932).

[85] O'Crovley, "Idea compendiosa," f. 150.

[86] Because it is more widely available, I have used the Spanish version: *Historia antigua de Mexico*, ed. R. P. Mariano Cuevas (Mexico City, 1964), p. xvii. The work is dedicated to the University of Mexico. For a more extensive treatment of Clavigero's use of the Mexica past, see Anthony Pagden, *An Eighteenth-Century Historian of Mexico: Francisco Javier Clavigero and the Storia antica del Messico* (Leiden, 1983).

prevents them, Clavigero argued, from producing "philosophers, mathematicians, and theologians" is merely their present condition, their "miserable servile life." Any culture, no matter how splendid, can be brought low by the conquest and enslavement of its people. Would anyone, he asked, on seeing the Greeks today, ever imagine that these people had produced Plato?[87] The conclusion to be drawn from this argument was that the Spaniards—which for Clavigero meant the gachupines—were to be compared to the Turks, who for any writer of the eighteenth century were the embodiment of that "oriental despotism" that had long been used as a metaphor for the "tyranny" of absolute monarchy by its opponents.

Clavigero's work was in many respects, some of them self-conscious, a continuation of Sigüenza y Góngora's. The Aztecs of the *Storia antica* are the bearers of a classical past whose very existence was a refutation of all those Europeans—Buffon, the Abbé Raynal, the Scottish historian William Robertson, and the Prussian naturalist Cornelius de Pauw in particular—who claimed that the Americas were, by their very nature, incapable of producing anything of lasting cultural value, that any New World culture whether autochthonous or transplanted must be inferior to the cultures of the Old World.

Clavigero was a Jesuit and the Jesuits, before their expulsion in 1767, helped to encourage the criollos in their cultural and ultimately political aspirations more than any other ecclesiastical body. They had arrived too late to reap any of the initial spiritual benefits of the conquest, and although they succeeded in seizing substantial numbers of Indians from the Franciscans and Augustinians and later gained control of some of the more remote areas, most notably Paraguay, their prime concern was the education of the white population. During the seventeenth and eighteenth centuries the Jesuits thus became the intellectual elite of the colony, the voice of its aspirations and the most self-consciously patriotic of all "Mexicans."

Men like Clavigero were able to reestablish some connection between the Indian past and the realities of the Indian present. By the end of the century other less reflective criollos had even come to regard the plight of the Indians as a metaphor for their own oppressed condition. The piece of anti-Spanish doggerel popularly known as "Our decree" (*Nuestra cédula*) that sparked off the so-called *comunero* uprising in New Granada in 1781 referred at more than one point to the Peninsular tyranny against the Indians.

> The greatest cause for horror
> In all these deeds of tyranny
> Was to see how, filled with villany,

[87] Clavigero, *Historia antigua*, p. 34.

They treated the poor Indians with such rigor,
That, under the guise of their protector,
They destroyed them with cruel treachery."[88]

This was not simple rhetoric or even the survival of a language of revolt, echoing the demands made by the original comuneros in 1520 that the Indians be set at liberty (though it may have been that too). The rebel leader Juan Francisco Berbero repeated in more exact terms the same message in the "capitulations of Zipanquira," calling there for a reduction in the tribute paid by the Indians to four pesos per Indian per year, because of their "most deplorable and miserable condition."[89] For these comuneros the plight of the Indians was essentially the same as their own: both groups were seen as "natives" afflicted by tyrannous outsiders and in this respect, if in no other, their interests were identical. It was this striking, if inaccurate, message that in 1812 Hidalgo would convert into an ideology of independence.

By the 1780s some members of the white elite in Mexico had become aware that the Indians had been deprived of their rights both as Christians and as men. In part this was due to a relatively new concept of the value of labor. "They prefer hunger and nudity rather than suffer others to take from their hands the fruits of their labors," wrote José Ortega de Texada in 1789. He proposed an elaborate system of redistribution, in which "the fruit of their sweated [labor] would be their most sacred property."[90] But it was also due to the recognition, implicit in Berbero's demands, that the Indians and the castas, long considered an inert mass, could be mobilized in defense of criollo interests. For the ideologues of the comunero revolt, as later for those of the first insurgent movements, identification with the political status of the tyrannized bearers of a once noble past became a means to express their own condition. For Fray Servando Teresa de Mier, the earliest historian of what he called "the revolution" in New Spain, there existed an unwritten charter, a "magna carta" as he put it, that derived from a pact made between the first conquistadores and the ancient Indian "kings." This "constitution," which guaranteed both the rights of the criollos and those of the Indians, had been violated in later years, not by the native-born Spaniards (though elsewhere Mier made no attempt to gloss over their individual cruelty) but by royal despotism.[91] The three centuries of Mexican

[88] All the documents are printed in Pablo E. Cardeñas Acosta, *El movimiento comunal de 1781 en el Nuevo Reino de Granada*, 2 vols. (Bogota, 1960), 1:125.

[89] Ibid., 2:20.

[90] José Ortega de Texada, "Methodo para auxiliar y formentar a los Yndios de los Reynos del Peru y Chile," BL Add. Ms. 13,976, ff. 120–134, at ff. 124–125v.

[91] "José Guerra" [pseudonym for Fray Servando Teresa de Mier], *Historia de la revolución de Nueva España antiguamente Anahuac*, 2 vols. (Mexico City, 1922), 2:342–46. The work was

history could, said Viscardo, be summed up as *"ingratitude, injustice, servitude* and *desolation."*[92]

Association with real Indians, however, was always uncertain and frequently perilous for the pure, or purer, of the white groups. Indian uprisings tended to be revolts against white rule whether criollo or gachupín; and an Indian rebellion always threatened to carry with it the mestizo, mulatto, and black masses that comprised the bulk of every colonial population. The comuneros of New Granada employed a political language that drew heavily on the concept of Indian rights to legitimate their own claims, but there were very few real Indians in their army. Similarly, the leaders of the "Inca" uprising of 1750, though they wished for an independent Indian state, accepted that this would still be a state ruled by the same white elite. What they claimed as their rights were only the political dues owed to every European polity. They had, they said, risen in revolt "for God and our honor . . . as other nations have done to restore their kingdoms, as Portugal did and the Kingdom of the Two Sicilies."[93] The Tupac Amaru revolt of 1780–1783, however, alienated the Peruvian criollo elite forever. Although Tupac Amaru had promised only to "extinguish the corregidores in the public interest,"[94] to abolish taxes and internal customs duties, and with one exception of doubtful authenticity, had made no explicit claims to his ancestor's "empire," the image that lay behind the revolt, the so-called *Imperio del Tahuantinsuyu*,[95] was a mestizo fantasy. Had it ever been realized, it would have excluded the white population from what they believed to be their political and cultural heritage. Indians, like the peasants of Europe, might provide rebels against royal authority with a justification, even a descriptive vocabulary, for their rebellion. But once the rebellion was over they, like their European counterparts, were supposed to return quietly to their villages to occupy the same social position as before. The threat posed by men like Tupac Amaru—and indeed by the leaders of the first insurgent movements in Mexico, Morelos and Hidalgo—lay in ambitions that were built upon an image of a new social order in which the downtrodden would ultimately become the rulers; this was something the criollos feared far more than the officers of the Spanish crown. Like the Tupac Amaru rebel-

---

first printed in London in 1813. On the Mexican "Magna Carta," see Brading, *Los orígines*, p. 71.

[92] Viscardo, *Carta*, p. 2.

[93] "Copia de la carta que se cogio a un indio . . . ," BL Add. Ms. 13,976, ff. 195–198 at ff. 197v–198.

[94] See Lillian Estelle Fisher, *The Last Inca Revolt, 1780–83* (Norman, 1966), p. 135.

[95] See John H. Rowe, "El movimiento nacional inca del siglo XVIII," *Revista universitaria* [Cuzco], 107 (1954), pp. 17–47. After the rebellion had been crushed the use of any imagery relating to the Inca past was banned from all public places.

lion, that of Morelos and Hidalgo in Mexico failed to win the support of the colonial elite because it too, by its invocation of the names of Moctezuma and Cuahautemoc, threatened to mobilize a mass that in the real world of experience was, as the criollos well knew, far removed from the noble Aztecs of Sigüenza y Góngora and Clavigero.

V

The role of the changing relationship between Indians past and present, living criollos, and dead conquistadores in the formation of a criollo identity can also be seen in the terminology used by the members of the colonial societies to describe both themselves and the other peoples among whom they lived. As with so many groups, initially uncertain of their own identity and status, the criollos rapidly adopted Spanish terms of abuse as descriptive labels. These generally drew close parallels between the Indian population and the white, or near-white, settlers. A "native" (*natural*), for instance, at first described only an Indian. By 1588, however, the Jesuit General Aquaviva was using it of the criollos; [96] and in 1619, Ortíz de Cervantes declared proudly and tautologically that the criollo elite was composed of "legitimate native sons by nature."[97] The word *criollo* itself, though its etymology is innocent enough (meaning simply native-born), rapidly became a term of gachupín abuse, so that the Jesuit visitor to New Spain in 1579 forbade its use in the schools. "Do not allow our brothers to be called 'criollos,' " he wrote, "rather they should be held in the high esteem which is proper among the religious."[98] Yet in 1634 Luís de Betancurt y Figueroa described the white population of Mexico as constituted by two separate nations, "*criollos* and Castilians";[99] and by 1681, as we have seen, Sigüenza y Góngora was talking proudly of "our *criollo* nation."

The term "Americano," which seems to have been a relatively late coinage—it does not appear in Sebastían de Covarrubias's dictionary of 1610 (although both *criollo* and *perulero* do)—also shifted in meaning. Sigüenza y Góngora uses it sometimes to mean criollo, sometimes as a synonym for "Mexican" (though never to mean merely "Indian"). Similarly, Clavigero employed it to designate both criollos and Indians, ancient and modern. For him the terms served to distinguish between two distinct cultures rather than two races; the counterpart to "American" is not "Spaniard" but "European."[100] *Español*, the term by which all whites were known until Inde-

---

[96] Letter of January 1588, *Monumenta mexicana: Monumenta historica societatis Iesu* [hereafter MM] (Rome, 1956), 4:286–87.

[97] Ortíz de Cervantes, *Información*, f. 9v.

[98] MM, 1:420.

[99] Betancurt y Figueroa, *Memorial i información*, f. 13.

[100] See e.g., Clavigero, *Historia antigua*, pp. 45, 318.

pendence, was first employed to distinguish between the so-called "two republics"—that of the Spaniards and that of the Indians—and implied both cultural and racial differences. By the end of the seventeenth century if not before, however, it had come to acquire a narrowly racial definition. The pardos, mulattoes, and mestizos who succeeded in acquiring the status of white became not "blancos" but "españoles."

In general there was a tendency, which became more marked toward the end of the seventeenth century, both to apply to criollos terms that were once used only of Indians and to employ more precise terms when describing the Indians themselves. The early chroniclers of the Indies had either, like Bernal Díaz del Castillo or Fernández de Oviedo, lumped all Indians together under a single generic heading or, like José de Acosta and Juan de Torquemada, had been careful to distinguish between particular tribes. Men like Clavigero, as part of their quest for a single cultural identity for both Indian and criollo, abandoned both tribal and generic descriptions in favor of national ones. Clavigero employed the word "Mexicano" of the Mexica and "Peruleros" of the Inca (though he also used both Azteca and Inca). "Mexicano" had been used by Cortés in the same sense but, at least by 1570,[101] it had come to describe the criollo population. Similarly "Perulero" was originally the name given to the Spanish settlers in Peru, but it gradually came to be used to describe the Indians there.[102] By using the adjectives of nationality in this way, Clavigero succeeded in suggesting the existence of a single national culture shared in different ways and to different degrees by both criollo and Indian. Both groups took their identity from the land where they had been born. The nation of Mexico, the *patria* Clavigero had been compelled to leave, was multiracial, multifaceted. To be, as he proudly claimed himself, a "Mexican" meant to have a share in both the white and the Indian worlds.

VI

The attitudes of the criollo toward the Indian both past and present was always paradoxical, shifting, ambiguous. The attitude of the peninsular Spaniards, however, was quite clear. Just as the New English in Ireland found an expression for their contempt of the Old by ascribing to them the supposed cultural characteristics of the "very wild Irish," as Nicholas Canny notes below, so the gachupín sought for, and inevitably discovered,

[101] In Pedro de Trejo's *Canción de una dama* of 1570, a deserted Peninsular wife laments having given her love to a "mexicano"—which suggests that by then the word was in common use. *Poetas novohispanos: Primer siglo (1521–1621)*, ed. Alfonso Méndez Plancarte (Mexico City, 1942), 1:7.

[102] See e.g., Clavigero, *Historia antigua*, p. 159.

similarities in behavior between the criollos and the very wild Indians. This correlation was grounded in a theory of climatic determination that was given a measure of scientific respectability by the appearance between 1768 and 1769 of the *Recherches philosophiques sur les Américains* of the naturalist Cornelius de Pauw. De Pauw argued, in crudely reductionist terms, that America was in all respects a degenerate world, geologically and botanically as well as humanly.[103] The *Recherches* were followed in 1777 by the Scottish historian William Robertson's *The History of America*, which though more moderate in its language and better informed about Indian life made much the same point. Both works caused a howl of indignation from the criollos, who regarded the translation of "the detestable work of Robertson" by the Royal Academy of History in Madrid as an act of open aggression by the crown.[104]

The thesis set out by de Pauw and Robertson, however, repeated a much older theory of climates that had been used on several previous occasions to explain the peculiarities of Indian behavior. This was loosely based on a classical solution to the problem of how to provide a causal explanation for the wide variety of human social practices, which postulated that a man's innate disposition to action was determined to a very large extent by the physical environment in which he had been born. The stars at his birth, the soil, and the climate itself all contributed to the formation of his character.[105] The association between physical environment and mental disposition upon which the theory was predicated made its transference from Indians to criollos a relatively simple matter. "Those who are born in [New Spain]," noted the great Franciscan ethnographer Bernardino de Sahagún in the 1570s, "are born very much like the Indians, for in appearance they are Spaniards, but in disposition they are not . . . and I believe that this is due to the climate and the constellations of the land."[106] It became possible to ascribe to the criollos all those supposed shortcomings of the Indians that were thought to derive from psychological weakness or deformation, above all their moral and social instability. In 1681, Juan de Saevata warned the king that because the leaders of the militia were criollos, he feared a rebellion "for although they are attended by loyalty and a sense of duty the strength of the stars and the constellations is terrible."[107] Similarly in Bra-

---

[103] The most detailed study of the debate over the newness of the New World is Antonello Gerbi, *The Dispute of the New World* (Pittsburgh, 1973).

[104] "Carta a Bernardo Iriarte," Valladolid, 1784, BL Add. Ms. 13,976, f. 3.

[105] See Anthony Pagden, *The Fall of Natural Man: The American Indian and the Origins of Comparative Ethnology*, 2d ed. (Cambridge, 1987), pp. 137–40.

[106] Bernardino de Sahagún, *Historia de las cosas de la Nueva España* (Mexico City, 1938), 3:82.

[107] Quoted by Torero, *El quecha*, p. 201.

zil, the Council of the Benedictine order required in 1600 that "because of the humor of the people" the fathers should go about in pairs. The sign of Venus was, as Stuart Schwartz observes above, "simply too strong in the tropical skies" for them to be allowed out on their own.

By the eighteenth century such accusations had become an integral part of the language of criollo-gachupín relations. One of the greatest offenses the people of America has ever had to suffer, complained the *Representación* of 1771, looking back over a long history of calumny, was the supposition that the Indians "despite all the evidence" were irrational beings. "With no less injustice," the document continued, "they pretended that those of us who have been born of European parents on this soil have barely sufficient reason to be men."[108] Even those who did not take such an extreme view were nevertheless willing to accept the possibility of the existence of a number of cultural similarities between Indians and criollos.

Spaniards born in the Indies, wrote the duke of Linares, echoing commonplace accusations against the Indians, lived by subterfuge and deceit: "lying is their common style, giving false testimony a general custom and envy and emulation common practice."[109] Although, as one observer noted, the criollos were "for the most part of a better disposition than those born over here [i.e. in Spain]," they acquired after one generation "the complexion of the land . . . and it seems that they incline toward very little truth."[110] For the same reason the Jesuits, who generally supported the criollos in their conflicts with the peninsular Spaniards, considered them to be fickle and unreliable when it came to admitting them to the Society. After a number of early defections, the provincial council of Lima, in 1582, advised that criollos should not be admitted to the order until they were twenty (instead of the usual eighteen) and should then be subject to a more rigorous training than the Peninsulars,[111] because they were "little capable of mortification because of the liberty and vice in which they are reared and from this comes their inconstancy; and they are very changeable as regards their good intentions."[112] Although one Jesuit claimed that the criollos were less trouble than the Peninsular recruits,[113] it was generally agreed

[108] "Representación," p. 428, and cf. Clavigero, *Historia antigua*, p. 45.
[109] *Instrucciones que los vireyes de Nueva España dejaron a sus sucesores*, 1:234.
[110] "Apuntaciones muy curiosas para la descripción de la Nueva España," ENE, 15:60.
[111] *Monumenta peruana: Monumenta historia societatis Iesu* [hereafter MP] (Rome, 1954), 3:687. The debate over the age of entry, however, had been going on since the 1570s. See, e.g., the recommendations of the visitor Juan de la Plaza "that they should be known for a year or more and have passed their twentieth year" (MP, 1:536). The same situation applied in Mexico. Pedro de Ortigosa in a letter to Aquaviva of May 1592 and the third provincial council both recommended the same course of action (MM, 4:415).
[112] Juan de la Plaza to Aquaviva, Mexico, October 1583, MM, 2:183.
[113] Pedro Díaz to Aquaviva, Mexico, May 1585, complaining of the rector's treatment of the criollos, MM, 2:596.

that "the condition of those who are born here is an inclination for liberty and license in their food, their games, their music, and their recreation" to such a degree that, not surprisingly perhaps, they were believed to have contaminated the Spanish novices.[114]

VII

It is evident from comments such as these that the use of analogies with the given behavioral characteristics of the Indians was not merely a means of denigration; it was also a device to explain the very real, and to the peninsular Spaniards very mysterious, cultural differences that, even by the last two decades of the sixteenth century, had grown up between gachupines and criollos. The love of ostentation and display, the criollo custom of allowing their women far greater freedom than those in the Peninsula (so that they could, as one scandalized observer recorded, be seen playing cards in mixed company), or the criollo passion for tobacco, which priests were reported to indulge in immediately before mass and women at all times ("even the most delicate ladies," remarked Fray Francisco de Ajofrín, "could be seen smoking in the street")—all such deviations from what the peninsular Spaniards regarded as immutable cultural norms suggested not merely a different world but a world inverted.[115] "Here," mocked Ajofrín, "everything is the reverse of Europe, skirts worn inside and petticoats out; children carried on the backs [of their mothers], barefooted men who sell shoes; naked men who sell clothes; the lakes provide more meat [a reference to the wildlife] than they do fish, and the mosquitoes live in the water."[116] For Ajofrín, the visitor, this was merely a joke, but for the average gachupín such apparently deviant behavior required a serious explanation, which could only be provided by some kind of psychological or environmental determinism.

Criollo reactions to these accusations were varied. Some accepted the basic premises of the theory but argued that the conclusions drawn from it by hostile gachupines were generally false. The American climate, argued the *Representación* of 1771, far from making men foolish, weak, or wicked,

[114] Juan de la Plaza to Aquaviva, Mexico, October 1583, MM, 2:174.

[115] On love of ostentation: Israel, *Class, Race and Politics*, p. 94; on women playing cards: "I must add," wrote the itinerant English Dominican Thomas Gage in 1648, "the liberty they enjoy for gaming which is such that the day and night is too short for them to end a *Primera* when once it is begun" (*The English American, His Travail by Sea and Land: Or, a New Survey of the West Indies* [London, 1648], p. 56); on priests and tobacco: Archivo General de la Nación, Mexico City, *Inquisición*, 141, no. 18, Yucatán, March 1584. The inquisitors seem to have understood the nature of addiction. "In this province," they reported, "it is a custom among the religious to take tobacco smoke compelled by necessity"; on women and tobacco: Ajofrín, *Diario del viaje*, 1:82.

[116] Ajofrín, *Diario del viaje*, 1:84.

made them wise and gentle. The temperate air, in the opinion of Henrico Martínez, had provided the criollos with good minds and elegant speech.[117] Even wild men living on the fringes of the civilized world in "harsh and intemperate regions," such as the English, the Danes, and the Muscovites, were made more tractable by the air of America.[118] Some rejected the whole theory as epistemologically unsound or as a threat to the freedom of the human will that had been guaranteed by the Church. "Every man," wrote Antonio de Ahumada, "has *merum et mixtum imperium* over his will as defined in the sacred council of Trent." Nothing, he went on, is wholly without some imperfection; neither the Catholic church, which was compelled to tolerate Arians, Pelagians, Lutherans, and Calvinists, Noah, who sired Ham, nor even the Apostles, who counted Judas among their number. There was, he concluded, no land on earth "which is not a theater of virtues and vices."[119] But few took such a dispassionate view. Presented with a theory whose authority it was difficult to reject, in the intensively conservative intellectual atmosphere of Mexico City, men like Sigüenza y Góngora had no alternative but to acquire, define, and defend a separate identity that took some account, however fancifully interpreted, of the *land* where they had been born and therefore of the condition of its aboriginal inhabitants. As Betancurt y Figueroa told the crown in 1634, "if fathers and sons are correlative and are born not only for our fathers but also for our fatherland [*patria*] . . . love of the fatherland is even to be preferred to the love of one's father."[120]

This "Mexican" or "Peruvian" culture that the criollos had created for themselves by the end of the sixteenth century, though frequently accused of being lax and too fond of pleasure, was in the opinion of most of them in no sense inferior to the culture of Spain. It was also, even by Spanish standards, a culture that was intensely orthodox and ostentatious in its religious devotion. This was at least in part a response to accusations, whose force the criollos could not deny, that during the course of the sixteenth century Spanish America had become, like Brazil, something of a refuge for heretics, Iberian Jews, and what Dorantes de Carranza called "many peoples of suspicious lineages and opinions."[121] Faced also with the knowledge that the mass of the Indian population was Christian in name only, the criollo elite responded to what they saw as a stain upon their honor by attempting

---

[117] Henrico Martínez, *Repertorio de los tiempos y historia natural desta Nueva España* (Mexico City, 1606), p. 81.

[118] "Representación," p. 443.

[119] Ahumada, *Representación política-legal*, ff. 6v–7.

[120] Betancurt y Figueroa, *Memorial i información*, f. 2.

[121] Dorantes de Carranza, *Sumaria relación*, p. 104.

to create, at least among the white community, a model Christian society. It seemed to the English traveler Gage "that in their superstitious worshipping of God and the Saints they exceed *Rome* itself."[122] It was also a society with a passion for church building and one whose population practiced public charity on a lavish scale. All the inhabitants, wrote Alonso de Zurita in 1585, "are very liberal and generous although many of them live in great need." On every Sunday and feast day of obligation the women would visit the hospitals and take food to the poor, "not trusting to send their servants."[123]

Religious display reinforced the criollo sense of belonging to a society that was observant of its duties and conscious of the honor of its god. In the Virgin of Guadalupe, who became the patron saint of New Spain, the criollos of Mexico also had their own protector. For the lay clergy, who were almost entirely of criollo origin, the Virgin provided a focus for their devotions and a champion in their rivalry with the regulars who, until the middle of the seventeenth century at least, were predominantly gachupín. The shrine of Guadalupe owed its special holiness to the miraculous apparition of the Virgin to Juan Díaz, an Indian. Because of its explicitly "national" character, it bound in a sometimes uneasy and potentially dangerous manner the white elite to the Indian and mestizo masses, like so many other aspects of the emergent criollo identity. In 1812 she would even be used by Hidalgo and Morelos as a political symbol, a specifically Indian Virgin, prepared to guide the fortunes of the rebel armies against the Spanish Virgins of the viceregal troops.[124]

VIII

During the late sixteenth and seventeenth centuries, New Spain came to acquire not only a political and religious but also a technical culture of its own. Criollos were forced to diversify their agriculture and to widen the basis of the colony's economy. In the process they developed quite distinctive styles of dress; their horses—which because of strict sumptuary laws governing who could ride them were important symbols of status—were caparisoned quite differently than the horses in Spain; their buildings were generally more highly decorated than those in Spain; their manners, mode of eating, and terms of address were all distinctive. Though evidently Spanish in inspiration, the culture that both New Spain and Peru had acquired

---

[122] Gage, *The English American*, p. 57. Gage wrote his book after he had been converted to Protestantism; it is full of the renegade's loathing for his former beliefs.

[123] Alonso de Zurita, *Historia de la Nueva España* (Madrid, 1909), p. 181.

[124] See Jacques Lafaye, *Quetzalcoatl et Guadalupe, la formation de la conscience nationale au Mexique* (Paris, 1974).

by the beginning of the seventeenth century was recognized by all visitors as sui generis. Above all Mexico and Peru had cities. Mexico City—the Rome, Athens, Rhodes, and Corinth of the New World[125]—was a European capital built upon the ruins of an Indian one; for both Cortés and all his descendants it was a place of great symbolic importance, made magnificent, as Sigüenza y Góngora claimed, "by the opulence and valor of its ancient kings."[126] On looking down on the wonders of Mexico City, Alfaro, the criollo in one of Cervantes de Salazar's dialogues on the glories of Mexico, remarks, "with every reason I dare to affirm that both worlds here find themselves encompassed and that one might say of Mexico what the Greeks said of man, by calling him a microcosm or small world."[127] It was a symbol, as another of Cervantes's characters makes plain, of the criollos' claim to form a worthy but independent part of "Greater Spain."[128] Its inhabitants had, by the end of the sixteenth century, come to regard it as the greatest city in the world, a view shared by Gage. Though he thought the place a "second Sodom," he claimed that it surpassed even Venice and Florence in its splendor.[129] In Mexico, wrote Juan de la Cueva in a verse letter to Laurencio Sánchez de Obregón, first corregidor of Mexico, you will find everything there is to be seen in Spain—good houses, good horses, beautiful women, wide streets, fine coaches, excellent food, and "you will [also] find a thousand other things besides that are lacking in Spain and that are, to sight and taste, delightful."[130]

Both New Spain and Peru, unlike Brazil, also had their own universities. Just as the Portuguese insistence that the colonial elite should be educated only in Portugal had, as Stuart Schwartz has noted, the effect of enforcing "the intellectual dependence of the colony on the mother country and [socializing] the colonists in political as well as intellectual terms," so the founding of universities in Mexico and Lima in 1553 helped to create an independent criollo intellectual and ecclesiastical elite, together with a specifically criollo academic culture, which its beneficiaries regarded as the equal of those of the Old World. "Alumnus of Minerva, glory of your homeland, envy of all others" trumpeted Sigüenza y Góngora over the Uni-

---

[125] Bernardo de Balbuena, *La grandeza mexicana*, ed. John Van Horn, University of Illinois Studies in Language and Literature, 15 (Urbana, 1930), p. 30.

[126] Carlos de Sigüenza y Góngora, *Parayso occidental plantado y cultivado por la liberal benefica mano de los muy Catolicos y Poderosos Reyes de España, Nuestros Senores . . .* (Mexico City, 1684), p. 47.

[127] Cervantes de Salazar, *Mexico en 1554*, p. 65.

[128] Ibid., p. 66.

[129] Gage, *The English American*, p. 57.

[130] Higinio Capote Porrua, "Epistolario quinto de Juan de la Cueva," *Anuario de estudios americanos* 9 (1952), pp. 597–616 at p. 608.

versity of Mexico; and the Peruvian Diego de León Pinelo wrote an entire treatise in protest against the fact that Justus Lipsius had never once mentioned the University of Lima in his writings.[131] These universities certainly could boast a number of distinguished men, such as the theologian Alonso de la Veracruz, among their professors. But the sheer physical distance that separated America from Europe and their inescapable intellectual dependence on the universities of Spain, which went into rapid decline during the seventeenth century, meant that their curricula were narrow and parochial.

The absence, furthermore, of the independent aristocratic patronage for new learning of the kind that had emerged in Spain by the end of the seventeenth century severely restricted the growth of an intellectual community independent of either the church or the university. As late as 1789, for instance, the courses in philosophy at Lima still rejected all forms of Cartesianism and accepted Copernicanism only as a hypothesis.[132] But criollos were not, at least until the late eighteenth century, often conscious of having to compete with a wider European world of learning. Their standards remained Iberian, and they took pride in their own home-bred versions of the fearful pedants who made up the academic body of most seventeenth-century Spanish universities, men like Pedro de Vasconcelos, who is said to have dictated four separate commentaries on four Church Fathers simultaneously and to have known the works of Aquinas by heart.[133]

No matter how backward these universities may have been, their role in the creation of culturally independent and self-aware criollos can be measured against the failure of the Brazilians to detach themselves from the influence of Coimbra, discussed above by Stuart Schwartz. Mexican and Peruvian criollos, unlike their Brazilian counterparts, were conscious of possessing an independent intellectual community worthy of defense against the mockery of its gachupín detractors. In 1755 Juan José de Eguiara y Egurén, angered by the implications in a book by Manuel Martí, dean of the cathedral of Alicante, that Mexico was a place without books, "a country covered in the darkest mists of ignorance, home of the most barbarous peoples that have ever existed, or will ever exist in future," set out to compose "a Mexican library" that would "repudiate so foolish and atrocious an

[131] Sigüenza y Góngora, *Triumpho parthenico*, f. 2; Diego de León Pinelo, *Semblanza de la universidad de San Marcos* (Lima, 1648) quoted by Francisco Stastny, "The University as Cloister, Garden and the Tree of Knowledge: An Iconographic Invention in the University of Cuzco," *Journal of the Warburg and Courtauld Institutes* 46 (1983):94–132.

[132] Félipe Barreda Laos, *Vida intellectual del virreinato del Peru* (Lima, 1964), pp. 227–28, cited by Stastny, "University as Cloister."

[133] Ahumada, *Representación política-legal*, f. 7v.

insult to our *patria*."[134] Eguiara y Egurén's "Biblioteca Mexicana" begins, significantly, with a lengthy account of Indian pictorial scripts and then lists the works of all the criollo literati. These include the poets Francisco de Terrazas, Bernardo de Balbuena, and most outstanding of all, Sor Juana Inés de la Cruz. "In one single individual," wrote Sigüenza y Góngora, who knew her well, "Mexico now enjoys that which in centuries past the Graces have shared out between all the learned women who were the veritable wonder of history."[135] Part of the "wonder" was due simply to the fact that Sor Juana was a woman, but it was her Mexicanness that made her truly remarkable.

IX

American culture, American architecture, American learning, and American piety could all compete with and even surpass their Spanish counterparts. Toward the end of the sixteenth century criollos also became highly conscious that the language they spoke was no longer the language of Castile. Like the supposed psychological differences between the criollos and the Peninsulars, differences in speech were often explained by reference to contemporary perceptions of the Indian world. Because language was held to be the most perfect reflection of a man's innate abilities, its structure, like the mind of its user, was believed to be conditioned by the nature of the climate in which the speaker had been born. Although the grammatical properties of Castilian clearly remained unchanged when transposed to America, the style and rhetorical habits of the Spanish spoken by the criollos was believed to have been influenced by the conditions that helped form the languages of the Amerindians. In the minds of most Spaniards, these possessed three salient characteristics: they were numerous, syntactically complex, and although weak in philosophical and theological terms, nonetheless possessed of considerable metaphorical power.[136] Of these characteristics only the last could be translated from one form of the same language to another. Criollo Spanish, in the opinion of the doctor Juan de Cardenas, was rich in its range and rhetorical expression in precisely the same way that the great Jesuit historian José de Acosta had described Quechua to be. Put a criollo, said Cardenas, reared "in a poor and barbarous village of Indians," next to a newly arrived gachupín and you will notice that the Spaniard born in the Indies "speaks in a manner so polite,

[134] Juan José de Eguiara y Egurén, *Prologo a la biblioteca mexicana*, ed. Agustín Millares Carlo (Mexico City, 1944), pp. 57–58.

[135] Sigüenza y Góngora, *Obras*, p. 23, and see Juan José de Eguiara y Egurén, *Sor Juana Inés de la Cruz*, ed. Emilio Abrey Gómez (Mexico City, 1936).

[136] See Pagden, *The Fall*, p. 181.

courtly, and elaborate, and with so many delicate preambles and such a rhetorical style, neither forced nor artificial but natural, it will seem that he has spent all his life in the court in the company of well-spoken persons."[137] The criollos' use of metaphor also struck him as both unusual and "well polished." He recorded the story of "a certain Mexican hidalgo," who in telling him that he had little fear of death with such a doctor, remarked that when the fates decided to cut the thread of his life, "I will have your worship at my side who will know how to tie it up again."[138] What Cardenas was in all probability hearing in the Mexico of 1591 were the speech habits of the Spain of 1500-1510 or a regional phraseology with which he was unfamiliar. But elaborate forms of speech persisted. Fray Francisco de Ajofrín noted that the phrases Mexicans used when taking leave of each other were "very friendly and to European seriousness very strange. For even when a man is speaking to a woman, they say, 'farewell my soul,' 'farewell my life,' 'farewell my consolation,' 'farewell mirror of mine.' "[139] Such modes of address became for the criollos a further mark of their distinctiveness, the precise means of their innate and unique "capacity." The speech of the people of Mexico, claimed Balbuena, was "the most courtly and pure, the most chaste and measured, that the Spanish nation possesses and uses, demonstrating in this as in other well-known things, the superiority of their minds over the most famous in the world."[140]

Language was not the only social expression of the criollos' essential Americanness. There were also other forms of cultural display that were put to the same end. One of these, which had a more exact political significance, was conspicuous expenditure. "Both men and women are excessive in their apparell," wrote Gage, "using more silkes than stuffes and cloth; pretious Stones and Pearls further much this their vain ostentation."[141] But it was not only in personal adornment that they spent their money. The great baroque churches, the Jesuit schools, the ornate private residences, and the elaborate coaches, on which every visitor seems to have remarked ("they do exceed in cost the best in the court of Madrid and other parts of Christendom," noted Gage) were all the outward symbols of a society that by the seventeenth century had become what Pierre Chaunu has described as "superconsummatrice."[142] These displays of great wealth were particularly marked among the members of the *cabildos* (city councils).

[137] Juan de Cardenas, *Problemas y secretos maravillosos de las Indias* (Mexico City, 1591), f. 177.
[138] Ibid., f. 177v.
[139] Ajofrín, *Diario del viaje*, I, p. 67.
[140] Balbuena, *La grandeza mexicana*, p. 70. Not all criollos, however, took this view; see above.
[141] Gage, *The English American*, p. 56.
[142] Ibid.; H. Chaunu and P. Chaunu, *Séville et l'Atlantique, 1504–1650* (Paris, 1955–59), 8 (I), p. 751.

Since the conquest the cabildos of America had been the criollo communities' social and political center. Many of the cities of America had been founded by the conquistadores and their civic bodies were highly conscious of their origins. The royal decree of 1523, which stated that the councillors should be elected by the entire citizen body, had had the long-term effect of creating a political body that was, and would remain until independence, dominated by either encomendero or hacendados. [143]

This criollo patriciate, however, spent very little of the money at its disposal on public works and very little of its time in administration. Like most, if not all, colonists the criollos used their considerable wealth for display in a way that seemed to peninsular Spaniards further evidence of their improvident nature. Like the Barbadians described by Jack Greene, they too were consumed with an "extravagant Passion for Riches." The bulk of cabildo funds and many private resources as well went to finance fiestas and public ceremonies. [144] For the white elite, even for those of its members who held royal office, display, because it was the stuff of reputation which was the mark of kings, constituted power far more strikingly than did either the business of administration or the visible willingness to act in the public good. In a society where many of the instruments of political authority were in the hands of outsiders, the dramaturgy of political ritual had had, even since the days of Martín Cortés's symbolic coronation, a particular appeal. The authority of the *criollo* elite rested upon its identity as a group of urban aristocrats who comprised the community's natural leaders, and the most effective demonstration of that identity was their ability to stage astounding public festivals that left no one in any doubt about the independence of their political power. On such occasions, as one contemporary observed, the members of the cabildo of Lima even decked their servants in ostentatious finery "to show off in this way the power of their masters." [145] The costliest of these festivals were the fiestas held in honor of the arrival of a new viceroy. When the marqués de Falces arrived in Mexico in 1556, he was greeted by two hundred horsemen clothed in blue and orange and by the cabildo members themselves decked in new red and white taffeta robes, all of which had cost 25,000 pesos—considerably more than the cabildo's

[143] Constantino Bayle, *Los cabildos seculares de la América española* (Madrid, 1952), p. 101.

[144] Fredrick B. Pike, "The *Cabildo* and Colonial Loyalty to the Habsburg Rulers," *Journal of Inter-American Studies* 2 (1960):405–420. Pike argues that the crown encouraged criollo ostentation in order to divert attention from "real" politics. This seems an improbable conclusion to draw from the fact that, on numerous occasions, the crown attempted to curtail this manifestation of status and that the criollos frequently responded to such action by raising the necessary funds from their own pockets.

[145] *Actas del cabildo de la ciudad de México* (Mexico 1889–1911), 7:296, 303, 452.

entire annual budget.[146] As with Sigüenza y Góngora's triumphal arch, such a display was a vehicle for a political commentary on the worth and status of the criollo nation.

X

By the middle of the seventeenth century this nation had established its own cultural and, insofar as it was permitted to express it, political identity. It had also acquired an independent, diverse, and flourishing economy. By the end of the sixteenth century, as the result of improved agricultural methods and consequently higher outputs from the haciendas, the major colonies had become independent in foodstuffs.[147] For much of this period, as we have seen, most criollo wealth derived from the traditional economic resources, the land and Indians who provided tribute in the form of both subsistence foods and marketable goods. A sizable number remained loyal to these pursuits, as hacienda replaced encomienda. As late as 1812 Juan López de Cancelada was complaining in El telégrafo americano that the criollos, all of whom were born to be hidalgos and nothing more, still persisted in seeing themselves as a landed aristocracy.[148] But it would be false to characterize the entire criollo population, despite its social aspirations and claims to be the heirs of a conquistador past, as wholly wedded to antique values. The production of both Mexico and Peru's staple economic product, silver, was in the hands of peninsular Spaniards and produced few forward or backward linkages from which criollos might benefit (the major exception being the cultivation of coca for the miners of Potosí). But, after the beginning of the seventeenth century, Mexico (unlike Peru) became increasingly less dependent upon a single staple. As early as 1605, for instance, silver export accounted for 65 percent of the total value of exports to Spain. The remaining 35 percent was in cochineal, hides, indigo, wool, dyes, and medicinal plants, and this trade was, for the most part, in criollo hands.[149] The rich intercolonial trading triangle—Mexico, Manila, and Peru—in particular had become the greatest single source of criollo wealth by the middle of the century.

The colonies also developed local industries that catered to local markets and consequently reduced dependence on goods imported from the mother

[146] Quoted in John Preston Moore, The Cabildos in Peru under the Bourbons (Durham, 1966), p. 89.

[147] Peter Bakewell, Silver Mining and Society in Colonial Mexico: Zacatecas 1546–1700 (Cambridge, 1971), p. 235.

[148] David Brading, Miners and Merchants in Colonial Mexico, 1763–1810 (Cambridge, 1971), p. 211.

[149] John Lynch, Spain under the Habsburgs (Oxford 1964–69), 2:185, and see Chaunu, Séville et l'Atlantique, 2(bis), pp. 1499–1500.

ANTHONY PAGDEN

country. By the second decade of the seventeenth century Mexico seems to
have created a largely independent economy through import substitution;
as Peter Bakewell has argued, it was probably this rather than any supposed
decline in silver production that was the principal cause for the crisis in the
Atlantic trade in the 1620s.[150]

This economy, which by the end of the seventeenth century criollos had
come to regard as a further mark of their independence of, and superiority
to, the hated gachupín, had to be protected. Criollos were understandably
indignant at the crown's 1630 embargo on intercolonial trade, a wholly un-
justifiable attempt, in their view, to protect the interests of the Seville merchants.[151] They also began to resent not only that their nation's mineral
wealth was largely in gachupín hands but also that so much of it flowed out
to Spain. As early as 1597 the audiencia of Mexico had protested to the
crown against the constant flow of wealth that left the country in the pockets of greedy gachupines, of "the merchants of Castile of which they are
natives, with the result that this land is ruined, poor, without people who
can sustain it in the service of your majesty."[152] The author of this complaint, the oidor Antonio de Maldonado, was typical of the second generation of settlers. As an officeholder whose fortunes clearly lay with the future of the colony, he resented the alienation by outsiders of the wealth
that he regarded as a criollo patrimony. Such complaints increased in volume and pitch as criollos came increasingly to regard the Mexican economy
as a domestic affair. As one eighteenth-century critic observed, the staple
wealth of America had, for over two centuries, gone either to line the pockets of short-term immigrants or had flowed to Spain in order to finance
"wars in Flanders, France, and England." These wars, he said, had drained
the natural wealth of the country to foreign places, creating the economic
vacuum that had drawn in "the active commerce of foreigners,"[153] so that
by the eighteenth century New Spain had become a virtual condominium,
defended and administered by Spain but exploited by every nation in Europe.[154]

The creation of an independent economy served to enhance the criollos'
sense of belonging to an independent culture and finally to an independent

[150] Bakewell, *Silver Mining*, p. 299.
[151] J. Israel, "Mexico and the 'General Crisis' of the Seventeenth Century," *Past and Present*
63 (1974):33–57 at pp. 38–39.
[152] Antonio Maldonado, oidor of the audiencia of Mexico, in reply to a questionnaire
"sobre el estado en que se encontraba la sucesión de las encomiendas de indios y la convenien-
cia de hacer el repartimiento perpetuo," ENE, 13:131.
[153] "Reflexiones sobre el comercio libre de la América, que produce el amor público de un
zeloso profesor del comercio. Ano 1789," BL Add. Ms. 13,984, ff. 135–67 at f. 136v.
[154] Pierre Chaunu, *L'Amérique et les Amériques* (Paris, 1964), pp. 198, 203.

92

nation. The crown's largely unsuccessful attempts to suppress the intercolonial trade created separate interest groups who, in the eighteenth century, were arguing not only that the new laissez-faire economics were the only just and efficient ones but that Spain's attempts to shore up its own declining fortunes by restricting trade were, like its efforts to exclude criollos from office, against the dictates of nature. "When commerce," wrote a "zealous professor of economics" in 1789, "can be conducted without restraint by all individuals in a nation, it is most useful to the state, for the wider the trade extends within a nation the greater is the benefit to its native sons." Any restrictions, any limitations, he continued, could only be of benefit to "foreigners," by which he meant peninsular Spaniards, and any government that favored foreigners was, almost by definition, an "unnatural" one.[155]

By the time the "zealous professor" came to write his memoir, loyalty to the crown could only be purchased with a large degree of political and economic self-determination that Spain, because of its own domestic needs, was in no position to provide. The Spanish American viceroyalties had become de facto independent communities and they remained loyal to Spain only as long as that independence was respected. For the criollos of the closing years of the eighteenth century, Montesquieu's observation that "the Indies and Spain are two powers under the same master; but the Indies is the principal one and Spain nothing but an accessory" had become all too obviously true.[156] The crown's attempts to break the political power of the criollo elites by restricting their right to office and its simultaneous efforts to gain a tighter hold on colonial trade had, by the first decade of the nineteenth century, made exit the only possible course available, once the loud protesting voices of the petitioners had been ignored.

[155] "Reflexiones," f. 148.
[156] De l'esprit des lois, bk. 21, ch. 22, Oeuvres complètes, ed. Roger Caillois, Bibliothèque de la Pléiade (Paris, 1951), 2:648.

4 ❧ Nouvelle-France / Québec / Canada: A World of Limited Identities

Gilles Paquet and Jean-Pierre Wallot

THIS VOLUME raises the question of the nature and timing of the process through which European colonists in several situations in the Atlantic world came to perceive themselves as distinct and different peoples—how they came to acquire a cultural identity and a political structure of their own and an economy of an idiosyncratic type.[1] Various models have been suggested to assist in explaining phenomena on such a scale,[2] but the mechanism through which the colonial identity is supposed to be shaped, whether by external or internal forces, is neither precise enough nor necessarily compelling as an explanation of the character of the colony. What has to be explained is not clear, the explicandum is vague, and the link between them is of necessity somewhat imprecise. These models are also unsatisfactory because they take insufficient account of institutional realities. We are convinced that a major factor in explaining the uniqueness of the Canadian experience is that Canada endured a sequence of intruders from different metropolises, each of which left behind a successive layer of institutions. The nature of this particular experience contributed to the development of a fragmented society, and the inhabitants of each socioeconomic segment never developed anything but a weak sense of belonging to a larger corporate entity. Indeed, the central hypothesis developed in this essay is

[1] This essay reports on part of a broader research project on the evolution of the Canadian socio-economy from the seventeenth to the twentieth century. Our research program has been financed by Le Ministère de l'Education du Québec (programme F.C.A.C.), by the Social Sciences and Humanities Research Council, and by our institutions. Other results of this work have been reported in G. Paquet and J-P. Wallot, "Pour une méso-histoire du XIXᵉ siècle Canadien," *Revue d'histoire de l'Amérique française* 33, 3 (December 1979):387–425; ibid., "Canadian Cities as Social Technologies: An Exploratory Essay" in W. Borah, *Urbanization in the Americas*, ed. W. Borah, J. Hardoy, G. A. Stelter, National Museum of Man (Ottawa, 1980), pp. 57–62; ibid., "Sur quelques discontinuités dans l'expérience socio-économique du Québec: Une hypothèse," *Revue d'histoire de l'Amérique française* 36, 4 (March 1982):483–521; ibid., "Le système financier bas-canadien au tournant du XIXᵉ siècle," *Actualité économique* 59, 3 (September 1983):456–513. We wish to thank A. Burgess, J. Dickinson, R. Girard-Wallot, and P. Neri-Johnston for their assistance and the editors for their critical help.

[2] See, for example, the Canadian application of the Turner hypothesis in *The Frontier Thesis and the Canadas: The Debate on the Impact of the Canadian Environment*, ed. M. S. Cross (Toronto, 1970), and the Canadian application of the Hartz thesis by K. D. McRae, "The Structure of Canadian History," in *The Founding of New Societies*, ed. Louis Hartz (New York, 1974).

that the inhabitants of the political entity now known as Canada never developed anything but limited identities, but that paradoxically those limited identities, rather than reducing "national" communicative competence, may have improved it.[3]

Identity formation has often been stylized schematically as a steady passage of colonists from the status of explorers and temporary residents to the status of a community in which each individual shares a self-awareness and a new self-conscious and independent identity. This presumes that the transition process is smooth and that it generates some sort of convergence on a subset of special characteristics common to all the members of the community. The stylized model would appear to place great emphasis on the psychological dimensions of the notion of identity, on the consciousness of such identity as the determining factor. It also assumes that identity formation proceeds in stages: after a phase of negative identity formation—a period of identity building in opposition to indigenous or other communities or metropolitan groups, there is posited a phase of positive identity building—a period of cultural identity construction when identity becomes a collective (consumption or investment) good sought by the citizenry for the benefits it generates.

The Canadian case does not fall into the standard pattern for a variety of reasons. First, Canada was subjected to two successive waves of colonization by two different European countries—France in the seventeenth century and Britain in the second half of the eighteenth. Second, these experiences injected into the country (on top of the indigenous population) two separate communities that until perhaps 1800 lived almost separate lives. Finally, at the turn of the nineteenth century, the duality of language, religion, and values developed into a major struggle between these communities for organizational power at the economic and political level. This further crystallized the so-called Canadian dualism.[4]

This does not mean, of course, that there were no identity-formation activities in Canada: as we shall see, around 1700 some identity formation of both a negative and a positive nature had already materialized. Later, in the eighteenth century, one may detect evidence of some positive identity formation by *les Canadiens*. A second colonization process was under way from the 1760s on and the British settler presence was greatly strengthened two decades later with the arrival in Canada of substantial numbers of British Loyalists fleeing from the recently established United States of America. It

---

[3] For convenient summaries of the literature on the quest for a Canadian identity see M. Ross, ed., *Our Sense of Identity* (Toronto, 1954) and H. Hardin, *A Nation Unaware* (Vancouver, 1974).

[4] G. Paquet and J-P. Wallot, *Patronage et pouvoir dans le Bas Canada* (Montreal, 1973).

was then clear that two distinct settler communities existed in Canada and that the suspicions each fostered of the other produced a process of negative identity formation in each. It is our contention that the *Canadien* identity was already blossoming into an active nationalism by the time the Canadian socio-economy experienced its second major discontinuity about 1800.[5] The second settler community underwent a not too dissimilar process with appropriate lags: the first part of this process was negative identity formation in opposition both to the French-Canadian population and to the population of the United States during the American Revolutionary War and the War of 1812; this was followed by some positive identity formation later in the nineteenth century with the strengthening of an East-West socioeconomic structure.

This parallel development may have prevented the early emergence of one Canadian identity, but it did not hinder the development of limited identities. What had existed in English America during its earlier historical experience and what some have labelled "a confused jumble of ethnic, economic, religious and nationality attachments, usually pulled together by a pervasive sense of localism," produced "the articulation of regional patterns in one transcontinental state."[6] Regions, classes, and cultures sought and attained only limited identities because they recognized that the cost of going further would prove too high. The Canadian limited identities and differentiated ethos have instituted geographical, linguistic, cultural, and other obstacles to communication between the Canadians, but although Canadians have communicated less, they may, for all we know, have communicated better.[7]

The progressive crystallization of these limited identities from the seventeenth century on is discussed below. One may detect three dimensions to this process of identity formation: (1) the moment when colonists shaped their identity by eluding the metropolitan planning process that previously constrained them; (2) the moment when they more or less passively distilled new forms of organization; and (3) the moment when they actively constructed new elements of the Canadian social architecture (or tried to do so) as an investment in identity, that is, as an instrument of their

---

[5] On the content of this nationalism see J-P. Wallot, *Un Québec qui bougeait: Trame socio-politique au tournant du XIXᵉ siècle* (Montreal, 1973), chs. 2, 4, and 8. To avoid confusion we use the term "Canadiens" to refer to the French-speaking community in Canada as opposed to the whole of Canadian society.

[6] The first phrase comes from R. D. Cowen, "New World Colonization and Old World Loyalties" (mimeo, November 1969) and the second from J.M.S. Careless, "Limited Identities," in *Canadian Historical Review* 15 (March 1969):1–10.

[7] For the theoretical underpinning of this conjecture, see J-P. Dupuy "Le signe et l'envie," in P. Dumouchel and J-P. Dupuy, *L'enfer des choses* (Paris, 1979).

praxis. It is the mingling of these three sets of forces acting in an overlapping manner that has shaped the Canadian colonial identities.

Colonists as Planners

When colonists first went to North America, they were the actors in an unwritten "plan" that had been devised by a metropolitan government, or by some of its officials, to serve its ultimate purposes. From the correspondence and dispatches back and forth between the continents, one can follow the continuous dialogue between planners and plannees through which the plan was more or less successfully implemented. The planners were usually ignorant of local circumstances, and their plans idealistic or faulty in other ways. As a consequence, the plannees had to interpret, adapt, and recast those messages or orders to render them meaningful in context.

This process can be witnessed in the French colonial experience that got seriously under way in the early seventeenth century. There had been French fishing and even trapping contact with the New World long before this time, but permanent settlement began only with this second round of exploration into the North American continent via the St. Lawrence River and the Great Lakes. Even then, there was limited emigration from France, the settlers did not exploit Indian manpower, and they saw no need to displace the indigenous population and take over their land. To this extent the French experience was in sharp contrast to the Spanish and English endeavors in the Americas.[8] Those who have studied the French–Indian contacts in the sixteenth and seventeenth centuries have come to the conclusion that on the whole "relations remained friendly" between these communities.[9] Although the dictum of Francis Parkman that "Spanish civilization crushed the Indian; English civilization scorned and neglected him; French civilization embraced and cherished him" may be excessive, there is a grain of truth in it.[10]

The French settlers began with an explicit plan to assimilate the Indians and to convert them to the Roman Catholic faith, but this program failed unequivocally. The segregation of the native population in "reserves" (as a socially controlled environment in which the Indians might adapt to the French way of life at their own rate) also failed. The facts of life dictated an

---

[8] When France established permanent settlements there were few Indian tribes inhabiting the St. Lawrence valley, if one excepts the Montagnais near Tadoussac and Quebec and the Algonquins, near Three Rivers and Montreal. Furthermore, the French neither settled on Indian territory nor used the natives as laborers. See Bruce Trigger, ed., *Handbook of North American Indians* 15 (Washington, D.C., 1978).

[9] C. J. Jaenen, *Friend and Foe* (Toronto, 1976), p. 192.

[10] F. Parkman, *The Jesuits in North America in the Seventeenth Century* (Toronto, 1899), 1:131, cited in Jaenen, *Friend and Foe*, p. 7.

altogether different outcome. The French not only came to be dependent on the Indians "for supplies of furs, for allies in wartime, and for their own safety and convenience" but also learned a great deal from the Indians and borrowed much from them, so much so that it was possible for Peter Kalm in the eighteenth century to write that "the French in Canada in many respects follow the customs of the Indians."[11]

If the particularly positive relationship between the French colonists and the Indian population did not promote any strong sense of negative identity, the borrowing of Indian customs and techniques tended to generate in turn two adjustments in opposite directions: a change in the ethos of the French settler, tending to establish some distance between him and the typical metropolitan *paysan français*, and a reaction to this erosion that resulted in increased efforts by the French government to create in Canada "a society according to plan" in the image of metropolitan France.[12] But however detailed and rational may have been the plan to create an organization in New France that would satisfy the norms of order, symmetry, and harmony, it was bound to fail, as did the earlier plan to assimilate the Indians into French settler society. Sigmund Diamond has shown the degree to which France revealed its "passion for rationality" in the design of the plan and also the reasons why it failed.[13]

Before the end of the seventeenth century, the colonists, both through their contacts with and their borrowings from Indian customs and through an effective shaking off of the constraints of the metropolitan plan, had managed to create new social types in Canada. The *coureurs de bois* and the *habitants* were not only the dominant figures, but they had many traits in common: freedom and independence might be regarded as the leitmotif characterizing their actions and their self-image.[14]

The "gentility" (seigneurs, high officials, and military officers) were closer to metropolitan values than the rest of the community, and this was probably true also of the merchants who, although exploiting the fur trade in the St. Lawrence valley, were still dependent upon the French market and on French credit. They found it difficult on occasion to distinguish

---

[11] Jaenen, *Friend and Foe*, esp. ch. 5.

[12] Sigmund Diamond, "An Experiment in Feudalism: French Canada in the Seventeenth Century," in *William and Mary Quarterly* (1961):3–34.

[13] Diamond, "An Experiment in Feudalism," sections 2 and 3.

[14] Diamond, "An Experiment in Feudalism," and P. G. Roy, ed., *Ordonnances, commissions des gouverneurs et intendants de la Nouvelle France, 1639–1706* (Beauceville, 1924). For an analysis of these two social types see R. M. Saunders, "The Emergence of the Coureurs de Bois as a Social Type," in *Canadian Historical Association Annual Report* (1939), pp. 22–33; R. C. Harris, *The Seigneurial System in Early Canada: A Geographical Study* (Madison and Quebec, 1966); W. J. Eccles, *The Canadian Frontier, 1534–1760* (New York, 1969).

French from Canadian interests, but new social types emerged even in these social strata during the early decades of the eighteenth century. These social types differed dramatically from anything existing in France and, as has been demonstrated by Diamond, they made "a mockery of the behaviour defined for them." The *bourgeois gentilshommes*, a class of individuals sharing traits with the traditional nobility, the bourgeoisie in the usual sense, and the general class of functionaries, are a case in point.[15]

At the turn of the eighteenth century, New France faced serious difficulties in its major economic activity, the fur trade, at the same time that it experienced an important increase in the size of its population. These factors as well as the opening of Louisbourg as a market for New France's agricultural products drove larger numbers toward agriculture. This in turn triggered the emergence of an almost dual socio-economy: one segment with an agricultural base and Continental roots, developing its own particular ethos, and the other with a commercial base and maritime connections linked with the Atlantic system. Already some might say the fragmentation in the process of identity formation was under way.[16]

The evolution of new social types suggests that the process of positive identity formation was taking place. The Canadiens had already moved that far by the beginning of the eighteenth century. One may also find evidence of concurrent negative identity formation, especially vis-à-vis the English colonists south of the border. With the short occupation of Quebec by Kirke and his sons in 1629 and the disturbances that followed, some sense of negative identity had developed. But it is worth noting that in reaction to such threats, colonists were less tempted to leave for France than to take refuge in Indian communities. The hospitality that was afforded them, even from somewhat xenophobic tribes, contributed to the forging of positive bonds with the indigenous population and thus with the place of settlement.

This process was disturbed by the second wave of colonization, which came from Britain and the American colonies in the 1760s and the two subsequent decades. At first, as Trevor Denton has argued, this did not trigger any transformation in the original colony, because of the substitution of a new metropolis for the old.[17] There was significant change at the top of the

---

[15] C. Nish, *Les bourgeois gentilshommes de la Nouvelle France, 1729–48* (Montreal, 1968).

[16] For an examination of certain aspects of this first discontinuity see Paquet and Wallot, "Sur quelques discontinuités," pp. 493–500, and F. Ouellet, "La mentalité l'outillage économique de habitant Canadien-Français: A propos d'un document sur l'encan," *Bulletin des Recherches Historiques* (1956):131–39.

[17] T. Denton, "The Structure of French Canadian Acculturation, 1759–1800," *Anthropologica* (1966):29–42.

social pyramid, but without much consequence because the bottom part had already begun to define its own elements of identity in reaction to the merchants, seigneurs, and officials who had previously dominated the community. Thus the new group of British merchants and officials who reached Quebec in small numbers did not seem to threaten the existing population. Nonetheless, the British presence contributed to a strengthening of the French-Canadian sense of difference and also to the maintenance and consolidation of a sort of social division of labor that produced a de facto and seemingly peaceful establishment of quasi-separate facilities for the two communities. Soon after the Conquest, the British government saw the need to bestow much more identity-forming capital upon the Canadiens, with a view to mobilizing their support during the American Revolutionary War. These included the linguistic, religious, and legal concessions granted under the Quebec Act of 1774 and subsequently some political concessions under the Constitutional Act of 1791.

The first substantive wave of new colonists came from the United States at the end of the American Revolution, armed with a strong sense of negative identity vis-à-vis the Americans. They also reacted rather strongly to being required to live under French-Canadian laws and customs and almost immediately demanded a separate government. For most of them, this was obtained in 1791 with the creation of Upper Canada.[18] But already one could see signs from the administrators, both in the colony and in England, of a dream emerging—the dream of constructing a new British North American empire to compete with the rebel colonies. This political objective was strengthened by the "dream" of the merchants of the St. Lawrence to channel all trade from the west through the St. Lawrence to Europe.[19]

It is tempting to see in this "program" of the St. Lawrence merchants evidence of positive identity formation, but it would be a mistake. For the new "English Canadians," there is little evidence of identity formation. Indeed, some might even say that before 1760 there was some identity erosion

---

[18] Except between 1763 and 1774, the Old Province of Quebec, like New France, covered not only the northeastern tip of the North American continent but also much of the unexplored territory to the west of the British-American colonies. The American Revolution altered the geographical boundaries of the continent by truncating the British North American empire at the 49th parallel. The Constitutional Act of 1791 caused still further fragmentation by dividing what remained to the British in North America into two separate political units: a northeastern segment, Lower Canada, with a population of perhaps 150,000 French Canadians and 15,000 new settlers, and a southwestern segment populated largely by Loyalists and American immigrants. Both Lower and Upper Canada enjoyed a distinct elective legislative assembly in 1791.

[19] D. G. Creighton, *The Commercial Empire of the St. Lawrence, 1760-1850* (Toronto, 1937), esp. ch. 2.

in Canada. The new Canadians had a fear of an American invasion, which fuelled antirepublican and antidemocractic sentiments. These feelings tended to become somewhat confused with allegiance to conservative and monarchic values, with a strengthening of the British connection, and with a distinct distaste for anything Canadien. It can be said that these new Canadians wished to remain part of an explicitly British program of action. For them there was also a self-interested identification with Britain's interests. Britain poured very large sums of money into British North America at the time; Howard Temperley has estimated that "close to half a million pounds was granted to North American residents during the first decade of the Loyalist settlement and in excess of £1,300,000 between 1783 and 1842."[20] Under these circumstances, it is hardly surprising that the process of identity formation was somewhat slowed down: the cost of identity affirmation would have been high, for it might have entailed the loss of important benefits. It was not until waves of have-nots from the United Kingdom arrived in Canada after 1815 and until Britain began the process of disengagement from its mercantilistic policies in the first third of the nineteenth century that one could see signs of the negative identity of the new colonists (vis-à-vis Americans and Canadiens) being extended to include the old country.

Any exact timing for this shift is difficult to establish, but there may have been signs of some negative/positive identity formation in the 1830s, when the *Montreal Herald* threatened secession from Britain rather than submission to the rule of a French Canadian majority and, in the 1850s, with the debates on the Galt tariffs. But the fact that national debates could still be carried on late in the nineteenth century about the importance of the "British connection" would appear to provide some contrary evidence that the process of positive identity formation for the new Canadian colonists proceeded rather slowly.[21]

The native population for these new colonists was the French Canadians. If at first there was peaceful coexistence, it had become a somewhat hostile coexistence, at least for the lower classes, by the nineteenth century. For many, the roots of the second round of Canadien positive identity formation can be traced to the debate over the control of the public finances of the colony that went on from the end of the eighteenth through the first half of the nineteenth century and to the struggle over the choice of which economic, political, and sociocultural development strategies to

[20] H. Temperley, "Frontierism, Capital and the American Loyalists in Canada," *Journal of American Studies* 13 (1979):5–27.

[21] For a different view, see W. L. Morton, *The Canadian Identity*, 2d ed. (Toronto, 1972), p. 111.

implement.[22] As to the relationship with the Indian population, it is interesting to note that the new Canadians, in many ways, "appropriated the apparently friendly French relations with the tribesmen after the conquest of Canada and the American Revolution." This would suggest that environmental circumstances might have much to contribute to an understanding of different modes of cultural accommodation.[23]

The cleavage between the French Canadian population and the British and their English Canadian allies became more evident in the 1830s. One could talk of the *britannisme des patriotes* and document it from speeches of Louis-Joseph Papineau, the leader of the Patriotes, until the late 1820s; after that it was no longer possible. In the Résolutions presented to the legislative assembly of Lower Canada in 1834 and in many contemporary texts, one can recognize that the French Canadian majority had started to praise, through its parliamentarians and others, the republican ideas borrowed from the United States, to reaffirm the "grandeur" of the French civilization from which it had evolved, and to mention the possibility of separation from Britain.[24] The difficult financial and economic circumstances of the late 1830s and Britain's decisive political interventions (the Russell Resolutions of 1837) accentuated the rift between the different parties, and contrasting strategies for the development of the colonial socio-economy were developed and put forward. This led to sharp differences of opinion and the French Canadians rebelled formally and militarily against the British and their English Canadian representatives. This was not, however, a global, total rebellion: the radical elites succeeded in mobilizing only a portion of the French Canadian population into military action.[25]

If the rebellions did not carry the whole population, the violent quashing of the uprising and the political implications of the acceptance by Britain of the recommendations of Lord Durham for the creation of the Province of Canada—merging Lower and Upper Canada into a single political

[22] Paquet and Wallot, *Patronage et pouvoir dans le Bas Canada,* esp. ch. 5. See also G. Paquet, *Histoire économique du Canada* (Société Radio-Canada, 1980–81), cahier 20.

[23] Jaenen, *Friend and Foe,* p. 192.

[24] F. Dumont, *Chantiers* (Montreal, 1973), pp. 98ff.

[25] There exists no definitive study of the 1837–1838 rebellions in Lower Canada and their feeble parallel in Upper Canada. However, it is clear that although the French Canadian distinctiveness, their majority in the Lower Canadian House of Assembly, and the more violent character of the Lower Canadian rebellion would suggest the uniqueness of the rebellion in that segment, there is nonetheless some similarity of sentiment between the two rebellions, especially in the sense of republicanism manifested by both movements. See Dumont, *Chantiers,* p. 100, for quotations from F-X. Garneau, a participant observer in 1837–1838. For a comparison of the two contrasted economic development strategies (fundamentally Continental for the English Canadians and more rooted in local development for the French Canadians), see Paquet, *Histoire économique,* cahier 10.

unit—confirmed the suspicions of the French Canadian colonists that they were being betrayed by Britain. Etienne Parent, one of the leading patriote journalists, wrote in 1838 in *Le Canadien,* the patriote newspaper, that the project of a union of the two Canadas was bound to eradicate the "French Canadian nationality."[26]

The result of this experience was the emergence of a new sense of militant and "nationalistic" identity. Although previously the French Canadians had been satisfied to affirm their separate identity and to foster the hope that they would someday achieve political autonomy with the help of Britain, this *sentiment national* was suddenly transformed into a "militant nationalism" by the quashing of the rebellions.[27]

But even when the British authorities chose to support the economic development strategy of the "new" colonists, thereby alienating the old, the process of industrialization was to play havoc with their plans. Urbanization accelerated, social classes crystallized somewhat differently than they expected, and it became obvious that retaining the allegiance of Canadians (of whatever origin) had a price tag. To the extent that economic progress began to slow down in Canada relative to its southern neighbor, both the old and the new colonists began to migrate on a larger scale to the United States. This process revealed that even though both groups had developed a certain sense of proprietorship over the administration of the community and had been willing to fight to confirm these rights, these rights were not absolutes, and they could therefore be traded for higher wages, better economic conditions, and manufacturing jobs. Indeed, the border between the United States and Canada remained very porous until the 1930s.[28]

One might say that the lower cost of exercising the exit option (in the sense of Hirschman) after the transportation revolution, may have further weakened the development of the voice option, and thereby the process of identity formation. For the use of voice is a key instrument of identity formation, and the unattractiveness of the voice option might have become clearer at a time when the "Canadian game" appeared to be drifting into a phase of "conflictive equilibrium" and when it began to prove more and more difficult to invent better ways to influence events.[29] But although some were attracted by the exit option, others—from both communities—had strong reasons to remain at home.

[26] Quoted in Dumont, *Chantiers,* p. 102.

[27] M. Séquin, *L'idée d'indépendance au Québec: Génèse historique* (Trois Rivières, 1968); Dumont, *Chantiers,* section 4.

[28] G. Paquet and W. R. Smith, 'L'émigration des Canadiens françaises vers les Etats-Unis, 1790-1940: Problématique et coups de sonde," *Actualité économique* 59 (1983):423–53.

[29] The drift into "conflictive equilibrium" is analyzed in Paquet and Wallot, *Patronage et pouvoir.* On the exit and voice options see A. O. Hirschman, *Exit, Voice and Loyalty* (Cambridge, 1970).

Colony as Home

For the descendants of the French settlers, Canada was a home because it was a society that was largely of their own creation after they had refashioned the institutions provided them by the French metropolis to serve their own purposes. Subsequent to the British conquest of Canada, the French Canadian community remained in control of a portion of its own destiny as a result of the unintended consequences of the British administrative system. The British concern to exclude French Canadians from the lucrative fur trade and other specialized economic activities in the Atlantic segment of the economy left the French population in control of the local agricultural sector. What ensued was "stabilized pluralism": two cultures "side by side but almost completely independent of one another."[30] Moreover, when political concessions to the French community were made in 1791, the unintended result of lowering the eligibility requirements for voting was to give the right to vote to most French Canadian family heads (male and female) when the ratio of the French to the British was ten to one. This meant in effect that the French Canadian population was given control of the legislative assembly; what other populations in the Atlantic would have to seek by revolutionary means was virtually granted to the French Canadian population.[31]

These unintended consequences served to accelerate the process of identity formation and to assist the crystallization of a particular life style for French Canadians. One cannot perceive a parallel development of anything like the same strength on the English Canadian side. Furthermore, when the French Canadians began to challenge the British connection, whether implicitly or aggressively, it became clear that the British conquest of Canada could never become the centerpiece in a "unifying national myth" in the way that the American revolutionary experience brought the diverse elements of the United States together into a single national unit. In fact, the British conquest of Canada became a divisive factor to the extent that for the Loyalists and English Canadians the British connection was their lifeline and "loyalty meant loyalty to Britain and British values."[32]

Although this would suggest that the English Canadians, unlike their French counterparts, owed no loyalty to Canada itself and in this sense had

[30] T. Denton, "The Structure of French-Canadian Acculturation, 1759-1800," *Anthropologica* 8 (1966):29-42, esp. pp. 31, 34.
[31] Paquet and Wallot, *Patronage et pouvoir*, ch. 2.
[32] R. Cook, *The Maple Leaf Forever* (Toronto, 1971), p. 200; P. Berton, *Flames across the Border, 1813-14* (Toronto, 1979), p. 428.

a weak sense of identity, the reality was that they cultivated and focused their loyalty on what George Grant has aptly termed a "British dream of Canada."[33] Most English Canadians, from the beginning of the nineteenth century until perhaps even the 1920s and 1930s, cultivated a romantic dream that British traditions would enable them to build a Canadian community in North America that would be different from and much better than that achieved in the United States. This idealized Canada was for them always derivative and could never stand on its own as a homeland, but the cultivation of the dream nonetheless assisted the development of an English Canadian identity. The tragedy for English Canadians was, however, that at the very moment when they were constructing this ideal, the British government was commencing a long process of disengagement from its colonies; English Canadians depended on the assumption that the mercantilist and moral links between the metropolis and the colony were intact even when the principles of free trade were supreme in Britain.[34]

The development of these separate identities goes some way also toward explaining the different concepts of nationhood that emerged within the two communities. The French Canadian community developed a concept of nation that is rooted in blood ties, in affectual and traditional feelings, and in the substantial ethos that binds the community together. This is very close to the notion of *Gemeinschaft* in Ferdinand Tonnies's sense. On the other hand, the concept of nation for English Canadians was and is much closer to the notion of *Gesellschaft* à la Tonnies—a social relationship of an "associative type" resting "on a rationally motivated adjustment of interests or a similarly motivated agreement, whether the basis of rational judgment be absolute values or reasons of expediency."[35] Although reference continued to be made to the broader British community of values and traditions as values that might provide a base for a Canadian nation, it is clear that English Canadians favored a *Gesellschaft*-type construct and that Canada for them has remained a contract-type group.[36]

It is much easier to develop a territorial sense of identity from a community to which one belongs by birth, kinship, culture, or status than it is to develop loyalty toward a political organization that concedes rights and imposes duties that derive from bilateral arrangements. In the first instance, "group rights" are easier to identify, as can be seen in the case of

[33] G. Grant, *Lament for a Nation* (Toronto, 1978), p. xi.

[34] A. Faucher, *Québec en Amérique* (Montreal, 1973), ch. 3.

[35] The expressions "communal" and "associative" are used in translation to convey the meaning of the labels used by Tonnies. See Max Weber, *The Theory of Social and Economic Organization* (Glencoe, Ill., 1947), pt. 1, sect. 9.

[36] For a recent discussion of this point, see F. H. Underhill, *The Image of Confederation* (Toronto, 1964).

French Canadians. This historical divergence between French and English Canadians regarding group rights in general has lasted until now. For French Canadians, the struggle for collective rights began in the very early days of the colony under British rule, and by the time militant French Canadian nationalism had emerged in the nineteenth century, the homeland was well defined around Quebec. For English Canadians, more attached to British values and "English liberty" à la Acton, collective rights have been undesirable and undemocratic privileges. This may explain in part why their homeland is still a less well defined and "precarious homestead."[37] The degree of tangibility of the English Canadian homeland has remained lower and, accordingly, their identification with the territory has been less. If anything, the sense of homeland of the English colonials became "regionalized" very early. This paved the way to a compromise that was to be central in the definition of the "Canadian identity."

Colonial Identity as Social Technology

During their historical development, both groups of colonists tried to escape from the plans of their metropolitan governments and to react more or less passively to the transplantation of metropolitan institutions; but they also tried actively to intervene to mold their sociocultural environment according to their own interests and ideals. One way in which this manifested itself was in the attitude of the two communities to government involvement in Canadian affairs. Although on one level, one can see how the settlement communities sought to frustrate the efforts being made to have them serve metropolitan interests, account must also be taken of how the colonists have been able to harness the state apparatus to serve their purposes and to win from public institutions what they could not obtain from private enterprise.[38]

An early example of such a phenomenon may be the development of an independent monetary policy by the colonists in New France. New France, like all colonial societies, was plagued by scarcity of specie. In the seventeenth century, coins sent to pay the salaries of officials and soldiers were almost immediately returned to France to pay bills and buy goods. After unsuccessful attempts to overvalue coins in order to keep them in the colony, the local authorities became more imaginative and began to experiment with paper currency (in fact with playing-card currency).[39]

[37] A. Rotstein, *The Precarious Homestead* (Toronto, 1973).
[38] J. F. Bosher, "Government and Private Interest in New France," *Canadian Public Administration* 10 (1967):244–57.
[39] R. A. Lester, *Monetary Experiments* (Princeton, 1939), ch. 2; J. Hamelin, *Économie et société en Nouvelle France* (Quebec, 1960).

From the middle of the 1680s to the period of the Conquest, paper currency was used in a recurrent way in New France. Although this has been regarded by some as a simple expedient to solve the cash-flow problems of the local authorities between specie shipments from France, one may also read those experiments as a specific and deliberate attempt to free the colonists from the discipline of the metallic monetary system of the metropolitan country—a discipline that linked the money supply and the price level in the colony to the monetary and financial circumstances in Europe. That such a conscious effort was being made by the French colonists has been argued forcefully by Richard Lester,[40] and we can see how, subsequent to the Conquest, the English colonists exploited the public sector in much the same way. Then the colonial authorities introduced a public form of paper money under the Army Bills of the 1810s and thereby used public enterprise as an explicit instrument in the elaboration of their development strategy.[41] But in witnessing this, we see the tendency only in embryo; it took considerable time for the Canadian public enterprise culture to crystallize explicitly and ideologically as a form of self-expression for the British colonists.[42]

Prior to the 1840s, the British North American colonies were part of a protected imperial trade network tightly woven around Britain by all sorts of preferential tariffs and trade restrictions. The movement of Britain toward a free-trade regime in the middle third of the nineteenth century played havoc with the protected status of the colonies and meant that the British North American colonies had to develop some sort of response. The existence of a Canadian government capable of pursuing an independent economic policy was probably the major new feature of the Canadian scene from the 1840s on, and one can discern a rapid alteration in the perception of the government's role in private affairs. The reaction in Canada to Britain's move was to take three main forms: a foreign trade policy, a policy of social overhead capital formation, and a settlement and land policy.[43] All these might be regarded as deliberate ways by which the colonial governments and, even more so, the government of the Province of Canada (the unit created from the union of Upper and Lower Canadas) sought to modify the rules of the game in line with the needs of Canadians. Through these

[40] R. A. Lester, "Playing-Card Currency of French Canada," in *Money and Banking in Canada*, ed. E. P. Neufeld (Toronto, 1964), p. 17.

[41] Paquet and Wallot, "Le système financier," sect. 5. See also H. T. Manning, "The Civil List of Lower Canada," *Canadian Historical Review* 24 (1943):24–47.

[42] Hardin, *A Nation Unaware*, ch. 6.

[43] V. C. Fowke, *The National Policy and the Wheat Economy* (Toronto, 1957), pt. 1; R. Pomfret, *The Economic Development of Canada* (Toronto, 1981), ch. 5.

actions, the objectives Canadians *qua* Canadians wanted to pursue were re-vealed; it was shown also that the instrument of these policies would be public enterprise.

The role of the state was already important within each of the fragments of British North America before Confederation. Hugh Aitken has chroni-cled the way in which this plurality of government bodies has influenced the pattern of development in Canada.[44] In each case, state action and public enterprise took different forms as a result of different economic bases, and the inner contradictions of the colonies were not worked out through the market mechanism acting as the referee of the divergent plans. It is as if the series of contradictions that Canada has been seen to represent could only find a resolution through the intervention of the public sector.

Aitken has labeled this Canadian tonus "defensive expansionism," to underline the reactive nature of this panoply of government interventions in Canadian colonies to threats and challenges coming from the growth and development of the United States. Although this is in great part true, at least for the post-1820 period, it would be unwise to presume that public enterprise has emerged only as a reaction from those external challenges.

A long tradition had existed in Canada dating back to New France, fed by the experience of the fur trade and the lessons in social relations it had taught the colonists, which drove home the point that the market mechanism and private enterprise were only one of many forms of social organization and coordination of socioeconomic activities, and that these institutions were often inefficient and untrustworthy agents.[45] The uncertainties and fears triggered by the American western expansion and the consequent negative identity sentiment it ignited had helped make ex-plicit the recognition that public enterprise was the only way out if the frag-ile Canadian existence were to be preserved, but this fed on a strong and deep-rooted sentiment that had been present for quite a long time.

In British North America each region, with its own government and dif-ferent resource base, attempted alone and then collectively, after 1867, to evolve an effective response to the end of the mercantilistic era, but these "national policies" tended to promote further the Balkanization of the country.[46] To a great extent, these policies were to strengthen the degree of specialization of the different areas of the country as a result of regional

[44] H.G.J. Aitken, "Defensive Expansionism: The State and Economic Growth in Canada," in *The State and Economic Growth*, ed. H.G.J. Aitken (New York, 1959), pp. 79–114.
[45] A. Rotstein, "Innis: The Alchemy of Fur and Wheat," *Journal of Canadian Studies* (1977):6–31.
[46] Pomfret, *The Economic Development of Canada*, ch. 5.

pressures by private interest groups, who used the government to promote their special interests.[47]

The federal structure of 1867 made an attempt to bring the mosaic of colonies in British North America under one general set of rules. However, despite the limited financial resources devolved to the provinces and the apparently clear allocation of responsibilities between the different levels of government, what was established was a regime much closer to competitive federalism than was first anticipated. In turn, the consequent horizontal (among regions) and vertical (between levels of government) concurrency and competition was to lead to administrative growth, executive federalism, and increasing Balkanization.[48]

But concomitant with this fragmentation process, there were strong reactions from those portions of the country that were on the losing side of the ledger. Though the western area was hardly populated until late in the nineteenth century, representations were heard rather early about the maleffects attached to the tariff policy. This led to a new role for the federal government as a broker: in the language of the Rowell-Sirois Commission, "When as a result of national policies undertaken in the general interest, one region or class or individual is fortuitously enriched and others impoverished, it would appear that there is an obligation, if not to redress the balance, at least to provide for the victim."[49] This in turn led to "the adoption and the elaboration, as a fundamental mode of Canadian life, of the *un-American* mechanism of redistribution as opposed to the . . . American mechanism of market rule."[50]

In the same way that Canadians had come to rely on public enterprise as their instrumentality, they came to develop some sort of redistribution norm or insurance policy, which enabled the country despite its lack of homogeneity to construct some mechanism of reciprocity outside the marketplace. This was to serve as a bond defining Canadianness, a way for Canadians to reconcile their separate regional lives with a need for collective security. Interregional redistribution became a way to define the new unity in this great diversity. This second set of institutions, developed mostly in the 1860s, was to take ever richer forms in the pre–World War II period.[51]

[47] T. W. Acheson, "The National Policy and Industrialization of the Maritimes," *Acadiensis* 1 (1972):3-28; K. H. Norrie, "The National Policy and Prairie Economic Discrimination, 1870–1930," in *Canadian Papers in Rural History* 1, ed. D. H. Akenson (1978):13–32.

[48] D. V. Smiley, *Canada in Question: Federalism in the Eighties* (Toronto, 1980).

[49] The Rowell-Sirois Commission was a royal commission on Dominion-provincial relations. The quotation from the report, published in 1940, is cited in Hardin, *A Nation Unaware*, p. 307.

[50] Hardin, *A Nation Unaware*, p. 300.

[51] V. C. Fowke, "The National Policy—Old and New," *Canadian Journal of Economics and Political Science* 18 (1952):271–86.

This redistribution ethic may be at the core of the Canadian identity, but it has not always been consciously, explicitly, and appropriately understood as such. There have been redistribution schemes elsewhere and it may be claimed that the issue is not Canada-specific. What is particular in the Canadian case is the way it is "so umbilically tied to our unique internal contradictions."[52]

In a sense, the redistribution ethic has found a way to become a non-market norm that serves as the underpinning of the effective working of market relationships. It has become the basic tenet of Canadian federalism as a social technology. Although it generates as much friction as it does solidarity, it does provide a bond and a basis for Canadian identity. Central to an understanding of this bond is the notion of rights: there are maritime rights, Quebec rights, and western rights to be honored, and even if the explicit argument that by leaving Confederation one would leave "the dense and potentially rich redistribution culture of solidarity" has not been made openly and explicitly, it might be said that the regions live by that norm implicitly.

Conclusion

Canadians of different vintages have developed "limited identities": regional, ethnic, and cultural identities that crystallized more or less quickly for the different segments of the community as a result of various configurations of forces. It evolved more quickly for Canadians of French extraction, who were able to develop a sense of negative and positive identity within a century of the arrival of Samuel de Champlain in 1608 and whose sense of identity was heightened by the arrival of the second wave of colonists. We have drawn attention to some indicators that would appear to demonstrate that their colonial ethos had been transformed rather early. For Canadians of British/American extraction, the process was much slower and we have referred to a number of factors explaining this retardation. Most certainly, the formation of their colonial identity did not progress as quickly as for the French Canadians during the first century after their arrival and the strength of the British connection remained strong late in the nineteenth century and into the twentieth.

Yet, in the nineteenth century, as a result of ethnic and regional contradictions (which were the very fabric of the country), some features of a "new Canadian ethos" emerged. Those features were the outgrowth of different strands emanating from the experience of the two founding groups, but they acquired, through the circumstances of the postmercantilistic pe-

---

[52] Hardin, *A Nation Unaware*, p. 303.

riod and of the industrialization drive in Canadian development, something of a new twist. Without its being possible to find any particular moment when collectively the fragments of Canada came to decide that they would make practical use of public enterprise and that they would honor a system of redistribution of resources, it was through these means that Canada found modes of accommodation for those fragments with limited identities and distilled at least some elements of a "national character."

Some have suggested that those features had become the governing relations of the Canadian society—the hard core of robust and resistant subprocesses, with the net of all other relations becoming adjusted to this more resistant core. The temptation to put a label on this core and call it the "Canadian identity" has been great and not always successfully resisted. Yet, despite this hard core, the Canadian identity has remained elusive and the Canadian personality split in many ways. It is easy to illustrate Canadian diversity; it is more difficult to identify any dominant, widely shared feeling that could be labeled "national character" and would be perceived by *all* as the distinguishing feature separating Canadians from their European forebears.

What has emerged from the nineteenth-century experience is some "Canadian order," based on a fragmented society bound by a few rules and joined by very incomplete interaction. The segments of the country had different economic bases; they had developed a limited identification as a regional/sectional/ethnic group and disunity more than unity was the rule. But it would be unwise to conclude from this that stability was not achieved and/or that communication between these segments was difficult because it was limited. Quite the contrary, the Canadian society evolved in the nineteenth century as a multistable system, one in which a great ability to adapt is ensured through discontinuities between the subsystems. The fragmentation of the overall process led to additional costs of transaction and friction, but the overall cost of adjusting the system was lowered.[53]

The paradox of this fragmentation, leading to an overall greater capacity to adapt and therefore to some "macrorationality" of the Canadian system, has been noted already by observers of the Canadian scene, albeit in rather different terms. "Our Canadianism, from the very moment of its real birth, is a baffling, illogical but compulsive athleticism—a fence-leaping which is also, and necessarily, a fence-keeping. . . . There are, of course, on both sides of the fence, those who will not make the leap, those who are un-

[53] For the notion of a multistable system, see W. R. Ashby, *Design for a Brain*, 2d ed. (London, 1960), ch. 16, and for the application of this concept to Canadian society see G. Paquet, "The Regulatory Process and Economic Performance" in *The Regulatory Process in Canada*, ed. G. B. Doern (Toronto, 1978), pp. 34–67.

moved by the creative irony of our unique nationhood. There are even those who would wish it away. Such people are not Canadians. Not yet. . . . Ours is not, can never be, the 'one hundred percent' kind of nationalism. We have always had to think in terms of 50–50. No 'melting pot.' Rather the open irony of the multidimensional structure, and openness to the 'larger mosaic'. . . . The diversity, the proper diversity of full Canadianism, has opened out from that irony of the fence-leaping and the fence-keeping . . . we can see vividly the actual movement from the dual irony to the multiple irony, from the expansive open thrust of the French–English tension to the many-coloured but miraculously coherent, if restless, pattern of the authentically Canadian nationhood."[54]

There is almost a sense of euphoria in such a statement, and a sense of confidence that particular Canadian "creative irony" knows no bounds, that it can remain the permanent feature of Canadianness even in the turbulent world of the twentieth century: "the foreshadowings of the new Promethean age of the technological, foreshadowings which threaten with extinction the parochial, self-centered, encrusted sense of identity of the older nations, but which set to tingling that sense of identity to which no bounds are set, need to be set, can be set. *Our* sense of identity. Dynamic irony opening outwards against—and through—a world of shut-ins. A hope, confronting both the anarchic and the totalitarian. . . ."[55] With the benefit of hindsight, this sounds like a somewhat presumptuous statement made at a time when the echo effects of major transformations in the Canadian society were observable but not yet fully understood by Canadians. A storm was brewing in the socioeconomic underground that was to affect the social order as the fire consumed the phoenix. Demographic forces would play a central role in this transformation.

The third wave of immigrants coming to Canada in the twentieth century and most especially in the post–World War II period did not find an absorptive Canadian identity but added to the multiplicity of tensions within Canada. The "founding nations" felt threatened by this new wave; a sense of peril for this precarious cultural identity developed. The passage from dual irony to multiple irony proved more difficult and the powers of dynamic irony, perhaps, more feeble than had been anticipated.

The multistable order of the Canadian society is a reality, but the practice of "compulsive athleticism" has not necessarily produced a subjective mix of self-image, life style, and collective future that one might identify as

[54] M. Ross, *Our Sense of Identity* (Toronto, 1954), pp. x–xi.
[55] Ross, *Our Sense of Identity*, p. xii.

113

the Canadian identity. Some have even suggested the existence of an "identity vacuum." This would lend a particularly ironic twist to the title of Herschel Hardin's book, *A Nation Unaware*, and it might explain the difficulty in arriving at firm conclusions about the formation of the Canadian colonial identities.

5 ◆ Identity in British America: Unease in Eden

Michael Zuckerman

SEVERAL ESSAYS in this volume trace the emergence of a common identity among a settler group in a colonial situation and investigate the connection between this process of identity formation and a subsequent bid for political independence. This essay, in contrast, argues that the colonists of British America always strove to be Britons and that they attained political independence at the end of the eighteenth century without ever declaring their common character or distinctive identity. Such a proposition can be advanced because the American break with Britain was essentially if not entirely political and sprang from administrative and diplomatic sources rather than from any deeper disconnection between the antagonists.

And yet the bid for independence by the American colonists did touch upon discontinuities in experience and in the understanding of experience. Though Americans were neither able nor willing to see themselves as a people with a cultural identity of their own, they faced a far different world than those they took for fellows across the Atlantic, and they faced it in very different ways. Though the colonists never sought any awareness of such differences, let alone any larger conception of themselves as an encompassing community, their peculiar ways imparted a special flavor to subsequent American modes. Though the colonial experience of English Americans did not determine the subsequent shape of national consciousness, it was, nonetheless, profoundly formative. In some crucial ways it set the very terms in which notions of national character would eventually arise.

It is a measure of how minimally a state of self-awareness matured among Americans that divergences between the colonists and the mother country were as deep—and as deliberate—at the moment of settlement as they would ever be during the colonial period. Descendants of the original pioneers did their best to recover the culture their parents had left behind,[1] but the pioneers themselves often embarked upon the ocean passage in willful rejection of the emerging English modes. They projected colonies in regressive determination to resist what they perceived as the capitalistic ini-

---

[1] Jack P. Greene, "Search for Identity: An Interpretation of the Meaning of Selected Patterns of Social Response in Eighteenth-Century America," *Journal of Social History* 3 (1970):189–220.

115

tiatives of the great merchants and magnates or the centralizing enterprise of the Stuarts. [2]

Such emigrants aimed to escape all that was eroding their accustomed insularities. Puritans fled the alluring corruptions of their native land; patroons sought sovereignty in New York; Catholics envisioned a feudal retreat in Maryland. All of them, and others elsewhere, refused the real England of their experience in order to try to re-create the archaically idealized England of their imagination.

John Clarke might complain in 1652 that, "while Old England is becoming new, New-England is become old," but many of the early migrants celebrated the development he lamented. Colonial leaders from the Sagadahoc in Maine to the Sea Islands in Georgia had sought such a consummation from the first. Gorges and Mason projected sixteenth-century plans for their vast claims in northern New England. Ministers and magistrates enacted "essentially medieval" assumptions and ambitions in Massachusetts. Gentleman adventurers took up feudal manors in Maryland, under a proprietor who laid claim to powers that had been obsolete in England for a century. Shaftesbury and his gifted secretary ordained an intricate array of fantastic titles in the Fundamental Constitutions of Carolina. [3]

Settlers themselves sought the same consummation. Artisans and craftsmen from the diversified economy of England frequently reverted to farming in the colonies, [4] and some colonial farmers and landowners spurned the innovative techniques of intensive agriculture that were fairly widespread in England, in favor of traditional and less productive methods of farming and land management. [5] What was true of economic activity and social relations was equally true of material culture. Forms that were fading in Britain were revived in the colonies. Post-built homes, shingle roofs, clapboard walls, and connecting service wings between houses and barns were

[2] T. H. Breen, "Persistent Localism: English Social Change and the Shaping of New England Institutions," *William and Mary Quarterly*, 3d ser., 32 (1975):3–28.

[3] John Clarke, *Ill Newes from New-England* (London, 1652); Charles Clark, *The Eastern Frontier: The Settlement of Northern New England, 1610–1763* (New York, 1970), pp. 16–20; Howard M. Jones, *O Strange New World: American Culture: The Formative Years* (London, 1965), p. 75; "Instructions to the Colonists by Lord Baltimore, 1633," in *Narratives of Early Maryland, 1633–1684*, ed. Clayton Hall (New York, 1910), p. 14; Hall, *Narratives of Maryland*, pp. 66–68; *Virginia and Maryland, or the Lord Baltimore's Case Uncased and Answered* (1655), in Hall, *Narratives of Maryland*, pp. 196–97; Clarence Ver Steeg, *Origins of a Southern Mosaic: Studies of Early Carolina and Georgia* (Athens, Ga., 1975).

[4] T. H. Breen and Stephen Foster, "Moving to the New World: The Character of Early Massachusetts Migration," *William and Mary Quarterly*, 3d ser., 30 (1973):189–222; see also Clark, *Eastern Frontier*, pp. 9–10.

[5] Darrett Rutman, *Husbandmen of Plymouth: Farms and Villages in the Old Colony, 1620–1692* (Boston, 1967), esp. pp. v, 52–62; Harvey Jackson, "The Darien Antislavery Petition of 1739 and the Georgia Plan," *William and Mary Quarterly*, 3d ser., 34 (1977):622–25.

only a few of the artifacts of everyday life already outmoded in the Old World that were refurbished in the New.[6]

Nonetheless, the past could not be brought back intact, and the transformation of traditional society could not be arrested so easily. Archaic ideals could be carried across the Atlantic and reconstituted in America from the models in people's minds, but such deliberate recourse to tradition was, at bottom, the antithesis of tradition. The rich particularity of the past could not be remade from models. In the very effort to defend ancient insularities, settlers shattered the continuity with the past that was a hallmark of the localism they sought to conserve. For the communities that could be constructed on a wilderness coast were wholly new communities, without indigenous customs, without elders who had lived there all their lives, without ancient burying grounds or even any old buildings. Traditional ends had therefore to be achieved under novel circumstances by novel means. In the exigencies of existence three thousand miles from kings and archbishops and in the cause of serving customary ideals, the colonists improvised a variety of new institutional arrangements that had no parallels in their communities of origin. As they did, they precipitated a pattern of counterpoised extremities that has been characteristic of America ever since. Reaction entailed innovation. Conservation of tradition compelled cultural creativity. And the dialectic that emerged out of that initial dislocation only deepened over the years that followed.[7]

Just as their motives for emigration detached many settlers from the civilization they left behind, so too—and still more starkly—did the ocean

---

[6] Cary Carson et al., "Impermanent Architecture in the Southern American Colonies," *Winterthur Portfolio* 16 (1981):135–96; Dell Upton, "Toward a Permanence Theory of Vernacular Architecture: Early Tidewater Virginia as a Case Study," *Folklore Forum* 12 (1979):176; Henry Glassie, *Folk Housing in Middle Virginia: A Structural Analysis of Historic Artifacts* (Knoxville, 1975), p. 130; Henry Glassie, *Pattern in the Material Folk Culture of the Eastern United States* (Philadelphia, 1969), pp. 185–87. All of these developments were deliberate and explicit. Still other reversions to a real or imagined past may have been more unwitting or may at any rate have befallen the colonists more nearly unawares. See, e.g., Philip Greven, "Historical Demography and Colonial America," *William and Mary Quarterly*, 3d ser., 24 (1967):438–54. The secondary literature also hints that the settlers, once arrived in America, may have been less mobile than their fellows on the other side of the ocean, less class-conscious, and more inclined to live compactly. See, e.g., Breen and Foster, "Moving to the New World," p. 209; Richard Dunn, *Sugar and Slaves: The Rise of the Planter Class in the English West Indies, 1624–1713* (Chapel Hill, 1972), p. 341; Barry Levy, "The Light in the Valley: The Chester and Welsh Tract Quaker Communities in the Delaware Valley, 1681–1750" (Ph.D. diss., Univ. of Pennsylvania, 1976), p. 9. Such intimations of a more significant traditionalism in the New World than in the Old are only intimations and would have to be followed out more systematically, but they are suggestive.

[7] For a more detailed exposition of the dynamic and a causal hypothesis, see Michael Zuckerman, "The Fabrication of Identity in Early America," *William and Mary Quarterly*, 3d ser., 34 (1977):183–214.

117

crossing itself. The perils of the Atlantic passage impressed themselves vividly on all who contemplated it and unforgettably upon all who undertook it, whether in the seventeenth or the eighteenth centuries. The Huguenot exile Durand of Dauphiné provided a graphic description of the travails that could beset the voyager to Virginia, and he was a paying passenger who would have received more favorable treatment than the indentured servants and redemptioners who constituted the overwhelming majority of emigrants. Durand described himself as "stowed between decks, three in a bed, and once a day . . . fed pea soup, salt beef three times a week, and the remaining four days the most unsavory codfish that can be found." The ship advanced thirty leagues to sea on three occasions, only to return to port each time because of fierce contrary winds. During these wasted four weeks off the coast of England, the captain of the vessel attempted to steal Durand's belongings. And if the captain was a thief, the ship's company was no comfort either. Of the sixty hands on board, including crew, twelve were prostitutes "brought along to be sold" and another fifteen were "the boldest and most insolent young scoundrels in all England." These "shameless creatures" sang, danced, and carried on "shockingly" while Durand's woman and boy took sick and died. By the tenth week at sea, with supplies running short, a despondent Durand prayed God to "put an end to all this grief and suffering by a quick death." But his prayer went unanswered, even as his despair grew. A storm broke the hoops of the last barrel of salt pork, so that the meat spoiled and there was nothing left to eat but "moldly biscuit." The captain, an "inhuman master," not only put the passengers on a strict ration of biscuit and water but also held them punctiliously to it as "three or four people died for want of water, although there was still plenty." When the ship finally dropped anchor in Virginia, nineteen weeks after setting sail, Durand put on a suit he had not worn since leaving Europe and discovered that he "had to draw in the belt to his breeches sixteen inches."[8]

Durand's was hardly the most harrowing of early ocean voyages. Many travelers died; many more endured despair. If Durand and his shipmates had to ration their drinking water, the water itself was at least potable. Others on subsequent voyages were served a vile liquid "very black, thick, and full of worms, so that one cannot drink it without loathing." Still others ran so short of water that the rats themselves "could find no more" and therefore "came in great numbers into their sleeping room at night,

[8] Durand of Dauphiné, *A Huguenot Exile in Virginia*, ed. Gilbert Chinard (New York, 1934), pp. 89–100.

seeking the sweat on their faces." And still others were grateful even for rats that could be bought and cooked to relieve the pangs of hunger.[9]

Awareness of the dangers of the sea voyage was widespread in England. George Alsop, writing in 1666, told of impoverished tradesmen in England who would as "lief take a bear by the tooth" as attempt an Atlantic crossing. And the prospect of the passage continued to dismay people—even people who enjoyed relatively easy voyages—to the very end of the colonial era. Eliza Lucas Pinckney made an eighteenth-century voyage in a mere twenty-five days, a marvelously "fine" journey, as she acknowledged. Yet, once safely ensconced, she swore she "would not cross that frightful ocean" again "for the best fortune in England."[10]

New Englanders transposed such traumas into religious terms. Indeed, they were so shaken by their season on the high seas that they came to conceive it the decisive divide of their lives. Blasphemously mistaking a ship's progress for a pilgrim's, they declared an "equation of new life with New World" and let the migration to America "displace . . . conversion as the crucial event" of their spiritual careers.[11]

For men and women who could thus confound the story of their sea passage and the saga of their soul-passage, the ocean crossing was obviously momentous indeed, and its momentousness belies E. E. Rich's brilliant suggestion that "the most important thing about the peopling of British North America" was its very ordinariness. Rich, arguing from the regularity of geographic mobility in early modern England, proposed that the mass migrations to America were accomplished by unexceptional people who were not even "conscious that they were doing anything remarkable." Such folk, he felt, "were already accustomed to migration; emigration held few additional terrors." But New Englanders found terror enough in the transition, and the meaning and purpose of their lives besides. The Atlantic expedition represented a literal rite of passage for the Puritans. In its extremities of peril and promise, it presaged the exaggerations and the contrapuntal excesses that would distinguish American life from European.[12]

Whether colonists made for Maryland or Massachusetts, whether they

[9] Gottlieb Mittelberger, *Journey to Pennsylvania*, ed. and tr. Oscar Handlin and John Clive (Cambridge, Mass., 1960), p. 24; Henry Muhlenberg, *The Journals of Henry Melchior Muhlenberg*, tr. Theodore Tappert and John Doberstein (Philadelphia, 1942–58), 1:55; Carl Bridenbaugh, *Vexed and Troubled Englishmen 1590-1642* (New York, 1968), pp. 6–9.

[10] George Alsop, *A Character of the Province of Mary-Land* (London, 1666), pp. 41–43; *The Letterbook of Eliza Lucas Pinckney, 1739-1762*, ed. Elise Pinckney (Chapel Hill, 1972), p. 132.

[11] Sacvan Bercovitch, *The Puritan Origins of the American Self* (New Haven, 1975), p. 12.

[12] E. E. Rich, "The Population of Elizabethan England," *Economic History Review*, 2d ser., 2 (1949):263–64.

used secular speech or sacred, they countered their terror of the Atlantic from a "fund of revivifying images" of a "realm of harmony" awaiting them on the western shore. This dynamic of dread and regeneration ensured that British America would never be just another European or English province. The woods were dark in England, to be sure, and in Germany and Scandinavia as well, and there were bogs and wastes to be reclaimed everywhere. But none of them—with the possible exception of Irish woods and bogs— were depicted in such luridly denigrating tones or exalted in such edenic ones as the wilderness of America. Migration inspired extravagant ideas on every hand of what the migrants were, what they were engaged upon, and what they discovered.[13]

According to one image that had its origin with Richard Hakluyt and that continued to enjoy popularity in England throughout the colonial period, the American colonists were the dregs and refuse of English society. As one commentator put it, they were the population "farthest from conscience and moral honesty of any . . . in the world." On that image, an aura of outcast infelicity hung over the early settlements, coloring the colonists' preconceptions of their destinations and indeed discouraging would-be colonists from leaving Europe. Even friends of New England admitted that the reputation of the New World Puritans had come to "stink everywhere." Even promotional tracts for the Chesapeake colonies acknowledged that the area was "reported to be an unhealthy place, a nest of rogues, whores, dissolute and rooking persons; a place of intolerable labor, bad usage and hard diet."[14]

It was said from the outset that Virginia would "ease" the mother country "of a swarm of unnecessary inmates." It was conceded that the colony was corruptly governed, and that the mismanagement occasioned "many miseries to the undertakers and scandals to the business." And the "base reports and slanders" that beset the Virginian venture in its earliest years persisted for a century and more. A promotional tract of the Cromwellian period attempted to relieve the colony of "that odium that malicious tongues [had] thrown upon" it. A working paper for the Board of Trade at

---

[13] Wayne Franklin, *Discoverers, Explorers, Settlers: The Diligent Writers of Early America* (Chicago, 1979), p. 35. For a nice instance of the sea passage as a source of renewal, see Charles Wooley, *A Two Years Journal in New-York* (1701), ed. E. B. O'Callaghan, in *Historical Chronicles of New Amsterdam, Colonial New York, and Early Long Island*, ed. Cornell Jaray (Port Washington, N.Y., 1968), 1st ser., pp. 60–63.

[14] Richard Hakluyt, *Voyages and Discoveries*, ed. and abr. Jack Beeching (Penguin ed., Harmondsworth, Middlesex, 1972), p. 211; Fulmer Mood, "The English Geographers and the Anglo-American Frontier in the Seventeenth Century," *University of California Publications in Geography* 6, no. 9 (1944):375; *Winthrop Papers*, Massachusetts Historical Society, *Collections*, 4th ser., 6 (Boston, 1863), p. 537; John Hammond, *Leah and Rachel, or, the Two Fruitful Sisters Virginia and Mary-land* (1656), in Hall, *Narratives of Maryland*, p. 284.

the end of the seventeenth century confessed the "cursed bad character" under which the settlement still labored. A pamphlet of the early eighteenth century lamented that the ugly reputation the tobacco plantations had "long groaned under" caused "prejudice and aversion in the breasts of many against transportation to those colonies." And the same aversion still prevailed a generation later, when a planter who requested his brother in England to procure servants for him was rebuffed by the brother, who was fearful he might "be accounted a kidnapper." The apprehensiveness induced by all those forbidding images had made it seem that people could be procured for service in Virginia only by abduction.[15]

Similarly unsavory images attended every other colony, from the beginning of colonization to the time of the Revolution. Bermuda, Barbados, New England, the Carolinas, and Pennsylvania were all disparaged by critics, and the criticisms continued to the very end of the colonial era. In the second year of the Revolution, opponents of independence registered their disgust at Washington's military success "with a ragged banditti of undisciplined people, the scum and refuse of all nations of earth." Because of the ill repute of the colonies, would-be employers encountered difficulty in procuring servants to emigrate, and this in turn fostered the belief that "very few of good conversation would adventure thither."[16]

Coexisting with this image of America was its counterimage, which held that it was the Old World and its inhabitants that were decadent and degenerate and that it was England rather than any of the American colonies

[15] Alexander Brown, ed., The Genesis of the United States (Boston, 1890), 1:252; ibid., 2:601; William Crashaw, A Sermon Preached in London (London, 1610), p. H, verso; William Bullock, Virginia Impartially Examined (London, 1649), "To the Reader," p. 1; Michael Kammen, ed., "Virginia at the Close of the Seventeenth Century: An Appraisal by James Blair and John Locke," Virginia Magazine of History and Biography 74 (1966), p. 155; "A Plain and Friendly Persuasive to the Inhabitants of Virginia and Maryland for Promoting Towns and Cohabitation," Virginia Magazine of History and Biography 4 (1896–97), p. 255; Thomas Ludwell to Philip Ludwell, January 4, 1723/4, in William and Mary Quarterly, 1st ser., 3 (1894–95):198.

[16] Louis Wright, ed., The Elizabethans' America (Cambridge, 1966), pp. 194, 196–97; David Galenson, "The Social Origins of Some Early Americans: Rejoinder," William and Mary Quarterly, 3d ser., 36 (1979):271; Nathaniel Ward, The Simple Cobler of Aggawam, in The Puritans: A Sourcebook of Their Writings, ed. Perry Miller and Thomas Johnson (New York, 1963), p. 227; [Council for New England], A Brief Relation of the Discovery and Plantation of New England (London, 1622), p. 7; William Wood, New Englands Prospect (London, 1634), p. 39; Robert Weir, "The South Carolinian as Extremist," South Atlantic Quarterly 74 (1975):90; "A Letter from Doctor More, with Passages out of Several Letters from Persons of Good Credit, Relating to the State and Improvement of the Province of Pennsylvania: Published to Prevent False Reports," Pennsylvania Magazine of History and Biography 4 (1880):447; Letter of Doctor Nicholas More, 1686, in Narratives of Early Pennsylvania, West New Jersey and Delaware, 1630–1707, ed. Albert Myers (New York, 1912), p. 284. Quotations from The Journal of Nicholas Cresswell, 1774–1777 (New York, 1924), pp. 251–52, and Hammond, Leah and Rachel, p. 287.

that was a "dry, heathy, bare, barren wilderness . . . wherein virtue is an exile."[17] Enthusiasts for colonization extolled the opportunities that America offered to the skilled and the industrious who could "scarcely get a living" in England, and they promised opportunity for social and economic advancement far in excess of anything that could ever be imagined at home, where "toil and penury" were men's lot while they had vigor, and "begging and starving" when they reached old age.[18]

Against images of the colonies as a barren desert, apologists conjured up counterimages of the Old World as a "cold and blasty" place, "hideous" in its aspect, and of the New as a voluptuously lovely one.[19] Advertisement after advertisement portrayed the plantations as "earth's only paradise." Pamphlet upon pamphlet, poem upon poem pronounced its author's conviction that, "if there be any terrestrial Canaan, 'tis surely here."[20]

In opposition to the images of the inferiority of American conditions and commodities, publicists affirmed the excellence of everything American from mast trees to melons and wheat to wool.[21] Such puffery extolled fruit so fine "that they who once taste of it will despise the watery taste of that in England," horses so "beautiful and full of courage" that none at home could stand the comparison, and soil so rich that "the most fertile part of England is . . . but barren" by contrast.[22] A brief letter from Pennsylvania

[17] Daniel Price, *Sauls Prohibition Staide* (London, 1609), pp. 1–2. Puritans promoted migration to New England in identical accents, as Michael Walzer has shown; see "Puritanism as a Revolutionary Ideology," *History and Theory* 3 (1961):59–90. Price's position is the more striking because he was a staunch royalist and Anglican, as was Robert Gray, whose sermon of the same year spoke in a similar vein. See *A Good Speed to Virginia* (London, 1609).

[18] John Fenwick, *Friends, These Are to Satisfy You* (London, 1675), p. 2; Board of General Proprietors of the Eastern Division of New Jersey, *Advertisement, to all Tradesmen, Husbandmen, Servants, and Others Who Are Willing to Transport Themselves unto the Province of New-East-Jersey in America* (London, 1684).

[19] Beauchamp Plantagenet, *A Description of the Province of New Albion* (London, 1648), pp. 28–29; Durand, *Huguenot Exile*, p. 114.

[20] Michael Drayton, "Ode to the Virginian Voyage," in Brown, *Genesis*, 1:86–87; see also ibid., 1:494; Daniel Denton, *A Brief Description of New York* (1670), ed. Victor Paltsits (New York, 1937), pp. 19–20; Bullock, *Virginia Impartially Examined*, pp. 3, 52; R. W. Kelsey, "Swiss Settlers in South Carolina," *South Carolina Historical Magazine* 23 (1922):87–88; *A New and Accurate Account of the Provinces of South Carolina and Georgia* (1733) in *Collections of the Georgia Historical Society* 1 (1840):52; Robert Montgomery, *A Discourse Concerning the Designed Establishment of a New Colony to the South of South Carolina, in the Most Delightful Country of the Universe* (London, 1717), p. 6; Fenwick, *Friends*, p. 2; Board of Proprietors of Eastern New Jersey, *Advertisement*.

[21] [Thomas West, 3rd Lord De La Warr], *The Relation of the Right Honorable the Lord De-La-Warr* (London, 1611), p. 12; [William Loddington], *Plantation Work the Work of This Generation* (London, 1682), p. 18; "A Letter from Doctor More," p. 452; *A Perfect Description of Virginia* (London, 1649), pp. 1–2; *Proposals by Mr. Peter Purry . . .* (1731), in *Historical Collections of South Carolina*, ed. B. R. Carroll (New York, 1836), 2:133–35.

[22] B[ishop] Roberts, "Prospect of Charleston" (London, 1739), South Carolina Historical Society, Charleston, S.C.; Virginia Company, *A Declaration of the State of the Colony and Af-*

declared the superiority of its parsnips, thorns, sturgeon, and limestone. A lengthy treatise on North Carolina celebrated the supremacy of its water, fowl, crawfish, cornstalks, flowers, nuts, pork, pheasant, even its eels, beans, and millstones. An early account of South Carolina assured "any maid or single woman" that if she would "go over" she would think herself "in the Golden Age." A promotional portrayal of Pennsylvania and West New Jersey promised parents that children born by the banks of the Delaware were "better natured, milder, and more tenderhearted than those born in England." And a report from Massachusetts insisted that the very atmosphere of America excelled anything on the other side of the ocean. "A sup of New England's air," said Francis Higginson, "is better than a whole draft of old England's ale."[23]

All of these chiaroscuro constructions, damning European darkness and blazoning American brilliance, were responses to equal but opposite condemnations of the new continent. The condemnation sowed seeds of doubt that ripened into a deep unease that could be clipped only by an answering acclamation of America; yet the unease grew more luxuriantly every time it was cut back. It was exactly the sensitivity to derision that inspired the extravagant fancies of the real estate salesmen. The colonists recognized the reality of their odious reputation even as they attempted to offset it by tall tales and paradisaic images. They felt the force of metropolitan contempt for their primitiveness even as they tried to meet it with exaggerated assertions of economic growth and development. Again and again they were impelled to extremities of a haunting insecurity and a compensating compulsion to exalt their country in order to create it.

When the settlers exalted America, they exalted above all the indolent ease they professed to find there. In the New World as in the ancient garden, "everything seemed to come up by nature." Husbandmen lived "almost void of care and free from . . . fatigues." By the bounty of a benign providence, the earth brought forth "all things in abundance, as in the first creation, without toil or labor."[24]

---

fairs in Virginia (London, 1620), pp. 4–5; Douglas McManis, *European Impressions of the New England Coast, 1497–1620* (Chicago, 1972), p. 94.

[23] "A Letter from Doctor More," pp. 449–51; John Lawson, *A New Voyage to Carolina* (1709), ed. Hugh Lefler (Chapel Hill, 1967), pp. 37, 38, 50, 56, 66, 76, 82, 88, 96, 106–107, 144, 161, 165; Robert Horne (?), *A Brief Description of the Province of Carolina* (1666), in *Narratives of Early Carolina 1650–1708*, ed. Alexander Salley (New York, 1911), p. 73; Gabriel Thomas, *An Historical and Geographical Account of Pennsylvania and of West-New-Jersey* (1698), in Myers, *Narratives of Pennsylvania*, p. 332; Francis Higginson, *New England's Plantation, or a Short and True Description of the Commodities and Discommodities of that Country* (London, 1630), p. 10.

[24] Lawson, *New Voyage*, p. 69; "Arthur Barlowe's Discourse of the First Voyage," in *The Roanoke Voyages, 1584–1590*, ed. David Quinn (London, 1955), 1:108.

Effortlessness was, of course, the epitome of Eden. It would have been a literary necessity even if it had not been a literal reality. But the appeal of such idleness and ease extended far beyond the fulfillment of supernal metaphors. The blandishments of the "spirits" who swarmed London to entice the least lyric of men and women to the colonies were not cast in terms of wealth as much as of hedonic indulgence. "The usual way of getting servants" for Virginia was by means of such tempters, and their principal persuasion was the prospect of relief from labor. As one assured his recruits, they were bound for "a place where food [would] drop into their mouths." To the very end of the colonial era, in Ireland as well as in England, remonstrants against migration inveighed against "the misrepresentations of designing men" who "induced and inveigled" people "to leave their native country" on promises of a life "without labour and industry."[25]

And what these seducers expounded in Europe, settlers often swore they found in America. Whether shipwrecked on Bermuda or left without adequate provisions in Virginia, colonists claimed they were able to survive in the New World without difficulty.[26] In every province, pioneers declared their dependence on the bounty of nature. Domestic stock cost "nothing to keep or feed" because animals grazed freely in winter as well as in summer, sparing settlers the drudgery of fencing and the tedium of foddering. An ox could be "raised at almost as little expense in Carolina as a hen . . . in England." Feeding on the rich and self-renewing grasses of America, herds increased "abundantly . . . without any charge or trouble to the planter."[27]

Fish and fowl were even more accommodating. In the bays, Marylanders encountered "rich bosoms" of marine creatures, all "easily taken." In the rivers, Pennsylvanians saw sturgeon "leap into the boats" of the men angling for them. And in the islands, Bermudans found fish "so abundant" that, if a settler stepped in the water, fish came "round about him" to the point that "men were fain to get out for fear of biting."[28] Furthermore, as fish were "in numbers inexhaustible," so birds were "so numerous . . . that [one] might see millions in a flock." Just as New Englanders professed to be "pestered" by the cod that covered the decks of their ships, Pennsylvanians

[25] Bullock, *Virginia Impartially Examined*, p. 14; *Belfast News Letter*, no. 3411, April 27, 1770, typescript excerpts in South Caroliniana Library, Columbia, S.C., pp. 29–30.
[26] R. Rich, *News from Virginia* (1610) (New York, 1937), p. A verso; [West], *Relation of De-La-Warr*, pp. 8–9; [Joel Gascoyne], *A True Description of Carolina* (London, 1682), p. 3; Richard Hartshorne et al., *A Further Account of New Jersey* (1676; London, 1890), p. 2.
[27] Durand, *Huguenot Exile*, p. 122; Samuel Wilson, *An Account of the Province of Carolina* (1682), in Salley, *Narratives of Carolina*, pp. 170–73; Denton, *Brief Description*, pp. 5, 18.
[28] [Father Andrew White], *A Declaration of the Lord Baltemore's Plantation in Mary-Land* (1633) (Baltimore, 1929), pp. 3–4; [Loddington], *Plantation Work*, p. 18; Silvester Jourdain, *A Discovery of the Barmudas* (1610) (New York, 1940), pp. 11–12.

complained of being "cloyed with" birds that could be caught "by hundreds at a time."[29] Everywhere men marveled at the manna that awaited them. Everywhere also they reveled in their exemption from the Adamic curse, and everywhere they echoed the exultancy of the first English settlement at Roanoke that the land lavished its largess upon them without "toil or labor."[30]

Some settlers allowed their own labor literally no part at all in their prosperity, attributing it instead to "the rich land." But even those who acknowledged American industry acknowledged very little. They reported an "amazing increase" of their corn "though their husbandry is so slight that they can only be said to scratch the earth." New World grains were "so grateful to the planter" that they returned him "his entrusted seed" with a treble growth; and they were "so facilely planted that one man in 48 hours may prepare as much ground and set such a quantity of corn that he may be secure for want of bread all the year following." Men managed "very easily," though unwilling to work "above two or three hours a day" or more than "three days in seven."[31]

Indeed, under such circumstances, it was difficult to distinguish between work and leisure. John Smith's Virginia was a land in which planting was a pastime of "pleasure," "hunting and hawking" an "exercise" of "delight," and fishing a "pretty sport" for profit. Anthony Gondy's South Carolina was a country in which "nobody . . . works more than two m[onths]. The remainder of the time he may go fishing or hunting." William Byrd's North Carolina was a domain in which "everything" grew plentifully "to supply the wants or wantonness of man"; Daniel Denton's New York was a place in which woods and fields were "dyed red" with strawberries and springtime ardor.[32]

Nonetheless, such celebration of hedonic ease was perilous. It stirred once more the specter of corruption that had driven some settlers from Eng-

[29] Lawson, New Voyage, pp. 50–51; McManis, European Impressions, pp. 92–93; [Loddington], Plantation Work, p. 18.

[30] "Barlowe's Discourse," 1:108. See also, e.g., Lawson, New Voyage, pp. 69, 115; R[obert] F[erguson], The Present State of Carolina (London, 1682), pp. 3, 8–9; Letter of Doctor Nicholas More, p. 285; Bullock, Virginia Impartially Examined, p. 7.

[31] Proposals by Purry, 2:129; A New and Accurate Account, pp. 50–51; E. W., Virginia: More Especially the Southern Part Thereof, Richly and Truly Valued (1650), in Peter Force, Tracts and Other Papers Relating Principally to the Origin, Settlement, and Progress of the Colonies in North America (Washington, D.C., 1836–46), vol. 3, no. 11, pp. 12–13; Proposals by Purry, 2:127; Lewis Leary, "The Adventures of Captain John Smith as Heroic Legend," in Essays in Early Virginia Literature Honoring Richard Beale Davis, ed. J. A. Leo Lemay (New York, 1977), pp. 16–17.

[32] Leary, "Adventures of Smith," pp. 16–17; Kelsey, "Swiss Settlers," p. 86; William Byrd, The History of the Dividing Line, in The Prose Works of William Byrd of Westover, ed. Louis Wright (Cambridge, Mass., 1966), p. 290; Denton, Brief Description, pp. 3–4.

land in the first place. It invited anew the castigation of the colonists that had originally impelled the inflation of American excellences.

The problem with paradise was that it was "apt to make the people incline to sloth." The very exaggeration of effortlessness that was enticing was also unsettling. Emigrants uncertain of their own civility were sensitive to suggestions that they might be overwhelmed by the wilderness and lapse into self-indulgence. Their affirmations of abundance therefore evoked answering affirmations of the arduousness of clearing a frontier or establishing a farm.[33]

Puritans in particular wished to see the New World in straitened terms. They proclaimed it a "howling wilderness," the better to hold its attractions at a distance. They denied desire for "prelapsarian ease," the more effectively to accommodate their image of the continent as "a land preoccupied with toil."[34]

But Puritans were never alone in their willful emphasis on industry or their definition of themselves as people who had plunged into the dark forests to escape corruption. Promoters of Georgia as much as builders of the Bay Colony mourned the decay of discipline and morality in the mother country and anticipated the renewal of good order amid the diminished temptations of America. The trustees of the southern venture as much as the preachers of the northern one envisioned an enterprise that would transform "an uncultivated desert into a fruitful garden." In accents that might as easily have come from east of the Hudson, the organizers of the settlement on the Savannah admonished that their province might be "deformed by its own fertility," warned that they would not accept men and women who sought "a state of idleness and dependence," and advised more generally that "men were appointed to cultivate the earth," not bask in its bounty.[35] In similar fashion William Penn and his Quaker adherents expressed satisfaction that their colony did not provide men with "the least occasion or temptation" to follow "a lazy, scandalous life," while promoters in East New Jersey hailed simplicity in that province as a sign of "golden times" when men "newly entered into their possessions" would be "enforced thereby to labor."[36]

[33] John Archdale, *A New Description of that Fertile and Pleasant Province of Carolina* (1707) in Salley, *Narratives of Carolina*, p. 290.
[34] Daniel Rodgers, *The Work Ethic in Industrial America 1850–1920* (Chicago, 1978), pp. 4–5.
[35] John Burton, *The Duty and Reward of Propagating Principles of Religion and Virtue Exemplified in the History of Abraham* (London, 1733), p. 27; George Watts, *A Sermon Preached before the Trustees for Establishing the Colony of Georgia in America* (London, 1736), pp. 7–8, 12, 7. See also *Some Account of the Designs of the Trustees for Establishing the Colony of Georgia in America* (London, 1732), p. 3.
[36] William Penn, "The Benefit of Plantations, or Colonies," in *Select Tracts Relating to Colonies* (London, 1732), pp. 26, 28; Thomas, *Historical and Geographical Account*, pp. 332–33;

It was on just such advertisements of austerity that some men and women abandoned England. Quaker families embarked for Pennsylvania because they believed it would be "a good place to train up children amongst a sober people and to prevent" their corruption in England "by the loose behaviour of youths and the bad example of too many of riper years." Other parents set sail for Virginia on a similar conviction that their children "would be removed from the infinite temptations, false pleasures, snares, and delusions which everywhere abounded in Britain to a land . . . where industry, probity, and the moral virtues were only encouraged, cherished, or regarded."[37]

Throughout the plantations, then, colonists careened from one extremity to the other. They preened themselves on their effortless indolence in one breath and prided themselves on their exemplary industry in the next. This ambivalence was as real for John Smith and the early promoters of Virginia as it was for the first historians of New England because they all experienced similar indecision in their appropriation of the New World. Adventurers and clergymen alike understood the connection between men being "orderly turned to their trades" and a "well ordered commonwealth." But their very acknowledgment of the importance of labor fostered further centrifugality or, perhaps more nearly, recognized a centrifugality that already existed.[38]

The lot of laborers in the Old World was not an enviable one, but the lot of those who left was often worse. Motivated by "extreme misery" or "reduced to . . . poverty," they were forced to sell themselves into servitude to come to the colonies at all. The terms of their transplantation made plain that they had no attractive alternative in England. The often ruthless exploitation to which they were subjected in America disabused them of any hopes they might have held of a new and better home. More than a few of these self-made bondsmen came to "cry out day and night, oh that they were in England without their limbs. . . . yea though they beg from door to door."[39]

Francis D. Pastorius, *Circumstantial Geographical Description of Pennsylvania* (1700), in Myers, *Narratives of Pennsylvania*, pp. 382–83; George Scot, *The Model of the Government of the Province of East-New-Jersey* (1685), in William Whitehead, *East Jersey under the Proprietary Governments* (Newark, N.J., 1875), pp. 400–401, 381.

[37] James Levick, "The Early Welsh Quakers and Their Emigration to Pennsylvania," *Pennsylvania Magazine of History and Biography* 17 (1893):404; "Narrative of George Fisher," *William and Mary Quarterly*, 1st ser., 17 (1908–1909), p. 101.

[38] Virginia Company, *Declaration of the State of the Colony*, p. 3; Joshua Scottow, *A Narrative of the Planting of the Massachusetts Colony* (Boston, 1694), p. 49; Annette Kolodny, *The Lay of the Land: Metaphor as Experience and History in American Life and Letters* (Chapel Hill, 1975), ch. 2.

[39] "Roger Clap's Memoirs," in *Chronicles of the First Planters of the Colony of Massachusetts*

On the other hand, the exploitation endured by inferiors was only one side of the disjunctive development of servitude in the New World. As much as menials became mere commodities in the colonies, they were also imperative on the virgin land, where labor was everywhere in short supply. Consequently, the ones who stayed and survived were able to turn their situation to account and even acquired a sense of self-importance. Masters in New England grumbled that servants learned "to live idly, and work when they list." Manor lords in New York complained of their tenants' "hopes of having land of their own and becoming independent of landlords." Planters in Virginia had to exempt white servants from the slavishness of their original legal lot and accept them as political equals with themselves.[40]

In every colony, authorities were ultimately obliged to gratify the demands of their white subordinates in some degree—by legislation, adjudication, or common custom—in order to attract inhabitants at all. In every colony, "laboring men" emerged "who had not enough to bring them over, yet [were] now worth scores and some hundreds of pounds." And in many colonies, rival publicists vied in promoting their own province as the "best poor man's country," in an odd conflation of poverty and prepotency that was itself indicative of the antipodal tensions of early American life.[41]

As men and women of even the most servile stations came to matter in America, they came also, in Thomas Shepard's words, to "desire liberty." Though they probably expressed thereby a motive also emerging among their English counterparts, their craving for freedom certainly matured in America.[42]

Bay, ed. Alexander Young (Boston, 1846), pp. 354–55; Warren Billings, ed., *The Old Dominion in the Seventeenth Century: A Documentary History of Virginia, 1606–1689* (Chapel Hill, 1975), p. 305. See also Edmund Morgan, "The First American Boom: Virginia 1618 to 1630," *William and Mary Quarterly*, 3d ser., 28 (1971):169–98.

[40] Larzer Ziff, *Puritanism in America: New Culture in a New World* (New York, 1973), p. 86; Patricia Bonomi, *A Factious People: Politics and Society in Colonial New York* (New York, 1971), p. 195; Oscar and Mary Handlin, "Origins of the Southern Labor System," *William and Mary Quarterly*, 3d ser., 7 (1950):199–222; Edmund Morgan, "Slavery and Freedom: The American Paradox," *Journal of American History* 59 (1972):5–29.

[41] *Johnson's Wonder-Working Providence, 1628–1651*, ed. J. Franklin Jameson (New York, 1910), p. 212. The claims for New York, Pennsylvania, and North Carolina as premier poor people's provinces were almost proverbial; see, e.g., Bonomi, *A Factious People*, p. 196; James Lemon, *The Best Poor Man's Country: A Geographical Study of Early Southeastern Pennsylvania* (Baltimore, 1972), pp. xiii, 229; A. Roger Ekirch, *"Poor Carolina": Politics and Society in Colonial North Carolina, 1729–1776* (Chapel Hill, 1981), pp. 27–29. For comparable claims from other colonies, see, e.g., Board of Proprietors of Eastern New Jersey, *Advertisement*, pp. 20–21; Fenwick, *Friends*, p. 2; Hartshorne, *A Further Account*, p. 3; "Report of the Journey of Francis Louis Michel from Berne, Switzerland, to Virginia, October 2, 1701–December 1, 1702," *Virginia Magazine of History and Biography* 24 (1916):124; Samuel Wilson, *An Account of the Province of Carolina, in America . . .* (1682), in Salley, *Narratives of Carolina*, p. 167.

[42] Ziff, *Puritanism in America*, p. 87.

By the beginning of the seventeenth century, vagabonds, rogues, and roaring lads were merely the most visible embodiments of an unprecedented geographic and social mobility that was itself only an aspect of more extensive upheavals under way in England.[43] But even amid this general attrition of social attachments, the men and women who migrated to America may still be imagined as people apart. The traveler is, as Wayne Franklin has observed, "almost by definition an iconoclast; his departure, even if he goes in the service of 'home' purposes, hints not merely at the general authority of experience, but also (and more subversively) at the prospective power of individual life beyond the horizon." Such subversive individuality was not for everyone in seventeenth-century England, but emigration to America must have held a particular appeal for those who wished to break free of traditional constraints.[44]

Many of the men and women who crossed the Atlantic must therefore have been more concerned with their own designs and less considerate of the claims of community than the mass of their countrymen. Promotional appeals assumed that they were, and they themselves—where we can catch their thoughts—confessed as much. When, in 1765, John Rea praised South Carolina to his brother in Belfast, he identified especially the opportunity that existed to "get land" and "plenty of good eating and drinking," and he advised explicitly against migration for all who preferred "the pleasure of society" to the possibility of solitary economic gratification. When George Scot in East New Jersey published an account of the province in Britain, he promised that people could "live as comfortably" along the Raritan "as in any place in the world"; but he too acknowledged that the price of such economic ambition was the loss of "friends and relations and the satisfaction of their company." And when others cast the balance, they were not even as scrupulous of social bonds or as sensitive to their salience as Rea and Scot. British port authorities, polling passengers on the causes of their emigration, concluded that people bound for the New World sought solely "a better livelihood and employment."[45]

Nicholas Cresswell was a youth of no discernible distinction whose diary of his departure for the New World allows us our most extensive insight

[43] For a brief discussion and an indication of some of the pertinent sources, see Zuckerman, "Fabrication," pp. 190–92. For a recent consideration of similar issues from a different vantage, see Alan Macfarlane, *The Origins of English Individualism: The Family, Property, and Social Transition* (New York, 1978).

[44] Franklin, *Discoverers*, p. 12.

[45] *Belfast News Letter*, no. 2926, September 3–October 22, 1765, pp. 7–8; Scot, *Model of Government*, p. 462; Sharon Salinger, " 'Like a Blind Man without a Guide': The Servant Experience in Colonial Pennsylvania," paper presented to the Philadelphia Center for Early American Studies, Philadelphia, 1979, p. 5.

129

into the mentality of migration. He began his journal in 1774, on the day he "determined" to leave home. Recognizing that he would "meet with every possible obstruction" from his parents and associates, he "resolved to brave them all." Where others were attentive to the advice and appeals of family and friends, Cresswell coveted "improvements" in his "fortune" and sought to "follow [his] own inclination." As the days went by and he discovered that "all his friends" thought him "mad," he was undeterred. Even when he found the parson critical, his father "heartily vexed," and his mother shedding "many tears," he was unmoved. He was bent on being alone. He rejoiced in having "not one friend in the world" who approved of his "proceedings," and he even spurned an offer of companionship on the crossing. He would not, he declared, "be connected with any person whatever."[46]

But men and women like Cresswell soon found themselves "forlorn." Having neither "relations to comfort . . . nor friends to assist them," they discovered the Old World dream of autonomy a disturbing reality in America.[47] And as they did, their isolation stimulated a compensatory craving for comradeship.

The early colonists were at once more free and more controlled, more concerned about themselves and more sensitive to the opinions of others, than their European forebears had been; and those who came after them carried the initial fission further. They sought simultaneously a new purity of personal identity and a new consummation of conscious community. They pursued at once the self-possession that informs the modern psyche and the coercive mutuality that marks modern society. Almost from the first, therefore, they were impelled by contrapuntal forces of excess and insufficiency, exaggerated and attenuated fellowship. Even as they dissolved old ties of consanguinity and propinquity, they set themselves to search for "wider circles of solidarity."[48]

The search was most manifest among the Puritans of Massachusetts and

[46] *Journal of Nicholas Cresswell*, pp. 1–8. For another who came to America "contrary to the sentiments of all [his] friends," see *The Letters of Hon. James Habersham, 1756–1765*, in Georgia Historical Society, *Collections* 6 (1904):103. For further intimations of self-selection for economic individualism among the migrants, see Stephanie Wolf, *Urban Village: Population, Community, and Family Structure in Germantown, Pennsylvania, 1683–1800* (Princeton, 1976), pp. 327–37, and James Lemon, "The Weakness of Place and Community in Early America," in *European Settlement and Development in North America: Essays on Geographical Change in Honour and Memory of Andrew Hill Clark*, ed. James Gibson (Toronto, 1978), esp. p. 203.

[47] Ann Deas, *Recollections of the Ball Family of South Carolina and the Comingtee Plantation* (Summerville, S.C., 1909), p. 29. For Cresswell's own, equally poignant experience of his plight, see *Journal of Nicholas Cresswell*, p. 167.

[48] Francis L. K. Hsu, "Kinship and Ways of Life: An Exploration," in *Psychological Anthropology*, ed. Francis L. K. Hsu, (Homewood, Ill., 1961), p. 421.

Connecticut, for whom its result was, inevitably, to expose the individual to the strictures of those he embraced as brothers. His very attachment to them placed his outward behavior under their ceaseless surveillance and made his most inward experience, the vicissitudes of his regeneration, subject to their scrutiny. He could not count his own conversion complete or authentic until he had confessed its course to their satisfaction.

The result of the Puritans' search was also to impose upon them a range of obligations of intrusion and examination into the affairs of their fellows. Once admitted to a congregation of visible saints, the individual Puritan had in turn to hear the confessions of other candidates. Each had to be possessed of sufficient self-knowledge to obtain a "standard of sanctity" by which to judge the experience of others and carry on relations with spiritual kin. Each also had to display a daily "zeal for the morality of others" in order to uphold the social covenant on which the temporal prosperity of the community was predicated and in order to be confident of the covenant of grace on which his or her own eternal destiny depended. Alacrity in overseeing the reformation of neighbors was a test of the efficacy of the original conversion. "Whatever sins come within [the true convert's] reach," Thomas Hooker averred, "he labors the removal of them, out of the families where he dwells, out of the plantations where he lives, out of the companies and occasions, with whom he hath occasion to meet and meddle at any time."[49]

Puritans were therefore bound to be their brothers' keepers while they were prohibited any comparable tie to wicked worldlings. As believers, they faced always the "double requirement" of an "ardor of intimacy" within the fellowship and a fierce "heat of hostility" outside it, amid "the encircling mass of enemies." Sophisticated students of Puritanism have long recognized this power of the movement simultaneously to individuate and aggregate, and it is useful for present purposes to allude to Michael Walzer's observation that the "constant tendency" of the saints to "turn the theology of salvation into a sociology" produced "a collective discipline" that "created bonds in many ways more intensive than those of blood and nature."[50]

Nonetheless, few of these disjunctions were unique to the New England Puritans. Many of them developed even more fully among the Quakers, who legitimized "personal authoritative revelation" with an antinomian equanimity the Puritans never permitted and secured a "system of disci-

---

[49] Charles George and Katherine George, The Protestant Mind of the English Reformation, 1570–1640 (Princeton, 1961), pp. 102–103; "The Diary of Michael Wigglesworth," ed. Edmund Morgan, Colonial Society of Massachusetts, Publications 35 (Boston, 1951):316–17.

[50] George and George, Protestant Mind, pp. 103–104; Michael Walzer, The Revolution of the Saints: A Study of the Origins of Radical Politics (Cambridge, Mass., 1965), p. 170.

pline and church control" with a thoroughness the Puritans never managed.[51] Most of them were evident in some measure in all the colonies, since early English Protestantism in its entirety was at once a renewal of the old tribal temper and a symptom of the decay of the common life of preceding centuries. It brought both a new scrupulousness in the reconnaissance of conduct and a new freedom from such scrutiny. It subjected settlers of every plantation to more and, concurrently, less control than they had known in their native land.[52]

In all the colonies, the first settlers were impatient of conventional social ties and inclined to set their own advantage before the public good. In Massachusetts as much as in Virginia or Carolina, authorities had to contend with "self-love" that "forgot all duty" and with men who "neither feared God nor man." Indeed, such men often took their cues from the authorities themselves. Thomas Weston "pursued his own ends" assiduously in the Plymouth enterprise. Governor George Yeardly gave an impression of being "wholly addicted to his private [interest]" in Virginia. And men of all ranks found "their own conceived necessity" a "warrant sufficient" to take up lands where they pleased and to plant crops as they pleased, even if their fellows implored and the laws enjoined otherwise.[53]

At the same time, such determined affirmations of personal liberty evoked equally determined assertions of social control. In religious and social life alike, restraints evolved in the face of unprecedented freedom from sanctions.

In the churches, religious and lay leaders became uneasy as farms scattered into woods that whispered of the possibilities of privacy; and in every colony an answering church discipline of a strikingly similar sort emerged. Quakers, Puritans, and Anglicans all appointed ecclesiastical agents to pry into personal lives and attempt the repression of iniquity, under conditions of congregational communalism. For without effective episcopal order, individual churches everywhere in British America functioned essentially by themselves. They were not enmeshed in centralized hierarchies, and they were not organized as inclusive parishes. On the contrary, they were gathered by spiritual affinity out of much larger local populations. They reflected both the heightened individuality that led people to separate themselves from society at large and the augmented intensity of community life

[51] J. William Frost, *The Quaker Family in Colonial America: A Portrait of the Society of Friends* (New York, 1973), p. 49.

[52] George and George, *Protestant Mind*, pp. 82–83, 84.

[53] William Bradford, *Of Plymouth Plantation, 1620-1647*, ed. Samuel E. Morison (New York, 1952), pp. 54, 107, 254; *A True Declaration of the estate of the Colonie of Virginia . . .* (1610), in Force, *Tracts*, vol. 3, no. 1, p. 18; Edmund Morgan, *American Slavery—American Freedom: The Ordeal of Colonial Virginia* (New York, 1975), p. 123n.

that was embodied in the very churches to which these same people belonged.[54]

In the larger society, controls also contracted and expanded concurrently. The disruptive imbalance of reckless young bachelors among the early settlers was offset by their assignment to reputable families in New England and by their confinement to grinding servitude in the south. Enticements to self-interest were counteracted by exemplary penalties imposed on offenders as different as Robert Keayne and Thomas Morton. And inclinations to go off from settled society—ultimately, to go off to the Indians—were fought with maledictions on the wilderness and grisly executions of recaptured renegades "to terrify the rest for attempting the like."[55]

In a wilderness antithetical to everything they had left behind, settlers insisted on civility. As William Penn put it, they "came to a wilderness," but "it was not meet that [they] should continue it so."[56] In every essential sphere of life, therefore, they set out to reinstate the modes and manners they had known in the Old World.

They sought such reinstatement in the realms of food, clothing, and, especially, shelter, and they sought it in defiance of demonstrably superior indigenous adaptations and examples. In New England, for example, colonists scorned native building techniques more efficacious than their own in conserving warmth against the winter. They made plain their refusal of rapprochement with the wild by designing dwellings with such low ceilings, dark walls, and scant fenestration that they may well have had to burn candles even in daylight. Their very habitations implied the "radical disjunction" discerned by John Demos "between the natural and the man-made environments" of the Calvinists. Nature was to them as antagonist, and "they saw no reason to try to make place for her in their homes." Indeed, as early as 1624 and in sublime disdain of the forests all round them, the Pilgrims began to import prefabricated wooden houses from England.[57]

[54] Laymen gained control of all these churches, most completely, perhaps, among the Quakers and pietist sectarians, and more completely, in many ways, in the officially Anglican South than in ostensibly Congregational New England, where ministers maintained consociations and occasional synods and asserted a sacerdotal authority over the laity that would have been inconceivable in the Quaker colonies and literally laughable in Virginia. See Paul Lucas, *Valley of Discord: Church and Society along the Connecticut River, 1636–1725* (Hanover, N.H., 1976); David Hall, *The Faithful Shepherd: A History of the New England Ministry in the Seventeenth Century* (Chapel Hill, 1972); and, on the derision of such pretensions in Virginia, *Prose Works of William Byrd*, p. 344.

[55] Morgan, *American Slavery*, p. 74.

[56] Margaret Tinkcom, "Urban Reflections in a Transatlantic Mirror," *Pennsylvania Magazine of History and Biography* 100 (1976):296.

[57] John Demos, *A Little Commonwealth: Family Life in Plymouth Colony* (New York, 1970), p. 29; Charles Peterson, "Early American Prefabrication," *Gazette des Beaux-Arts*, 6th ser., 33 (January 1948):37–38.

In the middle colonies, town planning, house siting, and home building all reflected recourse to a repertoire essentially—and inappropriately—English. New Jersey colonists around Trenton, to take but a single example, were still erecting clapboard houses after the fashion of the mother country to the very end of the seventeenth century. Their persistence was revealing, for the Swedes who preceded them on the Delaware had been perfecting log cabins there for generations, while the English colonists' clapboard constructions were so "wretchedly" built that "if you were not so close to the fire as almost to burn yourself, you could not keep warm, for the wind blew through them everywhere."[58]

In the south, planters put up structures predicated on the cool damp climate of Britain for the better part of a century before a few of them began to build their ceilings higher and their windows larger. Far into the eighteenth century, they showed themselves still determined "to adhere to an intellectual model" derived from English experience. They were willing to endure discomforts "to live in a house that was a perfect reflection of an idea." And town dwellers clung even more ardently to Old World notions. In semitropical Charleston, to the time of the great fire of 1740, houses crowded closely upon one another in provincial approximation of metropolitan conventions and magnificent disregard for the demands of climate and sanitation. Maps and prospects of the early eighteenth century exhibited proudly the city's serried row houses. On the waterfront itself, from Granville's Bastion to Craven's, there were only nine buildings that were detached at all in 1739, and those were set off only by the barest of breezeways or the most minimal of alleys.[59]

In the Caribbean, English colonists refused for a century and more to accommodate themselves to the climate. Disdaining the heat and humidity of the tropics and the adaptations all about them of the Spaniards, Indians, and Africans, they held tenaciously to their own northern ways. In the country they built of mud and thatch, littering the landscape with low-walled, ill-lit, and highly flammable homes in which they sweltered horribly. In the towns they laid out lots without gardens or shade trees, cluttering the municipality with four- and five-story townhouses in which they pressed tightly together. In every sort of setting, in a latitude that cried out for airy rooms for optimal ventilation, the very finest houses were said by

[58] Stephanie Toothman, "Trenton, New Jersey, 1719–1779: A Study of Community Growth and Organization" (Ph.D. diss., Univ. of Pennsylvania, 1977), pp. 64–65; Henry Glassie, "Eighteenth-Century Cultural Process in Delaware Valley Folk Building," *Winterthur Portfolio* 7 (1972):38–39.

[59] Glassie, *Folk Housing*, pp. 136, 118–19; Roberts, "Prospect of Charleston"; Samuel Stoney, *This Is Charleston: A Study of the Architectural Heritage of a Unique American City* (Charleston, S.C., 1970), p. 17.

visitors to be "so low . . . I could hardly stand upright with my hat on." Rather than providing shade from the sun and access to the breeze, such houses were "airless cubes" unadorned by balconies or verandas. Rather than getting their occupants as far off the ground as possible, such houses put primary living quarters on the first floor. But to their owners, such houses were sources of pleasure and pride, precisely because they were not made in the Spanish manner. New-made merchants and parvenu planters commissioned them again and again, because they derived satisfaction from their "compressed verticality and steep roofs ready to repel snow which never came."[60]

In every quarter of English America, men and women feared the frontier they had ventured forth to find. Three thousand miles from all they took to be civilized, beset by a bewildering plenitude of possibility, they clung the more compulsively to accustomed English habits and set themselves the more resolutely against intrusions that whispered of other ways. Few yielded freely to the forest. Far more, as Oscar Handlin suggested, refused to give way and insisted instead on cultivating clearings in the darkness, hoping thereby "to re-capture the order that had gone out of life at their departure."[61]

With a view to excluding the wilderness and its inhabitants, the colonists built barricades about their communal settlements. They erected forts at Roanoke and Sagadahoc at the very commencement of colonization, and they built palisades around their private plantations in Virginia in the early decades of settlement. John Winthrop, while still at sea, sketched his model Puritan town as a walled stronghold on a hill. The founders of New York fortified themselves behind a Wall Street and a Battery. The planners of Charleston did the same, and their town remained within its palisades for decades, rather resembling a medieval fastness with moats, drawbridges, bastions, and demi-lunes. As late as 1717, a proponent of a buffer colony between Carolina and the Spanish settlements to the south projected the "whole plantation" as "one continuous fortress."[62]

The same siege mentality that prompted the erection of battlements also inspired verbal imagery. Puritans were particularly prolific of symbols of sanctuary; drawing a dichotomy between gracious civility and wayward na-

[60] Roger Kennedy, *Architecture, Men, Women, and Money* (New York, 1984), ch. 3; Dunn, *Sugar and Slaves*, ch. 8.

[61] Oscar Handlin, *Race and Nationality in American Life* (Anchor ed., New York, 1957), pp. 114–15.

[62] McManis, *European Impressions*, pp. 103–105; Annie Jester and Martha Hiden, eds., *Adventurers of Purse and Person: Virginia, 1607–1625* (Princeton, 1956), pp. 49–66; John Stilgoe, *Common Landscape of America, 1580 to 1845* (New Haven, 1982), p. 43; Stoney, *This Is Charleston*, p. 17; Montgomery, *Discourse*, p. 7.

ture, they hailed hedges, gardens, walls, and cities as images of order. But settlers further south also feared dispersion in the "remote desert" of America; depending on the same dichotomy, they envisioned their province as "a garden enclosed," a veritable "vineyard fenced."[63]

British settlers in America, like their counterparts in Ireland, prized such symbols of order because they craved counterweights to the "desolate places" of a "wilderness without any comeliness." Convinced as they were that only "wild creatures" would "ordinarily love the liberty of the woods," they feared the forests as "enemies, strange and evil, existing only to be cleared."[64]

Indeed, they feared all expansive, untamed land, forested and unforested alike. Their perceptions of the New World as a "dreary waste" were as pejorative as their apprehensions of the country as a trackless wood. They reserved their affection and enthusiasm for land they had domesticated or for domains that did not daunt them in the first place, such as the islands of the Caribbean. Initially, at least, the limitations of the Indies were more attractive than deterrent. Demure Bermuda rivaled vast Virginia in the days of the Virginia Company. Barbados alone enticed more migrants than all New England in the years of the so-called great migration to the Puritan provinces. Elsewhere as well, early adventurers displayed a desire for milder, more manageable environments where settlement could be circumscribed within finite boundaries.[65]

Such desire induced some striking alterations in prevailing British communityscapes. The tightly organized towns of New England were merely the most notable of these. West of the Hudson too, as Carville Earle has shown, British authorities pursued policies of urban concentration under auspices of monopolistic concession. Unlike the Dutch and the Spanish, who permitted free trading throughout their New World territories, the British franchised fewer towns and located them for administrative rather than economic convenience. Moreover, the British achieved in practice the cramped, confined development they sought in principle, in the quasi-countryside as well as in the civil centers. Quakers who had been scattered

[63] A. W. Plumstead, *The Wall and the Garden: Selected Massachusetts Election Sermons, 1670–1775* (Minneapolis, 1968); Peter Carroll, *Puritanism and the Wilderness: The Intellectual Significance of the New England Frontier, 1629–1700* (New York, 1969); R. G., *Virginia's Cure* (London, 1662), pp. 16, 19.

[64] R. G., *Virginia's Cure*, p. 19; Alan Heimert, "Puritanism, the Wilderness, and the Frontier," *New England Quarterly* 26 (1953): 369; Glassie, "Eighteenth-Century Cultural Process," pp. 56–57.

[65] Janet Schaw, *Journal of a Lady of Quality: Being the Narrative of a Journey from Scotland to the West Indies, North Carolina, and Portugal, in the Years 1774 to 1776*, ed. Evangeline Andrews and Charles Andrews (New Haven, 1921), p. 141; Wesley Craven, *An Introduction to the History of Bermuda* (Williamsburg, Va., 1938), p. 13.

thinly through the western counties of England and Wales "thought they were living uncharacteristically close together" in Pennsylvania. Indeed, they defended their departure from the mother country exactly in terms of the closer communion they enjoyed in Penn's model settlement. Frontiersmen of the south justified themselves in similar terms. In Georgia they spoke explicitly of "cities" as the units of settlement, accounting it an encomium from the first to be "English-like" and "regular." In the back country critics themselves conceded that density of settlement was often greater in the "Great Wagon Road migratory corridor" than in the older coastal regions. According to Carville Earle and Ronald Hoffman, "the lonely frontiersman" of legend, "living apart from all urban contacts," simply "never existed in any significant number" amid the "matrix of substantial towns" of the Carolina piedmont.[66]

Early Americans balked at living apart because they felt so palpably the enticement of the ever-beckoning woods and believed so earnestly that those who lived in isolation would "decay insensibly" there. They founded schools to keep their offspring from becoming "as ignorant as the native Indians." They established literary associations "to prevent [their] descendants from sinking" into a "rude and savage state." Yet for all their efforts they were unable to avert awareness of their proximity to the "savage disposition" that aroused their "horror and detestation."[67]

A powerful public official in Virginia, holder of almost seven thousand acres in four counties, called the colony in its golden age an "Indian country." A lady in the Low Country, affluent enough to avail herself of all the opportunities of the most glittering city in America, considered herself "an old woman in the wilds" and her urbane capital a "remote corner of the globe." The movers of the Charleston Library Society, gentlemen all, conceded it "impossible . . . to reflect without very mortifying sentiments" how little their inherent nature differed "from the brute." And other settlers also sensed the ease with which they might "lose the essential badge of Christianity" or "suffer a sort of transmigration of the wolfish and brutish nature to enter [their] spirits." Like their counterparts in Ireland, British settlers in America dreaded "how apt human nature is to degenerate."[68]

---

[66] Carville Earle, "The First English Towns of North America," *Geographical Review* 67 (1977):34–50; Levy, "Light in the Valley," p. 9; "Account of the British Settlements in America Concluded: New Georgia," *Gentlemen's Magazine* 26 (1756):19; ibid. 6 (1736):229; Carville Earle and Ronald Hoffman, "Urban Development in the Eighteenth-Century South," *Perspectives in American History* 10 (1976):52–55, 56

[67] "An Account of the Missionaries Sent to South Carolina," in Carroll, *Historical Collections,* 2:566; A *Short Description of the Province of South Carolina* (1763), in ibid., 2:489–90.

[68] Edgar Hume, ed., A Colonial Scottish Jacobite Family," *Virginia Magazine of History and Biography* 38 (1930):297; *Letterbook of Eliza Lucas Pinckney,* pp. 181–82; *Short Description of South Carolina,* 2:489–90; Archdale, *New Description,* pp. 309, 306; Lawson, *New Voyage,* p. 69.

137

In their anxiety, they were at one with their Elizabethan and Stuart forebears. Pessimism pervaded the world picture of the colonizing epoch, in
England as well as in America, and decay colored the cosmos. As Earle observed, "only a thin veil of culture kept Englishmen from descending the
great chain of being to the barbarian and animal." Establishment of urban
places was thus imperative to prevent the corrosion of culture. The very
nearness of the forests demanded redoubled devotion to civility. The danger of degeneration compelled congregation "as members of a community."[69]

Yet even as people pursued social solidarity, they persisted in the dream
of freedom that had first lured them. Even as they ached for order, they
yearned for autonomy. William Penn understood this when he proclaimed
"more and not less" liberty the reason "to plant this wilderness." Much as
he lamented the "clandestine looseness" of his colonists, he knew they had
not "come 3000 miles into a desert of original wild people as well as wild
beasts" to have "only the same privileges [they] had at home." John Smith
had seen the same thing when he declared of Virginia, "no man will go
from [England], to have less freedom" in America.[70]

From the outset, in every colony, settlers experienced the exhilaration
of unconstraint, the "joy of the wilderness," the "gladness that did break
forth of the solitary and desolate land." From the outset, also, they experienced the failure of all formulas of European order, and therefore they experienced the counterposition of disorderly release and integrative design.
Their every effort to comprehend their experience oscillated between poles
of "emptiness and fulfillment, chaos and composition."[71]

Such centrifugality was especially striking in the way colonists occupied
the land on which they lived. On the one hand, they appropriated it as personal possession, exhibiting an unruly individualism that defeated schemes
of corporate control in imperial Virginia, Pilgrim Plymouth, and Quaker
Pennsylvania alike. On the other, they fenced it and confined themselves
upon it, exhibiting a settled domesticity that left them dependent on the
opinions of their neighbors.

Land ownership in fee simple was obviously attractive to people previously bound by archaic personal as well as monetary obligations, and lavish
allotments of it were understandably appealing to people accustomed to

---

[69] Earle, "First English Towns," p. 36; see also Margaret Hodgen, *Early Anthropology in the Sixteenth and Seventeenth Centuries* (Philadelphia, 1964), pp. 354–85. *Short Description of South Carolina*, 2:489–90.

[70] Gary Nash, *Quakers and Politics: Pennsylvania 1681-1726* (Princeton, 1968), pp. 162–63; Perry Miller, *Errand into the Wilderness* (Cambridge, Mass., 1956), p. 137.

[71] Nash, *Quakers and Politics*, p. 48; Franklin, *Discoverers*, pp. 6, 75.

rent little parcels of land from their landlords. Some observers insisted, indeed, that those acquisitive incentives were all that moved migrants. Other observers allowed different motives yet also emphasized the ability of the day laborer or artisan to obtain a holding in America "more independent than a nobleman's estate" in the Old World.[72]

For all that, though, the ardor for extensive acreage in freehold was almost inexplicably excessive for people who had had no prior experience of such estate. Not one in a dozen smallholders had as much as four acres in England. Not even that many had any landed property at all in Scotland. The explosive desire for—and diffusion of—ownership in fee simple on the American frontier suggests something of the predicament of the pioneers.[73]

In this perspective, the apprehension of unallotted land as disordered domain acquires a different aspect. The act of settlement becomes, as Wayne Franklin saw so acutely, "a deed of mythic organization." Assertion of the soil's suitability for "all sorts of English grain" expressed a determination to anglicize the earth rather than accept it on its own terms. Attainment of expansive properties attested to a renunciation of more radical ambitions of autonomy. The ideal of individual ownership was, as Howard Mumford Jones reminds us, "in flat contradiction to the emotional appeal of the uncharted forest, the unfenced range, the trackless mountains, and the open sky."[74]

As settlers took possession of their own personal patches of the vast continent, therefore, they presented equal but opposite exaggerations of Old World ways. Their importunate appropriation of freeholds was at once an unprecedented realization of freedom and an unparalleled refusal of further freedom. Given how little the colonists had had in Europe, the diffusion of landed lots among them was surely liberating. Given how much they might have had in America, the conversion of the country into real estate was as surely limiting. It confined pioneers to particular plots of an immeasurable expanse, and it bound them also to the drudging routine of cultivating those enclosures.

Indeed, the tensions evident in systems of land tenure extended into the larger society. The very vision of the colonial enterprise apparent in the early accounts exhibited the same qualities. Settlers sought both opportu-

[72] Jacquelyn Wolf, "The Proud and the Poor: The Social Organization of Leadership in Proprietary North Carolina, 1663–1729" (Ph.D. diss., Univ. of Pennsylvania, 1977), p. 16; Stanley Kutler, ed., *Looking for America: The People's History*, 2d ed. (New York, 1979), 1:38.

[73] Alan Everitt, "Farm Laborers," in *The Agrarian History of England and Wales*, ed. Joan Thirsk (London, 1967), 4:400–401; Ned Landsman, *Scotland and Its First American Colony, 1683–1765* (Princeton, 1985), ch. 1.

[74] Franklin, *Discoverers*, p. 77; Denton, *Brief Description*, p. 16; Jones, *O Strange New World*, p. 352.

nity and order more extravagantly than they had in the Old World. They cherished change even as they shrank from it, inflaming aspirations of worldly ascent yet intoning assurances that the world would abide unaltered. They craved control even as they resented it, projecting plans for forts, mills, and other such devices of collective security yet spreading far and wide to their own farms. They valued authority even as they vaunted liberty, recognizing the necessity for discipline and common defense yet chafing at every constraint on their quest for private fortune.

None of these ambivalences was ever resolved. All of them tended to further extremities of authoritarian imposition and anarchic resistance. Political controls expanded and contracted concurrently, as leaders uncertain of their own authority demanded deference and settlers driven to discover their own powers declined to proffer such submission. Even as early as the first settlement at Roanoke, Ralph Lane bemoaned the "wild men of [his] own nation, whose unruliness is such as not to give leisure," and this sentiment was repeated almost word for word by the founders of each successive colony in the seventeenth century.[75] Experience was to show that insistence by subordinates on dominion and dignity was a concomitant of the colonization process because, as Sigmund Diamond has observed, the very blandishments held before men to entice their migration served also to diminish their susceptibility to discipline. "Instead of docility, there was disobedience; instead of stability, disorder. . . . Disobedience and disorder were both consequences of the means by which the country was peopled." And such disobedience and disorder evoked antipodal excesses of severity and subjection. Crews might concert to cut their captain's throat and "make themselves masters of the whole . . . so [as] to seek a new fortune where they could best make it." Captains could counter by ordering insurgents "put to sundry deaths, as by hanging, shooting, and breaking upon the wheel." A simple citizen might refuse a sheriff's demand for aid in apprehending a fugitive, beating the official's back and crying, "thou the sheriff, thou a turd" while the miscreant made off. Authorities could answer by sentencing a poor settler who stole a few pints of oatmeal to have "a bodkin thrust through his tongue" while "tied with a chain to a tree till he starved."[76]

[75] Quinn, Roanoke Voyages, 1:204–205; Miller, Errand, p. 131; Bradford, Plymouth Plantation, p. 75; Nash, Quakers and Politics, p. 174; Nicholas Wainwright, "Governor John Blackwell," Pennsylvania Magazine of History and Biography 74 (1950):472.

[76] Sigmund Diamond, Immigration, Citizenship, and Social Change: The American Experience (Tel Aviv, 1977), pp. 8–9; [Council for New England], Brief Relation, p. 14; "The Tragical Relation of the Virginia Assembly, 1624," in Narratives of Early Virginia, 1606-1625, ed. Lyon Tyler (New York, 1907), p. 423; H. Clay Reed and George Miller, eds., The Burlington Court Book: A Record of Quaker Jurisprudence in West New Jersey, 1680–1709 (Washington, D.C., 1944), pp. 176–77; "Tragical Relation," p. 423.

The fact that many of the settlers had slipped old ties by migrating to America and the fact that many appeared the offscourings of Old World societies prompted some of their masters to institute a stern regimen in the belief that they "would be useful only when subject to arbitrary rule." Such endeavors provoked obstinate opposition from the colonists and this, in turn, was decried as treasonable and was savagely suppressed.[77] Virginia in its early years oscillated incessantly between the libertinism of the first planters and the brutal leadership thought necessary to contain it. Governors imposed martial law on the settlers or were "thrust out" for trying to impose it. The air rang with recriminations of "extreme choler and passion" and "tyrannical proceeding" on one side and "mutinous meetings" and "treason" on the other. "Giddy headed and turbulent persons" rose repeatedly against the "oppressions" of "men in authority and favor," burning Jamestown itself to the ground in Bacon's Rebellion; and men in authority responded as repeatedly and heatedly, executing men for treason.[78] Massachusetts also experienced periodic sparring in its early decades between magistrates who were insistent upon extensive discretionary scope and more popular forces who sought legal guarantees of local rights and liberties. New York, Maryland, Pennsylvania, and the Carolinas too suffered from chronic instability that occasionally spilled over into chaotic disturbance that threatened the very survival of the colonies.[79]

Within these struggles the logic of polarization was apparent in the pronouncements of the partisans. In Pennsylvania, for example, Isaac Norris insisted that the government was unable to follow a middle course "between arbitrary power and licentious popularity." In Maryland, Lord Baltimore's opponents charged that he ruled "in such an absolute way and authority as no Christian prince or state in Europe exercises the like," while his supporters countered that the insurgents in Maryland enjoyed political liberties far in excess of anything they might have hoped for in England. And identical charges and countercharges were levelled by rebels and rulers in Georgia one against the other. The seditionaries there railed against a

---

[77] Nicholas Canny, "The Permissive Frontier: The Problem of Social Control in English Settlements in Ireland and Virginia 1550–1650," in *The Westward Enterprise: English Activities in Ireland, the Atlantic, and America, 1480-1650*, ed. K. R. Andrews, N. P. Canny, and P.E.H. Hair (Detroit, 1979), pp. 18, 27.

[78] Billings, *Old Dominion*, pp. 252, 253, 255, 265, 278; see, generally, pp. 236–87. More generally still, see Morgan, *American Slavery*, passim.

[79] Bonomi, *A Factious People*, pp. 111, 138; Archdale, *New Description*, pp. 282, 295; "Instructions to the Colonists by Lord Baltimore," pp. 16–17; *Virginia and Maryland*, p. 201; "Letter of Governor Leonard Calvert to Lord Baltimore, 1638," in Hall, *Narratives of Maryland*, p. 152; "Extract of a Letter of Captain Thomas Yong to Sir Toby Matthew, 1634," in Hall, *Narratives of Maryland*, p. 56; Hammond, *Leah and Rachel*, p. 300.

141

regime "as arbitrary . . . as Turkey or Muscovy ever felt," and Lord Egmont fumed in return that it was they who were the "ruling cabal" in Georgia.[80]

These same symmetries and centrifugalities that appeared in the founding of colonial societies persisted to the very end of the colonial era. Early America was, as Robert Wiebe observed, "a multitude of small fortresses" whose inhabitants resisted "efforts to integrate them into any sort of broader system." Their recalcitrance "perplexed and infuriated those on both sides of the Atlantic who for various reasons sought greater coordination in colonial life." Such men raged relentlessly against the settlers' insolence. More than that, they set themselves to curtail it. They devised schemes to order the unruly colonists by means of a stricter imperial system, a revival of religious piety, an appointment of a bishop, or an importation of troops. But as they did so, they aroused public anger to the point where Americans were convinced they were being threatened by despotism. The more strenuously these policies were pursued the more vigorously they were opposed, until eventually they precipitated a revolutionary crisis in mainland British America.[81]

Even before that conflagration, however, Americans had shown themselves incapable of reconciling authority and autonomy. Indeed, in their most idealistic envisionings of an appropriate public order in the New World, they were unable to imagine a regime that did not augment both the authoritarian and the libertarian tendencies of the time. The "true and absolute lords proprietors" of Carolina might wish to "avoid erecting a numerous democracy" and to that end establish Fundamental Constitutions that provided for a hereditary nobility and leet-men whose children would be leet-men "to all generations," but they also promulgated a charter that promised the inhabitants "full and free license" in religion and extensive rights in the political process. The proprietors of New Jersey might proclaim their lordly powers in the most "full and ample manner," but they also issued Concessions and Agreements that allowed their colonists "liberty of conscience," generous terms of landed settlement, and a representative assembly with decisive control over provincial taxation; and the purchasers of their privileges in West New Jersey issued further Concessions

---

[80] Nash, *Quakers and Politics*, pp. 292–93; *Virginia and Maryland*, pp. 199, 191; *The Lord Baltemore's Case, Concerning the Province of Maryland* (1653), in Hall, *Narratives of Maryland*, p. 174; Pat Tailfer and others, *A True and Historical Narrative of the Colony of Georgia, with Comments by the Earl of Egmont*, ed. Clarence Ver Steeg (Athens, Ga., 1961), pp. 20, 52–54, 58–59; Sarah Temple and Kenneth Coleman, *Georgia Journeys: Being an Account of the Lives of Georgia's Original Settlers and Many Other Early Settlers from the Founding of the Colony in 1732 until the Institution of Royal Government in 1754* (Athens, Ga., 1961), p. 107.

[81] Robert Wiebe, *The Segmented Society: An Introduction to the Meaning of America* (New York, 1975), pp. 98–99.

and Agreements that renewed the assurance of "full liberty of religious faith and worship," offered elaborate protections against corruption of the electoral process, and guaranteed that representatives would "act nothing in that capacity but what shall tend to the fit service and behoof of those that send and employ them." William Penn's charter for Pennsylvania might confer upon him a "free, full, and absolute power" of superintendency over his province, but his Frames of Government made every inhabitant a member of the assembly for the first year of the venture, provided for annual elections of as many as five hundred representatives thereafter, and established a representation not only proportional to population but also rotated so that "all may be fitted for government, and have experience of the care and burden of it." In all these colonies and in the others as well, the government grew more ambitious of control than the state had been at home even as it afforded its citizens a more effective participation in authority than they had had at home. Discipline and autonomy developed apace.[82]

Clashes over conceptions of appropriate social order and entitlement inevitably exacerbated the tensions arising from the other unprecedented extremities of frontier life. Americans were bound to try to mitigate those tensions, and they did so by exaggerated affirmation of their own civility. Because they could not fully face the implications of their emigration, they created a counterweight to their inadmissible impulses to savagery in an idealized identity as Englishmen. And because they founded that fictive identity upon denial of the wilder one within them and all about them, they developed a disposition to conceive the world in dualistic terms.

New Englanders especially distilled dichotomies out of the traditional multiplicities of medieval pluralism, but pioneers everywhere understood themselves in absolute antitheses. Saved and damned, Christian and heathen, civilized and savage, white and black were counterpositions that came congenially and, indeed, compellingly to the colonists, as though they could redeem their own enigmatic identities by disparaging the identities of others. In their peculiar logic of negation and self salvage, such counterpositions, and the counteridentities they betokened, contained the seeds of a new individuality as well as a new community.

Individual settlers, unable to accept their disordered experience in America, confined its complexity in disjunctions and then deliberately disavowed one side of those disjunctions. They attained identity by denying the undisciplined impulses that plagued them and by disowning the abundant opportunities that tempted them. Thus these settlers came to know

---

[82] William MacDonald, ed., *Select Charters and Other Documents Illustrative of American History: 1606–1775* (New York, 1899), pp. 122, 150, 151, 154, 123–25, 140, 142–43, 146, 176, 180–81, 186, 197, 202–203, 194, 201.

themselves by their negations. In their logic they distinguished ideas by "setting them against their opposites" while, in their lives, they discerned themselves by setting their assumptive civility against the unconditional abandon—the "license, sedition, and fury," as the Virginia Company put it—that they ascribed to others. Therefore they achieved a sense of their own moral ideal by conjuring up a contrast to the "degradation to which the spiritual thralls of the wilderness are brought"; and they preserved an assurance of their religious aspiration by emphasizing that they were "no Jews, no Turks . . . nor Catholics." They defined themselves less by the vitality of their affirmations than by the violence of their abjurations. Their apprehension of their individuality came to be encapsulated in such counteridentity and in the "identity-work" by which they managed the modicum of their inclinations that they would accept and the rest that they rejected.[83]

The temptation that they rejected most vehemently of all was the life of the indigenes on whom they intruded. As James Axtell has put it, they found in the Indians "sometime adversaries and full-time contraries."[84] Even before the British established permanent colonies in North America, many of them conceived of the occupants of the continent as creatures of Satan, and once arrived they persisted in such conceptions.[85] Other settlers saw the native peoples more nearly as dumb brutes. Despite the biblical account of the common creation of all humanity, few frontier dwellers would have disputed Samuel Purchas's description of the Indians as "bad people, having little of humanity but shape, ignorant of civility or arts or religion; more brutish than the beasts they hunt." Cotton Mather of Massachusetts, Roger Williams of Rhode Island, and Commissary Johnston of Carolina literally likened the indigenous inhabitants of the eastern woodlands to animals: "beavers upon our streams," "mad Dogs," "wolves and tigers." And

[83] Miller and Johnson, *The Puritans*, pp. 33, 480; *True Declaration of the Estate of the Colonie*, p. 15; Richard Slotkin, *Regeneration through Violence: The Mythology of the American Frontier, 1600-1860* (Middletown, Conn., 1973), p. 86. On the concept of "identity work," see Anthony F. C. Wallace, "Identity Processes in Personality and Culture," in *Cognition, Personality, and Clinical Psychology*, ed. Richard Jessor and Seymour Feshbach (San Francisco, 1967), pp. 62–89.

[84] James Axtell, *The European and the Indian: Essays in the Ethnohistory of Colonial North America* (New York, 1981), pp. 303–304.

[85] Bernard Sheehan, *Savagism and Civility: Indians and Englishmen in Colonial Virginia* (Cambridge, 1980), p. 47; Wright, *Elizabethans' America*, pp. 178, 184; *The Narrative of the Captivity and Restoration of Mrs. Mary Rowlandson*, in *Held Captive by Indians: Selected Narratives, 1642–1836*, ed. Richard Van Der Beets (Knoxville, Tenn., 1973), p. 45; Richard B. Davis, *Intellectual Life in the Colonial South, 1585–1763* (Knoxville, Tenn., 1978), pp. 654–55; Gray, *Good Speed*, p. C, verso.

one commentator even went so far as to describe American Indians as "game" for the colonists.[86]

With such creatures, the English could neither conceive of nor allow themselves comity. From New England to the Caribbean, they thought tribes terrifying that other Europeans did not. Englishmen everywhere kept indigenes at a distance while, to one degree or another, Spaniards, Portuguese, and French incorporated the American Indian into their colonial cultures.[87] In Virginia, the English strung palisades all the way from the James to the York in order to clear the lower peninsula of its native population. In Massachusetts and Carolina alike, colonists glorified God for the deaths by European disease that decimated the Indians before the invaders ever arrived; and in Massachusetts, missionaries tried to confine the few who survived in self-contained praying towns.[88] The first settlers never intended to have Indians among them, except perhaps as slaves, and they never meant to permit their own people to go among the Indians either. They forbade absence from their plantations without permission. They prescribed punishments even unto death for flight to the natives. And they consigned those who deserted in defiance of these penalties to a kind of cultural death even if they could not inflict upon them a literal one. Thus the colonies of Great Britain, unlike those of all other European nations in the New World, refused to accommodate men who mixed with the natives or embraced their ways in any measure.[89]

The interdiction on dealings with the Indians extended beyond the sphere of social relations to the realm of sexual intimacies. Despite dire shortages of women in the southern colonies and significant imbalances everywhere else, English pioneers prided themselves from the first on their self-denial. Raleigh reported of an early expedition that, though the Span-

---

[86] Gary Nash, "The Image of the Indian in the Southern Colonial Mind," *William and Mary Quarterly*, 3d ser., 29 (1972):222–23; Cotton Mather, *Magnalia Christi Americana; or, The Ecclesiastical History of New England* (Hartford, Conn., 1855, 1853), 1:559; Richard Drinnon, *Facing West: The Metaphysics of Indian-Hating and Empire-Building* (Minneapolis, 1980), p. 53; Frank Klingberg, ed., *Carolina Chronicle: The Papers of Commissary Gideon Johnston, 1707–1716* (Berkeley, 1946), p. 147; J. Frederick Fausz and Jon Kukla, "A Letter of Advice to the Governor of Virginia, 1624," *William and Mary Quarterly*, 3d ser., 34 (1977):127.

[87] Karen Kupperman, *Settling with the Indians: The Meeting of English and Indian Cultures in America, 1580–1640* (Totowa, N.J., 1980), pp. 43–44, 156; Dunn, *Sugar and Slaves*, pp. 16–19; Jones, *O Strange New World*, p. 49.

[88] Sheehan, *Savagism and Civility*, pp. 177–78; Davis, *Intellectual Life*, p. 207; *Johnson's Wonder-Working Providence*, pp. 39–42.

[89] Sheehan, *Savagism and Civility*, p. 114; Kupperman, *Settling with the Indians*, p. 156. In insisting on cultural purity as they did, the English differed not only from other Europeans but also from the Indians themselves; see James Axtell, "The White Indians of Colonial America," *William and Mary Quarterly*, 3d ser., 32 (1975):55–88.

iards took Indian women, not a single member of his crew ever did. He conferred credibility on his account when he added that the tribesmen who sought his alliance against rivals asked only the women for themselves and promised to leave the gold entirely to the English.[90]

The divergence in priorities that was transparent to those aborigines distinguished the English from every other people in the New World. In Brazil, a widespread concubinage of Portuguese males with Indian women prevailed for centuries, and the Jesuits there even demanded that the Europeans solemnize such liaisons by marriage. In Spanish America, a nomenclature of exquisite subtlety evolved to acknowledge and in some sense legitimate the proclivities of the conquerors by locating the products of their promiscuity in social space. In Canada, Champlain promised intermarriage from the outset, and the coureurs de bois accepted easily the sexual fashions of the forests.[91]

Only in English outposts was concubinage uncommon and intermarriage forbidden. Puritans and cavaliers alike testified to their execration of interracial attachment in legislation to prevent "abominable mixture and spurious issue" and in mandates that mixed couples "be banished forever." As late as 1717 the governor of Virginia told the Commissioners of Trade and Plantations that he could not "find one Englishman that has an Indian wife, or an Indian married to a white woman." A few decades later, John Bartram said similarly of Pennsylvania that he could not "remember . . . one English man to have married an Indian nymph. It would [be] reckoned a horrid crime with us."[92]

Such aversion was proverbial among Europeans, who knew "the inclinations" of the English to be quite unlike "the custom of the French" in that regard. It was provoking enough even to the Indians, who expected English visitors to their villages to accept hospitable offers of "trading girls," "Indian lasses," or their own daughters as "bedfellows" for the night, and who "flew into a passion" when the English refused such "kindness." Yet the colonists never overcame their aversion. In Byrd's words, they

<hr />

[90] Herbert Moller, "Sex Composition and Correlated Culture Patterns of Colonial America," *William and Mary Quarterly*, 3d ser., 2 (1945):113–53; Walter Raleigh, A *Voyage for the Discovery of Guiana*, in *The Works of Sir Walter Ralegh, Kt.* (Oxford, 1829), 8:430, 450.

[91] Dauril Alden, "Black Robes versus White Settlers: The Struggle for 'Freedom of the Indians' in Colonial Brazil," in *Attitudes of the Colonial Powers toward the American Indian*, ed. Howard Peckham and Charles Gibson (Salt Lake City, 1969), p. 24; Mason Wade, "The French and the Indians," in Peckham and Gibson, *Attitudes of the Colonial Powers*, p. 72.

[92] W. W. Hening, ed., *The Statutes at Large, Being a Collection of All the Laws of Virginia, 1619–1792* (Richmond, 1809–1823), 7:86–87; Wilbur Jacobs, "British-Colonial Attitudes and Policies toward the Indian in the American Colonies," in Peckham and Gibson, *Attitudes of the Colonial Powers*, pp. 91–92; John Bartram to Peter Collinson, 1757 (?), in John Bartram, *Correspondence*, ed. Edward Wildman, typescript, American Philosophical Society, p. 457.

never "brought their stomachs to embrace this prudent alliance" from con-siderations of policy or of passion.[93]

As the settlers spurned sexual union with the natives, so they scorned spiritual communion. Byrd believed the two contempts to be connected, "for after all that can be said, a sprightly lover is the most prevailing mis-sionary that can be sent among these . . . infidels." But even on a more ethereal understanding of the missionary enterprise, the English performed abysmally in the New World. Though Virginia avowed the primacy of pros-elytizing at its founding, a governor who reviewed the record at the end of the seventeenth century confessed that, in his colony, no efforts to convert the Indians to Christianity "had ever been heard of." Though Massachu-setts professed the promotion of the gospel to be the principal justification of its endeavor, the Bay colonists bent almost all their early efforts with the Indians to the killing of Pequots. By 1640, Puritan preachers were still ra-tionalizing or reveling in the bloody slaughter. By the same date, the Jesuits in Canada had already baptised more than a thousand Indians and estab-lished a hospital, schools, and a seminary for Montagnais, Hurons, and Al-gonquins, despite having come to America later than the Congregational-ists. By that time too, of course, the Spaniards had already claimed tens of thousands of Indians for the faith.[94]

Moreover, those paltry early gestures turned out to be the peak of English concern to convert natives. Succeeding generations fell ever further from even the rhetorical ideal to which they had once appointed themselves. Some gave up of their own volition, in wrathful resolution that Christianity was for rational creatures, "not for brutes . . . in the shape of men." Others abandoned the effort in despondent submission to the sentiments of their neighbors, wearily recognizing that their exhortations were only "words," and "little minded." Even the few who persisted did so in defiance of the antipathy of their peers. John Eliot had to endure the delight of the towns-folk when his boat ran down in Boston harbor. Eleazer Wheelock had to suffer the derision of the gentlemen of Middletown, who declared his work of decades "absurd and fruitless," and the still more pointed disdain of the churchgoers of Windsor, who passed his collection plate and returned it empty but for a bullet and flint.[95]

[93] Jacobs, "British-Colonial Attitudes," pp. 91–92; Lawson, *New Voyage*, pp. 46–47, 50, 77; Byrd, *History of the Dividing Line*, p. 160.

[94] Byrd, *History of the Dividing Line*, p. 160; Wesley Craven, *White, Red, and Black: The Sev-enteenth-Century Virginian* (Charlottesville, Va., 1971), p. 64; Wade, "The French and the Indians," pp. 73–74.

[95] Gerald Goodwin, "Christianity, Civilization, and the Savage: The Anglican Mission to the American Indian," *Historical Magazine of the Protestant Episcopal Church* 42 (1973):97; Ed-gar Pennington, "The South Carolina Indian War of 1715, as Seen by the Clergymen," *South*

English attitudes toward the American Indians were, by European standards, stern from the moment of first contact, and they became even more harsh following the massacre, in 1622, of some settlers in Virginia and the outbreak, in 1637, of hostility between Pequot tribesmen and New England Puritans. Each episode provided those in power in the individual colonies an opportunity to pursue a policy of extermination against the Indians, and this policy became so explicit in the New England context that the Connecticut assembly renamed the Pequot village New London and the Pequot river the Thames so as to cut off "all remembrance of [the Pequot] from the earth."[96]

The genocidal rage so rampant in the earliest settlements persisted into the eighteenth century, among Pennsylvanians and Carolinians as among Virginians and New Englanders. The gentle Quaker John Bartram concluded in the course of his travels that the only effective way with the "barbarous Indians" was to "bang them stoutly." The upright Anglican Francis Le Jau decided in the wake of the Tuscarora massacre of 1711 that the only efficacious course with "those murderers" was "to destroy the whole nation." The one concession Le Jau could conceive was that the Tuscarora women and children might be allowed to live, as slaves. In this notion he was not alone, for other colonists sought a similar fate for the Indians. New Englanders declared that they would "have those brutes their servants, their slaves, either willingly or of necessity, and docible enough, if not obsequious." The Virginia assembly once sold an entire tribe into involuntary servitude. And as late as 1708 there were 1,400 Indian slaves in South Carolina, fully half the number of African slaves in the colony at the time.[97]

In the end, of course, the natives refused to submit to slavery. As the

Carolina Historical Magazine 32 (1931):261–62; Alden Vaughan and Daniel Richter, "Crossing the Cultural Divide: Indians and New Englanders, 1605–1763," Proceedings of the American Philosophical Society 90 (1980):45; Axtell, The European and the Indian, pp. 102–103. Wheelock never could raise funds for his work in Connecticut, or anywhere else in New England, and was always dependent on British benefactions; see Axtell, The European and the Indian, pp. 102–103, 106–108. In this his experience was exactly like that of his seventeenth-century predecessors.

[96] Axtell, The European and the Indian, p. 103; Jones, O Strange New World, p. 60; Gray, Good Speed, p. C,; Kupperman, Settling with the Indians, pp. 78, 175, 184–85; Nash, "Image of the Indian," p. 218; Craven, White, Red, and Black, p. 55; Fausz and Kukla, "Letter of Advice," p. 108; Edward Neill, Virginia Carolorum: The Colony under the Rule of Charles the First and Second, A.D. 1625–1685 (Albany, 1886), p. 192; Vaughan and Richter, "Crossing the Cultural Divide," p. 45. Quotation from Drinnon, Facing West, p. 53.

[97] Bartram, Correspondence, pp. 607, 617, 619; Frank Klingberg, ed., The Carolina Chronicle of Dr. Francis Le Jau (Berkeley, 1956), p. 122; Drinnon, Facing West, p. 50; Tim Morgan, "The Sale of the Nansiatticoes: A New Look at Colonial Virginia's Indian Policy," paper presented to the Virginia Social Science Association, Radford College, 1977; Jacobs, "British-Colonial Attitudes," p. 97.

English lamented, Indian men "forced to labor" would "either hang themselves or run away." Because they were thus willing to die, the colonists concluded by killing them. But the original English intention had not always been so lethal. Many of the pioneers would have preferred, in the telling phrase of the time, to "reduce the savages to civility."[98]

Servile labor was to have been one evidence of such reduction. Settled agriculture was to have been another, and regular residence, English woolens, and Christian conversion still others. Conversion, as the English invaders and the Iberians before them idealized it, was meant to obliterate Indian culture, not to annihilate Indian populations. It was designed to subjugate the dangerous and distressful pluralism of the land and to set a safe and satisfying uniformity in its place. Whereas some French and Iberian missionaries met the Indians more nearly on their own ground and accepted a measure of aboriginal beliefs and observances into a syncretistic Christianity of the New World, the English were adamant in attempting to anglicize the natives before beginning to Christianize them. They wanted to "cure the natives . . . of their savage temper" and "purge all the Indian out" of them. As James Axtell wryly noted of such medical metaphors, "even a casual acquaintance" with sanatory practice of the period "will convey the full rigor of the treatment implied."[99]

If war is the continuation of politics by other means, then a policy of extermination was the continuation of conversion by other means. Sometimes the line between the two modes blurred, but even when it was quite clear, conversion and extermination were still just divergent means to an unquestioned end. The English meant to eliminate an alien presence they found unnerving. And if they achieved that end by causing demographic collapse among the Indians, they wrought cultural catastrophe on another race.

The Africans who were brought as slaves to British North America did not act on familiar terrain and could not run away to friendly forests. They had no option, therefore, but to suffer the enslavement that planters had once prepared for Powhatans and Pequots. They underwent the systematic program of cultural annihilation that the English inflicted on all who deviated from their norms while remaining within reach.

---

[98] Dunn, *Sugar and Slaves*, p. 74; James Axtell, "The Invasion Within: The Contest of Cultures in Colonial North America," in Axtell, *The European and the Indian*, pp. 39–86.

[99] Axtell, *The European and the Indian*, p. 98. See also, e.g., Francis Jennings, *The Invasion of America: Indians, Colonialism, and the Cant of Conquest* (Chapel Hill, 1975), pp. 43–57, 228–53; Neal Salisbury, "Red Puritans: The 'Praying Indians' of Massachusetts Bay and John Eliot," *William and Mary Quarterly*, 3d ser., 31 (1974):27–54; James Ronda, " 'We Are Well as We Are': An Indian Critique of Seventeenth-Century Christian Missions," *William and Mary Quarterly*, 3d ser., 34 (1977):66–82.

Yet even as blacks were detached from their cultural moorings and forced to conform to English ways, the colonists continued to deny all commonality with their slaves. In the islands and the staple-producing provinces of the mainland alike, there emerged "a growing racialist conviction that negroes were a non-human form of life." A pious woman of early Barbados maintained that "any minister who dared to baptise them might as well baptise a puppy." Another insisted that blacks "were beasts, and had no more souls than beasts." And in the Chesapeake and Carolinas, more than one planter actually named his Africans Ape or Monkey.[100]

Whereas settlers of the other European nations in the New World apprehended color categories in continua that reflected racial interbreeding, the English who colonized America acknowledged only the polarized alternatives of white and black. Whereas Spaniards and Portuguese evolved elaborate vocabularies that recognized the complexity of racial realities, Virginians and Carolinians put themselves radically apart from their slaves. Drawing a dichotomous color line between themselves and the Africans that denied all gradation or degree, they defied the abundant actuality of miscegenation and the evidence of the varied complexions before their eyes.[101]

Such oppositions alleviated anxiety and at the same time aggravated it. Once the colonists entered the vortex of extremity, their every effort to reduce tensions precipitated further tensions. The very comparisons of color that spared them the strain of dwelling on the disparity between their own practices and those they had left behind and the contraposition that sustained their psychic equilibrium by reassuring them of who they were when they were a long way from home simultaneously compounded their dilemma. Those contrasts intensified their conviction that they were poised on the edge of an abyss of barbarism and reinforced their disjunctive definition of the colonial situation as one in which civilized virtue stood always in awful temptation of descending into savage vice.[102]

---

[100] Gary Puckrein, "The Plantation Household and the Growth of a Racialist *Mentalité* in Seventeenth-Century Barbados," 14th Conference of the Association of Caribbean Historians, Puerto Rico, April 1982, p. 30; Craven, *White, Red, and Black*, p. 84.

[101] There was, to be sure, a more elaborate and complex set of color categories in the British West Indies than in the British colonies on the mainland; see, e.g., Winthrop Jordan, "American Chiaroscuro: The Status and Definition of Mulattoes in the British Colonies," *William and Mary Quarterly*, 3d ser., 14 (1962):183–200. But this is, in the exact sense of the phrase, the exception that proves the rule, since even in the British islands the intermediate categories were less elaborately and more grudgingly applied than in the French, Spanish, and Portuguese colonies; see, e.g., Donald Horowitz, "Color Differentiation in the American Systems of Slavery," *Journal of Interdisciplinary History* 3 (1973):509–542, esp. pp. 518–20.

[102] Winthrop Jordan, *White over Black: American Attitudes toward the Negro, 1550–1812* (Chapel Hill, 1968), esp. pp. 97–98, 110, 119–20, 143–44, 193.

150

By their dichotomies, the settlers made their moral bed. By their duplicitous displacements, they declined consciously to lie in it. Yet, inevitably and often explicitly, they apprehended in themselves the very defects that they disparaged in others. With both Africans and Indians, they were, as Winthrop Jordan said, "especially inclined to discover attributes in savages which they found first but could not speak of in themselves."[103]

By European standards of civility, only savages were improvident and without care for the morrow. By the same standards, the early settlers were less civilized than the natives they denigrated, because in the first decades of settlement they were the wasteful ones who battened on the food provided them by the Indians.[104] The psychic unsettlement entailed by such dependence was amplified by the settlers' recurrent practice of desecrating the graves of the natives for food and treasure.[105] The Indians exhibited their contempt for the perpetrators of this outrage when they wiped out a search party and left the corpses with their "mouths stopped full of bread." The colonists who recovered the bodies both interpreted aright the symbolic "scorn" of the Indians for the incessant importunity of the English and read its resonances. George Percy explicitly likened the incident to the fabled figure of the Spaniard whose throat the Indians filled with molten gold in gruesome gratification of his avarice.[106]

Indeed, the incapacity of the colonists to produce their own food impelled even more appalling grave robbing. One beleaguered band of Virginians, almost "entirely without provisions," not only ate their own dead but also dug up and devoured an Indian who had been buried for two days. Though the English constantly assailed the cannibalism of the Indians as the consummate mark of their barbarism, nothing in the settlers' stories of the natives approached such ghoulish behavior. And the episode was not unique. On one of the only occasions on record of early Virginia providence for the future, a husband killed his wife, hacked her up in pieces, salted the pieces, and put them away for subsequent consumption.[107]

---

[103] Jordan, *White over Black*, p. 40.

[104] Kupperman, *Settling with the Indians*, pp. 83–84; Brown, *Genesis*, 2:641–43; Sheehan, *Savagism and Civility*, p. 105. For the sophisticated food cycle of the Indians, see Gene Waddell, *Indians of the South Carolina Low Country, 1562–1751* (Spartanburg, S.C., 1980), pp. 37–43, and William Cronon, *Changes in the Land: Indians, Colonists, and the Ecology of New England* (New York, 1983), ch. 3.

[105] J. Frederick Fausz, "Indians and English at Jamestown: Culture, Race, and Ethnocentrism, 1607–1622," paper presented to the Duquesne History Forum, Pittsburgh, 1976, p. 7; Kupperman, *Settling with the Indians*, p. 125; Michael Zuckerman, "Pilgrims in the Wilderness: Community, Modernity, and the Maypole at Merry Mount," *New England Quarterly* 50 (1977):264.

[106] Sheehan, *Savagism and Civility*, p. 150.

[107] Brown, *Genesis*, 1:392; Morgan, *American Slavery*, p. 73.

The more the colonists fell short of their own standards of civility, the more vehemently they inveighed against the savagery of others. Only savages, in the settlers' view, lived straggling and scattered in rude residences in the woods. But in Virginia it was the Indians who occupied settled towns and the English who soon spread far and wide for seventy miles on both banks of the James. It was the Indians who had houses so fine that John Smith bought one of them for Virginia's fort, the Virginians whose homes were derided as "mean and poor" by their own House of Burgesses. In New England too, it was the English who dispersed. From the first decades, Bradford bewailed the abandonment of Plymouth Town for private farms, Winthrop worried over flight from his city on a hill to a host of tiny encampments about the Bay, and ministers and magistrates alike regretted the migration to Connecticut. Everywhere the colonists' denunciations of the natives' wilderness way of life betrayed their doubts about themselves. By the beginning of the eighteenth century, observers could see clearly that the destructive "defect" in all the early enterprises was their willingness to allow landholders to pursue personal ends at "distances unsafe and solitary," in settlements "without any form at all."[108]

All those awarenesses ate at the settlers' sense of self-esteem, the more so because they had staked their sense of worth on embodying the sanctified state of being they had disjunctively defined. Inevitably they found themselves drawn—even driven—to the very impurities they professed to have put aside. They did not cease to be susceptible to the terrors of the irrational merely because they distinguished themselves in terms of an exaggerated sanity. They did not divest themselves of carnal desire merely because they conceived of themselves as civilized white men and projected their sensuality upon the "savage" blacks and red men. They had to have those they scorned—the Africans, the Indians, and all the idle, dissolute, and damned—to maintain the boundaries of their increasingly brittle identities. Precisely because they found themselves, and in truth created themselves, in their counteridentities, they required for their very sense of selfhood the outcasts they purported to abhor.[109]

Dependence on counteridentities enmeshed the colonists in vexing dilemmas, many of which revolved around those outcast peoples. There were

[108] Wilcomb Washburn, "The Moral and Legal Justifications for Dispossessing the Indians," in *Seventeenth-Century America: Essays in Colonial History*, ed. James M. Smith (Chapel Hill, 1959), pp. 23–24; Kupperman, *Settling with the Indians*, p. 120; Carson, "Impermanent Architecture"; Montgomery, *Discourse*, pp. 2–3.

[109] On the asymmetry of the civilized person's need for the idea of the "savage" and the lack on the part of the "savage" of any analogous need for the civilized, see Stanley Diamond, "Introduction: The Uses of the Primitive," in *Primitive Views of the World*, ed. Stanley Diamond (New York, 1969), pp. v–xxix.

simple discordancies of self-presentation and complex contrarieties of religious orientation and obligation. There were perplexing problems of how the settlers were to understand themselves and how they were to relate to others. There were crucial questions of what sort of world the emigrants had entered upon.

Disjunctions that promised to clarify somehow ended by clouding such issues. The colonists emphasized the heathenism of other races in the New World in order to reassure themselves of their own Christian character in the wilderness. But their Christian identity constrained them to convert the heathen and risk eradicating the very contrast on which they had predicated their religious conception of themselves.[110]

Similarly, the settlers emphasized the roughness of the Indians in order to convince themselves of their own refinement, but their stress on such savagery undid the promises that they made in their every advertisement for immigrants. Defense of endangered identities required distance from the blood-thirsty fury of the "barbarians." Promotion of colonial development demanded assurance to prospective settlers that the natives of the New World were cordial and kind. And since these disparate imperatives could not be encompassed in a single coherent conception, the colonists ended as they had begun, speaking of the Indians as Satanic "beasts" in the same breath in which they called them "loving and gentle." Early Americans were caught in a moral centrifuge of their own making, doomed to desire the Indians at once ferocious and friendly, treacherous and tractable.[111]

Similarly too, the colonists' insistence on the cruelty of the natives augmented their awe of aboriginal aggression and impaired their ability to make themselves at ease in Eden. The simplest walk in the countryside could stir a sense of a "paradise" suffused with wondrous colors, tastes, and fragrances, but the sight of a solitary Indian running through the woods could awake "mistrust" of "some villainy" and induce an entire company of colonists to quit the garden, making "all the haste away" that they could.[112]

The very readiness with which settlers abandoned such sensual pleasures on such paltry provocation betrayed the confusion that attended their condition. For the truth was that they could never decide whether they preferred to enjoy paradise or expel themselves from it. Often they exaggerated the differences between the Old World and the New, to attract immigrants and to assert their own moral excellence. They flattered themselves that they were "flying from the depravations of Europe to the American strand."

[110] Michael Kammen, *People of Paradox: An Inquiry Concerning the Origins of American Civilization* (New York, 1972), p. 142.
[111] Gray, *Good Speed*, p. C₂ verso.
[112] Brown, *Genesis*, 1:162–63.

Yet the very gratification they found in differentiating themselves from the Europeans by opposing innocence and corruption simultaneously jeopardized the identity they claimed as Europeans in opposition to primitive Indians.[113]

Early Americans experienced tension between claims of knowledge and innocence in other ways as well. They celebrated the bounty of the continent and its opportunities for indolent subsistence while at the same time they saw the promise of the west in its prospect of straitened circumstances and welcomed the necessity to work by the sweat of their brows. Even as they indulged in an idyll of idleness, they drew back. Their dependence on the "benign dispensation" of the new land disturbed them. The profusion of nature affronted their sensibilities as much as it offered fulfillment of their fantasies. For such superabundance intimated to the pioneers a willessness and passivity profoundly at odds with their determination to improve and order nature by conscious artifice.[114]

Also, exactly insofar as the invaders vaunted America as a world without work, they vitiated their justification for dispossessing the Indians. That justification depended on English assertion that the natives left the land "unused and undressed" by their disinclination to labor. America was, in the words of one Pilgrim, "a vast and empty chaos," and its emptiness was its uncultivation.[115]

The hypocrisy of such pleading was, of course, palpable; and so were the paradoxes it entailed. The Indians, supposedly unwilling to work when the English wished to strip them of their rights, suddenly became serviceable when the settlers sought to assure potential migrants of the availability of a labor force. The country that was at some times an unparalleled paradise became at others an ambiguous Eden that had to be "cultured, planted, and manured by men of industry" to come up to colonial anticipations.[116]

Civility as the English defined it demanded exertion, but the darkest desire of the pioneers was exemption from exertion. Unable, ultimately, to avow that desire openly and embody it in a legitimate way of life, they projected it onto the Indian. Whether they celebrated his noble savagery or castigated his indolent paganism, whether they idealized his passivity or complained of his incapacity "to use either the land or the commodities of it," they held that the native lived "with less labor and more pleasure and plenty" than they themselves did. Still they steadfastly denied themselves

---

[113] Martin Marty, "Reinterpreting American Religious History in Context," in *Reinterpretation in American Church History*, ed. Jerald Brauer (Chicago, 1968), pp. 200–204.

[114] Franklin, *Discoverers*, pp. 83, 64, 75–77, 80, 108, 224.

[115] Franklin, *Discoverers*, p. 220; Washburn, "Moral and Legal Justifications."

[116] Sheehan, *Savagism and Civility*, pp. 34, 35.

such ease and clung to imported ideals of toil in preference to availing themselves of imitable indigenous models of mixed labor and leisure.[117]

Colonists' uncertainties about how to demean the Indian reflected still more serious incoherences about how to idealize themselves. Early Americans clearly sought self-determination. They risked a remorseless ocean for it. But at the same time they were deeply ill at ease about it. They understood that the assertive self-seeking that had impelled them over the seas was subversive, and therefore they endeavored to disown it by displacing it upon the Indian.

Just because they ascribed such excessive fondness for freedom to the natives, they forced their own oppositionally defined identities into the realm of restraint. Just because they postulated that the Indians knew "nothing like government among themselves," they set their own self-image by that negative ideal. They condemned comrades who seemed to "shake off" such "yoke of government" and adopt "the manners of the Indians they lived amongst." They disdained those who lived "too like the heathen, without instituted ordinances." And they complained not of their own submissions and subjections but of the "sinful liberty" and "overweening pride" of the natives, who rendered "no homage to anyone whomsoever, except when they like," and who did not "know what is meant by bridle and bit."[118]

For all the insubordinate independence that had inspired their embarkation for America in the first place, the colonists came soon enough in the New World to value control and prize predictability. Anglo-American resentment of Indian spontaneity and inconstancy was genuine enough. And for all the insistence on autonomy that had motivated their migration, the pioneers came quickly enough in the provinces to concede the necessity and even the propriety of authority. Their antagonism to the "insufferable pride" of the Indians and their certainty that such self-respect was the source of native "contempt of all authority" was authentic.[119]

Yet the very individualism they reviled in the Indians still lingered in their own immoderate ambitions. The obstinate antiauthoritarianism that they imputed to the natives still lurked in their own hostility to hierarchy and its pretensions. The mobility that so disconcerted them in the indigenes still survived in their own proclivity to pull up stakes when a better opportunity offered or simply when the spirit moved them.

Only when the colonists commenced a revolution could they acknowl-

[117] Axtell, "Invasion Within," p. 49.

[118] John Sergeant, *A Letter from the Rev. Mr. Sergeant to Dr. Coleman of Boston, August 1, 1743* (Lancaster, Penna., 1929), p. 5; Heimert, "Puritanism, Wilderness, and the Frontier," p. 374; Axtell, *The European and the Indian*, p. 266; Axtell, "Invasion Within," p. 63.

[119] Axtell, *The European and the Indian*, p. 104.

edge such impulses. Only when they were ready to recognize the uses of attributes they had long dared contemplate only from afar, under cover of contempt, could they find any favorable figurative functions for the native. After decades of cultivation of a careful symbolism of control, rebel cartoonists all at once embraced the Indian as their preferred image of America. After generations of criticism of "creolean degeneracy," insurgent iconographers adopted the Indian as their emblem of unyielding independence and fierce love of liberty.[120]

As they did so, they declared not only a transformation of politics but also an abrupt inversion of the colonial sense of self. If only for a Revolutionary moment, Americans would cease to be virtuous communards and become ungoverned and ungovernable liberals, embracing the very values their pre-Revolutionary predecessors had anathematized.

None of these oscillations ever ended. None of these dilemmas ever dissolved. None of these incoherences ever cleared. None of them ever really could. And all of them contributed to the deep disquietude of early American psychic life. All of them underlay the settlers' readiness for extremity, their disposition to passionate outburst and awakening, their hair-trigger sensitivity to insult, their virulent animosities toward racial and religious out-groups, and their incessant eruptions into intergroup conflict and assaults on authority.

At the same time, all of them engaged elements specific to life in the wilderness. Englishmen did not have to deal with native tribes or black slaves. Englishmen did not confront vast tracts of free land. Englishmen did not enter into society only at the peril of a terrifying ocean transit.

On that account, the tensions that defined American life and defied the fabrication of coherent identity also heightened colonial disconnection from the metropolis. After an odd fashion, Frederick Jackson Turner was right. The Americans *were* a frontier people. Insofar as they attained any distinctive identity, it arose from their encounter with the wilderness. Insofar as their experience diverged from that of the Old World and their consciousness from that of the mother country, they did so in response to predicaments presented by the wilderness.

But the colonists could scarcely allow themselves to come to any awareness of all this as individuals, let alone arrive at any common consciousness of it as Americans. They failed to forge a new national identity because their disconnections from England were always discrete. To the time of the

---

[120] E. McClung Fleming, "The American Image as Indian Princess," *Winterthur Portfolio* 2 (1965):65–81; Hugh Honour, *The New Golden Land: European Images of America from the Discoveries to the Present Time* (New York, 1975), ch. 6. Quotation from Bernard Bailyn, *Education in the Forming of American Society* (Chapel Hill, 1960), p. 79.

Revolution itself, each colony maintained its primary economic and cultural relations with England rather than with other colonies; and each had also a separate sense of its own Americanness. Few provincials felt a sense of common fate with Americans in other provinces, and no comprehensive conception of American singularity ever achieved wide currency before the final crisis. Thus although it would be possible to trace the emergence in the eighteenth century of a sense of communal identity in the more densely settled areas of the British American colonies, the people who arrived at such a notion of self-awareness had come to think of themselves as Pennsylvanians or Virginians rather than as Americans.

Even when due allowance is made for this development, and account taken of the growing pride that people evinced for their colonial institutions, one must also emphasize that not all white inhabitants of any given colony shared in this communal self-perception. The middle colonies, for example, were inundated in the eighteenth century with hordes of non-English immigrants who were always ready to challenge existing authority; all the densely populated colonies were riven by religious dissent; and settlers in the back country of each colony defied the will of the colonial government, sometimes by an appeal to arms.

It is clear, therefore, that Americans were still very far from being a people bonded by a shared sense of purpose and identity by the third quarter of the eighteenth century. It was, ironically, almost solely in this regard that the colonial experience prepared the consolidation of a national identity in the years after the accomplishment of national independence. The very fragmentation of the country that had occurred in the colonial era made all the more imperious, and poignant, the craving for social solidarity that attended the creation of a nation. And since that craving could not be satisfied in a social reality that was already too heterogeneous for successful centralization, it had to be gratified in symbolic ways. The symbols would begin to be forged in the maelstrom of revolution.

6 ❧ Identity Formation in Ireland: The Emergence of the Anglo-Irish

Nicholas Canny

THE IRISH historical experience presents rich possibilities for those who would understand the process by which colonizing groups come to perceive themselves as a people distinct both from those resident in their country of origin and from those indigenous to their place of settlement. By the seventeenth century, Ireland had already been so engulfed by a series of waves of conquest that all groups who still maintained a foothold there had come to accept that it was the experience of conquest that provided the essential dynamic to the country's historical development. Like conquering groups in other parts of the Atlantic world, each asserted that it was its involvement in a particular conquest that legitimized its presence in the country and each distinguished itself by making reference to that conquest.[1]

Those who will engage our attention are the English settlers and their descendants who asserted their authority over Ireland during the period 1560–1660 and who were to maintain a political ascendancy over the country from then until the mid-nineteenth century. They saw themselves as engaged in a colonial endeavor, and they frequently likened their position to that of their contemporaries who were simultaneously engaged in the

THIS PAPER has been long in gestation and has undergone many revisions. In addition to those who criticized the initial version at the Princeton conference, I would like to thank Tom Dunne, Pat Sheeran, and Hubert McDermott, who commented on a subsequent draft. Most helpful of all was Thomas Bartlett, who offered a searching criticism of the text and who guided me to several references from eighteenth-century sources that made it possible for me to state my case with greater confidence.

[1] The extent to which the historical view of the Gaelic Irish was dominated by the model of conquest made a particular impression on the Dutch planter Matthew de Renzy, who made a special study of Gaelic attitudes and responses. On de Renzy see Brian MacCuarta, "Newcomers in the Irish Midlands, 1540–1641" (M.A. thesis, University College, Galway, 1980). De Renzy recognized that the model of conquest that so inspired the Gaelic Irish derived largely from the twelfth-century text *Lebor gabála Érenn* [The Book of the Conquests of Ireland], and it is significant that a new edition of that text was being prepared in the early seventeenth century by the Gaelic scholar Mícheál Ó Cléirigh. The best example of New English appreciation of the pattern that was imposed by the Irish historical experience by successive waves of conquest is John Davies, *A Discovery of the True Causes why Ireland was never entirely Subdued* (London, 1612). The Old English would appear to have been less impressed by this model and at least one of their number in the early seventeenth century fostered a cyclical notion of the historical process, with "Divine Providence" determining the course of the wheel: Anonymous, *Advertisements for Ireland*, ed. George O'Brien (Dublin: Royal Society of Antiquaries, 1923) esp. pp. 2–3.

conquest and settlement of what was to become British North America. To this extent, their experience was analogous with that of the other groups discussed in this volume; but their endeavor was unique in that they were resuming an earlier effort at colonization in the twelfth century. Thus, as well as having to contend with the Gaelic Irish inhabitants of the country, this more recent wave of settlers felt the need to distinguish themselves from the descendants of those from England who had undertaken the earlier task of occupying the country. The experience of the English in Ireland was also unique in that their effort at settling (but not at conquering) the country was powerfully reinforced by lowland Scots who, after 1603, were common subjects with the English of the same British monarch. The colonization endeavor of these Scots was presented in a positive light by the English-born settlers and administrators whenever it was seen to be supplementary and subordinate to that of the English themselves, but the English in Ireland generally viewed the Scots as rivals and this consideration drove them with even greater urgency to forge an identity that would serve to legitimize their emergence as the dominant social group in Ireland. But, by a strange irony, the very success of the English settlers in becoming the dominant group in Ireland marked their failure there because, as we shall see, their mission was defined as one of advancing the existing population to such a point of civility that it would no longer be necessary to rule over it.

It was the presence in Ireland of an already anglicized population that first mobilized the more recent English settlers to engage in the process of identity formation. These anglicized people were the descendants of the Anglo-Normans who had partially conquered Ireland in the twelfth century and who had maintained a secure foothold there, even subsequent to the Black Death and the accompanying Gaelic resurgence of the fourteenth century. These survivors were known collectively as the Old English in Ireland, a nomenclature first employed by Edmund Spenser in 1596 and one that came into common currency in Ireland, particularly during the seventeenth century. Many of the lesser landowners of Anglo-Norman descent in the provinces had so far succumbed to the influence of their Gaelic neighbors that they were hardly distinguishable from them in dress, language, and culture, but this process of degeneracy, as it was termed, was bewailed by the great feudal magnates in the provinces and even more so by the merchants, lawyers, and landowners in the Pale. This latter area, which included the city of Dublin and most of the rich agricultural land in the four counties that abutted it, was the heartland of English influence in Ireland. The inhabitants of the Pale, or at least those who claimed to be their spokesmen, were acutely conscious of being culturally superior to their Gaelic neighbors and they belabored the fact that they and their forebears had, over the centuries, upheld the authority of the crown in Ireland against the persistent onslaught of their Gaelic neighbors. Furthermore, down to 1534, it was one of this Old English community who had traditionally served as the king's representative in Ireland, and younger sons from the Pale (some of whom had obtained legal training in England) held a virtual monopoly over positions in the Dublin administration.[2]

The efforts of the Old English to sustain or consolidate their position in Ireland were greatly assisted from England during the 1540s, when it became the expressed intention of the English crown to extend its authority beyond the confines of the traditional lordship of Ireland to cover the entire island. This purpose seems first to have been identified by a few English-born officials in Ireland, but it was immediately grasped by a group of Old English lawyers who believed that their promotion of this cause would justify the privileged position under the crown to which they aspired. Apparently with this in mind, these lawyers provided a constitutional framework for their favored policy when they had Henry VIII and his successors declared to be kings rather than, as hitherto, lords of Ireland. This change in title, which was ratified in the Irish parliament in June 1541, involved a fundamental constitutional change. Previously, when the monarch was referred to as lord of Ireland, the implication was that only those living within the part of the country described as the lordship of Ireland were subjects of the crown and that all living outside that jurisdiction were not provided with the protection of the crown and might therefore be attacked with impunity. In 1541, however, it had been made clear that all inhabitants of the country who acknowledged the English monarch as their sovereign were entitled to the protection of the law.

What was decided in 1541 was therefore that those Gaelic elements of the Irish population who previously had been designated "Irish enemies" were being provided with the opportunity to become subjects of the crown. To facilitate this process the government encouraged a succession of Irish lords to make their peace with the government. In doing so, they surrendered their lordships to the crown and were in turn regranted them with English-style titles and with the assurance that they, and all who resided within their lordships, were entitled to the full protection of the law. The immediate benefit for the government in this scheme, known as the policy of surrender and regrant, was that the surrendering lords agreed to limit

---

[2] For a description of the Old English community at this point see T. W. Moody, F. X. Martin, F. J. Byrne, eds., A New History of Ireland (Oxford, 1976), 3:1–38; Nicholas Canny, The Formation of the Old English Elite in Ireland (O'Donnell lecture of the National University of Ireland, Dublin, 1975). For a fresh account with emphasis on administrative matters see S. G. Ellis, Reform and Revival: English Government in Ireland, 1470–1534 (London, 1986).

161

their authority to their designated lordships; and there was further hope of political stability deriving from these arrangements because it was expected that succession to political power within each lordship would be according to the principle of primogeniture rather than, as previously, after a contest among the more ambitious members of the ruling family.[3]

The adoption of this policy by the government was particularly favored by the Old English officials, both because they were the ones who usually acted as intermediaries between the government and those Gaelic lords who agreed to surrender and because they were most active in providing for the future by bringing the designated successors of the surrendering lords into their own households to be educated after the English manner and familiarized with English legal procedures. The policy of surrender and regrant therefore provided the Old English with a new role and purpose in their country of birth. It was favored by them also because its gradualist character meant that there was less need of the English army to advance crown authority in Ireland; the Old English argued that English soldiers and officials were required merely to supplement their own efforts to make this objective a reality. This attitude naturally provoked resentment among certain English-born governors in Ireland, and tensions were heightened by the expressed belief of some English-born officials and soldiers that the reform of the country could not be achieved with such ease. Still others of the English-born in Ireland were concerned that little opportunity for self-advancement would exist while the surrender and regrant policy was adhered to, and these reservations of the New English combined to produce tensions between those appointed from England and the traditionally loyal population of the Pale, who repeatedly displayed their ability to exert influence at court and to effect the recall of a lord deputy whose policies did not meet with their approval. Such endeavors naturally produced friction between the Pale community and the English followers of the lord deputy, but a total breakdown in relations between Old and New English was avoided as successive governors were forced to combine whatever policy they favored for Ireland with some variant of the surrender and regrant strategy that had become *une idée fixe* with Old English reformers. Governors who wished to step outside this strategy usually advocated limited colonization of the Gaelic provinces, and an appropriate rationalization for this purpose was devised that traced a genealogical stemma for the Gaelic Irish, linking them with the most barbaric people known to western man.[4] But although

---

[3] Brendan Bradshaw, *The Irish Constitutional Revolution of the Sixteenth Century* (Cambridge, 1979).

[4] For the politics of successive governors in Ireland see Ciarán Brady, "The Government of Ireland, c. 1540–83" (Ph.D. diss., University of Dublin, 1980). The effort to trace a genealogy for the Gaelic Irish was carried furthest in Edmund Spenser, *A View of the Present State of*

the New English sought to justify a more harsh treatment of the Gaelic Irish than was permitted under the surrender and regrant formula, they were careful to mention that those in the provinces of Anglo-Norman descent who had become Gaelicized could be recalled to civility by stern but nonetheless persuasive methods. Sir Henry Sidney, whose rule was particularly associated with a hardening in attitude toward the Gaelic Irish, in offering an appraisal of the condition of Ireland in 1566 concluded that "all (doubtless) that is amiss is reformable, tractable and repairable, saving [the Gaelic chieftain] O'Neill, with this that the earls of Ormond and Desmond relinquish their pretended palatine liberties without which it is never to be looked for that Munster shall be reformed."[5]

Such tactful comments did much to reconcile the politically conscious of the Pale community with continued rule from England, and whenever the less tractable Old English lords in the provinces resisted the changes that were being forced upon them, they did so within the context of continued loyalty to the English crown.[6] The fact that most administrative and judicial posts in Dublin continued to be held by people of Irish birth also contributed to the maintenance of cordial relations between Old and New English, as did the fact that some English-born officials allowed themselves to become absorbed into the Pale community even to the extent of marrying into Old English families or joining the leaders of the Pale in their criticism of a particular lord deputy. This last development was facilitated by the conformity of most prominent Irish-born officials with the established church even when the general community of the Pale was displaying a conspicuous lack of enthusiasm for the Protestant state religion, and Old and New English were generally united by their mutual contempt for the Gaelic inhabitants of the island. Interest rather than principle thus explains the occasional breakdown in relations between the Pale community and their succession of governors; such estrangement usually occurred when the governor's call for financial support from the Pale toward the maintenance of the army exceeded the communal perception of what was just and equitable. Relations between the Dublin government and the Old English provincial lords were more frequently strained, but an irreparable collapse was

---

Ireland [1596], ed. W. L. Renwick (Oxford, 1970), but the idea was by no means original to Spenser as is evident from Nicholas Canny, *The Elizabethan Conquest of Ireland: A Pattern Established, 1565–76* (Hassocks, Sussex, and New York, 1976) esp. pp. 117–36. For the more general application of this concept see Michael T. Ryan, "Assimilating New Worlds in the Sixteenth and Seventeenth Centuries," *Comparative Studies in Society and History* 23 (1981):519–38.

[5] Sidney to Privy Council, 5 Apr. 1566 (Public Record Office [hereafter P.R.O.], S.P. 63/17/13, ff. 30–4).

[6] Canny, *The Elizabethan Conquest*, pp. 141–53.

also avoided there through the careful operation of compromise and tact on both sides.[7]

The sudden collapse, in 1579, of this tense but highly predictable relationship between government and community resulted in the alienation of both the Old English lords and the Pale community from all English-born servitors in the country. Events of the following year exacerbated an already difficult situation, so that by the mid-1580s it was acknowledged on both sides that mutual trust and understanding would never again be restored. Each side strove for total victory, and it was against this background and in this atmosphere of all-out verbal warfare that a sense of self-awareness was developed by New English settlers and officials in Ireland, a sense that was to make them increasingly conscious of their distinctiveness from both the apparently civil Old English and the clearly uncivil Gaelic Irish. Religious considerations—the increasing attachment of English servitors to a more stridently Protestant position and the gradual penetration of Counter-Reformation ideas within the Pale—no doubt contributed to the polarization between government and community, but of far greater importance was the chain of events that followed upon the outbreak of the second Desmond rebellion in 1579.

Gerald Fitzgerald, the fourteenth earl of Desmond, had resented what he regarded as the intrusion upon his authority by the recently erected provincial presidency in Munster, but he had been studied in his hostility and the government had made some tactful compromises to retain his allegiance. However, this tentative policy of compromise was abandoned by the government once the earl's cousin, James Fitzmaurice Fitzgerald, returned from the Continent with a papally appointed force and accompanied by Nicholas Sander, an English seminary priest charged with proclaiming the notorious papal bull *Regnans in Excelsis*. Initially the earl of Desmond, in accordance with his earlier actions, attempted to stand aloof from this rebellion against government authority in Ireland, but he was soon forced to make common cause with the rebels after his brother, John of Desmond, hitherto the government's most consistent supporter in the lordship, murdered Henry Davells, an important English official in the province, and thus symbolized his renunciation of allegiance to the crown. These developments indicated to the English-born officials in Dublin that a general revolt of the Irish population against English rule was in prospect.

[7] The most strident English-born critic of a lord deputy was John Parker, who became an accepted leader of the Pale community in opposition to Lord Deputy Sussex. On general developments see Brady, "The Government of Ireland, c. 1540–83," and on religious developments see Nicholas Canny, "Why the Reformation Failed in Ireland: Une question mal posée," *Journal of Ecclesiastical History* 30 (1979):423–50.

Further proof for the existence of a general conspiracy, master-minded by the pope, was provided by the outbreak in July 1580 of yet another religiously-inspired revolt, this time within the Pale itself and led by James Eustace, Viscount Baltinglass.[8] The coincidence of these two Old English revolts, led by men who could contemplate no further association with the English crown, provided the New English in Ireland with the opportunity to break the constraints that had previously limited the politics open to them. This opportunity should be seized, they urged, to make an example of those of English descent who had so flagrantly disobeyed the crown, and no further trust should be placed in individuals of Irish birth unless they were willing to prove their allegiance by publicly displaying an earnest commitment to the state religion.[9]

Such challenges, in addition to the ruthlessness with which the earl of Desmond and his followers were pursued, threw the entire Old English community into disarray. Obviously, their first concern was that the hitherto clear distinction between the respective treatments appropriate for rebellious Gaelic and Old English lords was now being set aside; but more particularly they were vitally concerned lest the plantation policy—previously reserved exclusively for the punishment of Gaelic Irish rebels—would be applied to them. Their fears on this second score were more than justified, because the New English officials made no secret of their plans for Munster. Quite typical of their advice was that proffered by Geoffrey Fenton in 1583, after the earl of Desmond had been killed, to the effect that the queen should:

introduce into Munster a mere English government, and make it an English Pale with the same profits and stability which the Pale yieldeth, and by that government being carried under a moderate ruler or magistrate of English birth, her highness in time may have entrance into the other remote parts of the realm, to reduce them after the line and square of Munster.[10]

Faced with such a prospect, the Old English recognized that their very survival as a privileged elite was now at stake. To ensure their survival, they sought even more vehemently to distinguish themselves from the Gaelic Irish, while at the same time striving to discredit all New English servitors in the eyes of the queen. The severe measure taken by Arthur Lord Grey de Wilton to suppress the rebellions in both Munster and the Pale provided the Old English with an ideal subject on which to base their allegations,

[8] *A New History of Ireland*, 3:105–15; Ciarán Brady, "Faction and the Origins of the Desmond Rebellion of 1579," *Irish Historical Studies* 22 (1981):289–312.

[9] See, e.g., "Book of Barnaby Rich on the Reformation in Ireland," 1589 (P.R.O., S.P. 63/144/35, ff. 104–113); Rich to Burghley, 20 May 1591 (P.R.O., S.P. 63/158/12, ff. 21–23).

[10] Geoffrey Fenton to Burghley, 6 Dec. 1583 (P.R.O., S.P. 63/106/4, f. 6).

and they pressed also for an official investigation of the conduct of Sir Richard Bingham as president in Connacht.[11] Essentially the Old English argued that far from being involved in conspiracy they were, in fact, well disposed toward the crown. However, they claimed that the Old English in the provinces were being goaded into rebellion by the harsh, ill-advised, and frequently extralegal actions of English officials and soldiers whose concern was self-advancement rather than the interests of the crown. This charge and the investigations that produced evidence to substantiate it were pursued with such persistence that the New English, thrown back on the defensive, were forced to provide elaborate justifications for their actions.

Because the Old English had taken the initiative, the New English authors were forced to defend themselves in the terms that had been selected by their opponents. The extent to which the terms of the exchange were set by the Old English is evident from a letter composed in 1581 by Sir Nicholas White, an Irish-born barrister who served in Dublin as Master of the Rolls during the late sixteenth century. Borrowing the medical metaphors so beloved by the New English when discussing the condition of Ireland, White contended that his long service in the country had taught him "by experience what things the stomach of that body can and cannot digest." The reform of the Gaelic Irish was, he admitted, a near impossibility unless severe measures were employed, and his purpose in writing was to persuade the queen that the "violent and warlike government" that might be appropriate for the Gaelic Irish should not be extended to the Old English population. The policy being pursued by the queen's officers in Ireland would, he averred (rather presciently, as it happens), "exhaust her Majesty's treasure, waste her revenue, depopulate the Pale, weaken her [Old] English nobility, that have been and may be made the security of this state, leave the wild Irish to their desires that be the peril thereof, and consume with misery of the wars her soldiers which she sendeth hither." Among these possible consequences, the most serious in White's eyes was that of losing the traditional allegiance of the Old English nobility, and he emphasized "what a strong garrison without pay the seed of English blood hath made to her crown since their first planting, which are easier reformed than supplanted and more to be esteemed for the priority of their tenures than others that seek by posteriority to go before."[12]

The "others" here referred to by White were of course the New English

---

[11] On Connacht during this period, see Bernadette Cunningham, "Political and Social Change in the Lordships of Clanricard and Thomond, 1569–1641" (M.A. thesis, University College, Galway, 1979).

[12] Nicholas White to Burghley, 23 Dec. 1581 (P.R.O., S.P. 63/87/55, ff. 151ʳ–152ᵛ).

servitors, and as well as providing details of their corruption and insensitivity, White questioned the motives that underlay their forward military policy. Those who advised the queen "to spare for no cost to translate this kingdom of the new" were likened by White to "artisans that persuade owners of ancient houses to pull them down for altering of fashion, wherein they seek more their own setting a work than to do the owners' profit." As White warmed to his theme he contrasted himself, a native of Ireland who through years of service had proven his concern for his country, with the New English "malcontents" who would "seek to better [their] state by change." He concluded with the aphorism that "innovations hath been in all ages accounted dangerous, and the busiest men that way be not the profitablest ministers." White's words were carefully chosen; in accusing the New English of being innovators he in effect identified them with the political philosophy of Machiavelli, which he knew to be repugnant to the queen and her advisors in England. The queen should, he claimed, avoid committing the government of Ireland "to such as cannot govern themselves," lest it lose her the loyalty of her subjects; she should avoid "the rooting out of ancient nobility" lest it alter the situation whereby she was "of all her nobility feared for love, and not loved for fear"; she should avoid the appointment of "judges that be bloody" lest their severe judgments "work things of dangerous effects"; and he warned that the queen should particularly avoid applying "the uttermost of her correction" to those who were wanting in duty lest "it may so happen that, thinking all law were ended there might arise other men" more difficult to control. In short, although pleading the merits of "a temperate and peaceable government," White clearly hoped that by drawing attention to the chaos that would result from innovation, he could deflect the queen from the policy being recommended to her by her English-born officials in Ireland.[13]

Some seem to have been even more explicit than White in suggesting that the New English were being guided by the godless Machiavelli; William Herbert, a New English author, was so incensed that he repudiated the charge of "being Italianated," stating there was "nothing more swerving from [his] conscience and course of life."[14] Denials, however, could avail them little; the New English could not conceal the fact that innovation was now their aim and necessity their guiding principle. This in turn explains their need to argue that a policy of innovation was dictated and justified by the moral imperatives of the particular situation in which they found themselves.

[13] Ibid.

[14] Sir William Herbert to Sir Valentine Browne, 1 Jan. 1588/9 (P.R.O., S.P. 63/140/14).

There is nothing to suggest that charges such as those of Nicholas White did anything to deflect the New English from their intended course of action; but they did force them to justify themselves and, in doing so, hastened the process by which they came to define their position in relation to other groups in the country. As before, they continued to revile the Gaelic Irish for their barbarism. Andrew Trollope, writing under the pen name Republicae Benevolus, surpassed all previous writers in his depiction of their barbarous traits. Trollope concluded, on the basis of his description, that the Irish were "not thrifty and civil or human creatures, but heathen or rather savage and brute beasts"; he then contended that they were even "worse than dogs, for dogs do but their kind," whereas the Irish who had "degenerated from all manhood [and] humanity" were "very apt, subtle and politic and very stout in performing of it." The real novelty of this invective lay not in its ferocity but in the fact that for the first time it was extended to all the inhabitants of the country. This was hinted at by the use of the term degenerate, which was usually applied only to those of the Old English who had adopted Gaelic customs, but Trollope soon made it clear that even those Old English who lived after a civil fashion were included within his condemnation. In the first of his two treatises, for example, he began conventionally by exempting the residents of "the walled towns" from his blanket condemnation of the Irish, but he conveniently ignored this exclusion as he accused the Old English generally of being intent on "treason or mischief" and of fostering a "burning hatred and malice against all the English nation." Support for this charge was provided by reference to an attack made by a mob in Waterford, significantly regarded as "one of the civilest towns in Ireland," upon the wife of Sir William Drury, then lord deputy of Ireland, and to the popular expectation in Dublin that "the throats of all the English nation" would be "cut at one instant."[15]

This "evidence" was sufficient to satisfy Trollope that the outward appearance of civility presented by the Old English was no more than a veneer to cover their evil intent. Those who attended Protestant services but declined communion were declared hypocrites, while those Old English officials who did partake of communion, and even Old English bishops, were still found inadequate because some of their relatives were notorious Catholics. But for Trollope the true measure of the unreliability of the Old English as subjects was their recent drift to the Counter-Reformation; this explains his remark that he would "undertake sooner reform of religion . . . among the wild Irish than the English pale."[16]

[15] Andrew Trollope to Walsingham, 12 Sept. 1585 (P.R.O., S.P. 63/85/39, ff. 96–102'). The descriptive passage occurs at f. 99'.

[16] The same theme as above was continued by Trollope in Trollope to Burghley, 26 Oct. 1587 (P.R.O., S.P. 63/131/64, ff. 200'–204'). This second letter concentrated more on the religious inadequacy of the Old English than on the barbarism of the Gaelic Irish.

Charges such as Trollope's were by no means exceptional in those tracts composed at the end of the sixteenth century. It is significant that Trollope's sentiments were repeated in Edmund Spenser's A *View of the Present State of Ireland* (1596), which might be regarded as a synthesis of the opinions of the New English in Ireland during these decades. Like Trollope, Spenser devoted considerable attention to the barbaric condition of the Gaelic Irish, but he said little that was new and his comments are echoed in literally scores of compositions by English or Old English authors from the time of Giraldus Cambrensis forward. In identifying a series of stages of social development and in situating the Irish, with their supposed progenitors the Scythians, at the least-developed stage, Spenser was merely advancing a notion that had become a commonplace among those engaged in the conquest of Ireland during the previous thirty years. Of more recent provenance, however, was his contention that many of the Old English population had degenerated from their original placement of about midway on the scale of social development to a position so lowly that it could be concluded that "the chiefest abuses which are now in that realm are grown from the English, and the English-that-were are now much more lawless and licentious than the very wild Irish."[17] Spenser was suggesting that the Old English who had become degenerate were more formidable opponents and less susceptible to reform that the Gaelic Irish, who were barbarians by descent. Such views were consistent with general European ethnographic thinking of the time, but Spenser then followed Trollope to argue that even the Old English of the Pale and the towns were far from being the civil men they appeared to be. He offered several explanations for this, but the most telling of his contentions was that their ancestors, the Anglo-Norman invaders of Ireland, had been only half-civil and certainly had not been capable of promoting a civilizing mission. Spenser concluded that the only ones in Ireland who were in fact capable of promoting the uplift of the Gaelic population of Ireland were those recently arrived from England, because it had been "but even the other day since England grew civil."[18]

The immediate purpose behind this attack on the Old English was to denigrate that element of the population of Ireland who had the most influ-

---

[17] Spenser, *View*, p. 63. Hyphens added for clarity. He returns to the same theme on p. 151.

[18] Ibid., p. 67; Ryan, "Assimilating New Worlds in the Sixteenth and Seventeenth Centuries." For a contextual analysis of Spenser's *View* see Nicholas Canny, "Edmund Spenser and the Development of an Anglo-Irish Identity," in *The Yearbook of English Studies: Colonial and Imperial Themes, Special Number* 13 (1983):1–19. A more recent appraisal of Spenser's work, which is at variance with the interpretation offered here is presented in Ciaran Brady, "Spenser's Irish Crisis: Humanism and Experience in the 1590s," *Past and Present*, no. 111 (1986):17–49. For a reaction to Brady's position, see Nicholas Canny, "Edmund Spenser as Political Theorist," *Past and Present*, forthcoming.

ence with the queen and her government in England and who had recently shown themselves to be bitter opponents of the New English presence in Ireland. But by denying the Old English the claim to be civil, the authors of these treatises were also discounting them as would-be reformers of the Gaelic Irish; Spenser's further effort to reveal the shortcomings of the surrender and regrant strategy was merely intended to give strength to his argument. The essential inadequacy was, he asserted, that it proceeded from the false assumption that law could be employed as an instrument for the uplift of a people who lived in a corrupt environment. Spenser argued that each legal system was suited only to the particular society that produced it. The drive to achieve the improvement of any degenerate people should, therefore, begin with the forceful alteration of the corrupt environment that bound people to their depraved condition, and in the particular case of Ireland Spenser outlined a series of stages that he considered necessary to release the population from being thralls to their lords. Only if the bonds that bound men to their masters were shattered, he contended, would the way be open for the implementation of a reform that would of necessity be extended to the seemingly civil Old English as well as to the barbaric Gaelic Irish.[19]

Spenser's was a particularly methodical account, matched only by the treatise *Croftus Sive de Hibernia Liber* composed in Ciceronian Latin by William Herbert, a fellow planter with Spenser in Munster and his associate on the provincial council of that province. For most of the New English authors the shortcomings of the surrender and regrant policy were self-evident, and they drew up and recommended a clearly defined program of action. This may be termed radical, for it involved the erection of a completely new commonwealth to replace the corrupt society that they sought to destroy. Metaphors abounded in these discourses: although one original spirit likened Ireland to an old cloak that had been mended with such frequency that it would bear with no further repair, most contented themselves with surgical or horticultural terms and proposed "cutting off the rotten and infected parts with swords."[20]

Such radical proposals were justified because by representing Ireland as a place where no civil population existed, the authors could make a plausible case for a suspension of the constraints that would operate in a properly ordered commonwealth. The first innovation they called for was the summary dismissal of all Old English officials who held positions of trust in the

---

[19] Canny, "Edmund Spenser and the Development of an Anglo-Irish Identity."

[20] The quotation comes from Anonymous, "Discourse for the Government of Ireland," c. 1581 (P.R.O., S.P. 63/87/81, f. 28). For a printed edition of the Herbert text see William Herbert, *Croftus Sive de Hibernia Liber*, ed. W. E. Buckley (London, 1887).

government of the country. It was even obliquely suggested that the parliament in Dublin be suspended and that Ireland be governed directly from London through the English-born officials in Dublin. Most argued that religion should become the true test of loyalty, thus leaving open the possibility of having some Irish-born officials in Dublin, but a minority considered even this too daring. They insisted that Irish birth ought to preclude government service because "the chronicles and common experience doth make it manifest that there hath never been Irishman in authority which upon trial had proved a true subject." In short, with only minor differences all agreed that Ireland would never be reformed until "true English hearts would rule there."[21]

But while insisting that only they should bear responsibility for government in Ireland, the New English were able to justify their stepping outside the law in pursuit of their reform program by arguing that they were a small unwanted group, surrounded by enemies whose plans meant their ruination. Richard Beacon, another colleague of Spenser's on the provincial council, devoted particular attention to the defense of Sir Richard Bingham, who had frankly acknowledged that as president of Connacht, he had gone outside the law to prosecute those whom he had suspected to be plotting insurrection against the state. In Beacon's allegorical account of this episode, Bingham was likened to a Roman general, forced by necessity to take summary action against the rebellious Gauls who, if given time, would have been able to achieve his overthrow.[22]

Necessity was also invoked by Spenser as a justification for the severe measures taken by Lord Grey de Wilton in his treatment of the rebels in Munster. In defending him, however, Spenser was careful to insist that there was no basis for the charge that Grey had been a "bloody man" who regarded the queen's subjects as "no more than dogs." Far from it, claimed Spenser, who portrayed Grey as an exemplary and clement ruler who had chosen to employ the sword rather than the halter when the circumstances of the rebellion and the crimes of rebels would have fully justified the widespread use of hanging. The devastation of the province of Munster and the frightening loss of population through famine, which Spenser depicted in touching and graphic detail, was not, he said, a consequence of Grey's action but a result rather of the perversity of the rebel leaders, who chose to have their followers starve rather than surrender to the government forces.[23]

The New English devoted much attention to the defense of both

[21] Trollope to Walsingham; see note 15 above.
[22] Richard Beacon, *Solon his Follie* (Oxford, 1594).
[23] Spenser, *View*, pp. 104–106.

171

Bingham and Lord Grey de Wilton, because on their vindication depended the explanation and justification of New English involvement in Ireland. One measure of the popularity of those views (usually associated with classically trained scholars such as Spenser, Herbert, and Beacon) among the less well educated of the New English is the advancement of similar rationalization in cruder form by John Merbury, a captain who served under Bingham in Connacht. Eschewing metaphor and classical illusion, Merbury came quickly to the point. "It was necessary," he wrote, "to make war in Connacht," and he justified Bingham's taking the offensive because war was the means "to have that province, and her realm of Ireland replenished with people." "Rigour," wrote Merbury, "hath its times in all government" and its employment in the particular circumstances was justified because the number who would suffer was "so small in respect of the multitude of the rest, that in good policies and in the use of many old commonwealths the lives of so few have been thought well given for the preservation of so many." Realizing, however, that this robust secular argument would provoke moral objections, Merbury threw up the rhetorical question whether it was "against Christian policy for the safety of all the rest to punish by justice and utterly to root out a few inveterate tyrants, ravening robbers, and violent murderers of mankind?" The question required no answer for Merbury, and he was able to conclude that the government was required by moral no less than by pragmatic considerations to dispense with due legal process whenever circumstance dictated that this best served its purpose.[24]

Although Merbury appeared to recognize that conflict could occur between the moral code by which officers of the crown should always be bound and the secular expedients that seemed to provide a solution to their difficulties, others would not admit of even this possibility. Some went so far as to suggest that no tension would exist as long as men were guided by logic in choosing their ends. Sir John Perrott, who served as lord deputy of Ireland from 1584 to 1588, coolly remarked that when discussing secular expedients "a man should set aside God, who in government admitteth no policy that is besides, much less directly against, His will," but he then demonstrated that, when argued "with good reason," the policy that would emerge would be in full conformity with Christian principles.[25]

This argument proved the most compelling for the New English, who were satisfied that by engaging in the innovative and revolutionary actions they had been accused of by their Old English critics, they were in fact ful-

[24] Captain John Merbury on Revolt in Connacht, 27 Sept. 1589 (P.R.O., S.P. 63/146/57, ff. 177–79).
[25] E.C.S., *The Government of Ireland under Sir John Perrott, 1584-88* (London, 1626), sig. D¹–D².

filling God's purpose. "The least duty" that was owed by the New English "to God, her Majesty or the commonwealth" was, said Trollope,

earnestly to pray to Almighty God, and to do the best they can that it might please her highness and her honourable council to take some good order that Ireland may be inhabited with Christian and civil people and that the youth thereof may be brought up in the knowledge of God and His word, some godly exercises and occupations, or to labour honestly thereby to get their living, and that all Irish councillors, Irish judges and all Irish officers and especially which have any thing to do touching her Majesty or the commonwealth may be abolished.

Failure on their part to fulfill this duty would, claimed Trollope, provoke God's vengeance, not only on the New English in Ireland but also upon "those magistrates under whose government God hath committed" the inhabitants of Ireland. Even as things stood, claimed Trollope, there could be "no doubt" that God was offended with successive English monarchs for their toleration of barbarism in one of their realms "which if they did inhabit and govern would be restored to order, and thus to prosperity."[26]

It had been one of the tacit assumptions underlying all English observations on Ireland since the twelfth century that Ireland was well endowed with natural wealth. However, a new element now crept into this old theme and it was argued that the failure of the inhabitants of the country to exploit these resources was further proof of their barbarism. A definition of barbarism in terms of a people's apparent inability to make use of the bounty with which God had provided them was employed by every European colonizing power. The English in North America, as Michael Zuckerman shows above, condemned the Indians for their supposed incapacity to make adequate use of nature's potential, although they were quite clearly far better husbandmen than the colonists themselves. The same account of what it was to be a barbarian had also been advanced in a more general context by Thomas More in his *Utopia*, so it is not surprising to see it emerge in relation to Ireland in Spenser's *View*. As always, however, Trollope was the most forthright on the subject. We can be certain that his was not an isolated opinion, because points taken up by him were developed independently by John Perrott. There were, claimed Trollope,

as many good blessings of God in Ireland as in most realms in the world, as good ground, rich mines, good waters, well replenished with all kind of fish, good moulds and many woods, which notwithstanding the people which are there (having respect to their estates) (which are not half a quarter of the number of those which England continuously maintaineth) live very hardly, yea the most part most miserably and many have and many more would have starved for food (albeit that many

[26] Trollope to Walsingham; see note 15 above.

live with grass in the field like brute beasts and spend no corn) if great store of vict-ual had not been sent over thither out of England.[27]

But while arguing this backwardness as proof of Irish barbarism, the New English were able to cite the material benefits that would derive from the implementation of the proposed conquest and colonization of Ireland as evidence of its godly purpose. Lest men should think his recommendations exceedingly destructive and negative, Perrott emphasized the fact that he did not seek after any "extirpation, but rather that all might be saved that were good for the country to be saved." Thus, in Perrott's opinion, nothing should be permitted to stand in the way of their proposed course of action because the existing condition of Ireland was "neither godly, nor honour-able" whereas "a reformation will breed competent wealth, and competent wealth containeth men in a liking [of] obedience where desperate beggary runneth headlong to rebellion."[28]

In focusing attention on the material and moral improvements that were in prospect for Ireland and by contrasting Ireland's glorious future with its shameful and ignominious past, Perrott was careful to draw a veil over the questionable means that were necessary for the attainment of these desira-ble ends. Others, notably Spenser and Herbert, were not so reticent. These were admittedly insistent that they strove for nothing less than the uplift of the Irish to that level of civility already attained by Englishmen, but in the final analysis they offered no apologies for the draconian measures that they believed necesssary for the attainment of this laudable objective. These measures, according to Spenser's prescription, involved uprooting the peo-ple from their traditional places of habitation, breaking up and dispersing the traditional kinship groups, and resettling them as individuals within the new social and political framework where, "in short time" each would "learn quite to forget his Irish nation." All of this was seen to be a necessary preliminary to the launching of an educational program that would then ensure that the next generation of the Irish would be indistinguishable from the English in language, religion, and morals.

The alternative to this strategy was described by Spenser as the policy of the halter. This, as its name suggests, would have involved the execution of large numbers of the Irish as undeserving or incapable of regeneration and the assignment of the remainder to a permanently inferior position seg-regated from their English overlords. This policy, which in fact had been

---

[27] Trollope to Walsingham; see note 15 above, f. 98. For the advancement of a similar util-itarian opinion in More's *Utopia* see Thomas More, *The Best State of a Commonwealth and the New Island of Utopia* in *The Complete Works of Thomas More*, ed. Edward Sturtz and J. H. Hex-ter (New Haven, 1965), 4:137.

[28] E.C.S., *The Government of Ireland under Sir John Perrott*, sig. A⁴, B³, D².

advocated by several Englishmen who had had dealings with Ireland, was now rejected on the grounds that it was the counsel "rather of desperate men far driven, to wish the utter ruin of that which they cannot redress, than of grave counsellors which ought to think nothing so hard but that through wisdom may be mastered and subdued, since the poet says that the wise man shall rule even over the stars, much more over the earth."[29] Here we see the ultimate statement of humanist purpose; and for those who might have doubted whether such ambitious aims could be accomplished within a reasonable period of time, Herbert solved this difficulty by advancing the educational and missionary endeavor by several stages. This was possible in his scheme because he recognized both the importance and the possibility of training missionaries to preach in the Irish language and of translating the Bible and religious discourses into Irish as well. In stating the necessity for these religious measures and in giving them practical demonstration on his Munster estate, Herbert was of course merely exploiting the Irish language as an instrument to hasten raising the Irish population to a level of civility equal to that of the English, at which point presumably they would abandon their native language in favor of that of the conqueror.[30]

In this the English in Ireland were also pursuing, whether in emulation of or in response to a similar set of circumstances, a policy that was an integral part of every European colonial enterprise. For the Spaniards, the French, the English, and the Portuguese in America, no less than for the English in Ireland, the need to transform the indigenous inhabitants of the land they occupied into civil people was held to be crucial to any attempt to mold a new civil society. Conquest, as the conquerors saw it, involved eventual acculturation; all conquering groups, like the English in Ireland, could legitimize their actions in Christian and humanist terms. Yet no matter how they might argue that they were being guided or even inspired by humanist principles, there was no denying the fact that the task in which the New English were engaged and the measures that they sought to pursue set them apart from their counterparts in England as well as from all elements of the Irish population. The New English had seen themselves as distinct from the Gaelic Irish even before their arrival in Ireland and they had distanced themselves from the Old English by rejecting their claims to be the historical promoters of English standards in the country. The elaborate rationalizations advanced by the New English served their purpose in vindicating their actions to the government in England and also offered some

---

[29] Spenser, *View*, pp. 140–50; quotations at pp. 155–56 and 2.
[30] Herbert, *Croftus*, esp. pp. 54–55.

solace to the tender consciences of those engaged upon the gruesome final episode of the Elizabethan conquest of Ireland. But by depicting themselves as conscious promoters of revolutionary change the New English were also isolating themselves from the English moral community, where no matter how it might be disguised, innovation was synonymous with social dislocation and was therefore regarded with horror. In these ways the ideas that the New English in Ireland adopted under the force of circumstances served also to provide them with a fresh identity; they came to see themselves as a distinct people engaged in a special mission barely understood by those resident in England.

Such arguments and justifications served their purpose in sustaining the ever-growing number of English who became actively involved in implementing the final conquest of the country during the closing decades of Queen Elizabeth's reign. By the 1590s the number of English in Ireland had increased from some hundreds to several thousands, and most of these were now soldiers or landowners and tenants on confiscated land rather than officials. But although the proportion of officials among the English-born population had declined, their actual numbers had so increased that they virtually monopolized the posts in the Dublin and provincial administrations. Also by the late sixteenth century a significant number of Englishmen had been appointed to the bishoprics in the Irish state church; and Englishmen or the sons of English-born parents who had been educated at the English universities or at the recently established Trinity College, Dublin, held almost all the church benefices in those parts of the country where plantations had been established. Moreover, the army was partially disbanded after the cessation of hostilities in 1603 and many of the demobilized soldiers were welcomed as tenants on the plantation estates. Further opportunity for settlement in Ireland was provided after 1610 when the government undertook the plantation of six escheated counties in Ulster, and between then and 1641 the English settlers there were joined by as many as 30,000 Scots who were not subjects of the same ruling monarch.[31] There was, at the same time, a substantial migration from England into the planted areas of Munster and a migration of English, Scots, and even Dutch

[31] For these developments, see A New History of Ireland, vol. 3, esp. pp. 168–232; Raymond Gillespie, Colonial Ulster: The Settlement of East Ulster, 1600–1641 (Cork, 1985); D. B. Quinn, "The Munster Plantation: Problems and Opportunities," Cork Historical and Archaeological Society Journal 71 (1966):19–40; M. Perceval Maxwell, The Scottish Migration to Ulster in the Reign of James I (London, 1973); Nicholas Canny, "The Irish Background to Penn's Experiment," in The World of William Penn, ed. R. S. Dunn and M. M. Dunn (Philadelphia, 1986), pp. 139–56; Michael MacCarthy-Morrogh, The Munster Plantation: English Migration to Southern Ireland, 1583–1641 (Oxford, 1986); Nicholas Canny, From Reformation to Restoration: Ireland 1534–1660 (Dublin, 1987), esp. pp. 108–187.

into all areas, whether planted or not, where the landowners wished to increase their incomes from rent or wished to transform the environment to an English appearance. The settler population in Ireland was thus growing appreciably through the first half of the seventeenth century and was in some places, particularly in planted areas of Munster, becoming self-sufficient. Nevertheless there was a palpable sense of failure among the settlers; and their more perceptive spokesmen were aware that the recommended conquest had fallen short of full implementation because whole tracts of the country, including most of the provinces of Leinster and Connacht, remained under the control of Old English proprietors or Gaelic landowners who had remained loyal to the crown during the decades of revolt.

For their part, the Old English naturally made much of the assistance they had provided the government in suppressing the most recent revolt. They argued more forcefully than they had in the sixteenth century that their attachment to Catholicism was entirely compatible with their loyalty to the crown. Such professions rang hollow, however, when account was taken of the recent influence of the continentally trained Counter-Reformation missionaries in Ireland. Their influence, which had been greatest at the upper levels of Old English society, meant that the Old English landowners found themselves unable in conscience to attend occasionally at services of the state church as their fathers and grandfathers had done. As a means of further bolstering their position the Old English denounced the self-aggrandizement of the British settlers and administrators in Ireland; they claimed that it was these people rather than the crown who had benefited from the forceful pursuit of a plantation policy.[32]

These developments explain why the debate that had taken place between spokesmen of the Old and New English groups in the sixteenth century continued into the following one, and why opinions such as those advanced by Spenser and Trollope continued to have relevance for the settler population in Ireland long after the conquest had been implemented. Even recent arrivals who had not participated in the conquest saw the usefulness of the opinions of Spenser and his contemporaries when they sought to defend themselves against the barbs of their Old English adversaries. The best means of defense was obviously to attack, and they were best able to discredit their opponents by reiterating the need to persist with the conquest of the country until all surviving proprietors had been forcefully removed.

[32] Aidan Clarke, "Colonial Identity in Early Seventeenth-Century Ireland," in *Nationality and the Pursuit of National Independence*, ed. T. W. Moody (Belfast, 1978), pp. 57–71; D. F. Cregan, "The Social and Cultural Background of a Counter-Reformation Episcopate 1618–60," in *Studies in Irish History Presented to R. Dudley Edwards*, ed. A. Cosgrove and D. MacCartney (Dublin, 1979), pp. 85–117.

The most articulate of these authors was Sir John Davies, successively Irish solicitor-general (1603–1606) and attorney-general (1606–1619). Davies presented his opinions to King James in his 1612 treatise, *A Discovery of the True Causes why Ireland was Never entirely Subdued, and Brought under Obedience of the Crown of England, until his Majesty's Happy Reign.*[33]

Davies, as is clear from the title, chose a historical framework for his discourse, but his concern was far from antiquarian. In revealing his discovery of past failures he was in fact explaining how the recent military success might be turned to the crown's advantage. Davies believed "the principal mark and effect of a perfect conquest" was the extension of "laws to a conquered people" but, like Spenser, he did not think this development was possible until the people had first been brought to subjection through military means. This had first been achieved in Ireland, he believed, by King Henry II, but those who had accompanied that king to Ireland had refused to take advantage of the situation and by denying law to the Irish this early group of settlers

did cause a perpetual war between the nations: which continued four hundred and odd years, and would have lasted to the world's end; if in the end of Queen Elizabeth's reign, the Irishry had not been broken and conquered by the sword, and since the beginning of his Majesty's reign had not been protected and governed by the law.[34]

But an even more alarming consequence of the failure of these original settlers to pursue the conquest to the limit was, claimed Davies, that by permitting Gaelic law to continue and by tolerating the corrupt environment that produced it, they had themselves succumbed to that corruption and had become "slaves to that nation which they did intend to conquer." This belief provided Davies with reason for joining with Trollope and his associates in rounding upon the Old English, whose "pride, covetousness, and ill counsel" had been "the chief impediments of the final conquest of Ireland."[35]

There was no doubt in the mind of Davies that the conquest pursued by Queen Elizabeth had made "a barbarous country . . . capable of good government." In acknowledging this, however, Davies was equally convinced that if, in the aftermath of the conquest, the country was "not well planted and governed" it would "eftsoons return to the former barbarism." Furthermore, Davies believed that the plans laid by himself for "a mixed plantation

---

[33] Sir John Davies, *A Discovery of the True Causes why Ireland was Never entirely Subdued, and Brought under Obedience of the Crown of England, until the beginning of His Majesty's Happy Reign* (London, 1612).

[34] Davies, *Discovery*, pp. 100, 112.

[35] Ibid., pp. 150, 144, 164–65.

of British and Irish" in the province of Ulster would produce a more prosperous and harmonious outcome there than any previous effort at colonization in Ireland, and he derived particular satisfaction from the eagerness with which the general population of the country came forward to claim the benefit of English common law in the aftermath of war.[36] He was, however, sufficiently a realist to recognize that this was but a superficial compliance and that true obedience would have to await a comprehensive conquest of all the provinces and the educational and missionary endeavor that would follow it.

The experience gained by Davies in Ulster certainly gave him reason to believe that the plantation scheme would produce the beneficial effects expected of it, and it was on the basis of his experience in that province that he permitted himself to "conceive a hope that the next generation would in tongue and heart and every way else become English so as there will be no difference or distinction but the Irish sea betwixt us."[37] Belying this optimism of Davies was, however, his distrust of those parts of the country that had escaped the full thrust of confiscation. Like Spenser before him, Davies was anxious lest these groups would "assemble, and conspire, and rise in multitudes against the crown" or would "even now in the time of peace" frustrate the development of an impartial jury system "by reason of this general kindred and consanguinity."[38] This admission that Spenser's prescription for reform had not yet been implemented in every detail was an acknowledgment by Davies that all could still be lost because, if left in a corrupt environment, the newly established settlers would become contaminated and would degenerate as all previous English settlers in Ireland had done.

Although Davies merely hinted at this prospect, it was stated explicitly by one of his contemporaries, obviously a planter in Munster, who donned the mantle of Edmund Spenser under the pseudonym E.S. and presented King James with "A Survey of the Present Estate of Ireland, Anno 1615." The author's purpose was to demonstrate that conditions in Munster in the seventeenth century were little different from what they had been in the previous one and that the settlers who had recently been established there had, like all previous waves of English settlers in Ireland, "by marriage with the Irish, or by purchase or custom become mere Irish again." This nativization had occurred, claimed E.S., because the educational and missionary aspects of the program of conquest had been neglected and because the settlers had been placed in an environment still dominated by the indigenous

---

[36] Ibid., pp. 4–5, 281, 264–67.
[37] Ibid., pp. 271–72.
[38] Ibid., pp. 172–73.

lords who gave lip service to English law, cynically exploiting it to strengthen their already excessive authority over their traditional follow- ers. Worse still, the king's "lenyty and the people's innate obstinacy and repugnancy in matters moral and divine" had made it possible for the Irish lords in Munster to provide support and patronage to seminary priests who, in turn, took it upon themselves to adjudicate on disputes among the king's subjects and so hold them back from enjoying the benefits of royal justice.[39]

The promotion of common law, the advancement of English to displace Irish as the dominant language of the country, and the progress of the Ref- ormation in Ireland were all thought to be hindered by these impediments to reform. Even more disastrous, in the opinion of E.S., was the decay of the recently established plantation in Munster, and he contended that if any trace of that plantation was to survive it was essential that the settlers be strictly segregated from the natives until the latter had been freed from the tyranny of their lords and had been exposed to the full thrust of the pro- jected educational and reform effort. Failing that, claimed E.S., there was nothing in prospect but a relapse of Ireland to its former barbarism.[40]

Matthew de Renzy, another contemporary planter, said much the same thing, but his views were jaundiced by his experience as a settler in the Gaelic Irish Midlands. A German by birth, de Renzy had come to Ireland after he had failed as a merchant in Amsterdam and London. He was en- gaged during the years 1613-1620 in attempting to promote a plantation in the Irish midlands. He soon came into conflict with Sir John MacCoghlan, a local lord of Gaelic background who had remained loyal to the govern- ment and had even conformed to the established church during the late six- teenth century, and who consequently still retained title to his estates dur- ing the reign of James I. We know of de Renzy's views through his extensive correspondence with successive governors in Ireland rather than through any formal treatise. The point that he constantly stressed was that, for all his professions of loyalty and religious conformity, MacCoghlan was still a dynastic lord who sought to mediate between the king's subjects and their monarch and was, therefore, inimical to the English presence in the coun- try. In order to substantiate his claim, de Renzy took the trouble to acquire a knowledge of literary Irish, and from his study of the classical Irish texts was in a better position to contend that anyone who fostered Gaelic culture

<hr>

[39] "A Survey of the Present Estate of Ireland, Anno 1615, Addressed to His Most Excellent Majesty James the First . . . by His Most Humble Subject, E.S." (Huntington Library, San Marino, Calif., El. 1746), ff. 11, 18–19, 9. This vellum-bound tract was obviously the work of someone very familiar with developments in Munster. The tract was the property of Sir Thomas Ellesmere, as was a manuscript copy of Spenser's *View* in similar binding.

[40] Ibid., f. 14.

was an enemy of civilization. Equipped with this insight, de Renzy argued that if the military effort of the previous century was to bear fruit it was necessary that lords such as MacCoghlan be swept aside. If this was not done, de Renzy saw nothing in prospect but the degeneration of the recent English settlers, and he was convinced that this process was already under way. As far as he was concerned, the main grounds for anxiety were the materialism and drunkenness of the Protestant clergy; the competitiveness of the planters toward one another; and the generally unsuitable characters who were being attracted to settle in Ireland, being, as he put it, "the scum of a nation." All of this pointed to the need for continuing with the conquest of Ireland. He argued, moreover, that if any trace of the earlier achievements were to remain, it would be necessary for the settlers in Ireland to withdraw from the corrupting environment and develop a nucleated settlement, or "little Bohemia," within what was still a predominantly barbaric society.[41]

No doubt a desire for the personal gain that would accrue from further confiscation lay behind these outbursts against Irish lords; equally it is clear that these self-appointed spokesmen of the planters in Ireland were seeking to undermine the claims for a privileged position under the crown that were being put forward by the surviving Catholic landowners in Ireland during the first half of the seventeenth century;[42] but a rehearsal of the arguments of Spenser and his contemporaries served also to establish an identity and sense of purpose for the English who had made their careers in Ireland. Now that peace had been restored to Ireland it was important that those who had recently settled there should be recognized as distinct from the remainder of the Irish population, at least until the projected uplift of the native population had been implemented. Denunciation of the native population such as that offered by E.S. and de Renzy clearly served this purpose, but the New English were painfully aware that their further claim to be engaged in a continuing revolution would have little meaning for their countrymen who remained at home and who had no immediate knowledge of circumstances in Ireland. This point was put specifically by the planter/official Sir William Parsons in 1622 when he remarked:

[41] This account of the views of de Renzy is based principally on the analysis provided in Brian Mac Cuarta, "Newcomers in the Irish Midlands, 1540–1641," pp. 49–88, esp. 63–64. This study of de Renzy's "colonial mind" is based principally on the relevant section of the de Renzy mss (P.R.O., S.P. 46/90, ff. 8ʳ–176ᵛ). The hostility expressed by de Renzy toward McCoghlan was by no means exceptional, as is clear from the difficulty experienced by the O'Haras of Annaghmore in winning acceptance among the ranks of the settler population in Connacht. See Thomas Bartlett, "The O'Haras of Annaghmore, c. 1600–c. 1800: Survival and Revival," *Irish Economic and Social History* 9 (1982):34–52.

[42] On the negotiations of the Old English see Aidan Clarke, *The Old English in Ireland, 1625–42* (London, 1966).

It might be thought unfit to take such a course [as he was recommending] in England, or any country governed by any certain law; but the case much differs in England: though some be ill yet the people generally are sound in the root. In Ireland they reject laws and have many times in several ages whole counties and whole provinces at once renounced their obedience, little weighing the king's expense of millions in a season to make them quiet.[43]

The claims for the degeneracy of the recent settlers in Ireland were greatly exaggerated by those who wished to alert the government in England to the need for completing their program of conquest and colonization. But although such claims did succeed in arousing interest in Ireland at the English court, the spokesmen for the settlers did not succeed in persuading either the king or his officials of the need for persisting with the conquest. On the contrary, the crown was satisfied that Ireland was at peace, and it was reluctant to approve any further large-scale plantation lest it provoke unrest among the compliant Old English and Gaelic proprietors. Insofar as the government at Whitehall was willing to countenance any further confiscation in Ireland, it was insistent that this should be on a limited scale and carried out merely with a view to rewarding courtiers and favorites who had no intention of residing in Ireland but would satisfy themselves with collecting rent from the traditional occupiers of the confiscated lands. This made it clear to the New English settlers that the king and his officials were not convinced by their rhetoric, but worse was to follow when it became evident that the government in London intended to turn the information that was available to them on conditions in Ireland against the planters themselves. What had been said of the developing degeneracy of the recently established plantations was taken not as proof that further confiscation was necessary but rather as evidence that the plantation conditions had not been complied with. Furthermore, once this point had been recognized in London, it was realized that the failure of the planters in Ireland to fulfill the conditions that had been prescribed made them liable to dispossession or fines. The opportunity for profit that this presented to the crown was not lost on the officials at Whitehall, who were becoming ever more concerned that Ireland had never produced the financial return to the exchequer that had been blithely promised by those who had first advocated the conquest of the country.[44] This realization prompted a series of investigations into the management of Irish affairs and of all recent plan-

---

[43] "Reasons for the Plantations in Ireland by Sir W[illiam] P[arsons], 16 May 1622" (British Library [hereafter B.L.], Harley Ms. 3792, ff. 26–31, esp. f. 31).

[44] This subject is treated in Terence Ranger, "Richard Boyle and the Making of an Irish Fortune, 1588–1614," *Irish Historical Studies* 10 (1957):257–97 and ibid., "Strafford in Ireland: A Revaluation," *Past and Present*, no. 19 (1961):26–45.

tations in the country, culminating in the 1622 survey of civil, ecclesiastical, and military affairs. Not surprisingly, these investigations revealed that much of the landed wealth that ought to have enriched the crown and the church in Ireland had been filched by the New English officials and planters and that what these same people had acquired legitimately had not been developed according to the strict conditions laid down under the plantation schemes.[45]

The New English were represented on most of these investigatory commissions, but the formal reports that issued from them merely stated problems rather than proposed solutions. However the commissioners did have an opportunity to file private reports and recommendations, and the Englishmen who served on these commissions frequently availed themselves of this to offer individual criticism and recommendations on what they had witnessed in Ireland. Almost all such private reports by the 1622 commissioners were addressed to Lionel Cranfield, earl of Middlesex, and these generally castigated the New English as a group for having unscrupulously defrauded the crown and church. Furthermore, the social deficiencies in Ireland that had been highlighted by the New English discourses (now confirmed by the findings of the commission) were attributed in these private reports to the rapacity of the New English themselves rather than, as previously, to any shortcoming in the strategy for effecting the reformation of the country.[46]

The English officials also showed themselves resentful of the social pretensions of what was in effect an emerging Anglo-Irish ascendancy, and they were particularly scornful of the titles that had come within the reach of this group by means of their ill-gotten gains. Quite typical of the reportage made to England was that of Sir Dudley Norton, who in complaining of some embezzlement conducted by Charles Coote in Connacht described how "about a little more than a year since from the provost marshal of Connacht, which he yet holdeth, he proceeded to be raised so high as a baronet and a privy councillor. A stirring man fuller of wit than judgement, very pragmatical but his own ends so much in his eye as he is become an eye-sore to the country who have grievously complained against him for extortion."[47]

Complaints were also made concerning the lack of enthusiasm among

[45] For the 1622 survey see B.L., Add. Ms. 4756, ff. 1–155.

[46] The relevant papers of Lionel Cranfield, earl of Middlesex, are kept among the Sackville Manuscripts at the Kent Archives Office [hereafter K.A.O.], and further details of the day-to-day proceedings of the commission are available in the library of Exeter College, Oxford, in Exeter College, Mss. 95 and 174.

[47] Sir Dudley Norton to Cranfield, 14 June 1622 (K.A.O., Sackville Mss., O.N. 8459).

the New English commissioners for the work of the commission, as when Sir Dudley Digges mentioned that they contributed "little light or help." But this general observation was given a more practical application when it came to discussing the suitability of New English candidates for positions of trust in the Dublin administration. Dudley Norton was, for example, particularly concerned that the Master of the Court of Wards in Dublin should be "an eminent person and free from taint" because he would "have the absolute disposing of the children of the nobility and gentry for their education and breeding in Protestancy, which is not in use here in England so much." Having thus described the necessary qualifications for the post, he found that none of the New English was able to meet them, and in commenting on the particular suitability of Sir William Parsons who was striving for appointment, Norton described him as one who had "very good abilities and never (that I know of) deserved ill of me. But having had the unhappiness to put himself upon several pardons (in one of which murder is contained and all else but coining and treason against the king's person) it hath so stained him, together with some other general hard conceipts held of him, as men are very sorry and afraid to have him put over them in their estates."[48]

In the opinion of Norton, what held true of Parsons held equally true of the entire group of New English officials in Ireland, and if it had been up to him he would have had all the existing officeholders dismissed from office. Furthermore, as well as questioning the suitability of the New English to hold positions of trust under the crown, Norton and his English associates cast doubt on the need for continued plantation. Norton did object to "the scandal of toleration," and to this extent was at one with the New English in criticizing the privileged position that was being negotiated by Irish Catholic landowners, but he sympathized with the position of such as Sir John MacCoghlan, the individual who had been the target of de Renzy's hard-hitting attack, "who in time of war was faithful and a brave servitor." Norton was especially concerned lest men like MacCoghlan, with a consistent record of loyalty to the crown, should be dispossessed of their lands to provide for the further enrichment of those British settlers who had already cast away the opportunity of civilizing the Irish by diverting the various plantation schemes to serve "private turns." Thus although he agreed that

---

[48] Sir Dudley Digges to Cranfield, 18 Apr. 1622 (K.A.O., Sackville Mss., O.N. 8442); see also James Perrott to Cranfield (same collection, O.N. 8445) where he complained of the New English that "we have had little help from them, more than what we have by industrious inquisition collected rather than by their ready offerings." On the subject of the Court of Wards see Abstract of five letters received by Cranfield from Ireland, 24 May 1622 (K.A.O., Sackville Mss., O.N. 8453); Concerning the Office of Wards in Ireland (same collection, O.N. 7550).

plantations were the most effective means of achieving the desired uplift of the Irish population, Norton thought it "strange" (clearly an understatement) "that there should be fresh essays when there are so many plantations yet unsettled and imperfect."[49]

The general purport of what Dudley Norton and his fellow English commissioners were saying was that the social inadequacies of Ireland could be attributed as much to the shortcomings and failures of the New English themselves as to the innate barbarism of the native population. Incidentally, they were also making a case for fresh involvement from England in Irish affairs, and the general findings of the commission revealed clearly how the failures of the New English could be turned to profit by the crown. This message was not lost to Cranfield and his associates in England, and as the finances of Charles I worsened it became ever more tempting to act upon the advice that had been offered by the commissioners in 1622 and to seek to exploit all elements of the population of Ireland, planter as well as Catholic, to provide extra revenue for the crown. This background explains the arrival of Thomas Wentworth (later earl of Strafford) as governor of Ireland in 1633. Fresh from his triumphs on the Council of the North, where he had cowed the Yorkshire gentry into compliance with the crown's wishes, Wentworth went to Ireland with the specific purpose of recovering for the crown and the church everything for which a legal claim could be advanced, and he made it clear from the outset that he would show favor to no interest group, whether Protestant or Catholic, who stood in the way of the fulfillment of this ambition.[50]

By 1633, most of the prominent New English officials had been in Ireland for as many as thirty years, and some were the children of those who had effected the Elizabethan conquest. There had been a high degree of intermarriage among the successful settler families, and the cohesion that resulted from this was further consolidated by a strident attachment to Protestantism that did not inhibit marriage with Old English or even Gaelic Irish spouses when this was dictated by economic expediency. English would still have been the exclusive vernacular of the principal officeholders, but their long sojourn in Ireland and their close association with an Irish-speaking population, not least in matters of wet-nursing and fosterage, must have resulted in an accent very different from that used at the English court. Those who lived in the provinces would, of necessity, have come to understand Irish, and there is plentiful evidence, principally among the 1641 depositions, that the Irish language was widely understood

---

[49] Sir Dudley Norton to Cranfield, 10 Dec. 1621 (K.A.O., Sackville Mss., O.N. 7508).

[50] See Ranger, "Strafford in Ireland: A Revaluation," and Hugh F. Kearney, *Strafford in Ireland, 1633–41: A Study in Absolutism* (Manchester, 1959).

and sometimes spoken by the settler population in Ireland.[51] These consid-erations must have made an immediate impression on Wentworth and those who accompanied him to Ireland, but what must have struck them most was the wealth and ostentatious vulgarity of the principal New Eng-lish officials and planters. Most of these had arrived penniless in Ireland but were now holders of recently purchased titles and wielders of political influ-ence. It was these people, more than the native population, that Went-worth resented, not least because of what he had previously learned of them from reports such as those made by the 1622 commissioners. Even before he departed for Ireland, Wentworth had decided that he would never as-sociate with such colonials as equals, and shortly after his arrival he dis-missed them as "a strange people, their own privates [private interests] al-together their study without any regard at all to the public [interest]."[52]

The New English were fully aware of the implications of these criticisms, but their response served to make them even more conscious of their dis-tinctiveness as a people. The initial reaction of the more prominent settlers in Ireland was to devote greater attention to establishing and cultivating court connections with a view to obtaining absolute control of the admin-istration in Dublin, and thus to stave off the assault that was threatened. Marriage alliances were forged and those in England who had offices in their gift were approached with offers of money. Both these expedients seemed to serve their purpose but, had they but known it, the New English were merely purchasing a stay of execution because the extravagant sums they laid out in England, far from winning them the respect of English cour-tiers excited their contempt and in fact convinced these same courtiers that the reports of the 1622 commissioners had been substantially correct.[53]

It may have been the recognition that their overtures at court were not producing the desired result that explains the general tendency of the New English to close ranks and to rely increasingly on their own resources to pro-

---

[51] This statement derives its authority from the frequent reports made by the deponents in 1641 of conversations that they overheard spoken by the rebels in the Irish language. There are a total of thirty-two volumes of depositions preserved in the library of Trinity College, Dublin, and the volumes for the province of Munster that I have studied in detail may be iden-tified as follows. Depositions for County Waterford (T.C.D., Ms. 820); depositions for County Tipperary (T.C.D., Ms. 821); depositions for County Cork (T.C.D., Mss. 822–25); depositions for County Limerick (T.C.D., Ms. 829). Further depositions were collected in the early 1650s but these shed little light on conditions before 1641 and have been disregarded for the purpose of this essay. On the question of intermarriage see the outburst against it by George Andrew, A Quaternion of Sermons preached in Ireland . . . 1624 (Dublin, 1625), p. 36.

[52] Nicholas Canny, The Upstart Earl: A Study of the Social and Mental World of Richard Boyle, First Earl of Cork, 1566–1643 (Cambridge, 1982), pp. 9–19. Quotation cited at p. 11.

[53] For a specific example of these developments see Canny, The Upstart Earl, and for a more general appraisal see Ranger, "Strafford in Ireland: A Revaluation."

vide them with a sense of moral purpose and well-being. From the moment they had set foot in Ireland, almost all of the New English had identified closely with Protestantism, and had obtained moral sustenance from their belief that the mission on which they were engaged had equally a religious as well as a civilizing purpose. Notwithstanding this religious dimension to their mission in Ireland, few of the first arrivals possessed a profound knowledge of theology, and the generally poor quality of the clergy of the established church meant that little help could be looked for from this quarter. The introduction of some well-educated clergy from England and the appointment of graduates of Trinity College, Dublin, to endowed positions in the church led to some improvement, but it still emerges from the literary evidence as well as from occasional surveys of the condition of the established church that circumstances in Ireland were far from conducive to the development of a lay Protestant spirituality.[54] The most telling indicator of the low intellectual level of lay Protestants in Ireland is the fact that hardly any of the 1,381 Protestants in the province of Munster who provided inventories of the goods that were lost in the 1641 rebellion listed bibles or other religious books among their possessions. The surprising absence of such literature is explained by the somewhat low literacy levels that prevailed among the settler population in Ireland as compared with their social counterparts in England. Only noblemen, knights, esquires, and clergymen can be assumed to have been literate, since of those who made depositions in Munster following the 1641 rebellion, as many as 11 out of 204 gentlemen and 13 out of 57 merchants and traders acknowledged illiteracy by making a mark. The true state of affairs is revealed by the figures for Protestant yeomen and husbandmen in Munster, where slightly over 57 percent of the deposing yeomen and husbandmen in Munster and little short of 70 percent of the deposing husbandmen made a mark (see table, p. 188). These were generally high illiteracy figures by English standards, and we can assume that the percentage of illiterates would have been altogether higher among the lower ranks of the planter settlement.

The fact that most Protestant settlers in Ireland were closed out from the printed word did not prevent them from developing a crude providentialism based loosely on the ideas expounded by the few theologians in their

---

[54] For the sober appraisal of the church by the 1622 commissioners see B.L., Add. Ms. 4756, ff. 19–31, 64–80. For more graphic accounts of clerical inadequacy see Sir Matthew de Renzy to Lord Deputy, 6 Jan. 1616/7 (P.R.O., S.P. 46/90, ff. 43ᵛ–44ᵛ); and it was admitted by E.S., as it had been by Edmund Spenser, that "their priests take more pains to preserve them than ours do to win them to our religion" ("A Survey of the Present Estate of Ireland, Anno 1615," f. 10). On the general question of the recruitment of clergy to the established church see Alan Ford, *The Protestant Reformation in Ireland, 1591–1641* (Frankfurt am Main, 1985), pp. 63–98.

Ability to Sign among Protestant Deponents
in the Province of Munster, c. 1641

	Total number	Made signatures	Made mark	Signed by proxy	Neither signature nor mark
Knights and Esquires	43	29	0	12	2
Gentlemen	204	166	11	18	9
Merchants and traders	57	36	13	4	4
Clerks	77	68	0	6	3
Yeomen	307	105	176	11	15
Husbandmen	124	22	86	5	11
Craftsmen	222	65	125	17	15
Widows and wives	144	18	107	5	14
Servants	1	1	0	0	0
No status cited	167	66	74	5	22
Irish Protestants	35	16	15	2	2
Totals	1,381	592	607	85	97

SOURCE: Based on the depositions taken for the province of Munster (see note 51).
NOTE: A strict comparison with England is not possible, because there historians have attempted to establish the percentage of those who could *read*; the estimates for East Anglia about this period are that over 65 percent of yeomen and over 21 percent of husbandmen could read.

midst. Of these, at least two, George Downham, Bishop of Derry, and James Ussher, Archbishop of Armagh and Primate of the Irish Church, enjoyed international reputations and were recognized as exponents of predestinarian theology. The Calvinist notion of predestination as filtered through the writings of such as Downham and Ussher seems to have enjoyed widespread support among the planter population in Ireland, and by vulgarizing what was an intricate theological doctrine some of the lay spokesmen of the settler society could argue that they, as the chosen people of God, were distinct both from their countrymen in England and from their less worthy neighbors in Ireland.[55] Some historians have been so impressed by the solace that the planters derived from the doctrine of predestination that they have concluded that some settlers used this doctrine to justify the suspension of their own efforts to bring about the uplift of the Irish population by arguing that the degenerate condition of the Irish was

[55] This point has been developed in relation to Richard Boyle in Canny, *The Upstart Earl*, pp. 19–40. In more general terms Sir Dudley Norton cast aspersions on the religious style favored by the clergy who ministered to the New English when he advised against the continued appointment of "hot, fiery persons whose zeals (for the most part) do exceed their discretion for such a one will do much hurt and no good amongst those people." Norton to Cranfield, 13 [ ] 1621 (K.A.O., Sackville Papers, O.N. 7543).

proof that they were unredeemable and hence destined for damnation.[56] It is true that the more conscientious of the Protestant clergy in seventeenth-century Ireland were driven almost to despair by the lack of response to their efforts to promote the Reformation among the Irish population. However a more common view was that the promised social and spiritual transformation of the Irish population would take place only if the government in England would recognize and facilitate the uniquely difficult task to which they, as reformers, had been assigned. Those who argued in this fashion were in fact advancing the claim that their behavior should not be judged by the standards that prevailed in England and, like de Renzy who had been writing in the pre-1622 period, the later writers continued to insist that until they were allowed to overthrow all surviving dynastic families in Ireland the task of reforming the population would "be ever but a new beginning."[57] The post-1622 writers, however, broke new ground. De Renzy and his associates had stressed the need for an ongoing conquest by citing the onset of degeneracy in their own ranks; after 1622 the emphasis was placed on the positive achievements of the planters in Ireland.

This turnabout is explained by the awareness of the planters that self-criticism would be used to their detriment by officials in England, whom they knew to be unsympathetic to their case. Those defects in their society that they had already admitted and that had been confirmed by the 1622 survey were now attributed to the neglect of English and Scots favorites who had sought land in Ireland solely for the purpose of making a profit. In contrast, spokesmen for the planters pointed to the productive use made of the land granted to servitors who had been rewarded in the plantations for their past service to the crown in Ireland in a civil or military capacity. This contrast was best developed by Sir Francis Blundell, a New English member of the 1622 commission, who specifically sought to counter the allegations of his English-born colleagues when he presented a detailed document on the six plantations "made in Ireland since the memory of man."[58]

Land in the midland plantation of Queen Mary's reign had been assigned principally to English soldiers in Ireland, and Blundell declared himself satisfied that these and their descendants had "by their civility made that the civilest county of the kingdom." It was "gentlemen of good quality in England" who had been the principal beneficiaries of the Munster plantation;

[56] Brendan Bradshaw, "Sword, Word and Strategy in the Reformation in Ireland," *Historical Journal* 21 (1978):475–502; Ford, *The Protestant Reformation in Ireland*, esp. ch. 8, "The Theology of the Church of Ireland."

[57] De Renzy to Lord Deputy; see note 54 above.

[58] Sir Francis Blundell about plantations, 1622 (K.A.O., Sackville Mss., O.N. 8540, ff. 40ʳ–45ʳ).

Blundell accounted for their inability to defend their position during the rebellion of the 1590s by reference to their laxity in drawing tenants from England to populate their estates. Nonetheless, he was satisfied that this original deficiency in the Munster settlement had since been rectified in the years of peace, with the result that the planters' "numbers are much increased, and the country doth begin to grow full of English." Blundell did nothing to disguise the deficiencies in the plantation in Ulster that the work of the commissioners had revealed, but he attached particular responsibility to English and Scots undertakers whose failure to meet the specified conditions had reduced what should have been a worthy work to being but "a poor quarter plantation." In contrast, he claimed, the more recent plantation of Wexford had been the most successful attempted so far because those selected as proprietors had been "all servitors, men of good ability, and such as know the danger of the work who, looking more upon their own safety than any present profits, had built according to their conditions many fair and strong castles, houses, and bawnes upon their proportions; and hereby made that part of the country strong and defensible against any Irish enemy."[59]

From this experience, Blundell concluded that "there cannot be a more easy and honourable way to reduce that kingdom to civility, than by plantation." Those deficiencies that had been discovered had resulted from "private profit" being put before "the public good of the kingdom"; similarly, the crown's persistence in using Irish land to reward Scots and English favorites had led to what he regarded as the total failure of the two most recent plantations in Longford and Leitrim. Thus the lesson to be learned from his historical account was "that his Majesty cannot place a gift so ill as land in Ireland upon a needy man."[60]

These views, which were endorsed by others of the New English commissioners, marked a new departure in New English thinking in that all shortcomings in the reform effort were now being attributed to official English misunderstanding of what was being undertaken in Ireland and to the consequent defective advice that was being presented to the king. It now appeared to the various New English authors that because of the misinformation being supplied to the crown their special role in Ireland was being disregarded, and they feared that if their behavior was judged by conventional standards everything that had been achieved so far would be threatened.

The New English desire to remind the king and his advisors of the special

[59] Ibid.
[60] Ibid.

mission that was under way in Ireland may be one factor that explains why Spenser's *View*, previously available only in manuscript, was published in Dublin in 1633.[61] But even before the *View* was available in print, echoes of Spenser's arguments had been making their appearance in the various compositions in which the New English pressed their claim to be treated as special subjects by reiterating the importance of their civilizing function in Ireland. The emphasis in these discourses was placed on the religious reform that would inevitably result from the fulfillment of the civilizing process and on the facility with which the native population would be brought to conform to the state religion once they had been resettled on plantations.[62] This marked shift in emphasis from the civil to the religious dimension of the colonizing effort is all the more significant because it coincided with and was a product of a new tendency of the New English to suggest that it was Divine Providence rather than the king who had appointed them to their special endeavor in Ireland. The case of Richard Boyle, earl of Cork and the wealthiest planter in Ireland, is the most striking example of one who could both explain every success of his career in providential terms and dismiss every challenge as evidence that God was putting his faith to the test.[63] But what Cork could argue in a personal capacity others extended to the collective. This emerges from a consideration of the discourse composed by Sir William Parsons in 1622 on the "Reasons for the Plantations in Ireland." Parsons, the man considered by Dudley Norton as unsuitable for the position of Master of the Rolls, prefaced his remarks on plantation with the observation that:

that course seems to be pointed unto us by the finger of God which appears thus.

The great Irish in Ulster took a general flight at once out of the kingdom whereby five counties at once fell into his Majesty's hands to be disposed at his pleasure without contradiction of any man of note or interest.

The English Irish of Ireland [i.e., the Old English] who heretofore seemed unwillingly to let in the English do now generally concur in this work and have many of them been actors in them.

---

[61] Edmund Spenser, *A View of the State of Ireland* (Dublin, 1633). The other factor that explains the publication of Spenser's *View* at this time is that the arguments formulated by Spenser supported Wentworth's ambition to proceed with the Connacht plantation, an enterprise that had long been advocated by the New English in Ireland.

[62] Anonymous, "On Natives in the Plantation of Ulster" (K.A.O., Sackville Mss., O.N. 7535). This author was confident that conformity in religion would follow once the natives were resettled upon plantations because "to say the truth, most of the people are not unwilling to go to church if they might be so provided for that they need not fear their lords' displeasure for doing it."

[63] Canny, *The Upstart Earl*, esp. pp. 19–41.

The Irish themselves who in all former times have been furious and given to warlike disturbance have since his Majesty's reign so yielded to peace as there is now little noise of war among them.

The very fact that the attitude of the various elements of the Irish population had thus been altered in a dramatic fashion was taken as evidence of divine intervention, but Parsons was also convinced that the same power had brought the king himself to conform with his plan. What else, he asked, could explain the clemency shown by James I toward the erstwhile rebels, "who deserved nothing but extirpation" for their "crying murders, rapes of women and oppressions of the weak?"[64]

Such instances of the workings of Providence in human affairs constituted proof for Parsons and his associates that it was God who had appointed them to their task in Ireland. This provided them with a shield against increasing criticism from England, but the New English still saw the need to disarm their critics by providing some tangible evidence that their efforts were continuing to enjoy divine support. A spontaneous participation by the native population in the services of the established church would have been one such proof, but not even the most optimistic of the New English authors saw any likelihood of this occurring in the short term. They looked, therefore, for evidence of economic improvement to convince themselves and their opponents that they still enjoyed divine favor, and Parsons compared the condition of pre-Conquest Ireland with that which obtained in 1622 to show that dramatic advances had already been made. Even more impressive, he claimed, was the financial improvement of the crown's position in Ireland. He asserted that "the ten years since plantation began had almost doubled His Majesty's profit in casualties, customs and rents." This admittedly was not the total transformation that had been promised by the sixteenth-century projectors of conquest and colonization; Parsons himself acknowledged that, outside the planted counties, "every thing be yet in the natural, little or no improvement made by enclosing, planting fruits, making meadows, changing cattle, searching into mines or minerals, working the country commodities, bringing in trades, skilful ploughmen, traffic or learning." This was, of course, clearly unsatisfactory, but Parsons did not find it in any way surprising. He explained the neglect by saying that the recommended policy of plantation had not been proceeded with. Furthermore, he believed that Englishmen "of substance" had hitherto lacked confidence in the security of Ireland and consequently had been reluctant to settle there. Now that it had been demonstrated that peace would become a permanent feature of Irish life, he looked forward to

[64] "Reasons for the Plantations in Ireland by Sir W.P.," f. 26.

concerted English settlement outside the previously planted areas. This would achieve the long-awaited uplift of the native population who, he claimed, in language reminiscent of the sixteenth-century authors, would be drawn from their former barbarism to live with the English planters in "the same frame of government and manner of life" and would "speak all one language, and dwell all in one form, and be answerable to the same order of usage and conversation."[65]

Once these new benchmarks of success had been set by Parsons and accepted by his associates in Ireland, the New English endeavored, as never before, to produce evidence that their work enjoyed God's blessing. In Munster, a large number of English tenants had already been introduced, particularly on the extensive Boyle estates, and the favorable notice that this received from the 1622 commissioners was used by the earl of Cork to support his contention that his life was dedicated to a godly purpose. More attention was now devoted by the earl to promoting what he described as works of charity, by which he meant anything from bridge building and the erection of manufacturing towns to the construction of elegant residences and the development of orchards, ornamental gardens, and deer parks. But more to the point, the earl of Cork insisted that his recently appointed tenants improve the land that they rented from him and devote themselves to advanced agriculture. His insistence, and the enforcement of the same requirements by most other principal planters in Munster, resulted in the physical and economic transformation of the better lands of the province on which the planters had settled.[66]

The most striking physical change was the destruction of the woods for the purpose of iron smelting and the manufacture of pipe staves. The ironworks that dotted the planted areas of Munster must have been an impressive sight, but hardly as imposing as the residences of the more successful planters. In addition to the principal proprietors, those tenants-in-chief who fell into the social categories of gentleman and esquire invested money in the construction and furnishing of residences appropriate to men of their rank, and each of these was surrounded with an extensive area of ornamental ground. The demesne land attached to them was, in almost every instance, developed as a model farm, and the level of cultivation there bore comparison with the most advanced tillage in contemporary Europe. But the principal commercial commodity on these farms was livestock, and the agricultural revolution introduced by those planters to Ireland was essentially in the realm of animal husbandry. They introduced cattle and sheep

---

[65] Ibid., f. 30.

[66] Canny, *The Upstart Earl*, passim; the commissioners' report on Munster is treated in B.L., Add. Ms. 4756 ff. 85^r–97^r.

of English breed to replace or cross with the despised native varieties, and their success made possible the trade in live cattle (and subsequently in barreled meat) that became an increasingly important element in the Irish export trade during the seventeenth century.

Evidence for all this comes from the inventories that were taken from Munster Protestants who made depositions in the aftermath of the 1641 rebellion. Most Munster settlers who made depositions came from the social categories of husbandman and above, and these provide plentiful evidence that the advanced agriculture exemplified by the proprietors and tenants-in-chief was imitated by the yeomen and husbandmen who farmed most of the better quality planted land in the province. No data exist on which to base a reliable estimate of the settler population in Munster, but the fact that 1,381 heads of households were still available to depose in the aftermath of a rebellion that forced most settlers off the land suggests that their total numbers were well up to the level of any contemporary English transatlantic settlement. More significant, however, is the fact that they were a wealthier, more socially diversified and more self-sufficient community than that which developed in any English overseas settlement during the seventeenth century.[67]

What occurred in Munster during the 1620s and 1630s was far in advance of the other planted areas in Ireland. Although Ulster absorbed more settlers, few were capable of promoting the economic improvement that was effected in parts of Munster. But if the other plantations failed in this respect, the principal proprietors throughout the country were still concerned to develop residences, home farms, and manufacturing enterprises that would present evidence of their civilizing and godly purpose in Ireland.

Testimony to these developments is again available among the 1641 depositions, but descriptions of what was achieved can also be found in Gerard Boate's work, *Ireland's Natural History*. Regarded as an exemplary manual of the new science that came to the fore in seventeenth-century England, it was in fact based on practical observations made in Ireland during 1644–1652 by the eminent Dutch emigré scientist Arnold Boate, brother to Gerard. His purpose was to gauge the economic potential of Ireland, now that the 1641 rebellion had been crushed. In conducting his observations Boate made special note of what had been accomplished by the pre-1641 planters, because he believed that their achievements under adverse conditions would provide some measure of the economic potential that Ireland would offer once English domination had been asserted in a truly comprehensive

[67] These remarks are further developed in Nicholas Canny, "The Irish Background to Penn's Experiment."

fashion. Having made his inquiry, Arnold Boate reported on what had been narrated to him after he had discussed the material "with several gentlemen who had been to Ireland, especially Sir William Parsons and Sir Richard Parsons."[68]

What was published in *Ireland's Natural History* was, therefore, as much a self-appraisal of their achievements by several of the New English as an estimate of Ireland's economic potential taken by the Boate brothers. Attention was drawn to the houses, gardens, enclosures, orchards, and hedges that had been destroyed by the "barbarians" who, during the 1641 rebellion, had "endeavoured quite to extinguish the memory of them [the New English] and of all the civility and good things by them introduced amongst that wild nation." It was said that "all parts where the English did dwell or had any thing to do had been filled with as goodly beasts, both cows and sheep, as any in England, Holland, or other the best countries in Europe." Special attention was devoted to the advanced scientific techniques that had been applied by the New English to the enclosure and fertilization of land as well as to mining, iron smelting, bog draining, and the development of inland water transport. Exemplary estates were isolated for particular discussion, and an extensive passage was devoted to the improvements promoted by Emanuel Downing, and further advanced by Sir Charles Coote, in the lordship of Mountrath in Queen's County.[69]

The New English contribution to the promotion of civility in Ireland was described along the lines desired by people like William Parsons. Indeed, it might be said that Parsons and his associates were concerned to cooperate with the Boates because their statements would provide seemingly independent scientific support for the claims the planters had long been making that their involvement with the country had led to its improvement. Associated with this attempt to document their own achievements and justify the privileged position to which they had long aspired was the effort by particular members of the New English population to uncover and describe the archaeological remains from Ireland's prehistoric past. Like the analogous activities of the criollo intellectuals of Mexico described above by Anthony Pagden, the purpose of this endeavor was to demonstrate that Ireland had once produced a highly developed civilization. The point was thus being made that, given the right conditions, Ireland would again sustain a sophisticated culture.

The glorification of Ireland's ancient past was made easier for the planters because the past being glorified was not that of their adversaries the Old

---

[68] Gerard Boate, *Ireland's Natural History* (London, 1652), preface to the reader by Arnold Boate.

[69] Ibid., pp. 89, 96, 97–98, 114, 121–22, 124–30, 134–35, 136–37, 151.

English, whose ancestors had only come to the country with the Norman conquest. But while striving to withhold credit from the Old English for any of their achievements, the spokesmen for the planters could not but admire and covet what the Old English had accomplished. They were particularly envious of the separate Irish peerage that had been developed by the ancestors of the Old English and they sought to take over this system of honor for themselves. This they did by the purchase of new Irish titles from the crown and by the absorption of existing titles into their own ranks through the process of intermarriage. The court of wards was a particularly effective instrument for the latter, because by controlling the nurture and disposition-in-marriage of young Catholic heirs the New English were able to effect the conversion of many Irish noblemen to the Protestant faith while at the same time winning them as husbands for their own daughters. The New English also came to admire the parliamentary and administrative institutions that had been devised by the Old English, and they strove to seize these institutions to serve their own purpose. In doing so they displayed considerable respect for the traditions and procedures of these bodies, which, like the separate peerage, highlighted the distinctiveness of Ireland from the mother country.

Although some Old English achievements could be praised and taken over for their own, the planters were equally concerned to isolate religion as the single factor that made it impossible for them to accept the Old English as equals. This strategy raised a dilemma, however, because there could be no denying that the statutes governing the Irish church were closely modeled on those first introduced in England. An ingenious solution to this problem was devised by Archbishop James Ussher, who contended that the church over which he was primate was no mere transplant of the English church but rather the church that had been introduced to Ireland by St. Patrick and now recently restored to its pristine purity. To substantiate his claim, Ussher made a study of early Christian Ireland and came away with the impression that what had been erected by St. Patrick in the fifth century and had survived until corrupted by St. Malachy, under Roman influence, in the twelfth, was an independent national hierarchy with a theological position that roughly approximated that of the established church of Ussher's generation.[70]

[70] James Ussher, *A Discourse of Religion Anciently Professed by the Irish and Scottish* (Dublin, 1622). On the antiquarian movement see J. G. Simms, *William Molyneux of Dublin: A Life of the Seventeenth-Century Political Writer and Scientist* (Dublin, 1982), esp. pp. 102–108; K. T. Hoppen, *The Common Scientist in the Seventeenth Century: A Study of the Dublin Philosophical Society, 1683–1708* (London, 1970), pp. 154–56 and 196–97; Norman Vance, "Celts, Carthaginians and Constitutions: Anglo-Irish literary Relations, 1780–1820," *Irish Historical Studies* 22 (1981):216–38; Ann de Valera, "Antiquarian and Historical Investigations in Ireland in the Eighteenth Century" (M.A. thesis, University College, Dublin, 1978).

The invention of an official myth greatly assisted the New English in their effort to identify with their country of settlement. So too did the creation of model settlements that further vindicated them in their claim that they were creating the conditions under which the Irish would be drawn to civility. This attachment to place provided the planter population with vital moral sustenance when their civilizing role in Ireland was called into question, especially during the years 1633–1641 when Thomas Wentworth, earl of Strafford, held office as lord deputy. When he openly challenged the position of the New English in Ireland, they pleaded their case for privileged treatment with even greater urgency and asserted that Wentworth's "tyranny" would undermine everything that had been achieved by them in effecting the reform of the Irish. Their conviction that right was on their side and that Wentworth was bent on their destruction provided them with the moral courage to exploit every stratagem, short of outright rebellion, to oppose the king's representative in Ireland. In doing so they portrayed themselves as men who were defending the interests of the Irish commonwealth against an interloper whose sole purpose was exploitation, and they carried their opposition to the extreme of engaging in an alliance with the Old English against their common enemy. In doing so they were careful to distinguish their particular struggle from the more general constitutional struggle that was taking place in Britain, and they proclaimed themselves loyal subjects to the king. Under the circumstances, the New English found it convenient to assume the description Irish. They could now do so with confidence because they had identified themselves as the exclusive promoters of an Irish commonwealth and had discredited the other would-be claimants as either papists or barbarians. This became all the more clear when their Old English allies-of-convenience were cast aside after Wentworth (by then earl of Strafford) had been defeated. The victory over him was cited as proof of the claims they had been making, and it set the final seal to the identity that they had been fabricating for the previous half-century. The point was not lost on William Parsons, who proclaimed that the defeat of "that strange man Strafford" would "let the world see and our own consciences tell us, we are the same men to the king and his service."[71]

To recapitulate, the crisis of 1579–1580 served only to provide a coherence to New English thinking on their role and purpose in Ireland; it took a second crisis, the challenge from Thomas Wentworth, to further quicken New English thinking and bring them to recognize and accept themselves as a people who were as distinct from the inhabitants of England as they

[71] Cited in Canny, *The Upstart Earl*, p. 137.

were from the indigenous populations of Ireland. But no sooner had this identity been forged than the New English were beset by the unforeseen uprising of 1641 when the Catholic rebels, Gaelic and Old English alike, joined forces to rid the country of the settler population. Grievances over land, religion, and exclusion from the political process were those articulated by the rebel leaders, but the factor that made most impression on the settlers was the religious one, because those attacked were given the choice of either attending Mass or departing stark naked from their houses and lands for the nearest port town or English garrison. Under these circumstances the settlers, who had so recently been fabricating an Irish identity and who were frequently Hibernicized to the extent that they could converse in Irish with their assailants, reverted to the description British Protestant and castigated everything Irish as base and barbaric. In doing this, they still revealed a strong attachment to the localities in which they had settled and that recently had been developed and improved by themselves. To this extent Ireland remained the focus of their attention and the settlers expressed every confidence that they would soon recover what had been lost and take revenge on the rebels.

It was only as the prospect of an early restoration of their property receded that some of the New English leaders began to take sides in the simultaneous conflict that had developed in England between the king and parliament. Even then, those who became engaged there seldom lost sight of their ambition to return to Ireland, and many of the erstwhile New English landowners came forward to participate in the Cromwellian effort to recover the country for the Protestant interest.[72] Revenge was the consideration uppermost in the minds of those New English who participated in the Cromwellian reconquest of Ireland, and only a few isolated Englishmen with no previous experience in Ireland devoted any sustained thought to the problem of achieving an uplift of the native population.[73] Even these made little impression on their fellow countrymen, and most Cromwellians in Ireland adopted an extremely hostile attitude toward the native population of the country. One product of this negative thinking was the pamphlet *The Interest of England in the Irish Transplantation, Stated*, composed in

[72] This appraisal of the rebellion is based on my reading of the 1641 depositions that relate to Munster. See also Nicholas Canny, "The Formation of the Irish Mind: Religion, Politics and Gaelic Irish Literature, 1580–1750," *Past and Present*, no. 95 (May 1982):91–116. The connection of Ireland with the politics of the English civil war has received some attention in J. R. MacCormack, "The Irish Adventurers and the English Civil War," *Irish Historical Studies* 10 (1957):21–39, but the role of Irish planters in English politics of the period still awaits its historian.

[73] On this subject, see T. C. Barnard, *Cromwellian Ireland: English Government and Reform in Ireland, 1649–60* (Oxford, 1975).

1655 by Captain Richard Lawrence, a Cromwellian officer who advocated a rigid policy of apartheid for Ireland and the abandonment of any further effort to reform the Irish. This stance was justified by the rebellion of 1641 when, according to Lawrence, the Irish, by participating in an unprovoked rebellion, had spurned the hand of friendship that earlier had been extended to them by the planter population in the country. Furthermore, he claimed, the rebels had symbolized repeatedly their inveterate attachment to barbarism when "even English cattle and horses were destroyed for their being of an English kind."

Most of the New English population would have agreed with Lawrence's strictures on the native population, but they were considerably taken aback by his attribution of the initial success of the rebellion to failures and shortcomings of the New English as planters. It was, he claimed, the planters' "promiscuous and scattered inhabiting amongst the Irish" that had encouraged the native population to rebel because they were "far the greater number, and in most a hundred to one." New English laxity had created the conditions that had ultimately encompassed their ruination. Furthermore, in the aftermath of the rebellion, Lawrence contended that if a more prudent course were not pursued the process would repeat itself whereby "the posterity of this present generation (if not themselves) shall after a few years come to be at the mercy and disposition of this bloody people again." The course he recommended was one whereby the native Irish would be corralled into a single province under the command of an English garrison; the remaining three provinces of the country would be reserved for the exclusive habitation of Englishmen.[74]

Such an arrangement must have had some appeal for the New English who had just endured the rebellion of 1641, but by 1655, when the shock of that rebellion had waned somewhat, they were less ready to endorse a formula that would have required them to forego their Irish tenants and to abandon their assumed role as civilizers of the Irish. Furthermore, they could see that their acceptance of the strategy proposed by Lawrence would have been an acknowledgment that their own neglect had been ultimately responsible for the rebellion. Rather than concede these points, which would have reduced their role to being mere functionaries of the government in London, the New English revived the argument that their attempt at advancing civil conditions had not produced the desired result in the years before 1641 because the British government had refused to permit them to press ahead with the comprehensive conquest of the country.

[74] Richard Lawrence, *The Interest of England in the Irish Transplantation, Stated* (Dublin, 1655), pp. 14, 15, 16–17, 18.

Since this was always represented by them as the essential prerequisite to the reform program, the New English were by implication blaming the rebellion of 1641 on the hindrances and interferences of the British government with their own efforts in Ireland. Furthermore, they contended that their position had been rendered all the more precarious because their ambition to suppress the potential Catholic rebels in Ireland had been vetoed by the government of King Charles I, lest it hinder official efforts to forge links with the Catholic monarachs of continental Europe. However, now that the comprehensive conquest of the country had been achieved by Oliver Cromwell and a government existed that could be trusted to place the Protestant interest before all others, the New English expressed themselves ready to implement the full program for reform and uplift that had been outlined by the first generation of New English settlers.

In 1652, when plans were already being laid for the Cromwellian confiscation of Ireland, one perceptive individual recommended that he who would advance the plantation in Ireland could hardly find better hints than in "Mr Ed. Spenser his *View of the State of Ireland*, published almost three score years ago, 1596."[75] The wisdom of this became fully apparent to the New English once the alternative strategy was outlined by Lawrence. Thus Vincent Gookin, a Munster planter and prominent political figure among the New English, rushed in 1655 to counter Lawrence's charge that "the Irish mixing with the English were the cause of their easy perpetrating their bloody resolutions." Mixed plantation was, protested Gookin, a sound method of settlement once political dominance had been achieved over the Irish. Now that a full-scale conquest had been implemented, he was satisfied that the planters might "safely taste the good of the Irish without fearing the ill" and might even "overspread them and incorporate them into ourselves, and so by an oneness take away the foundation of difference and fear together." He did not deny some shortcomings among the New English who had been involved in Ireland before 1641, but he upheld their strategy and cited the experience of ancient Rome and the more recent experience of the Spaniards in the Indies, both successes at colonization that derived from mixing "their colonies with the natives."[76]

What Gookin had to say was in strict conformity with what the New English authors had always been saying, and in rejecting the alternative

---

[75] *The Perfect Diurnall*, 7 June 1652, no. 130, p. 1928. Spenser's *View*, although entered on the Stationer's register in 1596, was not in fact published until 1633, as noted above. I am grateful to my colleague Dr. Tadhg Foley for this reference to *The Perfect Diurnall*.

[76] Vincent Gookin, *The Author and Case of Transplanting . . . Vindicated* (London, 1655), pp. 40–41, 37, 52. For general background on Gookin, see T. C. Barnard, "Lord Broghill, Vincent Gookin and the Cork Elections of 1659," in *English Historical Review* 88 (1973):352–65.

strategy of strict segregation he made specific reference to Sir John Davies, who had argued that the earlier pursuit of a segregation policy had sown "the seeds of an ever-lasting feud by perpetuating the distinctions of English and Irish." If Davies was the authority favored by Gookin, others among the planters identified more closely with Spenser, as is clear from the title chosen in 1673 by the anonymous author of *The Present State of Ireland, Together with Some Remarks upon the Ancient State Thereof*. This compilation was little short of a direct plagiarism of passages from Spenser, Davies, and Sir John Temple and dealt with the events leading up to and through the 1641 rebellion. That catastrophe had been caused, the writer believed, by the failure of the planters to adhere rigidly to the reform strategy prescribed by his favored authors. He was convinced from what he had witnessed in more recent years, however, that the reform of the country was well under way and that the secure position achieved by the settlers would ensure they would "no longer lapse to barbarism through intermarriage," while their "numerous habitations in most parts of the kingdom" would continue to draw "the Irish from their wonted barbarism." Thus the condition of the country in 1673 satisfied him that "the eternal peace of Ireland which was so solidly discoursed of and stoutly fought for in Queen Elizabeth's time; and very far proceeded in by King James I, had been absolutely perfected . . . according to all human appearance by the last settlement of Ireland confirmed by his gracious Majesty, King Charles the Second."[77]

By laying stress on the social and political transformation that had been effected following the suppression of the 1641 rebellion, this author was showing himself to be in the intellectual tradition of the Elizabethan authors to whom he had alluded. Furthermore, by invoking their ideas he was laying claim to a special role for the settler population in Ireland as the agents of a civilizing policy that could only be achieved in the aftermath of conquest. The settlers, however, were still referred to by the writer as English, although he admitted that they included "Welsh and Scots with some Dutch that yearly transported themselves hither to plant." This reversion to an earlier mode of identification is explained by the repugnance with which the term Irish was still regarded because of its association with the 1641 rebellion, but it was evident that English, or even British, was an inadequate description. Therefore the settlers gradually reverted to the label Irish, which was generally used by Irish-born Protestants to identify themselves throughout the eighteenth century.[78]

---

[77] The reference to Davies is cited in Gookin, *The Author and Case*, p. 39. Anonymous, *The Present State of Ireland Together with Some Remarks upon the Ancient State Thereof* (London, 1673), pp. 73-74.

[78] Ibid., p. 78. The reversion to the description Irish by the planter community began to

Although born in Ireland, the Protestants of the eighteenth century were less "Irish" in the cultural sense than their pre-1641 forebears had been. Some would still have been able to speak the Irish language and a very occasional gentleman might have provided patronage for Gaelic poets, but the big difference was that those at the upper levels of society did not have the same need, or even the opportunity, to learn Irish, because English was becoming widespread among the native population. The Irish Protestant gentleman would, however, have usually been educated at home, either in one of the several English-style schools or academies that were then established or at Trinity College, Dublin. It is probable that male literacy levels were greatly ahead of what they had been among the settlers of 1641. This would have been due not only to greater educational opportunity but also to the fact that, outside Ulster and the towns, the settler population was more thinly scattered than in the decades before 1641 and was comprised principally of landowners, wealthy tenants, and the subordinates who served and supported them. There was, of course, considerable upward as well as downward social mobility throughout the eighteenth century, but even those who reached the pinnacle of the social pyramid by dint of their own efforts would have been frequent visitors to England. Often those born into the social elite would have inherited estates in England as well as their larger holdings in Ireland, and marriages between British and Irish aristocratic families were not uncommon even though Irish peers were never accepted as social equals by their English counterparts. The settler population in Ireland was also regularly replenished by fresh arrivals from the neighboring island throughout the eighteenth century, and these included manufacturers and craftsmen as well as those equipped with special skills that related to estate management. All of these factors meant that the Irish Protestant community of the eighteenth century was much more closely linked with cultural developments in the mother country and even continental Europe than, for example, its North American counterparts. When an Irish Protestant gentleman visited England there would have been little besides his accent that set him apart from an English provincial squire. Although the eighteenth century is associated in Irish history with

---

occur in the late 1660s. The extent to which it had become a commonplace by the late seventeenth century is underlined by the fact that the earliest Irish novel, which describes the romance between the daughter of a Protestant settler in Ireland and a Protestant Continental prince who fought in the Williamite army, is entitled *Vertue Rewarded or The Irish Princess* (London, 1693). I am grateful to my colleague Dr. Hubert McDermott for this reference. The ease with which Irish Protestants could monopolize the description Irish for themselves is particularly striking in the pamphlet by Ezekiel Burridge entitled *A Short View of the Present State of Ireland . . . in the year 1700* (Dublin or London, 1708) where the expressions "the people of Ireland" and the king's "Irish subjects" are employed to describe the Protestant nation.

colonial nationalism, it was political rather than cultural developments (and the Irish Protestant perception of these political developments) that explain the strong sense of colonial identity that reemerged among the Irish settler population during the late seventeenth century and was sustained throughout the eighteenth.[79]

The most contentious political issue of the later seventeenth century re-lated to land, because the security of the Protestant interest in Ireland was seen to be associated with land ownership. The author of *The Present State of Ireland*, like the Protestant landowners whose views he represented, was willing to be reconciled with the Restoration land settlement because it had generally upheld the confiscation of Irish Catholic estates implemented during the Protectorate. There were admittedly some Catholic proprietors who had engaged in the 1641 rebellion who had recovered land from Charles II, but the overwhelming proportion of Irish land was in Protestant ownership after the Restoration settlement. The new wave of proprietors who had obtained Irish land under the Cromwellian confiscation were the owners of much of this, but many sold out their holdings to those Protestant landowners who were already established in the country. In practice, there-fore, the real beneficiaries of the land transfer effected by Cromwell in Ire-land were the New English who were previously settled there, and it seemed, after the Restoration, that these would enjoy the opportunity to apply the reform program that they had long espoused and that had con-tributed to their development of an Irish identity.[80]

Although these considerations explain why the Irish Protestants were willing to accept the land settlement of King Charles II, they also account for their unease when the king and his courtiers entertained further ap-proaches from dissatisfied Irish Catholic gentlemen to have the entire set-tlement renegotiated. When these overtures were being considered by the king, and when it became evident that he would be succeeded by his Cath-olic brother, the unease gave way to an acute sense among the Irish Prot-

---

[79] For a good sense of the social and intellectual life of the ascendancy in eighteenth-century Ireland see J. C. Beckett, *The Anglo-Irish Tradition* (London, 1976). A more balanced state-ment on the realities of ascendancy power will be derived from the several essays in *Penal Era and Golden Age: Essays in Irish History, 1690–1800*, ed. Thomas Bartlett and D. W. Hayton (Belfast, 1979). The extent to which Protestant landed society in Ireland during 1660–1801 was characterized by drastic upward and downward social movement emerges most dramati-cally from Ciarán Ó Murchadha, "Land and Society in Seventeenth-Century Clare" (Ph.D. diss., University College, Galway, 1982), esp. pp. 151–79 and A.P.W. Malcomson, *John Foster: The Politics of the Anglo-Irish Ascendancy* (Oxford, 1978), pp. 1–31.

[80] On the politics of land during the Restoration period, see *A New History of Ireland*, 3:420–54; Karl Bottigheimer, "The Restoration Land Settlement in Ireland: A Structural View," *Irish Historical Studies* 18 (1972):1–21; T. C. Barnard, "Planters and Policies in Crom-wellian Ireland, *Past and Present*, no. 61 (1973):31–69.

estant community that they were being betrayed by the British monarchy. Irish Protestants came increasingly to recognize that their security depended in the final analysis on their ability to defend themselves against both domestic insurrection and foreign invasion, and this conclusion was fully vindicated during 1688–1691, when King James II, backed by French forces, sought to use Ireland as a base from which to recover his English crown.[81]

The intervention of William III on the Protestant side was the crucial factor that tipped the balance in their favor, but Irish Protestants refused to recognize this and evinced little enthusiasm for William of Orange once he was firmly established on the British throne. Fear and suspicion of the intentions of the British government in relation to themselves was again aroused in their minds when they saw the principal spoils of the Williamite war go to courtiers and favorites of the king rather than to those in Ireland who had borne the brunt of the battle.[82] The settlers in Ireland lobbied for support in England to counter this development and, although partially successful, they continued to be wary and suspicious of any interference from Whitehall in Irish affairs. To this extent the Williamite episode placed a further wedge between the Protestant population of Ireland and the metropolitan government, but the Williamite experience also made the settler population more conscious of themselves as an Irish community because, thereafter, they could justly claim to be the only group in Ireland who should enjoy full political rights: a point, as we shall see, that was never conceded by the British government.

There was no doubt that those Irish Catholics who had sought to challenge the settlers' authority by supporting King James II had forfeited all claim to enjoy political rights, and they also lost most of the land that remained to them under the Protestant settlement that followed the Williamite war in Ireland. Furthermore, the elimination of this last remnant of a Catholic political nation provided the Protestant settler population with the final proof that they were the Israelites, the chosen people of God. This outcome also meant that they could now, for the first time, seek to control

---

[81] J. G. Simms, *Jacobite Ireland, 1685–91* (London, 1969). For a contemporary statement of Protestant unease with the disturbance of the initial land settlement see J. G., *The State of the Papist and Protestant Proprieties in the Kingdom of Ireland in the year 1641 . . . and how disposed in 1653 . . . and how disposed in 1662 . . . and how the Proprieties stand this Present Year, 1689* (London, 1689).

[82] J. G. Simms, *The Williamite Confiscation in Ireland, 1690–1703* (London, 1956); for evidence of the persistence of this resentment into the eighteenth century, see Ezekiel Burridge, *A Short View of the Present State of Ireland . . . in 1700.* For a good summary account of Irish political life in these years, see D. W. Hayton, "Ireland after the Glorious Revolution, 1692–1715" (Belfast, Public Record Office of Northern Ireland [P.R.O.N.I.], Educational Facsimiles, 221–40), introduction, pp. 2–27.

the instruments of government in Dublin without fear that their ambition would be frustrated by another group in the country. Under these circumstances the settlers could describe themselves as Irish with enthusiasm and could deploy traditional Old English constitutional arguments to defend the Irish parliament and administration from diminution or interference from England.[83]

These developments explain the emergence of individuals like William Molyneux and Jonathan Swift, who could argue the case for Ireland's legislative independence in strictly constitutional terms. In doing so, furthermore, they could look freely at the medieval history of these institutions, because now that the Old English had been eliminated as a political force, the New English who had succeeded them could adopt their traditions and achievements as their own and could represent the history of the two peoples as one long continuum in the promotion of English influence in Ireland from the time of the Norman conquest on. But these authors and their contemporaries were aware that the philosophical principles enunciated by John Locke and partly enshrined in the English revolutionary settlement could also be invoked to bolster their argument for greater freedom of action for the Protestant grouping that had achieved ascendancy in Ireland in the aftermath of the Williamite war.[84]

But just at the point when this freedom of action was becoming possible for the settler population, their position was again complicated by the arrival of a major influx of Scots Presbyterians into the northeastern part of the country. For the most part the newcomers were forced to seek a livelihood in Ireland because of the effective collapse of the agrarian economy of Scotland in the 1690s. They were readily received by the Protestant landowners in Ulster who, up to this point, had encountered considerable difficulty in attracting sufficient suitable tenants to their estates. Some of the landowners and their principal tenants were of Scots Presbyterian background, and the arrival of the new migrants meant that this group was now in a position of sufficient strength to challenge the indignities that they had previously endured and to claim equal status with their counterparts in the established church. This new assertiveness of the Dissenter group was

---

[83] On the constitutional arguments, see Simms, *William Molyneux of Dublin*, esp. pp. 102–119, and William Molyneux, *The Case of Ireland's being bound by Acts of Parliament in England, Stated* (Dublin, 1698), reprinted with introduction by J. G. Simms and afterword by Denis Donoghue (Dublin, 1977). For a good example of Irish Protestants likening themselves to the Israelites, see J. G., *The State of the Papist and Protestant Proprieties*, p. 19, where it is stated that "the fatal judgement . . . which last befel this kingdom, which next to the abomination of desolation which befel the Jews was the heaviest and sharpest that ever befel so small a spot of the world since the world began."

[84] Simms, *William Molyneux of Dublin*, esp. pp. 73–90, 102–119.

greatly resented by ascendancy Protestants, but even more alarming was the cynical exploitation by British government officials of these divisions within the Irish Protestant ranks.[85]

The fear among established-church Protestants in Ireland that the British government would side with the Dissenters against them was a prime factor in explaining their increased alienation from their mother country. To this was added concern over the economic policies pursued by the British government toward Ireland; a general suspicion of the British government's intentions in relation to the ownership of Irish land; and a resentment over the appointment of English fortune hunters rather than loyal Irishmen to the choice positions in the judiciary, the church, and the Dublin government. The combination of these factors provoked the spokesmen of the Irish Protestant ascendancy to engage in the composition of opposition literature. This literature and the opposition movement associated with it gave rise to the appellation *patriot*, and a series of events associated with the dispensation of government patronage during the eighteenth century provided those who would be patriots with the opportunity to prove repeatedly that their primary allegiance was to Ireland rather than to the government in London. Lockean principles continued to be cited whenever a new issue of contention arose between the British government and particular elements of the Irish Protestant elite, but the spokesmen for the Irish cause found even more cogent support among the arguments enunciated by the radical opponents to government in England. The growing self-confidence that derived from the repetition of these borrowed arguments combined with an increasing awareness of British corruption to produce a strident reform movement in late eighteenth-century Ireland. The immediate object of this effort was to end both the control exerted by the British government over Irish institutions and the privileges enjoyed by those elements of the Irish oligarchy who had succumbed to the corruption of the court.[86]

[85] On this migration of Scots, which one contemporary estimated as 50,000 families, see L. M. Cullen, "Population Trends in Seventeenth-Century Ireland," *Economic and Social Review* 6 (1974–75):149–65, esp. pp. 157–58. On the Irish Protestant hostility toward these Scots, see D. W. Hayton, "Ireland after the Glorious Revolution," esp. pp. 6–9.

[86] Some of the episodes that gave rise to tension are treated in *Penal Era and Golden Age*, ed. Bartlett and Hayton. The development of radical thinking in Ireland has received its best treatment in Caroline Robbins, *The Eighteenth Century Commonwealth Man* (Cambridge, Mass., 1959), esp. pp. 134–76. See also Seán Murphy, "The Lucas Affair: A Study of Municipal and Electoral Politics in Dublin, 1742–9" (M.A. thesis, University College, Dublin, 1981). The tendency of Irish Protestants to depict themselves as honest country folk free from the corruption of metropolitan society is graphically illustrated in the novel *Vertue Rewarded or The Irish Princess* where the heroine, an Irish Protestant, is described in the introduction, sig. A2ᵛ, as "an innocent country virgin, ignorant of the intrigues and tricks of the court ladies."

The ideology that inspired this movement has become known as colonial nationalism. It was strongly infused by the evangelical brand of Protestantism that continued to find favor with the settler population. This, in turn, made the Irish reformers even more conscious of the moral superiority of their own society, and they like their counterparts in British North America looked askance at what they believed to be the growing degeneracy of English urban and court society. Because of the premium that Irish Protestants attached to their moral integrity, some historians have faulted them for neglecting to undertake the religious reform of the native population, and these same historians have suggested that their failure in this matter, when circumstances most favored them in the eighteenth century, casts doubt on their very sincerity as reformers. To say this is to miss the point that for these, as for all previous generations of Protestants in Ireland, the task of religious reform was one that had to await the social and economic improvement of the country.

Furthermore, they could and did claim that the penal legislation against Catholics that had been enacted in the Irish parliament in the aftermath of the Williamite wars was designed to promote Protestantism in Ireland by eliminating those influences that had previously distracted the population from true religion. But in saying this, the Anglo-Irish political leaders were conscious that their efforts in this direction may have been too late, and they deplored the fact that their hands had previously been tied by British governments that had been more concerned with procuring the good will of their Continental allies than with promoting reformed religion in Ireland.[87] This meant that in the eighteenth century, even more specifically than in the seventeenth, the hopes for a general religious reform in Ireland were linked to the whole question of social and economic regeneration. Delay in the achievement of this was still attributed to unthinking interference from Britain, and the notion was fostered that once constitutional independence had been achieved the social amelioration of society would immediately ensue.[88] Indeed, this idea had become so fixed in the minds of Irish Protestants by the end of the eighteenth century that the radicals among them had come to attribute the survival of Catholicism to the constitutional limitations under which the country endured rather than, as previously, to the retarded economic and social condition under which the

[87] S. J. Connolly, "Religion and History," *Irish Economic and Social History* 11 (1984):66–80; Hayton, "Ireland after the Glorious Revolution," pp. 3–6.

[88] This simplistic notion of how economic and social improvement might be attained has been treated critically in L. M. Cullen "Problems in the Interpretation and Revision of Eighteenth-Century Irish Economic History," *Transactions of the Royal Historical Society*, 5th ser., 17 (1967):1–22.

native population lived. This argument was put most forcefully by Theobald Wolfe Tone, who believed that Catholicism in Ireland would wither away once constitutional reform had been implemented because "if the Catholics were emancipated, no matter on what compact with government, in a little time they would become like other people." This did not mean in any sense that Tone was relaxing the traditional Protestant animosity toward the Catholic church, which he always regarded as an instrument of tyranny, but he did believe that the hold that the institution exerted over the native population of Ireland would be weakened once it had been exposed to the counterattraction of enlightened liberalism. This he expressed most forcefully in a statement as notable for Tone's contempt of Catholicism as it is for his confidence in the inevitable triumph of social reform:

The emancipated and liberal Irishman, like the emancipated and liberal Frenchman may go to Mass, may tell his beads, or sprinkle his mistress with holy water, but neither the one nor the other will attend to the rusty and extinguished thunderbolts of the Vatican, or the idle anathemas, which indeed his Holiness is now-a-days too prudent and cautious to issue.[89]

Evidence that these arguments were taken seriously is provided by those Protestants who sought to prepare the ground for the social reform that would precede the moral uplift of the population. The comprehensive survey of the country that was conducted by William Petty as part of the Cromwellian confiscation was much appreciated by the Irish Protestant population at large, and his example was followed by those landlords who in ever increasing numbers in the eighteenth century undertook the mapping of their estates. But Petty himself had gone beyond mere mapping to provide some estimate of the quality and agricultural potential of land at the local level, and the desirability of a more comprehensive survey of this nature was admitted by those who were most committed to reform. The Dublin Philosophical Society actually devised a questionnaire for a natural history of Ireland that would supersede that of the Boate brothers, and more limited advances in agricultural and manufacturing technology were promoted, throughout the eighteenth century, by its successor, the Dublin

[89] The quotations from Tone, which I owe to Thomas Bartlett, are from *The Life of Theobald Wolfe Tone*, ed. W.T.W. Tone, 2 vols. (Washington, D.C., 1826), 1:187–88, 2:358. It is of interest that this same argument persisted among liberal Irish Protestants into the twentieth century, and received its most colorful expression from Captain Terence O'Neill, prime minister of Northern Ireland (1963–1969), who found it "frightfully hard to explain to a Protestant that if you give Roman Catholics a good job and a good house they will live like Protestants because they will see neighbours with cars and T.V. sets. They will refuse to have eighteen children . . ." (quoted in *The Conflict of Nationality in Modern Ireland*, ed. A. C. Hepburn [London, 1980], p. 182).

Society. Protestant landowners in Ireland were generally concerned to give a practical illustration of these advances on their estates, and all progressive landowners were dedicated to shaping their immediate domestic environments to recognized civil models. Some went beyond this to sponsor manufacturing on their estates, and many invested in the development of internal transport and the creation of artificial villages. All such endeavors were consonant with what had been recommended by those who had devised the blueprint for the conquest and reform of Ireland, and to this extent the Protestants of the eighteenth century were being guided by the writers of the late Elizabethan period.[90]

The improvements promoted by Protestant landowners in eighteenth-century Ireland demonstrated that some of these were abreast of the most advanced technology of the time. It is significant that as many copies of the *Encyclopédie* were sold in Dublin as in London and more than in "Enlightened" Edinburgh. The practical effect of the endeavors of the reformers in Ireland were most evident in Ulster, where the development of the linen industry added enormously to the wealth of a hitherto backward province, even if the price of this was the ruination of that province's agriculture. The fact that this was also the most Protestant, albeit Dissenter, province added further credence to the belief that religious reform would follow rapidly upon the country's social and economic improvement.[91]

This strange mixture of broad interest and particular concerns is also evident when one examines the outlook of the Irish Protestant population on European politics of the eighteenth century. The Continental military campaigns were followed with avid interest by Irish Protestant gentlemen,

[90] For a good example of Petty's continued concern with reform in Ireland, see Sir William Petty, *The Political Anatomy of Ireland, 1672*, in *A Collection of Tracts and Treatises Illustrative of the Natural History . . . of Ireland*, 2 vols. (Dublin, 1861), 2:3–126. For other efforts to arrive at a more scientific understanding of Ireland's resources with a view to promoting reform see Trinity College Dublin [T.C.D.], Ms. 883/1; Ms. 888/1; Ms. 889/1; Sir Henry Piers, "A Chorographical Description of the County of Westmeath, written A.D. 1682," in *Collectanea De Rebus Hibernicis* (Dublin, 1786), 1:1–126; "The Papers of the Dublin Philosophical Society, 1683–1708: Introductory Material and Index," ed. K. T. Hoppen, in *Analecta Hibernica* 30 (1982):153–248. See also L. M. Cullen, *The Emergence of Modern Ireland, 1600–1900* (London, 1981), esp. pp. 39–60; James Meenan and Desmond Clarke, eds., *The Royal Dublin Society, 1731–1981* (Dublin, 1981); and *Macartney of Lisanoure, 1737–1806: Essays in Biography*, ed. Peter Roebuck (Belfast, 1983), pp. 278–307.

[91] Robert Darnton, *The Business of Enlightenment: A Publishing History of the Encyclopédie, 1775–1800* (Cambridge, Mass., 1979), pp. 229–319. That a demand for the *Encyclopédie* should exist in Dublin is not surprising when account is taken of earlier intellectual developments, described in "The Papers of the Dublin Philosophical Society," ed. K. T. Hoppen. The concern with the promotion of manufacturing on his estate is well exemplified in the correspondence of Sir John Rawdon, whose lands lay in northeast Ulster and who was actively involved in promoting linen manufacturing among his tenants (Huntington Library, Hastings Mss., Box 34).

but it emerges from this correspondence that their eyes were firmly fixed on the fortunes of the British flag rather than on the resolution of the issues in dispute. In this they may not have been very different from English squires, but their particular concern was over the presence in the army of France of an Irish Catholic regiment led by the Irish supporters of James II and their descendants. This gave rise to the fear that a French victory over the British armies on the Continent could lead to an attempt by the dispossessed Irish Catholic landowners to recover their estates with the support of the French.[92]

That the motivating force of Irish Protestants was fear of the French rather than support for the British cause is underlined by the fact that their sympathy was firmly on the side of the revolutionaries in the thirteen mainland colonies of North America. Irish Protestants could see the parallel between their own situation and that of the disgruntled colonials, and the struggle there acted as a mobilizing point for the Irish reform movement. But the struggle in America served the purpose of the Irish reformers in another sense, in that it enabled them to advance a plausible case for the raising of a volunteer army from their own resources to provide for the defense of the country in the event of an attempted French invasion. These volunteers sprang from the militia network that had enjoyed the support of Irish Protestants until it was allowed to lapse by the British government in the early 1760s. When the militia was revived under this different guise, it was used by the Protestant political nation to extract constitutional concessions from the British government that would never have been granted under normal conditions.[93] The more radical of their number wished to go beyond concessions to follow the example of their North American counterparts and strive for independence. The majority of the reformers, however, recognized that their interest would not be served by this and they reduced their demands to a limited reform of government and parliament that they believed would further consolidate their position.

[92] Hayton, "Ireland after the Glorious Revolution." What was a nightmare for the Irish Protestants was, of course, a dream for some Irish Catholics, as is evident from the Gaelic poetry of the period. See Seán Ó Tuama, Filí faoi Scéimhle [Poets under Duress] (Dublin, 1978), pp. 88–204. It is clear from Hayton's writings that Irish Protestants came to accept that the possibility of French invasion was extremely remote, and they were then confident that they could, from their own resources, curb any rebellion that might arise in Ireland. This confidence and complacency emerges dramatically in the letters of Richard Boyle, second earl of Shannon to his son Henry, Viscount Boyle, at the height of the 1798 rebellion, in which the insurrection assumed the dimension of a curiosity hardly more important than local estate and family gossip; see Lord Shannon's Letters to his Son: A Calendar of the Letters written by the Second Earl of Shannon to his son, Viscount Boyle, 1790–1802, ed. Esther Hewitt (Belfast, 1982), esp. pp. 46–180.

[93] On the politics of the volunteers see P.D.H. Smyth, "The Volunteers and Parliament, 1779–84," in Penal Era and Golden Age, ed. Bartlett and Hayton, pp. 113–36.

When the more radical element did make a bid for revolution, they soon discovered that support for their cause was largely confined to those parts of Ulster in which large numbers of disgruntled Dissenters accounted for more general dissatisfaction with the status quo. Potential supporters in the remainder of the country had come to recognize that they and their coreligionists were essentially a *rentier* class who, regardless of their resentment of Britain, could never aspire to complete separation from the mother country because this would result in their being eventually engulfed by the native population, who had never been assimilated into a civil condition and who far outnumbered them in every province except Ulster. Once this admission was made, the spirit of colonial nationalism was broken and most of those who had teetered on the brink of political independence settled instead for a union with Britain. This expedient, which became a reality in 1801, contradicted everything that Irish Protestants had previously striven to achieve, but in the heated atmosphere of the late eighteenth century this had come to be seen as the only arrangement that would assure a continuation of their privileged position in Ireland.[94]

This essay has identified the process by which the Anglo-Irish population came to see themselves as a distinct people, and the extent to which this growing self-consciousness brought these people to challenge the political authority of the dominant English parliament has also been discussed. It has been noted how the rationalizations that were devised to serve a particular purpose in the sixteenth century were commissioned to serve an entirely different purpose in the two subsequent centuries. These rationalizations alone were hardly sufficient to compel their exponents to recommend any challenge to English authority in Ireland, but when they were combined with crude Calvinist notions of the elect and with Lockean concepts of the corrupting influence of power, an ideology was created that made it almost inevitable that a challenge to English government authority would occur. This challenge was deferred until the later decades of the eighteenth century, when the development of a revolutionary situation in North America created the circumstances that made it possible for the Anglo-Irish political leaders to assert their independence. Once the challenge was launched, however, the British government forced the majority to reconsider their position by suggesting that they would contemplate the restora-

---

[94] The shift from a reform to a reactionary stance has received its best treatment in A.P.W. Malcomson, *John Foster: the Politics of the Anglo-Irish Ascendancy.* See also Thomas Bartlett, "An End to Moral Economy: The Irish Militia Disturbances of 1793," *Past and Present,* no. 99 (1983):41–64. For the best recent analysis of the writings of one of the radicals see Tom Dunne, *Theobald Wolfe Tone, Colonial Outsider: An Analysis of His Political Philosophy* (Cork, 1982).

tion of civil liberties to the Catholics. This prospect forced the Anglo-Irish population to take stock of the situation that would exist if their claims to independence should prove successful, and the more cautious recognized that in an independent state they would be hopelessly outnumbered by a subservient but hostile population that had never been assimilated into their dominant culture. Rather than permit this situation to develop, most of the Irish political nation recognized they would have to shelve the liberal reforms they had previously espoused because they had not implemented the civilizing endeavor that had justified their engagement in Ireland in the first instance. Thus the words of Sir John Davies had proven prophetic: by failing to assimilate the native population of Ireland, the Anglo-Irish had been deprived of their own freedom of action and had, like the Old English before them, become "slaves to that nation which they did intend to conquer."[95]

[95] Davies, *Discovery*, p. 150. This conclusion implies that the concern of the Anglo-Irish population in the centuries after 1801 were quite different from what they had been previously, but there was naturally a considerable carryover in their interests and obsessions, as is neatly illustrated in Seamus Deane, "Civilians and Barbarians" (Derry, A Field Day Pamphlet, no. 3, 1983).

7 ❧ Changing Identity in the
British Caribbean: Barbados as a Case Study

Jack P. Greene

Dimensions of Identity

STUDENTS of the European colonizing experience have long insisted that
one of the most attractive aspects of their subject is the opportunity to observe the development of the new social entities they study from their very
beginnings. In contrast to the European societies from which they ema-
nated, the origins of which are no longer recoverable, early-modern colonies in America and elsewhere all have identifiable beginnings, about
which, in many cases, the documentary record is sufficiently detailed to
permit a reconstruction of the basic processes of social formation. Especially in recent years, considerable attention has been devoted to the economic, social, and cultural institutions and structures created by colonists
in this process. With the notable exception of Puritan New England, however, much less consideration has been given to the ways in which those
colonists acquired coherent identities as peoples and societies knit together
by a series of common aspirations and experiences in particular places.[1]

Each time a group of Europeans occupied a new segment of America,
they encountered what was for them "a strange Country," but it is important to recognize that in no instance was the region encountered a tabula
rasa.[2] Not only was it a physical entity with its own distinctive ecosystem,
topography, animal and vegetable life, and climate but, in most cases, the
physical landscape had also already been organized into an articulated social and cultural landscape inhabited by one or more particular groups of
people. By determining to an important degree what could and could not
be done there by its new occupants, by both presenting them with certain
opportunities and depriving them of others, these preexisting physical and
social attributes of place constituted one of the most important ingredients
in defining the identities of the new societies that would be constructed in
them. At the same time that they were coming to terms with their new
spaces, learning both how to manipulate them for their own survival and
material advantage and how to describe them in terms that would enable

[1] On New England, see in particular Sacvan Bercovitch, *The Puritan Origins of the American
Self* (New Haven, 1975), and Michael Zuckerman, "The Fabrication of Identity in Early
America," *William and Mary Quarterly*, 3d ser., 34 (1977):183–214.
[2] The quotation is from Richard Ligon, *A True & Exact History of the Island of Barbadoes*
(London, 1673), p. 121.

them and others to comprehend them, European settlers also became active agents in changing them, in creating new social landscapes.

The shape and content of these new landscapes as well as of the identities that they sustained were determined not just by characteristics of place. Three additional sets of variables also had a powerful influence. First were the short-term and long-term social and economic goals that had initially drawn and, as revised in the light of local potentialities, would continue to draw European settlers to specific places. Second were the standards of what a civilized society should be and how its members should behave. These standards had initially been brought by the earliest settlers from their metropolis, but they were subsequently revised or updated through a process of continuous cultural interaction with that metropolis. Third were the collective experiences—the history—that successive generations of inhabitants shared in their particular place.

Out of the interaction among these four sets of variables—attributes of place, goals, standards, and history—the inhabitants of each new society in the early-modern colonial world gradually acquired a well-articulated definition of itself. This definition involved the settlers in considering themselves as belonging to a corporate unit and in viewing themselves as a collection of people who shared not just common membership in a given social order in a particular place but also a set of commonly held values and orientations. These latter provided the inhabitants with a shared basis for approved social behavior and equipped them to interpret both contemporary events and developments and the social meaning of their own individual lives. Only as this definition of the collective self was, little by little, first articulated and refined by both the inhabitants and those who observed them from the outside and then internalized by the inhabitants did they come to some clear understanding of what they and their society were about. Finally, through that understanding and the reputation that comprised its external face, the inhabitants achieved a coherent corporate identity, that is, a well-defined sense of themselves and their society and a distinctive reputation by which they were known by the outside world.

This corporate identity was necessarily stereotypical, but it is nonetheless worthy of analysis because it constitutes the only coherent expression of what a particular collectivity of people thought of itself and how it wished to be regarded by outsiders. To this extent, each colony's corporate sense of self provides a key to the contemporary meaning of its inhabitants' collective experiences in founding and developing the new society in which they lived. At the same time, no collective identity is static, and an analysis of its changing content reveals, perhaps as well as can the study of any other single phenomenon, the character of a given colony's responses

214

to the successive social, economic, cultural, and political transformations it underwent. Based upon reflection on some of the voluminous published contemporary descriptions, analyses, and histories, this essay seeks to describe and to explain the changing identity and reputation of colonial Barbados and Barbadians from the colony's first founding during the second quarter of the seventeenth century through the first eight decades of the eighteenth century.

No doubt it would be possible to work on a more general level and to explicate a British Caribbean, British plantation colony, British American, or even pan-British identity during the period considered in this essay. Indeed, some preliminary effort will be made to relate the Barbadian experience to that of other British plantation colonies in the Caribbean and on the mainland. But one of the central assumptions underlying this essay is that, notwithstanding certain manifest similarities, the emerging identity of each new early-modern American society was powerfully shaped by a distinctive set of place-specific and time-specific experiences that gave it a content unique to the place, society, and people it had been constructed to describe.

This assumption has been confirmed by a much more ambitious, though as yet unfinished, study of the same subject for the same period in three other British-American plantation societies, those of Virginia, Jamaica, and South Carolina,[3] as well as by a shorter analysis of colonial Georgia.[4] The corollary of this assumption is, of course, that a more general understanding of the formation and acquisition of identity in these early plantation societies, of the common elements of what might be designated as a plantation self in early-modern colonial British America, can best be undertaken on the basis of careful reconstructions of the identities of specific societies.

"By all the sweet Negotiation[s] of Sugar"

A small island of only 166 square miles (106,000 acres), Barbados had been ignored by Iberian colonizing powers for more than 125 years prior to its occupation by the English in 1627. Even then, it was settled without any of the fanfare that had characterized the establishment of Virginia two decades earlier or would accompany the founding of Massachusetts Bay a few

---

[3] The tentative title of this study, which is still in progress, is "Paradise Defined: Studies in the Emergence and Changing Character of the Plantation Self in Virginia, Jamaica, and South Carolina, 1660 to 1815."

[4] Jack P. Greene, "Travails of an Infant Colony: Searching for Viability, Coherence, and Identity in Colonial Georgia," in *Forty Years of Diversity: Essays on Colonial Georgia,* ed. Harvey H. Jackson and Phinizy Spalding (Athens, Ga., 1984), pp. 278–309.

years later or the settlement of Jamaica, Carolina, and Pennsylvania following the Restoration. With Jamaica, which was captured from the Spanish in 1656, and the four Leeward Islands of Antigua, Montserrat, Nevis, and St. Christopher (St. Kitts), Barbados was one of the six permanent English colonies settled in the Caribbean during the seventeenth century. Though its claim to have been the first English Caribbean colony has been challenged by both St. Kitts and Nevis, its early success as a staple colony made Barbados a model for all subsequent English settlements in the region, albeit a model that was never fully imitated by any other colony.

During its first decade and a half, Barbados quietly attracted from England a substantial population of yeomen farmers and servants who managed both to raise enough provisions to feed themselves and to develop a modestly lucrative export trade in tobacco, cotton, and ginger.[5] During the 1640s, its inhabitants began to raise sugar cane, and within fifteen years they were producing large quantities of sugar for export. With this sugar revolution came more settlers—adventurers in search of their fortune, white servants from the home country, and black slaves from the coast of Africa—and, among English colonies up to that time, unparalleled wealth. By the 1660s, Barbados was probably the most densely populated and intensely cultivated agricultural area in the English-speaking world, and it had acquired a widespread fame as a place of abundance and riches—at least for its free inhabitants.[6]

By 1670, however, Barbados was already losing its position as England's leading sugar-producing colony to Jamaica. More than twenty-six times as large as Barbados, with soils not previously subjected to intensive sugar cultivation, Jamaica offered its free inhabitants greater opportunities for acquiring even more substantial fortunes as well as for constructing a richer and more extensive social and cultural life. With similarly "new" soils, even smaller islands during their early decades of settlement (including both the four Leeward Islands, the four new colonies—Dominica, Grenada, St. Vincent, and Tobago—acquired by the British in the 1760s, and the still newer colonies of Trinidad and St. Lucia conquered during the Napoleonic wars) enjoyed a comparative economic advantage over Barbados, yielding both more sugar per acre and higher rates of profit.[7]

Notwithstanding its relative decline in relation to these newer sugar col-

<hr>

[5] See F. C. Innes, "The Pre-Sugar Era of European Settlement in Barbados," *Journal of Caribbean History* 1 (1970):1–22.

[6] Richard S. Dunn, *Sugar and Slaves: The Rise of the Planter Class in the English West Indies, 1624–1713* (Chapel Hill, 1972), pp. 46–116.

[7] Richard B. Sheridan, *Sugar and Slavery: An Economic History of the British West Indies 1623–1775* (Baltimore, 1974), pp. 30–35, 97–147. See also Richard Pares, *Merchants and Planters* (London, 1960), pp. 14–25.

onies, Barbados continued to be an important sugar producer throughout the early-modern period, producing in its much smaller area between a fifth to a third of the quantity of sugar produced in Jamaica. Perhaps more important, it also continued to be the most densely settled and most intensively cultivated colony in British colonial America and to have a much higher ratio of whites to blacks and, in all probability, a higher proportion of creoles (native born) among both its white and black inhabitants than any other British Caribbean colony. Though we lack detailed studies of the social and political development of Barbados during the late eighteenth and early nineteenth centuries, it also seems to have retained vigorous political and social institutions and an active white creole elite population and, in comparison with other British plantation colonies at comparable stages in their development, to have enjoyed a rich cultural life.

Elsewhere in colonial British plantation America, the process of identity formation seems to have involved three sequential, if not always sharply distinguishable, phases. During the first phase, characteristics of place usually assumed primacy. That is, settlers and their sponsors tended to identify their society in terms of the nature and potentialities of the place in which they lived. During a second phase, they tended to define themselves more in terms of how they were actually organizing their social and cultural landscapes and the extent to which those landscapes did—or did not—conform to inherited notions and standards of how such landscapes should be organized. Finally, during a third phase, they gave increasing emphasis to their predominant characteristics as people and to the common experiences shared by themselves and their ancestors.

Because it neither attracted widespread attention in England nor achieved a visible identity until after it had already become a thriving concern, Barbados seems largely to have skipped the first phase in this process. In marked contrast to the experience of most other early-modern colonies in colonial British plantation America, the observers and interpreters who first began to characterize Barbados for themselves and the outside world emphasized less its special attributes as a physical entity than its most prominent features as a sugar-producing society. Through its first eight decades, the predominant image of Barbados as it was set forth in a large variety of reports, descriptions, and travelers' accounts[8] as well as in extended histo-

---

[8] These works, citations to which will be found in the notes below, are listed in Jerome S. Handler's excellent *A Guide to Source Materials for the Study of Barbados History, 1627–1834* (Carbondale, Ill., 1971), and in Handler and Samuel J. Hough, "Addenda to *A Guide to Source Materials for the Study of Barbados History, 1627–1834,*" published in six parts in the *Journal of the Barbados Museum and Historical Society* 36 (1980–82):172–77, 279–85, 385–97; 37 (1983):82–92, 296–307; 38 (1987):107–116.

ries by Richard Ligon[9] and John Oldmixon[10] was that of a rich, populous, and flourishing settlement, whose enormous economic value to England and extraordinarily rapid development had almost entirely been accomplished through what Ligon referred to as "the sweet Negotiation[s] of Sugar."[11]

This is not to suggest that either earlier or later writers on Barbados ignored its tropical character. Indeed, although the island's comparatively gentle terrain was reminiscent of home, they could scarcely fail to note the sharp contrasts with England in climate, animal and insect life, and vegetation. Like northern Europeans elsewhere in the tropics, new settlers found the unrelieved and "torrid heat of the Sun," which "scorch't up" the island "from morning till night," especially debilitating, and they complained about the excessive humidity that seemed to produce instant rust on metal tools and implements, the annoying attacks of the numerous populations of mosquitoes and chiggers, the extensiveness of the heavy forests that covered the island, and the fecundity of both animal and vegetable life. In the spring, ugly land crabs were so thick upon the ground that it was impossible to walk without stepping on them, while vicious withes grew so fast that they would cover a ten-foot clearing overnight and could be kept from invading cultivated ground only with enormous labor and diligence.[12]

For all its fruitfulness, moreover, Barbados was not well suited to produce many of the foods to which Englishmen were accustomed. It wanted the "English man[']s grasse," complained one writer in 1648, "and so the English man[']s Beef, Mutton, Milk, Butter and Cheese." Having no wheat for bread, they had to make do with flour made from cassava roots, "whose juice is poyson, so [that] the negligence of a servant or slave in the right making of it may cost the whole family a poysoning." Though infrequent, hurricanes, such as that which struck the island on August 31, 1675, brought "Pestilential Blasts" of an intensity and duration unknown in England. Finally, although Barbados was thought to be both the "healthfullest

[9] Ligon's extensive work was first published in London in 1657 and republished there in 1673. A full citation will be found in note 2. All citations to this work in this essay are to the second edition.

[10] John Oldmixon, *The British Empire in America*, 1st ed., 2 vols. (London, 1708), 2:1–196. Devoting far more space to the history of Barbados than to any other colony, Oldmixon's account, updated in a second edition published in London in 1741 (2:1–171), was the most extensive history of the colony published prior to the early nineteenth century.

[11] Ligon, *True & Exact History*, p. 96.

[12] Ibid., pp. 24, 27, 62, 66, 97, 102, 106, 110, 117; Alexander Gunkel and Jerome S. Handler, eds. and trans., "A Swiss Medical Doctor's Description of Barbados in 1661: The Account of Felix Christian Spörri," *Jo. Barbados Mus. and Hist. Soc.* 33 (1969):5; Samuel Clarke, *A True, and Faithful Account of the Four Cheifest Plantations of the English in America* (London, 1670), p. 58.

in all the westerne islands" and far less lethal than Virginia during its early decades, its illnesses, as Ligon lamented, were "more grievous, and mortality greater by far than in *England*, and these diseases many times contagious." All newcomers lived in dread of the "*Contrey Diseas*," probably yellow fever, and dysentery, malaria, various fevers, and other "dire Disease[s]" killed hundreds and in some years even thousands. "Black Ribbon for mourning," wrote Ligon, "is much worn there."[13]

For all of "Old Nature's Crimes" in Barbados, however, for all of the island's physical dissimilarity from England, its new inhabitants displayed a ready appreciation of its virtues as a tropical paradise. Never cold, it seemed to be "perpetual[ly] springing."

> Whilst the Sun in Northern Clime
> Posts, as if he grudg'd his Time,
> Robbing all of Life's Delights,
>   In Short Days and tedious Nights,

one local poet declared in celebratory rhyme early in the eighteenth century. Barbadians were

> Curst with no Cold Winter here,
>   Nature shines Serene and Clear,
> Fresh Spring and Summer smiling
>   all the Year.

Not only, in happy contrast to England, was Barbados always warm and always green. It had also been endowed by the "great Gardiner of the World" with a rich variety of exotic and glorious flowers, fruits, and trees. There was "not a more Royal or Magnificent tree growing on earth, for beauty and largeness," Ligon noted, than the palmetto royal, and the pineapple, which rarely failed to captivate palates of Europeans wherever they encountered it, contained "all that" was "excellent in a superlative degree, for beauty and taste."[14]

Indeed, by Caribbean standards, proponents of Barbados rarely failed to point out, Barbados had a temperate climate, the usual heat of the tropics being tempered by a constant breeze from the gentle trade winds that flowed

[13] Ligon, *True & Exact History*, pp. 21, 23, 25, 29–30, 33–34, 110, 117; Spörri, "Account," pp. 5–6; Beauchamp Plantagenet, *A Description of the Province of New Albion* ([London], 1648), p. 5; Thomas Verney to Sir Edmund Verney, Feb. 10, 1638, in *Letters and Papers of the Verney Family down to the end of the year 1639*, ed. John Bruce (London, 1853), p. 193; *An Ode Pindarick on Barbados* ([London, 1710]), p. 1; Neville Connell, "Father Labat's Visit to Barbados in 1700," *Jo. Barbados Mus. and Hist. Soc.* 24 (1957):164, 171.

[14] *Ode Pindarick*, pp. 1–2; Ligon, *True & Exact History*, pp. 75, 80, 82, 84–85; Verney to Verney, Feb. 10, 1638, in Bruce, *Verney Family Papers*, p. 194.

across the island. Together with these cooling breezes, sweet fruits, and fragrant blossoms, verdant prospects and brilliant night skies contributed to make Barbados an "extremely beautiful" and "Pleasant Place." Notwithstanding the many, for newcomers, unpleasant, even malignant, qualities of the island's climate, Barbados thus came to be routinely depicted by residents and visitors alike as an appealing habitation, a place that was so "happy" in its physical characteristics that its inhabitants might live in ease and comfort in a setting that was more fruitful and more inviting than any that could be found in the more temperate regions of Albion.[15]

If, as one resident avowed shortly after the Restoration, God had "made our Island Habitable and Fruitfull," its new European inhabitants brought the sugar cane that made it rich. From the beginning of settlement, people had come to Barbados for the principal purpose of improving their economic situations. Independent adventurers, like young Thomas Verney, expected to raise large "fortunes in a few years," and impecunious servants hoped to escape the desperate circumstances in which they found themselves in England. To these ends, Barbados early attracted a considerable population. By the mid-1640s, it was said, almost certainly with exaggeration, that the island had 20,000 European inhabitants. Yet, few Barbadian proprietors became wealthy until after they had discovered in the late 1640s that "nothing . . . succeed[ed] better than sugar." When he arrived in Barbados in September 1647, Ligon reported, the "great work of Sugar-making" was "but in its infancy, and but faintly understood." By the time he left, just three years later, however, sugar was being produced "to a high perfection." As it became increasingly clear that sugar would be "the main Plant, to improve the value of the whole Island," Barbadian landholders "bent all their endeavours to . . . planting, and making Sugar," which rapidly became the "soul of Trade" for the island.[16]

Once its landholders had "learned the Art of making Sugar," Barbados "in a short time . . . grew very considerable," increasing dramatically in

---

[15] Ligon, *True & Exact History*, pp. 20–21, 106; Clarke, *True, and Faithful Account*, pp. 59–60; Jerome S. Handler, "Father Antoine Biet's Visit to Barbados in 1654," *Jo. Barbados Mus. and Hist. Soc.* 32 (1967):64; Verney to Verney, Feb. 10, 1638, in Bruce, *Verney Family Papers*, p. 194; N. Darnell Davis, ed., "An Early Impression of Barbados," *West India Committee Circular* 28, no. 395 (1913):539; Peter Heylyn, *Cosmography in Four Books* (London, 1703), p. 1118; John Speed, *A Prospect of the Most Famous Parts of the World* (London, 1676), p. 48; Dr. Thomas Towns, "Observations made at Barbadoes" [1676], *Philosophical Trans-Actions of the Royal Society of London, 1672–1683* (London, 1809), 2:228–29.

[16] Davis, "Early Impression of Barbados," p. 539; Verney to Verney, Feb. 10, 1638, in Bruce, *Verney Family Papers*, p. 192; Handler, "Father Biet's Visit," pp. 66, 69; Ligon, *True & Exact History*, pp. 24, 85–86; J. Davies, trans., *The History of Barbados, St. Christophers, Mevis, . . . and the Rest of the Caribby-Islands* (London, 1666), pp. 8–9; John Ogilby, *America: being the Latest and Most Accurate Description of the New World* (London, 1671), p. 377.

both "Reputation and Wealth." Though some of them had begun with small investments, many planters had, as a result of the sugar boom, acquired "very great and vast estates." With large work forces of servants and, increasingly, African slaves purchased from their substantial sugar profits, they were able to establish sturdy foundations for the economic security of their posterities while themselves living in ease and affluence without the excessive toil that had been the lot of the first settlers. The most "Industrious and painful" among the planters, men who, like James Drax and Thomas Modiford, had the most "percing sights, and profound judgments," had been able to raise their "fortune[s] to such a height" that they "lived like little princes" and could confidently expect in just "a few years" to have enough money to purchase an English estate valued with an income of £10,000 per annum.[17]

Vast and sudden fortunes for the most successful proprietors were not, however, the only byproducts of the sugar revolution in Barbados. Most commentators who had been to the island agreed that its great wealth was being built on the cruel exploitation of its burgeoning labor force. Even among the free population, Ligon observed, "long and tedious hard labour, sleight feeding, and ill lodging" often depressed the spirits of "the meaner sort of Planters" and gradually brought them "to a declining and yielding condition." The unfree seem to have fared much worse. White servants and black slaves alike were reportedly subjected to "very hard labour," fed as little as possible, housed in conditions scarcely fit for animals, and treated with "a great deal of severity." "Truly," wrote Ligon, "I have seen such cruelty there done to Servants, as I did not think one Christian could have done to another." "All are very badly treated," agreed a French visitor: "When they work the overseers, who act like those in charge of galley slaves, are always close by with a stick with which they often prod them when they do not work as fast as is desired."[18]

Ligon claimed that "as discreeter and better natur'd men" had gradually "come to rule" in Barbados as a result of the sugar revolution, the lives of servants had "been much bettered." But the experiences of Marcellus Rivers and Oxenbridge Foyle, two men accused of royalism and rebellion and shipped to Barbados for sale as servants in the mid-1650s, seemed to render Ligon's claim little more than a naive and as yet unfulfilled hope. Along

[17] Handler, "Father Biet's Visit," pp. 64, 66, 69; R[ichard] B[urton], *The English Empire in America, or a Prospect of His Majesties Dominions in the West Indies* (London, 1685), p. 199; Heylyn, *Cosmography*, p. 1118; Plantagenet, *Description*, p. 5; Ligon, *True & Exact History*, pp. 34, 43, 86, 96; Spörri, "Account," p. 7; Speed, *Prospect*, p. 48.

[18] Ligon, *True & Exact History*, pp. 41, 43–44, 91; Handler, "Father Biet's Visit," pp. 66–67; Spörri, "Account," p. 7; Speed, *Prospect*, p. 48.

with many other political prisoners, they complained to the English reading public in 1659, they had fallen into the hands of the "most inhuman and barbarous persons," who worked them hard, fed them meagerly, and in general reduced them to the "most deplorable, and (as to Englishmen) . . . unparalleled condition" in which they were "bought and sold . . . from one planter to another, or attached as horses and beasts for the debts of their masters, . . . whipped at the whipping-posts (as rogues) for their masters' pleasure," forced to sleep "in sties worse than hogs in England, and [in] many other ways made miserable, beyond expression or Christian imagination."[19]

If Christians met with such "extream ill usage," the African slaves who year by year after 1650 came to comprise a larger share of the island's labor force and total population had to endure even worse. Because their permanent enslavement gave their masters a strong material incentive to keep them alive and well enough to work, Ligon thought that slaves were "kept and preserv'd with greater care"; a later writer even argued in the early 1670s that they were "well contented with their Conditions." But most other contemporary testimony pointed to the contrary. Even those, like Ligon, who appreciated the intellectual capacities of blacks and advocated their conversion to Christianity, still considered them to be "as near beasts as may be." Furthermore, blacks were said to have been worked harder and provided with less food, clothing, and shelter even than white servants. Indeed to blacks, it appeared, as one slave was said to have declared, that *"The Devel was in the English-man, that he makes every thing work; he makes the* Negro *work, the* Horse *work, the* Ass *work, the* Wood *work, the* Water *work, and the* Winde *work."* This remark underlines how thoroughly exploitative Barbadian free society was. The fact that it was reputedly "much quoted by the [white] Inhabitants" powerfully suggests that they took considerable pride in their exploitative abilities.[20]

For slaves as well as for servants Barbados was thus not a bountiful mine of white gold but a "place of torment." For them, its true character was symbolized less by the wealth of the greater planters than by the story of Yarico, an Indian woman from the mainland. Having fallen in love with and saved the life of a young Englishman from her own people, she was repaid for her act of love by being brought to Barbados and there sold into slavery. First

---

[19] Ligon, *True & Exact History*, p. 44; Marcellus Rivers and Oxenbridge Foyle, *England's Slavery, or Barbados Merchandize* (London, 1659), pp. 1–7.

[20] Ligon, *True & Exact History*, pp. 43, 45, 47; Richard Blome, *A Description of the Island of Jamaica; with the Other Isles and Terretories in America, to which the English are related, viz. Barbados, St. Christophers, Nievis* (London, 1672), pp. 84–85; *Great News from the Barbadoes* (London, 1676), pp. 6–7.

recounted by Ligon, this story was subsequently repeated and embroidered by many writers over the following century and a half. A seemingly telling commentary on the willingness of Englishmen in Barbados and elsewhere in the tropics to sacrifice all human feelings in the pursuit of their own avarice, the story of Yarico became for the outside world an emblem of the cruelty and inhumanity that was almost as strong an element in the emerging public reputation of Barbados as was its rapid rise to affluence.[21]

The harsh conditions suffered by the island's numerous laboring population inevitably translated into fear for white proprietors. They liked to think that the spirits of slaves and servants were kept in such awe and subjection as to prevent any effort at combination against their masters. No doubt, as one visitor noted in the early 1650s, many were sufficiently terrified as to "tremble when they speak." But the prevalence of military titles among plantation owners and the character of their houses testified to their underlying fear of "being murthered by" their own "unhappy" laborers. The houses, according to Ligon, were mostly "built in [the] manner of Fortifications, and have Lines, Bulwarks, and Bastions to defend themselves, in case there should be any uproar or commotion in the Island, either by the Christian servants or *Negro* slaves." That the planters were justified in taking such precautions was borne out by the frequent occurrence of flight, desperate acts of resistance and reprisal, and conspiracies of several shapes and sizes among both slaves and servants on the island. No less than the flammable canes in their fields, labor conditions in Barbados made the colony highly "combustible, and apt to take fire" at any moment.[22]

Fear of the wrath of their maltreated laborers and scorn from the outside world for the severity of their labor system were not the only problems confronting the free inhabitants of Barbados. As Ligon explained to his English readers early in the sugar revolution, sugar, no less than any other agricultural products, was a high-risk crop. Fire, drought, death of cattle or of laborers, and losses at sea were only the most important of many misfortunes that could wipe out a man's assets, destroy his credit, and bring him to an "inevitable ruine" from which, "if he be not well friended, he never can entertain a hope to rise again." Additionally, the high mortality in Barbados meant that planters put their lives as well as their fortunes at risk. Thus,

[21] Rivers and Foyle, *England's Slavery*, pp. 1–7; Ligon, *True & Exact History*, 55. On the frequent repetition and popularity of the Yarico story, see Wylie Sypher, *Guinea's Captive Kings* (Chapel Hill, 1942), pp. 122–37.

[22] Ligon, *True & Exact History*, pp. 29, 45–46; Blome, *Description*, p. 91; Handler, "Father Biet's Visit," pp. 66–67, 69; Plantagenet, *Description*, p. 5; *Great News from Barbadoes*, pp. 9–13. For a modern analysis of the prevalence of slave discontent in seventeenth-century Barbados, see Jerome S. Handler, "Slave Revolts and Conspiracies in Seventeenth-Century Barbados," *Nieuwe West-Indische Gids* 56 (1982):5–42.

notwithstanding the possibilities offered by sugar for the rapid accumulation of fortunes, the many hazards involved made it a venture fit only for those reckless and competitive men who, having always been "will[ing to] sell their lives at such a rate, as none shall out-bid them," had grown so accustomed to risk as to become "more valiant then other men." Barbados, Ligon warned, was obviously not a place for the faint of heart or for those who preferred to "live in a quiet security."[23]

According to Ligon and other early commentators, even those who succeeded in the sugar lottery faced lives in the colony that by conventional English standards contained few attractions. To be sure, they could afford anything money could buy. Visitors were invariably struck by their great extravagance. "They economize on nothing," declared one Frenchman during the early years of the sugar revolution. They paid outrageous sums for clothes, furnished their houses "sumptuously," went "well mounted on very handsome horses . . . covered with rich saddle-cloths," enjoyed abundant tables, and served "the best wines from more than six areas in Europe, brandy, *Rossolis*, and many artificial drinks." So high was the demand for luxury goods that virtually all of the "finest" products of England and Europe were available in the island.[24]

Yet if successful planters enjoyed "exceeding[ly] profuse and costly" material lives, in almost all other respects during these early years of sugar, their lives and their society were, from the perspective of metropolitan England, impoverished and crude. Their almost total concentration on sugar meant that they gave very little attention to any other kinds of husbandry, and their "ill Husbandry" with regard to food crops and livestock was matched by the irregular and contingent character of the social landscapes they were creating. Thus Bridgetown, the chief town in the colony, was built incrementally, house by house, without plan and with no regard either to the healthiness of its situation or any other consideration—except the convenience of trade. A similar "improvidence, or inconsideration" was revealed in the colony's architecture. Mostly crude wooden structures built without regard for the peculiarities of the climate, their houses, Ligon complained, largely consisted of poorly ventilated "low roofed rooms" that in the heat of the day were more "like Stoves, or heated Ovens" than human habitations. Barbados had stone for better and more permanent buildings. By the early 1650s, moreover, it also had carpenters and masons who were "very great Masters in their Art" and fully competent to "draw a plot, and pursue the design they framed with great diligence, and beautifie the

---

[23] Ligon, *True & Exact History*, pp. 117–21.
[24] Handler, "Father Biet's Visit," pp. 67–68.

tops of their Doors, Windows, and Chimney-peeces, very prettily." However, "though the Planters talk[ed] of building houses, and wish[ed] them up, yet when they weigh the want of those hands in their sugar work, that must be employed in their building," Ligon lamented, "they fall back, and put on their considering caps."²⁵

Nor, for the same reason, did wealthy Barbadians invest much time or energy in creating the cultural amenities enjoyed by their counterparts in urban England. The concerns of most people, Ligon observed, "were so fixt upon, and so rivited to the earth, and the profits that arise out of it, as their souls were lifted no higher." Thus, although Ligon met a few people who "had musical minds," most men, he reported, thought, as some had "been heard to say, that three whip-sawes, going all at once in a Frame or Pit, is the best and sweetest musick that can enter their ears; and to hear a Cow of their own low, or an Assinigo bray, no sound can please them better."²⁶

Conventional English moral standards were also reputedly little regarded in Barbados. Drunkenness was so common that it seemed to be the very "custom of the country." Lewdness, fornication, adultery, and incest were common, and fist fighting appeared to be the primary vehicle for settling disputes. Nor, according to many commentators, was such behavior much mitigated by either law or religion. Laws against immorality were "rarely put in execution," and, in any case, the legal system was said to be both loose and mutable, with justices making "laws one court, and break[ing] them the next." Although there were ministers in every parish, "very few people" came to hear them, and the tolerance some Catholic visitors found on this nominally Protestant island was, they thought, largely the product of religious indifference. "To tell the truth," one of them declared, "they have almost no religion."²⁷

So deep had "the sins of *Sodom*" penetrated into the island's life that some Quakers and others feared for the future of the colony. That the islanders were guilty of excessive wickedness, "Lewdness and [other] Abominations," extending even to their refusal to confer "the benefit and blessing of being Christians" upon their slaves, was undeniable. Reminding Barbadians that they had only recently been very "little in thine owne eyes, and in the eyes of all that knew thee," these critics both attributed the island's rapid rise to wealth to God and predicted that without a speedy ref-

---

²⁵ Blome, *Description*, p. 89; Ligon, *True & Exact History*, pp. 25, 34, 40, 42, 102; *Great Newes from Barbadoes*, p. 4.

²⁶ Ligon, *True & Exact History*, p. 107.

²⁷ Verney to Verney, Feb. 10, 1638, in Bruce, *Verney Family Papers*, pp. 193–95; Handler, "Father Biet's Visit," pp. 61–62, 68–69; Spörri, "Account," p. 6; Ligon, *True & Exact History*, p. 101.

ormation in their behavior He would sooner or later repay their ingratitude and rebellion against Him by "Blast[ing] their Endeavors, . . . bring[ing] them into Contempt," and "Otherwise . . . bring[ing] Our fruitfull Island [once again] into a Wilderness."[28]

Thus did the early image makers of Barbados endow it with an ambivalent identity. At the same time that they were celebrating its great natural beauty and fecundity and its remarkable capacity for generating wealth through sugar, they were depicting an ugly human environment in which mortality and risks of economic failure were high and the vast labor force cruelly exploited. They also portrayed the society created by the winners in the sugar lottery as extravagant, loose, morally and culturally debased, and riddled with fears of social revolt. Although one writer claimed that the "most considerable inhabitants" thought "themselves so well[-situated in Barbados], that [they] . . . seldom . . . ever remove[d] thence," their behavior as described by the vast majority of commentators bespoke the contrary. The contingent character of the towns and houses, the planters' heedless spending of labor in the quest for immediate profits, and their evident disinterest in investing in social and cultural amenities strongly suggested that they regarded Barbados as only a temporary abode to be escaped as soon as they had made their fortunes. According to Ligon, there were few "whose minds" were "not over-ballanc'd with avarice and lucre" who did not "hanker after their own Country" and did not intend, as soon as they had enough wealth and could sell their estates, "to settle themselves quietly in England."[29]

During the 1660s and 1670s, however, observers began to put more and more emphasis upon the colony's achievements in many areas, and Barbados gradually began to acquire a more positive image. Sugar, they stressed, had brought the island not only a severe labor system and substantial wealth for many of its proprietors but also a surging population. In less than a decade following the introduction of the crop, the white population was thought to have increased by 150 percent, from 20,000 to 50,000, and the last figure became the standard estimate offered in contemporary accounts of the island for most of the rest of the seventeenth century. At the same time, the number of black slaves was said to have jumped to 100,000 by the early 1670s. Although these figures, especially those for whites, were certainly much too generous, Barbados as one visitor remarked, had become

[28] Richard Pinder, *A Loving Invitation (to Repentance and Amendment to Life) Unto All the Inhabitants of the Island of Barbados* (London, 1660), pp. 3–5; Davis, "Early Impression of Barbados," p. 539; Ligon, *True & Exact History*, p. 82.

[29] Davies, *History*, pp. 8–9; Ligon, *True & Exact History*, pp. 22, 117.

"so heavily populated in such a short time" that virtually no contemporary commentator failed to stress the density of its population in comparison with all other English colonies in America.[30]

At a time when competition among European powers in the Caribbean was intense, such a large population made Barbados unusually strong; more important, it gave the island a settled character that, in terms of both its extent and the rapidity with which it had been achieved, was unparalleled among contemporary Anglo-American settlements. In the late 1640s, it still had a lot of uncleared forests, but by the mid-1650s a substantial portion of the island had been brought under sugar cultivation. By the mid-1660s, it was so intensively planted that from the sea it could be taken, in the words of one writer, "for one great City." By the mid-1670s, it had been "so taken up in Plantations, that there" was "no wast ground to be found," the "whole Isle for these many years" having had, as one earlier observer noted, such "a supernumerary glut of inhabitants" as to make it clear that Barbados was "too small a hive for such a swarm of people."[31]

Acknowledgment of this extraordinary progress in population as well as wealth was reflected in virtually every contemporary assessment of the colony's worth to England. Not only was it "one of the chief of our Plantations" and the "most considerable Colony the *English* hath amongst that Frye of *Isles* called the *Caribbee[s]*," it was also "certainly the most flourishing, and best peopled of all" the colonies "possest by the *English*," a plantation, almost every commentator agreed, that was "worth all the rest which are made by the English"—perhaps even, in the words of one of its most ardent champions, "the finest and worthiest Island in the World." With "not more than five and twenty thousand white Inhabitants," Dalby Thomas pointed out in 1690 in *An Historical Account of the Rise and Growth of the West Indies Colonies*, the small island of Barbados had "produced in Commodities above thirty Millions *Sterling*" and had "pay'd in Duties to support the [English] Government at a modest Computation, above 3/4 of a Million" which, he remarked, must "seem incredible to those that have not Employ'd thoughts on it." To the extent that, as another advocate of Barbados argued just a few years later, it was "the Planters and Settlers of

---

[30] Ligon, *True & Exact History*, p. 43; Handler, "Father Biet's Visit," p. 69; Spörri, "Account," p. 10; Davies, *History*, pp. 8–9; Ogilby, *America*, p. 377; Blome, *Description*, p. 84; Heylyn, *Cosmography*, p. 1118; *Great Newes from Barbadoes*, pp. 13–14; B[urton],' *English Empire in America*, p. 199.

[31] Ligon, *True & Exact History*, pp. 24, 106; Handler, "Father Biet's Visit," pp. 65–66; Edmund Hickeringill, *Jamaica Viewed* (London, 1661), pp. 16–17; Davis, "Early Impression of Barbados," p. 539; Davies, *History*, pp. 8–9; Ogilby, *America*, p. 379; Blome, *Description*, p. 79; Speed, *Prospect*, p. 48.

our America[n] Plantations, to whom England owes its greatest Riches and Prosperity," Barbados had contributed a greatly disproportionate share.[32]

Thus, through the agency of sugar, the unpromising island of Barbados had become "very famous in all parts" and had been transformed from a formidable wilderness into a "Spatious and profitable Garden." Ligon and his contemporaries at mid-century had depicted Barbados as a place of great natural beauty in which the industrious newcomer could make a fortune during the first phases of the sugar lottery. By the 1670s, Ligon's successors could no longer herald the island as a place of wide-open opportunity in which even industrious and intelligent servants had a chance "to get Estates." By that time, the English Caribbean frontier had shifted to the Leeward Islands and Jamaica. They still emphasized the island's astonishing capacity to generate wealth through the production of sugar, even to the point of giving it preeminence in any depiction of the colony. But they now gave almost equal weight to its settled character. They suggested, through the increasing use of the term garden to describe the colony, that Barbados, unlike England's other colonies both in the islands and on the mainland, had rapidly become a place not just of natural but of cultivated—that is, improved—beauty.[33]

People came to the new societies of colonial British America not merely to better their economic situation but also with the complementary hope of transforming those new places into improved ones. The language of improvement was ubiquitous in the early-modern British world. In England and Scotland, it referred primarily to schemes, devices, or projects through which the economic position of the country might be advanced, the estates or fortunes of individuals might be bettered, or existing resources might be made more productive. In the new societies of colonial British America, the term carried similar connotations. Settlers sought to "improve" their situations by securing the necessary capital and labor to develop their lands and fortunes; towns that would faciliate trade; roads, bridges, and ferries that would provide them with better access to markets.

But the term also acquired a much wider meaning: it was used to describe a state of society that was far removed from the savagery thought to be characteristic of most of America's original inhabitants, one that was not wild,

[32] Ogilby, America, p. 378; Blome, Desription, p. 65; Heylyn, Cosmography, p. 1118; Speed, Prospect, p. 48; Great Newes from Barbadoes, pp. 3, 13–14; B[urton], English Empire in America, p. 198; Dalby Thomas, An Historical Account of the Rise and Growth of the West India Colonies (London, 1690), p. 37; A State of the Present Condition of the Island of Barbadoes (London [1696]), p. 3.
[33] Davies, History, pp. 8–9; Great Newes from Barbadoes, p. 13; Towns, "Observations made at Barbadoes," p. 229; Ligon, True & Exact History, pp. 22, 86, 116–17; Handler, "Father Biet's Visit," pp. 60, 64, 67; Thomas, Historical Account, p. 27.

barbaric, irregular, rustic, or crude, but, like England itself, was settled, cultivated, civilized, orderly, developed, and polite. The concept of improvement thus enabled settlers in colonial British America as in early-modern Ireland to think of the societies they were creating in developmental terms. Their hope was that the simplifications of traditional social forms that were so obvious during the first phases of settlement would sooner or later be followed by a process of social articulation that would in turn lead ultimately in the direction of an ever greater assimilation to traditional paradigms derived from the socioeconomic, cultural, and political order of the world they had left behind.

By the 1670s, the proud boast of Barbados was that it was considerably farther into this process of social articulation and replication than any other English colony in America. Fully subdivided into fourteen parishes, each with its own church or chapel already built, it contained several urban settlements. Bridgetown, its capital and "principal *Emporium*," was, despite two devastating fires, a "flourishing City" with "many fair, long, and spatious Streets, furnish'd with a great number of noble Structures." The author of *Great Newes from Barbados*, published in 1676, was conscious that the social condition of the island in his generation contrasted favorably with that which had confronted Ligon, who, writing a mere twenty years earlier, had found little to praise in Barbados other than "that much Celebrated perpetual Verdure that Adorns the Native Trees of that warm World." Now, in 1676, the author described how both the towns and the countryside were full of "Houses which could boast a Grandeur much more considerable than those" of which "most of our [English] Villages are composed of." Furthermore, according to the proud announcement of another writer, virtually every plantation on the island was "delightfully situated" with "pleasant Prospects to the Sea and Land." Each one, "small and great," had "Sugar-works . . . with fair and large Buildings made of Stone and Brick" and "covered with Tiles or slate." Together with the dwelling house, many of which were also made of stone and roofed with tiles, this large collection of sturdy and permanent buildings made each plantation look "like a handsome town." To grind its cane, Barbados had about 400 windmills, "whose flying Sailes, besides the Profit they bring the Owner[s]," provided a "Remarkably pleasant . . . first Prospect from the Sea."[34]

Better and more permanent buildings and more intensive urbanization

---

[34] *Great Newes from Barbadoes*, pp. 4, 9–13; Davies, *History*, pp. 8–9; Ogilby, *America*, p. 379; Speed, *Prospect*, p. 48; Handler, "Father Biet's Visit," pp. 63, 65; Spörri, "Account," p. 5; Blome, *Description*, pp. 79–80; B[urton], *English Empire in America*, p. 202; Towns, "Observations," p. 229; Oldmixon, *British Empire*, 1st ed., 2:116.

were accompanied by other improvements. In the 1650s, Barbadian planters had been so preoccupied with producing sugar that they were content to drink contaminated water from ponds and to rely on the island's many superb natural fruits. By the mid-1670s, however, one correspondent told the Royal Society in London, "almost every sugar-plantation has a well that yields very good water," while some planters had enjoyed "Prodigious Success . . . in the Improvement of several newly introduced Fruits." The extension of sugar cultivation during the closing decades of the seventeenth century to more recently settled islands with newer and richer soils put Barbados at a serious competitive disadvantage in the race for sugar profits. As contemporaries appreciated, however, this development also had the beneficial effect of forcing Barbadians to become careful husbandmen. More and more after 1680, they had "to dung and improve their Plantations [until they were] like so many Gardens." In the process Barbados became the colony in the English Caribbean noted for having "the greatest Husbandry and Skill."[35]

At the same time, Barbadians had developed a network of roads that, in comparison with those elsewhere in the Caribbean, were "undoubtedly very fine." These roads linked the rural inhabitants closely to the towns, where shops and warehouses were "filled with all one could wish from all parts of the world" and where all manner of artisans, including even goldsmiths, jewelers, and clockmakers, provided many of the same specialized services enjoyed by the inhabitants of the largest English towns. Furthermore, in contrast to the simple yet relatively undifferentiated societies of England's other American colonies, Barbados had by the third quarter of the seventeenth century a fully articulated social structure. Like England itself, it had an enormous number of dependent laborers presided over by a small number of independent property owners, the wealthiest of whom, "Masters, Merchants, and Planters, live[d] each like little Sovereigns in their Plantations" in a manner "equal to many of our Nobility and Gentry, of the first Rank in *England*."[36]

At mid-century, Ligon had presented Barbados as a place where it was possible for people to grow rich and live a quiet, simple, retired life in beautiful tropical surroundings. But he had strongly advised those who loved "the pleasures of *Europe* . . . (or particularly of *England*) and the great variety of those . . . never [to] come there." The society was too crude, the climate too hot, and the landscape too dissimilar, he suggested, to permit

<hr/>

[35] Towns, "Observations," p. 229; *Great Newes from Barbadoes*, pp. 7–8; [William Cleland], *The Present State of the Sugar Plantations Consider'd* (London, 1713), p. 20.

[36] Connell, "Father Labat's Visit," pp. 163, 173; Oldmixon, *British Empire*, 1st ed., 2:111–14; Ligon, *True & Exact History*, p. 43; Blome, *Description*, pp. 83–84.

the inhabitants to engage in many characteristic English activities. Well before the close of the seventeenth century, however, one reporter after another emphasized that the simplicity of the 1650s had given way to a rich social and cultural life. Barbados was not yet itself a genuinely new England. But especially in comparison with other American colonies, these writers suggested, it was becoming in more and more ways recognizably English.[37]

This was particularly true in relation to the life styles of the wealthy. "Being *English*, and [by the 1670s and 1680s] having all their commerce from England," members of the island's white elite were always imitating "the Customes, and Fashions of *England*, both as to Apparell, household-Furniture, Eating and Drinking, &c." Their clothes were "fashionable and courtly," their diet, "the same with ours in *England*," their "Equipages . . . rich, their Liveries fine, their Coaches and Horses answerable; their Chairs, Chaises, and all the Conveniences for their travelling, magnificent." Though the heat obliged the islanders to be content for the most part with "sedentary Diversions more than active," the wealthy reportedly enjoyed a perpetual round of "Balls and Consorts," frequently employed their own "Pleasure-Boats, to make the *Tour* of the Island," and provided an avid audience when an English puppet theater company visited the island. Notwithstanding Ligon's prediction that the turf was neither "fine enough, nor the Ground soft enough to make a Bowling Green in *Barbadoes*," the island boasted two of them by the early eighteenth century.[38]

As Barbadoes had become more settled and more improved in all these ways, its independent proprietors reputedly had shown increased attention to both comfort and beauty in their lives. If houses in Bridgetown were mostly "well built in the English style with many glass windows" and "magnificently furnished," "houses on the plantations" were "better built [even] than those of the towns," one visitor observing that they were "large with good fenestration completely glazed; the arrangements of the rooms . . . commodious and comfort . . . well understood." Nor did Barbadians apply their vaunted agricultural skills strictly to sugar. All over the island, it was reported, proprietors took pride in the "Excellency" of their kitchen gardens and paid considerable attention to landscape. By 1700, according to one visitor from a nearby French island, this effort had resulted in a "beautiful countryside" in which "Nearly all" plantations exhibited "fine avenues of tamarinds, or, of . . . large orange trees . . . , or of other trees which give shade and make the houses very attractive." This attention to aesthet-

---

[37] Ligon, *True & Exact History*, pp. 58, 104–106.

[38] Thomas, *Historical Account*, p. 53; Oldmixon, *British Empire*, 1st ed., 2:114–15, 126–27; Blome, *Description*, p. 88.

ics reached even to the quarters of the slaves, whose habitations were "well laid out in lines and uniform."[39]

The growing civility of the Barbados elite and achievement of a more cultivated landscape were not the only evidence that Barbados was assimilating ever more closely to the English model of an improved society during the closing years of the seventeenth century and the opening decades of the eighteenth. By the 1670s, it already seems to have been characterized by a more settled family life. Following the shift to black slavery as the predominant form of labor between 1650 and 1660, white servant immigration tended to decline. The result was that over the next several decades the white population became less disproportionately male, with marriage more the norm and population replacement more the result of natural increase. By the end of the century, "everyone" among the white population was married and, because the women were so "very prolific," there were "swarms of children."[40]

If the social, cultural, and family life of Barbados was looking more and more like that of England, so were the island's public institutions. During the first decades of settlement, the political and legal systems had been unsettled. By the 1650s, however, Barbadians were taking pride in the fact that their government bore "a very near correspondence" with that of England. They had regular courts, were governed for the most part by the "Lawes of *England*, for all Criminal, Civil, Martial, Ecclesiastical, and Maritime affairs," and they had their own local legislature "in nature of the Parliament of *England*" to make additional laws to fit whatever conditions were "peculiar to the place." By 1700 judges, officials, and legislators were often creoles with an English education as well as considerable local expertise. "Of late Years," one writer claimed in 1713, even the legal profession was composed largely of "Men brought up at the Universities, and Inns of Court" in England. One native son, the younger Christopher Coddrington, had so distinguished himself as a classical scholar at Christ Church, Oxford, as to attract the attention and admiration of metropolitan intellectuals and to be appointed royal governor of the nearby Leeward Islands. Upon his death in 1710, he bequeathed £40,000 to establish a college in Barbados. A fitting capstone to the island's increasingly rich cultural life, this institution promised both to make it unnecessary for Barbadian youths to travel to England for advanced education and in general to "produce good Effects upon the Inhabitants, both with respect to Religion and good

[39] Connell, "Father Labat's Visit," pp. 163, 171, 173; *Great Newes from Barbadoes*, pp. 7–8.

[40] Davis, "Early Impression of Barbados," p. 539; Connell, "Father Labat's Visit," pp. 163–64.

Manners; and so by consequence [with respect to] the good Government of the Place."[41]

As they increasingly came to emphasize the extent to which Barbados had become an improved society, the colony's interpreters also painted a generally flattering portrait of the "natures and dispositions" of its wealthy proprietors. To be sure, they retained a reputation for extravagance. As one English merchant trading to the island remarked in 1695, "no People in the World have been more remarkable for a Luxuriant way of Living." The English economic and political writer Charles Davenant thought that the "rich soil, easy acquisition of wealth, and . . . warm climate" had "infected" all the English Caribbean colonies with "excess and luxury." Thus, notwithstanding a less favorable economic situation produced by declining soil fertility and increased competition from newer sugar settlements, the generation of Barbadians at the turn of the seventeenth century had not, "in any measure, retrench'd those Extravagant Excesses that were wont to abound amongst them, or have yet learn'd what Providence . . . is." If, however, later generations of wealthy Barbadians continued like their ancestors to live "at the height of Pleasure," they now did so, in contrast to their forebears, with considerably more "good taste," discrimination, and politeness.[42]

Besides, this profuse life style, as several writers noted, seemed to be closely associated with what they regarded as an admirable sociability and liberality. "Very sociable," they reportedly received both friends and strangers "with extraordinary expressions of civility." Nor, apparently, was this "good Hospitality" confined to the wealthy. Rather, according to one writer, it reached down from "those of the better rank to the meanest Inhabitants, who think it a great want of civility to dismiss any one from their houses, before they have presented them with somewhat to eat and drink." Ligon and later writers traced this "Loving, friendly, and hospitable" strain in the Barbadian character to the heterogeneity of the early settlers. Precisely because they were "of several Perswasions," Ligon suggested, they had found it necessary to bury their differences in the quest for sugar profits. Thus, during the English Civil War, they "made a Law amongst themselves, that whosoever nam'd the word *Roundhead* or *Cavalier*, should give

[41] Ligon, *True & Exact History*, pp. 50, 100–101; Spörri, "Account," p. 7; Ogilby, *America*, p. 380; Blome, *Description*, pp. 94–96; Speed, *Prospect*, p. 48; [Cleland], *Present State*, pp. 5, 12; William Gordon, *A Sermon Preach'd at the Funeral of the Honourable Colonel Christopher Codrington* (London, 1710), p. 22.

[42] Ligon, *True & Exact History*, p. 57; A Merchant, *A Discourse of the Duties on Merchandize, More Particularly of that on Sugars* (London, 1695), p. 11; Charles D'Avenant, *The Political and Commercial Works*, 5 vols. (London, 1771), 2:21–22; Blome, *Description*, pp. 84, 89; Connell, "Father Labat's Visit," pp. 163, 171–72.

to all those that heard him, a Shot and a Turky, to be eaten at his house that made the forfeiture; which," Ligon reported, "sometimes was done purposely, that they might enjoy the company of one another." "So frank, so loving, and so good natur'd were these Gentlemen one to another" that with only a few interruptions, the historian John Oldmixon averred during the first years of the eighteenth century, public affairs in the colony were remarkable for their concord and rarely "troubled with Factions and Parties." Barbadians, it seemed, vied with one another over nothing of any greater moment than the magnificence of their "Liberal Entertainment[s]," which, as one champion of the colony proclaimed, could "not be Exceeded by this their Mother Kingdome itself."[43]

But their commitment to good living did not mean, writers were careful to emphasize, that wealthy Barbadians were either soft or lazy. As their spirited help to other islands during the two major intercolonial wars between 1689 and 1713 seemed to demonstrate, Barbadian "*Creoleans* [were] . . . as brave Men as any in the World," and they prided themselves on their industry. Ligon had early stressed the extent to which "sluggard[s were] detested in a Countrey, where Industry and Activity" yielded such high premiums, and the vast estates still enjoyed by later generations stood "as glorious Proofs [both] of the Industry . . . of their Ancestors" and of their own continued diligence in a situation in which declining fertility forced them to triple their efforts to secure the same level of profits achieved by these same ancestors.[44]

During the half-century beginning around 1660, Barbados had thus gradually acquired an identity as an improved and settled society in which, in the words of the historian Oldmixon, "Wealth and Pleasure, which are generally Strangers, . . . dwell[ed] . . . together." Full of people who were rich, "civil, generous, hospitable, and very sociable," Barbados was rapidly achieving a reputation, in the words of a French visitor in 1700, as a "congenial society" whose "inhabitants were everywhere esteemed."[45]

Underneath all the surface glitter, however, at least some of the problems that had helped to tarnish Barbados's early image remained. In his extensive treatment of Barbados in his *British Empire in America*, Oldmixon defended the island's planters against the old charges of cruelty toward ser-

[43] Oldmixon, *British Empire*, 1st ed., 2:114, 126–27; Davies, *History*, pp. 198–99; Ligon, *True & Exact History*, p. 57; *Great Newes from Barbadoes*, pp. 7–8, 13–14; Speed, *Prospect*, p. 48; Handler, "Father Biet's Visit," pp. 62, 68; Connell, "Father Labat's Visit," p. 167.

[44] Oldmixon, *British Empire*, 1st ed., 2:111, 113; Ligon, *True & Exact History*, pp. 57, 108; Davis, "Early Impression of Barbados," p. 539; [Cleland], *Present State*, p. 20; Thomas Tryon, *England's Grandeur, and Way to get Wealth* (London, 1699), pp. 11–13.

[45] Oldmixon, *British Empire*, 1st ed., 2:111–12, 114; Connell, "Father Labat's Visit," pp. 163, 167.

vants and slaves. Because it contained little meat, the diets of servants, he admitted, were "not so good, as those who have been us'd to rich Farmers['] Tables in *England*." But in all other respects, he contended, their lives were "not very hard," their labor being "much less than our Day-Labourers in *England*, and their Encouragement much more; for if they are good for any thing when they come out of their Times, there are enough [who] will employ them on their own Terms."[46]

Similarly, Oldmixon dismissed the "Stories . . . told of . . . Severities" against slaves as gross exaggerations. He did not deny that their large numbers, their "frequent attempts to get the mastery," and what whites perceived as laziness, carelessness, and dissembling forced masters "to carry a strict Hand over them." He also admitted that slave treatment varied according to the "Nature or Understanding of the Masters." But he insisted that "few English have been so barbarous, as they are all represented to be, by the Enemies of the Plantations." "Their Whipping them with Thongs, till they are all a-gore of Blood; their tying them up by their Hands or Feet, to endure such Stripes, and the pickling afterwards with Brine" were all, he declared, nothing more than mere "Bugbears to frighten Children with, like Tales of *Raw-head, and Bloody-bones*." More commonly, he wrote, planters provided well for their slaves, seeing to it that they had good housing, adequate food and clothing, and family garden plots and that they were dealt with "humanely and prudently" by their overseers. Nor were the planters primarily responsible for the failure of the slaves to become Christians. The truth was, Oldmixon asserted, that slaves were "so fond of their own Idolatry" that few of them showed "any disposition to hearken to the Doctrine of the Christians."[47]

In this extended apology for the Barbadian planter class, Oldmixon also suggested that the gradual articulation of Barbados society and the creolization of the slave population were affecting the character of life on the island in ways that were beneficial to both masters and slaves. As slaves had grown more numerous and the economic and social demands of the free population more elaborate, new opportunities had opened up for the more able and assimilated slaves, who could now rise out of field labor into high-status skilled activities. These included key roles in sugar processing, all the major artisanal trades, and domestic service. Furthermore, according to Oldmixon, the "*Creolian* Negroes," who had been taught by the example of the whites to despise recently arrived "*saltwater* negroes," began both to "value themselves much on being born in *Barbadoes*" and to assimilate

46 Oldmixon, *British Empire*, 1st ed., 2:116.
47 Ibid., pp. 115, 118–20.

more fully to white culture. Thus, for example, did native slaves slowly move away from the "Diabolical Religion" of the "Foreign Slaves" toward that of the English. The implication in Oldmixon's analysis was that these social and demographic developments and the distinctions they had created within the slave population were rendering slavery less onerous, leading to the more complete adjustment of the slaves to slavery and enabling whites both to treat slaves more leniently and to enjoy more secure lives.[48]

But the testimony of other contemporary observers powerfully suggested that Oldmixon was far too sanguine in his accounts of relations between masters and their servants and slaves. The young French missionary, Father Jean-Baptiste Labat, visited Babados in 1700 and drew a generally favorable picture of life in the colony, which he subsequently published in France. Having served since 1694 in the French sugar islands of Martinique and Guadeloupe, Labat fully appreciated that conditions inherent in slavery "often compelled" the "inhabitants of islands of whatever nationality . . . to exceed the limits of moderation in the punishment of their slaves so as to intimidate" them. These measures, he believed, were necessary because the blacks, who outnumbered the whites by the ratio of ten to one, were "always ready to rebel and attempt to commit the most terrible crimes to regain their freedom."[49]

Nevertheless, Labat was virtually unstinting in his condemnation of the ways in which Barbadians treated their laborers. White servants, he reported, "groan[ed] under a harsh servitude of 7 or, at least 5 years, when they are compelled to begin a fresh term on pretexts which their masters always have ready, certain that they can do so because the judges never decide against them," and he predicted that in case of invasion, servants would "without fail . . . join with the invading force." And the condition of slaves was even worse. According to Labat, Barbadian whites yet regarded slaves "pretty nearly as beasts to whom every licence" was "allowed, provided that they perform[ed] their work satisfactorily." Uninstructed in the precepts of Christianity, they were "permitted to have several wives and to leave them as they please, provided that they produce[d] a large number of children, . . . work[ed] well and" did "not become ill." But such laxity was accompanied by the most severe labor discipline. It seemed to Labat that overseers appeared "to care less for the life of a negro than that of a horse," and he further charged them with working slaves "beyond measure and [with beating] them mercilessly for the least fault." Neither such rigorous punishment nor the knowledge that torture and death were

[48] Ibid., pp. 117, 121–24.
[49] Connell, "Father Labat's Visit," pp. 168–69.

the certain ends of unsuccessful rebellion prevented slaves from rising up against "their drunken, unreasonable and savage overseers." Those who were subsequently captured, Labat reported, were "burnt alive or exposed in iron cages in which they" were "attached to the branch of a tree, or, . . . left to die of hunger and thirst." This last practice, according to Labat, was known in Barbados as "putting a man to dry." Such harsh measures, the witness of Oldmixon notwithstanding, reveal that Barbadian whites still believed themselves to have everything "to fear from their negroes."[50]

In the very same year that Labat visited Barbados, Thomas Tryon, a London merchant who had earlier resided in the colony, published a series of letters in which he condemned sugar production as inherently "violent, I may say cruel." Predicting that Barbados could not long "thrive by such Oppressive Methods and Severities," he publicly urged Barbadian proprietors to "consider with your slaves, that the Groaning of him that suffereth Pain, is the beginning of the Trouble and Misery of them that laid it on." With this precept in mind, Tryon called upon Barbadians to abandon sugar for cotton, to stop mistreating their slaves, and to "begin a reformation in your selves, and cure the looseness and extravagancies of your Youth" before they felt the "Vindicative Hand of the Divine Power."[51]

If, as Tryon also remarked, such wickedness was "a sure Indication of Calamity and Misery to any Country," there were many signs during the three decades beginning in the early 1680s that Barbados was already suffering from divine retribution. Throughout these years, Barbados was beset by a variety of economic and demographic problems. Four to five decades of intense sugar cultivation had left some properties so "extremely barren, dry, and worn out" that their owners had to replant canes at least every other year in order to obtain satisfactory profits. They used so much manure on their lands that some planters began to specialize wholly in providing it to sugar producers. At the same time, lack of land for sugar expansion and consolidation of small estates into larger ones resulted in declining opportunity and considerable out-migration to newer colonies. Finally, a major epidemic of yellow fever broke out in 1691. Continuing intermittently for well over a decade, Oldmixon recounted, it indiscriminately "swept away . . . many . . . Masters, Servants, and Slaves." There had been a steady stream of some of the more successful planters back to England since the early days of the sugar revolution, and this persisting epidemic considerably accelerated this process as some of the colony's "most eminent" planter families migrated to escape the "fatal Disease." The result of all these de-

[50] Ibid.
[51] Thomas Tryon, *Tryon's Letters, Domestick and Foreign* (London, 1700), pp. 183–200.

velopments, according to Oldmixon and other observers, was a significant depopulation of the island. The numbers of both whites and blacks fell, perhaps by as much as 25 percent, to 25,000 and 60,000 respectively.[52]

Oldmixon predicted that with the abatement of the epidemic, the population would recover in just a few years, provided Barbadians were "not too much discourag'd from Home." His qualification derived from a widespread feeling in Barbados that, notwithstanding the great wealth it had brought to Britain and the alacrity with which it had contributed to the defense of the other Caribbean colonies during the intercolonial wars of 1689–1713, the island had indeed already suffered substantial discouragement from England in the decades after the Restoration. This feeling derived from three principal sources. First, in 1663, at the crown's insistence, the Barbados legislature had voted a 4½ percent duty on the export of all dead commodities from the colony to serve as a permanent revenue to cover the colony's civil and military expenses. Over the next twenty years, however, the crown diverted much of this revenue to other uses and thus forced the legislature to raise additional money to support the internal administration of the island. Second, at a time when Barbados was already finding it difficult to compete with newer sugar colonies, Parliament imposed a series of new duties on sugar products in addition to those it had previously levied in 1661. Finally, during the quarter-century following the Glorious Revolution, Barbadians complained that they were suffering under a string of oppressive royal governors, who, animated by "Avarice and Love of Power" and supported by the metropolitan government, seemed to be "intent upon nothing but their own private Gain." By promoting parties, engaging in a variety of arbitrary practices, and systematically ignoring the public welfare of the island, these men, defenders of the colony charged, were rapidly destroying its customary public tranquility.[53]

The many "great discouragement[s]" from England evoked deep resentments within Barbados. Not only did they threaten to bring social and economic ruin upon the colony but, equally disturbing, they also indicated that metropolitan officials regarded Barbados less as a distant society of kindred English people than as a source of immediate revenue and exploitation. By such measures, Edward Littleton, a Barbadian planter who had recently settled in England, charged in 1689, Barbadians were being "*com-*

[52] Ibid., p. 200; Connell, "Father Labat's Visit," p. 170; Oldmixon, *British Empire*, 1st ed., 2:111–13; Thomas, *Historical Account*, p. 53; *A Discourse*, pp. 11–12.

[53] Oldmixon, *British Empire*, 1st ed., 2:113; Thomas, *Historical Account*, pp. 42–43; [Cleland], *Present State*, pp. 8, 18–19; [Edward Littleton], *The Groans of the Plantations; or a True Account of their Grevious and Extreme Sufferings by the Heavy Impositions upon Sugar and Other Hardships Relating More Particularly to the Island of Barbados* (London, 1689), pp. 1–17.

manded as Subjects, and . . . crusht as Aliens." Despite their manifest loyalty, what Littleton referred to as their "Obsequious Devotion to our dear and native . . . Mother Country," they were being treated, he complained, as if they had no claim to the traditional rights, privileges, and benefits of Englishmen and could therefore be used as "miserable Drudges and Beggers" for the profit and pleasure of those who stayed at home. As he pointed out to his English readers, however, Barbadians believed that they had "as good English Bloud in our Veins, as . . . those that we left behind us. How came we to lose our Countrey, and the Priviledges of it," he asked, "Why will you cast us out?" Barbadians, another writer similarly declared in 1698, were "no other but *English* Men: They are your Countrey-Men, your Kindred and Relations, and they ought not to be thus Barbarously used."[54]

As these quotations suggest, "barbarous usage" by metropolitan officials not only stirred deep resentment within Barbados, it also touched a particularly sensitive nerve. Like colonists in other overseas territories, seventeenth- and early eighteenth-century Barbadians long had worried lest "the obscurity of their Origine, . . . the harshness of their Language, . . . the barbarisme of their Manners, . . . their strange course of Life, . . . the cruelty of their Wars, . . . their ancient Poverty, [or] . . . the unconstancy of their Fortune" should prevent their "favourable Reception" in England. Aspiring to parity of status with English people who had remained in England and thus already thinking of themselves and fearing that they would be thought of in England as "poor *Caribbeans*," Barbadians were deeply wounded by any suggestion that they were in any way inferior Englishmen. Yet, the common opinion within England during the late seventeenth century seems to have been, in the words of the economic writer Josiah Child, that both "*Virginia* and *Barbados* were first peopled by a Sort of loose vagrant People, vicious and destitute of Means to live at Home (being either unfit for Labour, or such as could find none to employ themselves about, or had so misbehav'd themselves by Whoring, Thieving, or other Debauchery, that none would set them on work)."[55]

In endeavoring to counter this negative image, Caribbeans and their supporters in England admitted "that, in peopling those Plantations, many persons of obscure Births and very indifferent Characters went, or were, from time to time, sent and transported thither, as Occasion required." But

---

[54] Thomas, *Historical Accounts*, pp. iii, 42; [Littleton], *Groans of the Plantations*, pp. 1–2, 15–17, 20–23; *State of the Present Condition*, p. 3; *The Case of the Inhabitants and Planters in the Island of Jamaica* (London, [1714]), p. v.

[55] Davies, *History*, dedication pages; Josiah Child, "A Discourse Concerning Plantations," in *The Most Delightful Country of the Universe: Promotional Litertaure of the Colony of Georgia 1717–1734*, ed. Trevor R. Reese (Savannah, 1972), pp. 106–107.

they adamantly denied that the early settlers "consist[ed] only of a sort of Vagabonds and persons of mean condition, as some fondly imagine[d]" in England. Rather, they maintained that "some thousands of Persons of very creditable Families, good Education, and loyal Principles, went thither likewise; some through Narrowness of their Circumstances; some to avoid the Miseries of the Civil War at home; and others to improve such paternal or acquired Fortunes and Estates, as they thought convenient to carry along with them, at the time." Certainly from the beginning of the sugar revolution, Barbados in particular had "tempted [many] Gentlemen of good Families and moderate Estates." "Whoever will look over the Map of *Barbadoes*," Oldmixon told his readers, would find the names of "Families . . . of the most ancient and honourable in England." To the further credit of Barbados, thirteen of its inhabitants had been knighted by the Crown following the Restoration, "more . . . than . . . all the rest of the *English* Plantations in *America*" combined. Thus, whatever might have been the case with other colonies, the "common Reflection made upon the Plantations, as to the Meanness of the Planters['] Origins," Oldmixon asserted, was "groundless as to the *Barbadoes*, where," despite the emigration of several of them to England, there were still "as many good Families as . . . in any of the Counties of *England*."[56]

As well as the fact that so many of them derived from prominent English families, the evident significance of their accomplishment in creating— with very little help from home—such an enormously valuable addition to the English world seemed to Barbadians to support their claims for an equal status with and the favorable opinion of metropolitan Englishmen, and their craving for metropolitan acceptance and for a status in the cultural and political center of the Anglophone world commensurate with their wealth and importance was driven by the failure of metropolitan Englishmen to appreciate the laudatory, even the heroic, character of their achievements. Too many people in England, complained the Quaker William Loddington in 1682, had "a sly . . . slighting way of Reflecting upon those that [had] Transplant[ed] themselves and [their] Interest[s] into America, as men of unsettled brains, wandering minds, [who were] void of Solidity and Gravity, &c." But he reminded his readers that "*England* was once as rough and rugged as *America*, and the Inhabitants as blind and barbarous as the *Indians*" and asked them to "consider, what a Country *England* it self had now been . . . if our *English* Ancestors had been so solid and staid as to keep in their own Countries." "If their brains had not been thus un-

[56] Davies, *History*, dedication pages, pp. 198–99; *The Groans of Jamaica Express'd in a Letter from a Gentleman Residing there, to his Friend in London* (London, 1714), p. v; Oldmixon, *British Empire*, 1st ed., 2:110–12.

settled," he contended, the "grave" stay-at-homes in contemporary England would never have "had such pleasant and profitable Setlements as they" then had. "Every Day, Age, or Generation," Loddington asserted, "hath some peculiar piece of Service to be carried on," which he called "*Generation Work.*" Because colonization was "an eminent part of the Generation Work of our Day," it and the people who engaged in it deserved not the scorn but the respect and admiration of the people who stayed behind.[57]

As a result of all their achievements during the first eight decades following the founding of Barbados, its inhabitants had gradually learned to value themselves and their new country. Given their heavy reliance upon their old country for standards of what a civilized—an improved—society should be, however, they could never hope to achieve a fully satisfying sense of themselves and their colony until they had won the approval of the metropolis itself. So poignantly revealed in the writing of Littleton and others of his contemporaries, this deep need for metropolitan approval was, perhaps, no less important than sugar, slavery, or the island's extensive wealth and population in the early stages of the formation of a Barbadian identity.

"*Prudence [is] . . . the prevailing Principle*"

During the seven decades beginning in 1710, a substantial literature on Barbados recorded the changing identity of the island and its dominant white inhabitants. Continuities abounded with the images that had characterized the colony's first eight decades. But there were many subtle yet powerful changes. Prior to 1740, these changes were mostly in a negative direction. As the colony's old economic difficulties became more severe, it was also beset by serious political discontents. After 1740, however, Barbados slowly began to exhibit a more positive self-image. An expanding local literature explored the inhabitants' collective experiences over time and tried to define their character as both a society and as a people. Increasingly, this literature emphasized not the vices but the virtues of Barbadians and not the problems but the achievements of their society.

This change in emphasis seems to have been closely associated with the establishment of the island's first press by the printer Samuel Keimer in 1731. By providing an outlet for local literary productions, many of which he brought together and published in the two-volume collection *Caribbeana* in 1741,[58] Keimer seems to have helped awaken local pride and interest in the island on the part of its native and long-resident inhabitants.

---

[57] [William Loddington], *Plantation Work The Work of this Generation* (London, 1682), pp. 3, 5–6.

[58] [Samuel Keimer], *Caribbeana: Containing Letters and Dissertations, Together with Political Essays, on various Subjects and Occasions*, 2 vols. (London, 1741).

In previous decades, local literary output had been confined to a few ephemeral and largely polemical pieces published in London. But the next four decades witnessed an outpouring of substantial works in other genres, including four short histories,[59] one natural history,[60] two book-length descriptive poems,[61] an agricultural treatise,[62] and a second volume of newspaper contributions.[63] Along with the number of polemical tracts and a growing volume of comment by outsiders, including especially the several general descriptions and histories of the British overseas empire that appeared after 1758,[64] these local productions provide a rich base from which to reconstruct the changing character of Barbadian identity during these years.

Prior to 1740, Barbados retained the reputation it had developed during the closing decades of the seventeenth century as an unhealthy place in serious economic decline. The malignant fever that had first visited the island in 1691 continued up to mid-century to be especially "fatal to new Comers" and occasionally even to carry off "a great many" oldtimers as well. Barbadians were also thought to age more quickly and to die earlier than people in England. "All the Infirmities of Threescore here," one commentator noted in 1732, were "frequently to be found upon one of five and forty there," while a person of "fifty or fifty four Years" was "a rarer Spectacle in *Barbadoes*, than one of sixty among the like Number of People . . .

[59] [William Duke], *Some Memoirs of the First Settlement of the Island of Barbados, and Other of the Carribee Islands* . . . (Barbados, 1741); Richard Hall, *A General Account of the First Settlement and of the Trade and Constitution of the Island of Barbados, Written in the Year 1755* (Barbados, 1924); [Henry Frere], *A Short History of Barbados from its First Discovery and Settlement to the End of the Year 1767* (London, 1768); [Sir John Gay Alleyne], *Remarks upon a Book, Intitled A Short History of Barbados* . . . (Barbados, 1768).

[60] Griffith Hughes, *The Natural History of Barbados* (London, 1750).

[61] [Nathaniel] Weekes, *Barbadoes: A Poem* (London, 1754); John Singleton, *A General description of the West Indian Islands* . . . *From Barbados to Saint Croix* (Barbados, 1767).

[62] William Belgrove, *A Treatise upon Husbandry or Planting* (Boston, 1755).

[63] [John Orderson?], [Extracts from the *Barbados Mercury*, 1772–1773] [Barbados, ca. 1773–1774]. The apparently only surviving copy of this work lacks a title page and is in the New York Historical Society.

[64] John Oldmixon, *The British Empire in America*, 2d ed., 2 vols. (London, 1741), 2:1–171; John Harris, *Navigantium atque Itinerantium Bibliotheca*, 2 vols. (London, 1748), 2:253–57 (citations in this study are to the 1764 edition); [Edmund Burke], *An Account of the European Settlements in America*, 2 vols. (London, 1757), 2:81–91; *The Modern Part of An Universal History*, 65 vols. (London 1747–66), 41:130–211; Daniel Fenning et al., *A New System of Geography: or a General Description of the World*, 2 vols. (London, 1765–66), 1:697–702; William Doyle, *Some Account of the British Dominions Beyond the Atlantic* (London, 1770), pp. 37–39; John Huddleston Wynne, *A General History of the British Empire in America* . . . , 2 vols. (London, 1770), 2:500–505; John Entick et al., *The Present State of the British Empire* . . . , 4 vols. (London, 1774), 4:480–84; Thomas Jeffreys, *The West-India Atlas; or a Compendious Description of the West Indies* (London, 1775), p. 20 (citations in this study are to the 1794 edition); *American Husbandry*, 2 vols. (London, 1775), 2:151–62.

in *England.*" The many risks that had always been associated with sugar production in Barbados were thus not all economic. Too often, one writer lamented in the early 1740s, new immigrants both "waste[d] their Health"
and forfeited their lives in that "distant and scorching Climate."[65]

Barbados was thought to be not only unhealthy but also, in the words of
the metropolitan political economist Joshua Gee, "very much worn out"
and no longer capable of producing the same "Quantity of Sugars as heretofore." With "every Inch of the Land having been long laboured to the
Height" and the soil under constant cultivation for six to ten decades, the
colony's planters had to employ "a vast Number of Slaves" and take infinitely greater care to secure profits that, even "in a fruitful Year," were "not
above half of what they used to be." Whereas during the seventeenth century sugar had produced such extravagant wealth as to enable the island's
planters either to support a luxurious life style in Barbados or to settle in
England, by the 1730s, "the Bulk" of the colony's sugar planters were "considerably in Debt" and it was questionable whether "*Barbadoes*, with all her
boasted Wealth," would much longer be "able to support herself in the Perfection to which she is arriv'd." By the mid-1750s, reported William Belgrove, a "regular bred and long experienc'd Planter of the Island," many
plantations had "proved not worth holding, and there" were "dismal Prospects of ruinous Buildings in the Island, that were at first very Commodious, which have by various Accidents been destroyed, and only the Land
[was any longer] . . . regarded as of Value by joining [it] to other Estates."[66]

In addition to its "drooping [economic] Pow'r" and its malignant disease
environment, the Barbadian social environment also helped to tarnish the
colony's reputation. Within the island, the institution of chattel slavery
was sacrosanct.[67] The successful suppression of a general slave uprising in
the early 1690s and the gradual creolization of the slave population during
the early years of the eighteenth century seemed to have allayed those
white fears of servile revolt that had been nourished by the frequency of
slave rebellions during the seventeenth century. Nevertheless, Barbadians
realized that "the constant Behaviour of the Negro-Slaves in *America*" left
no doubt that they would try to escape slavery whenever and wherever

[65] [Duke], *Some Memoirs*, p. 61; Hughes, *Natural History*, p. 37; [Robert Robertston], *A Detection of the State of the Present Sugar Planters, of Barbadoes and the Leward Islands . . .* (London,
1732), pp. 23, 26; [Jonathan Blenman], *Remarks on Several Acts of Parliament Relating More
Especially to the Colonies Abroad . . .* (London, 1742), pp. 124–25; Weekes, *Barbadoes*, p. 61;
Belgrove, *Treatise*, p. 45.

[66] Joshua Gee, *The Trade and Navigation of Great-Britain Considered* (London, 1729), p. 45;
[Robertson], *Detection*, pp. 15, 25, 81, 88; [Keimer], *Caribbeana*, 2:119; Belgrove, *Treatise*, p.
45.

[67] Weekes, *Barbadoes*, p. 14.

there was "the least Opening for them." Although some Barbadians warned that those who were tyrants in this world would themselves be condemned to chains in the next and urged more lenient treatment, this consideration seems to have been outweighed by lingering fears of slave revolt. Such fears in turn seemed sufficient to justify both the perpetuation of a harsh labor discipline and a continuing reluctance to provide slaves with the opportunity to become Christians. Englishmen at home might wonder how those in Barbados could "brook to live with so many Slaves as" were "necessary for carrying on a Sugar Plantation." They might lament how descendants of true-born Englishmen could rationalize "bringing our Fellow-Creatures, *who never did us any harm*, into a Condition so justly odious to ourselves." But the omnipresent possibilities of slave revolt prevented white Barbadians from changing their ways. Nonetheless, casual references to what was obviously a brisk sexual commerce between masters and slave women and complaints that continuing association with blacks was producing an Africanization of white language provided evidence of powerful cultural influences of blacks upon whites and illustrated the extent to which white Britons in Barbados were coming to terms with slavery and with the black majority among whom they lived.[68]

Yet another unflattering component of the changing identity of Barbados was its growing fame as a place of discord and contention. During its early generations, the colony had been noted for the tranquility of its public life. During the last decades of the seventeenth century, however, it had gradually become a scene "of perpetual Struggle and Contention." Throughout most of the early decades of the eighteenth century, it was "miserably divided into Factions," until by the 1730s it was so "full of Discord and Dissensions, perplexed with Parties and Animosities, and involved in such Difficulties of various Kinds" as to bring the island to its "lowest Ebb." Indeed, "the Good People of *Barbados*" seemed to have grown so accustomed to "venting Fals[e]hoods, Scandals, Absurdities, Scurrilities and Contradictions" in public life as to cause some of the more sober inhabitants to despair that the island would ever again learn "to treat *Public Business* with Decency and Temper" and to conclude that the island's "perpetual Round of Inconsistency and Tumult" must be attributable "to the Sallies of a warm Imagination in this Climate." But others denied that this "ill State" of af-

---

[68] [Keimer], *Caribbeana*, 1:56, 58, 61–62, 2:5, 105–16; Oldmixon, *British Empire*, 2d ed., 2:53–54; [Robertson], *Detection*, pp. 25–27, 80; Weekes, *Barbadoes*, pp. 33, 56; William Smith, *A Natural History of Nevis, and the Rest of the English Leeward Charibee Islands in America* (Cambridge, 1745), pp. 230–33; William Douglass, *Summary, Historical and Political, of the First Planting, Progressive Improvements, and Present State of the British Settlements in North America*, 2 vols. (Boston, 1749–53), 1:119; [Orderson], Extracts from *Barbados Mercury*, p. 157.

fairs was a product of a defect in the Barbadian character. Rather, they blamed it upon the oppression and evil machinations of a long succession of corrupt, greedy, and inept royal governors. As proof of their contention, they cited the brief administration of Lord Viscount Howe, whose generous, liberal, wise, open, and disinterested behavior in 1733–1735 had "soon lull'd asleep our jarring Factions" and produced "a general Calm . . . throughout" the "whole Government." Howe's success, Barbadians claimed, gave the lie to "the many Reproaches we have long suffered as a People whom no Governour could please" and showed that when they were "govern'd with Justice" they were peaceful and obedient subjects.[69]

Under Howe's immediate successors, however, the same "tedious Story of the Old Follies of *Barbados* [were] acted over again," and recurring dissensions once more made Barbadians "miserable within ourselves, and ridiculed by the rest of Mankind." The "intestine Divisions among the Inhabitants," lamented Henry Duke, clerk of the Assembly in the early 1740s, not only had produced "the greatest Mischiefs" but also had at "several Times" nearly effected "the utter Ruin" of the colony, and he undertook his brief history of the early years of Barbados specifically with the hope of recovering those "true Notions of the right Constitution of this Island" and the principles of social interaction that had enabled the early settlers to live in harmony without discord and partisanship.[70]

Many observers, including some Barbadians, traced all of these problems at least in part to the emerging character of the Barbadians themselves. Their early wealth had led them into luxury, "that Bane of States, . . . Great Foe of Health, and Source of ev'ry Ill." By the 1730s, "the receiv'd Notion" throughout the English-speaking world was that Barbadians, along with other West Indians, were "*the most opulent, most splendid, and gayest People of all His Majesty's Dominions,*" a people who, in the words of Joshua Gee, always lived "in great Splendor, and at Vast Expence." Their wealth had led them not only into an extravagant life style but also into indolence and "a certain Species of Vanity not uncommon among those who[,] subsist[ing] much on Credit and Reputation," desired "to be thought wealthier than they are." In turn, "this expensive Vanity of the Barbadians" drove them into ostentatious display, wantonness, improvidence, "willful Heedlessness," and unjustified optimism about the future. Reinforcing this un-

---

[69] [Robertson], *Detection*, p. 28; Oldmixon, *British Empire*, 2d ed., 2:64–65, 73–76; *A Pattern for Governours: Exemplify'd in the Character of Scroop Late Lord Viscount Howe, Baron of Clonawly; and Governour of Barbados* (London, 1735), pp. 3–5, 7; [Keimer], *Caribbeana*, 1:35, 219, 2:45, 200.
[70] Thomas Baxter, *A Letter from a Gentleman at Barbadoes . . .* (London, 1740), p. 2; [Keimer], *Caribbeana*, 1:219; [Duke], *Some Memoirs*, pp. i, 64–65, 70.

flattering list of qualities were the volatility and imprudence that also seemed to be deeply engraved upon the Barbadian character. Writers disagreed over whether this remarkable warmth of temper was traceable to the climate, as most people seem to have believed, or as Edmund Burke claimed, to the "fiery, restless tempers" of the original settlers, who, "put[ting] no median between being great and being undone" and loving "risk and hazard," found in the Caribbean "a fair and ample field" for the expression of their hot, rash, and visionary dispositions. But no one disputed that Barbadians were "of a more volatile and lively Disposition, and more irascible in general" than "*Phlegmatick Londoners*" or inhabitants of other areas "in the Northern Part of the World." Nor did they deny that this disposition discouraged application, persistence, self-discipline, and industry and encouraged "the many rash passionate Actions [that were so common] amongst the *Creols.*"[71]

Resentful that they were not "well spoken of, and esteem'd by others," Barbadians agreed that there were and had "been in *Barbadoes*, as in all other Countries, lazy, improvident, and expensive Men." But they argued both that it was unfair to take the "general Character of a People . . . from that of a few Particulars" and that the island's declining economy had long since driven all but the "more unthinking sort" to lead more sober, industrious, and frugal lives. Even the island's most resolute defenders had to admit, however, that the burden of ostensible evidence seemed to weigh heavily against them. They could not deny that Barbadians continued to import from Britain far more goods than they could afford; that some of them annually expended extravagant sums of £200 to £500 to keep their children in Britain, where "*most of them*" proved to be "Beaus *of the first Rate*" who only distinguished "*themselves by the Gaity of their Dress and Equipage*"; or that no less than a hundred Barbadians families had moved to Britain where they were "observed to live" much "more expensively than their Neighbours." From the historian Oldmixon, Britons at home and in North America learned that in 1721 the Barbadians, with their typical penchant for "Parade and Shew," had seized upon the occasion of a visit by the duke and duchess of Portland as an excuse for a profuse celebration to which the inhabitants came "*more richly habited*" than could be seen at similar events even in Britain itself. Such behaviors as these left observers with little doubt that the Barbadians' inability to quit the vain, extravagant, and im-

---

[71] [Keimer], *Caribbeana*, 1:35, 2:119; [Robertson], *Detection*, pp. 2–3, 16–17, 19, 29, 55; Weekes, *Barbadoes*, pp. 50, 63; Gee, *Trade and Navigation*, p. 45; [Orderson], Extracts from *Barbados Mercury*, pp. 47, 97; Oldmixon, *British Empire*, 2d ed., 2:75; Burke, *Account of European Settlements*, 2:128, 130, 133; Hughes, *Natural History*, pp. 9–11; Douglass, *Summary, Historical and Political*, 1:120.

provident habits they had acquired during the days of their great wealth was a principal reason why they could not compete with the frugal and industrious planters in the French sugar islands. These appearances also persuaded metropolitans and North Americans alike that West Indian demands during the 1720s and 1730s for the suppression of British trade with the French islands were at bottom a last-ditch attempt to force the rest of the British world to pay for their own degenerate life styles and deficiencies in character.[72]

Between 1720 and 1750 the fundamental question about Barbados thus seemed to be whether, despite all their early accomplishments, Barbadians had not already undone themselves by their own excessive behavior. To most outsiders and to some Barbadians, it appeared that their intemperance in drinking and eating was shortening their lives while their extravagance and vanity were bringing them into debt and the island to economic and social ruin. In their desperate efforts to keep up profits so they could maintain their luxurious living, they were importing far more slaves than was either safe or, from the point of view of the white inhabitants, congenial, and the volatility of whites not only made them contentious in public life but also contributed to make island society loose and permissive. Throughout the 1730s, contributors to the *Barbados Gazette* complained that respect for authority was slight, public disorder in the towns was rampant, thievery and commerce in stolen goods among slaves was both open and flourishing, gambling was widespread, and murder had become such a "truly heroick Diversion" that it was both "oftener committed on this little Spot that in any other Part of the World amongst the like Number of Inhabitants" and had "too frequently gone unpunished." Barbadians, in short, seemed to have become a "*foolish, ridiculous, inconsistent, scurrilous, absurd, malicious*, and *impudent*" people who, in their "extravagant Passion for Riches" and pleasure, made inadequate provision for education and other social amenities in their own island and wholly neglected all civilized moral standards, including "Honor and Probity, Modesty and Chastity." For a people thus interested in "nothing but the Gratification of their own Passions," one local writer lamented in 1732, the future contained nothing but social ruin. Without wholesale changes in behavior, he warned, it was "impossible [that] the Publick Good should [ever] be promoted, Industry encourag'd, or true Virtue establish'd amongst us."[73]

[72] [Keimer], *Caribbeana*, 1:64, 2:119; [John Ashley], *The British Empire in America Considered* (London, 1732), p. 26; [Robertson], *Detection*, pp. 3, 6–7, 13, 16–17, 24–25; [Blenman], *Remarks on Several Acts of Parliament*, pp. 124–25; Baxter, *Letter from a Gentleman at Barbadoes*, p. 3; Oldmixon, *British Empire*, 2d ed., pp. 75–76; Gee, *Trade and Navigation*, p. 45.

[73] [Keimer], *Caribbeana*, 1:10, 64, 86, 289, 353, 2:119, 123–24, 154, 195, 199–200, 289–

With so many problems with both Barbados and Barbadians, it was no wonder that some of the colony's white inhabitants wanted to flee from their once flourishing but now "degen'rate Isle" to Britain or to other colonies to the north. In conjunction with the decline in the number of wealthy white proprietors living in the island, moreover, the number of plantations reportedly fell, the number of abandoned buildings rose, the quality of public leadership and expertise in both politics and the law dropped sharply, and Barbados increasingly came to be regarded by whites as only a place of transitory sojourn rather than one of "settled Residence." Unless these trends were reversed, unless Barbadians learned, like New Englanders and other North American colonists, to shun luxury and vice and, by cultivating industry, parsimony, and strict self-discipline, endeavored to make the island a more attractive place to live, various commentators predicted, Barbados would soon consist only of "a few valetudenary white Men" and a numerous and "disaffected . . . herd of African slaves."[74]

Along with their economic travails, the slowly declining proportion of whites to blacks gave Barbadians a powerful sense of their own internal weakness. In their "declining State," their many long-standing complaints against the way they were treated by the metropolis seemed ever more grievous. Intermittently throughout the first half of the eighteenth century Barbadians continued to protest metropolitan duties and restrictions on the sugar trade, the misapplication of the 4½ percent duty "in Pensions to Courtiers," and their own systematic exclusion from all offices of trust in the colony in favor of "hungry" British deputies with "no Interest in the Welfare or Quiet of Barbadoes." They called for a return to the free and open trade that had contributed to the island's early economic successes and the elimination of political abuses. But they recognized that they were "under so constant, unalterable, and absolute a Dependance" upon Britain "in all Things," from food and credit to protection against their own slaves, that they had little leverage. If the metropolitan government would not redress their grievances, they had no choice but to endure them. Thus acutely aware that, as one anonymous writer put it in 1734, "our Situation" rendered any forceful course of action wholly "impracticable," islanders worried that Barbados was becoming a place where traditional British liberties were no longer "well understood" and "not fully enjoyed" and that Barbadians

---

91; [Robertson], *Detection*, pp. 6, 14, 53; Weekes, *Barbadoes*, pp. 36, 50; [Orderson], Extracts from *Barbados Mercury*, pp. 95–97; [Duke], *Some Memoirs*, Appendix, p. 3; Burke, *Account of European Settlements*, 2:90.

74 [Robertson], *Detection*, pp. 6, 31, 91–92; [Blenman], *Remarks on Several Acts of Parliament*, p. 125; Hall, *General Account*, pp. 8–9; Belgrove, *Treatise*, p. 45; [Keimer], *Caribbeana*, 1:123–24; Weekes, *Barbadoes*, p. 14; Douglass, *Summary, Historical and Political*, 1:119; Burke, *Account of European Settlements*, 2:141–42.

had themselves become little more than sycophants and dependents who were entirely reliant upon metropolitan pleasure for the preservation of their lives, liberties, and property. In view of their growing impotence, only Britain could any longer protect Barbados

> From Foes at Home, and Enemies Abroad,
> Protect her still! Her sacred Rights defend;
> Her Laws preserve; and save her from the Fate,
> Which PATRIOTS dread, and LIBERTY abhors.[75]

In their anguished efforts to comprehend and explain the reasons for their seemingly endemic political conflict and deep economic problems and in their pleas for metropolitan help to arrest the process of economic decline, Barbadians were themselves in large part responsible for their island's increasingly negative image between 1720 and 1740. Yet the burden of argument emanating from the island during these years was that this portrait had been considerably overdrawn by those who envied "and therefore hate[d] and slander[ed] the *British* Sugar Planter." Of all of its American colonies, they reminded people in the metropolis (and reassured themselves), the sugar colonies were the "most beneficial to *England*," and Barbados, "the Mother-Colony" of the British Caribbean, had "the Honour to stand foremost in the Sugar-Trade (as the first Founder of it)." Taking pride in the achievements of their predecessors, Barbadians stressed the colony's rapid rise in population and wealth during the seventeenth century and emphasized the remarkable extent of its contribution to British wealth, which they estimated as at least £24 million sterling, or an annual average of £240,000 during the century between 1660 and 1760. But their contention was not only that Barbados had once been, but that it was "still, a good *Milch-Cow*, or . . . *a Golden-Mine* to *England*" that "still Yearly yield[ed]" mighty sums. ". . . No County sure, / However large, in all Britannia's Realm, / Can Rival Thee in Worth," declared the poet Nathaniel Weekes in the early 1750s, "Great is thy Trade, / And by thy Produce still increasing more." "Those who prize[d] *Britannia's* Welfare," he added, obviously had to "prize this little *Isle.*" Barbados might have lost much of its old opulence. But even at its lowest economic ebb in the 1730s, its partisans insisted, it still had many inhabitants "possessed of affluent Fortunes." In terms of those "great Estates . . . whose yearly Profits exceed[ed] their Expences by many Hundreds, or rather some Thousands of Pounds," Barbados reportedly had three times as many as did all four Leeward Island colonies

---

[75] [Keimer], *Caribbeana*, 1:70, 75, 2:32–37, 219; Harris, *Navigantium atque Itinerantium*, 2:254; [Robertson], *Detection*, pp. 29–30; [Ashley], *British Empire*, p. 27; Weekes, *Barbadoes*, p. 63.

combined. Total capital improvements in Barbados, according to one estimate in 1732, exclusive of dwelling houses and town buildings, amounted to £5,500,000.[76]

But Barbados's claim that it was still "the most considerable . . . of the Charribee Islands" was not primarily based on its continuing productivity and wealth. Rather, it depended on the assertion, boldly advanced by Barbadians and widely endorsed by outsiders, that Barbados, as a British Board of Trade report announced in 1734, was yet more fully improved and settled "than any other of his Majesty's Territories in *America*." By the mid-eighteenth century, it had long been cultivated "as far as any Part of it can be cultivated," was fully stocked with slaves, and had three times as many plantations as it had had in the 1670s. Moreover, despite a precipitous decline in the number of white servants, most of whose places had been taken by blacks, and a slight drop in the total number of black slaves, Barbados was still, contemporaries liked to boast, "the best peopled . . . Spot of Ground, not in *America* only, but in the whole known World." Contemporaries in the 1750s put the number of whites at between 25,000 and 30,000, about half of the inflated estimates of the 1660s and 1670s. Though this number was also doubtless somewhat exaggerated, it was proportionately much greater than in any other sugar colony, none of which in ratio to its size had more shipping, more imports, or so large a population capable of bearing arms. "Whoever takes a full prospect of this place, views the number of plantations and small tenements, sees how near they are to one another, and how little land is uncultivated throughout the Island, and considers at the same time how well peopled the principal towns are," reported the native historian Richard Hall in 1755, "must suppose Barbados to be as fully settled and inhabited now as it ever was." In terms of both cultivation and population, then, Barbados was obviously both "at a *Ne plus ultra*, and the very best improved Sugar Plantation . . . to be met with any where." Neither Jamaica nor any of the Leeward Islands, declared one writer in the early 1730s, could possibly "for many Years to come be improved . . . to the Height *Barbadoes* is at present, or that it was fifty or sixty Years ago."[77]

[76] [Ashley], *British Empire*, pp. 26–27; [Robertson], *Detection*, pp. 14–15, 31–32; Harris, *Navigantium atque Itinerantium*, 2:253, 255–57; [Keimer], *Caribbeana*, 2:iv, vii, 33–34; Hall, *General Account*, p. 13; Oldmixon, *British Empire*, 2d ed., 2:166; [Dr. John Campbell], *Candid and Impartial Considerations on the Nature of the Sugar Trade . . .* (London, 1763), pp. 26–27; Weekes, *Barbadoes*, pp. 15, 61; [Blenman], *Remarks on Several Acts of Parliament*, pp. 124–25.

[77] Hall, *General Account*, pp. 1, 7–9, 23–24; [Keimer], *Caribbeana*, 2:62; Hughes, *Natural History*, p. 22; Harris, *Navigantium atque Itinerantium*, 2:253; Weekes, *Barbadoes*, p. 45; [Robertson], *Detection*, p. 82; Henry J. Cadbury, ed., "An Account of Barbadoes 200 Years Ago," *Jo. Barbados Mus. and Hist. Soc.* 9 (1941–42):83; *American Husbandry*, p. 436.

But the message of mid-eighteenth century Barbadians was that the improved state of their island extended considerably beyond the amount of its cultivated land, population, labor force, and capital improvements in mills, buildings, utensils, animals, roads, and bridges accessory to sugar production. Built for "Convenience more than Magnificence," the rural houses of the planters might not have been "so stately as one would [have] expect[ed] from the Riches of the Planters." But they were said to be "generally neat, and fit for the Habitations of Gentlemen." With tiled roofs, they were often three or four stories high and had rooms "as lofty as in England." "Sown thickly on every part of the island," these houses were, moreover, surrounded by gardens, "adorned with Variety of Orange-Walks, Citron Groves, Water-works, and all the lovely and pleasant Fruits and Flowers of that delicious Country, as well as the most curious of" England itself. Though its streets were irregular and narrow, Bridgetown by the mid-1750s had "about 1200 dwellinghouses and Stores." "Mostly built of brick or stone," with glazed windows and sashes, these urban buildings were constructed in the same substantial style and manner as the best houses in the country. Another "120 small wooden shingled tenements" housed the "lower class of the inhabitants." The annual amount of rents for these structures in 1755 was £37,000. About a quarter as large, Speightstown had about 300 houses that were every bit "as well built" as those in Bridgetown. Besides these private buildings in both country and town, the Anglican churches in each parish were "all handsom, regular Buildings of Stone" with cedar pews and pulpits and "Ornaments as decent as any where in the *British* Empire." The Bridgetown church, one visitor noted in 1741, even had "a fine Set of Organs and a Chime of Bells" with a high steeple that commanded "a fine prospect of the town, the Bay, and the country."[78]

Not just its architecture and its social landscape but its cultural life also seemed to be improving. Education, Barbadians had to confess, was inadequate, the college that had been so "well endowed" by Christopher Coddrington early in the century having remained unfinished. But the establishment in Barbados of the first press and the first newspaper in the British Caribbean in 1731 stimulated Barbadians to develop their literary talents. Their literary productions fostered local pride and, in terms of both quantity and quality, compared favorably with those of other British colonies south of New England. Moreover, though West Indians in general were notorious for living "without the least sense of religion," Barbadians, as earlier, continued to "provide very handsomely for their clergy" and to attend

[78] [Ashley], *British Empire*, pp. 26–27; Oldmixon, *British Empire*, 2d ed., 2:103, 105; Burke, *Account of European Settlements*, 2:90–91; Hall, *General Account*, pp. 6–7; Cadbury, ed., "Account of Barbados," pp. 82–83; Hughes, *Natural History*, p. 1.

251

church in considerable numbers. Though one writer reported in 1770 that he "heard many of the inhabitants say, [that] they went [to church] more to see and be seen, than out of devotion," such "public assemblies," he thought, had "contribute[d] much to civilize the people" in Barbados beyond those of other British Caribbean colonies. At the same time Barbados was becoming more civilized, it was also, according to many writers after 1740, becoming far less deadly. With virtually all of its trees felled and its bogs and marshes drained, the natural historian Griffith Hughes reported in 1750, the trade winds that blew constantly over the island purified the air and made the colony so "very healthy" that many "natives enjoy[ed] good health, and frequently live[d] to a very old age." Hurricanes were also said to be "much less frequent" than in earlier years or in other islands. If, as a result of all of these developments, Barbados was not yet, as its earliest printer suggested in 1741, "Great Britain *itself in Miniature*," it was certainly more "regularly settled" and had "in general an appearance of something more of order and decency, and of a settled people, than in any other colony in the West-Indies." "In point of numbers of people, cultivation of the soil, and those elegancies and conveniencies which result from both," Burke declared in the late 1750s, there clearly was "no place in the West-Indies comparable to *Barbadoes*."[79]

This growing emphasis upon the positive aspects of Barbadian society through the middle decades of the eighteenth century was associated with an expanded awareness of the remarkable achievements of the early generations of English settlers. Widely evident in the literature of the last decades of the seventeenth century, such an awareness had rarely been manifest while the colony was sinking into ever greater economic and political troubles during the first quarter of the eighteenth century. As natives and metropolitans began after 1730 to pay more and more attention to the history of Barbados, however, Barbadians once again began to exhibit a powerful admiration for their island's rapid "progress to power and opulence." In the process, they began to appreciate ever more fully that this extraordinary development could only have been the work of men of great ability, industry, and ingenuity. Barbados might have been first settled by "very indifferent Hands," but the men who were actually responsible for the sugar revolution and the transformation of the island from a wilderness into a golden mine were obviously of quite "another sort," men of "antient and opulent" English families who, having been displaced or impoverished by

---

[79] [Duke], *Some Memoirs*, Appendix, p. 3, *Caribbeana*, 1:iv, ix, 2:iv, 63; Weekes, *Barbadoes*, pp. 16, 20–21; Oldmixon, *British Empire*, 2d ed., 2:98; William Doyle, *Account of the British Dominions*, pp. 37, 39; Hughes, *Natural History*, pp. 3, 29, 32; [Frere], *Short History*, pp. 114, 128–30; Burke, *Account of European Settlements*, 2:90–91, 144; *American Husbandry*, p. 435.

the vicissitudes of the Civil War, came to Barbados to find a "safe retreat" or to retrieve their lost fortunes.[80]

Although they did not deny, as so many of the island's critics charged, that warm temperatures, wealth, and slavery had combined to produce "a great Deal of Indolence" and to weaken "that enterprising spirit" that had characterized those earlier generations, mid-eighteenth-century defenders of Barbados stressed the extent to which, notwithstanding widespread allegations to the contrary, most contemporary Barbadians were genuine heirs of these early giants. Productive and profitable sugar estates, they emphasized, could only be maintained by "incessant Industry"—on the part of planters as well as slaves. And, they contended, "their Sugar Works, built with so much Strength, Neatness, and Convenience, and every way fitted for the Uses intended; their Highways carry'd over Morasses, and cut thro' Mountains; their Bridges [built] over Swamps and Gullies; and their indefatigable Labour in the Culture of their Plantations" all revealed a degree of industry that could "not . . . be match'd, perhaps, by any other Planters upon Earth" and rendered ludicrous all attempts to "charge them with Idleness." Certainly, in comparison with Britain's other Caribbean colonies, Barbados was an "industrious . . . Isle."[81]

Mid-eighteenth-century Barbadians argued that they had become not only an industrious but also a prudent people. For generations, they had taken pride in their reputation for hospitality and generosity. They liked to believe that the "hospitable and generous Spirit of most Sugar Planters" in the island exceeded that of "Persons of like Estate or Wealth in Europe" and boasted that "no People on Earth" were "more hospitable to Strangers, kinder to their Friends and Neighbours, and more helpful to the Distressed." No doubt the manifest liberality expressed through this generosity had in earlier and more prosperous times often led them into excesses, which, along with the "*luxurious dissipation*" of the few proprietors wealthy enough to live in Britain, had fastened upon the entire island its undeserved reputation for extravagance and prodigality. In the less flush times of the mid-eighteenth century, however, such excesses, they explained, were "almost quite over." No longer able to live in "*Splendour and Magnificence*," Barbadians had made prudence "the prevailing Principle" of their lives, and the island's advocates praised Barbadian women for their "prudent Behaviour and Oeconomy" and even held them up as a positive counterimage to their frivolous and luxury-loving counterparts in Britain. As

---

[80] [Frere], *Short History*, pp. iv, 2–11; [Robertson], *Detection*, p. 90.

[81] Burke, *Account of European Settlements*, 2:141; [Blenham], *Remarks on Several Acts of Parliament*, p. 124; [Ashley], *British Empire*, p. 26; Weekes, *Barbadoes*, p. 13; [Orderson], Extracts from *Barbados Mercury*, p. 47.

further proof that Barbadians were showing a heightened concern for "Frugality and good Oeconomy," the island's proponents cited the diligence and ingenuity of the planters in adapting to continuing declines in soil fertility. With more careful and intensive cultivation, they had been able through the decades from 1740 to 1780 not merely to keep sugar profits respectable in the face of ever-growing competition from new sugar areas but also to economize further by producing an ever "large[r] portion" of their island's food requirements. In contrast to contemporary Britain, which was widely believed to be fast sliding into an all-consuming luxury, Barbados seemed to be moving in precisely the opposite direction, its inhabitants rapidly coming to terms with the island's economic limitations in ways that, they were persuaded, earned them both credit and reputation.[82]

Barbadians also associated a new emphasis upon self-control and moderation with this increased attention to industry and prudence. They acknowledged that they were "of a more volatile and lively Disposition" than Englishmen who remained at home, a phenomenon they attributed to climate and culture. At the same time that the warm temperatures of the island put their "Animal Spirits . . . in a high Flow," patterns of child rearing put few inhibitions upon the will. In particular, as Griffith Hughes explained, "Children, in these *West-India* Islands, are, from their Infancy, waited upon by Numbers of Slaves, who . . . are obliged to pay them unlimited Obedience; and . . . when they have thus their favourite Passions nourished with such indulgent Care, it is no Wonder, that by Degrees they acquire . . . an overfond and self-sufficient Opinion of their own Abilities, and so became impatient, as well as regardless, of the Advice of others." By the 1750s, however, Barbadians were suggesting that their traditional volatility had been transformed into a wholly benign and "cultivated Levity." Whatever might be the case in Britain's other Caribbean colonies, the "Liveliness and Activity" usually found among people resident in warm climates had gradually come to be expressed in Barbados through a warm and relaxed sociability, "a great Deal of good Nature," and a degree of self-control that enabled people, blacks as well as whites, to exhibit "most excellent Fronts" even in the most trying circumstances. Notwithstanding their straitened economic conditions, these admirable qualities in turn enabled

---

[82] Hughes, *Natural History*, p. 9; [Robertson], *Detection*, pp. 3, 53; Weekes, *Barbadoes*, pp. 16–19, 50; Blenman, *Remarks on Several Acts of Parliament*, p. 125; [Frere], *Short History*, pp. 60, 112–13, 116–17; [Alleyne], *Remarks upon a Book*, pp. 15, 33; Belgrove, *Treatise*, p. 45; Samuel Martin, *An Essay on Plantership*, 6th ed. (Antigua, 1767), pp. ix–xi; *American Husbandry*, pp. 439–41; [Orderson], Extracts from *Barbados Mercury*, p. 126.

Barbadians to preserve "that antient British hospitality, for which Great Britain [itself] was once so deservedly famed."[83]

Indeed, the message emanating from Barbados during the third quarter of the eighteenth century was that the colony had finally become what Ligon, a century earlier, had urged: a place where people "of middle earth" could "find moderate delights, with moderate labour." They had not become passively servile or cowardly. Their frequent battles with royal governors during the first half of the century had demonstrated that they could behave "with the honest Freedom" of Englishmen. Even more so, their behavior during the Seven Years' War, when "Barbadians bore no inconsiderable share in the glorious events which [then] distinguished the British arms," showed that they would, "like good Subjects . . . and Men of Honour," act with "Bravery and Gallantry in Defense of their Properties and Liberties" whenever it became necessary to do so. That they were, however, a fundamentally quiet people who eschewed contention and whose earlier public dissensions had been primarily the result of the malicious behavior of "oppressive rapacious governors" seemed to be fully proved by the "revival of unanimity and public spirit" in the mid-1730s under Lord Howe and again for a quarter-century beginning in 1747 under a succession of "quiet, easy governor[s]." By pursuing a "disinterested and truly patriotic Conduct" and behaving with "*Prudence* and *Uprightness*," Henry Grenville, Charles Pinfold, and William Spry each went "through his Office without a Murmur" as the colony "continued in great tranquility."[84]

As part of their increasingly positive identity, Barbadians also began to stress the extent to which their "little Spot" was "not without Capacities that would bid fair for the highest Rewards even in *England*." To be sure, they had produced only one Christopher Coddrington, who remained by "far the richest production and most shining ornament Barbadoes ever had." They also lamented that too many of their young had misspent educations that left them "[in] capable of serving their Country or themselves to purpose" and that Coddrington College had never, even as late as the 1770s, fulfilled the intentions of its founder. Yet as proof of the contention

[83] Hughes, *Natural History*, pp. 9–13; Weekes, *Barbadoes*, pp. 22, 43–44, 47, 50; [Orderson], Extracts from the *Barbados Mercury*, pp. 18, 47; [Frere], *Short History*, p. 113; Singleton, *General Description*, pp. 5, 19, 124; *The Life and Adventures of James Ramble*, 2 vols. (London, 1770), 2:217.

[84] Ligon, *True & Exact History*, p. 108; Burke, *Account of European Settlements*, 2:133, 143; Singleton, *General Description*, p. 158; [Keimer], *Caribbeana*, 1:69, 2:90–91, 155, 176; [Frere], *Short History*, pp. 20–26, 59–74; Hughes, *Natural History*, p. 9; Weekes, *Barbadoes*, p. 16; [Duke], *Some Memoirs*, Appendix, p. 15; [Orderson], Extracts from the *Barbados Mercury*, p. 94; *Universal History*, 41:116, 181, 206; [Alleyne], *Remarks upon a Book*, pp. 7, 9–10, 23–30, 55, 76.

that "few of the Youth of other Countries" responded to disciplined educational training "better than our *Creoles*," Barbadians cited many of their offspring in Britain who served "with great Applause in several Posts and Offices of the Government" and made "as good a Figure in the Regiment, on the Bench, at the Bar, and in the Practice of Physick, as any . . . that were born and bred in *England*" itself. Moreover, despite this early drain of talent, Barbados still had many men "with no small Share of Useful Learning, and Knowledge in Trade" and politics. "For near a century and a half," they pointed out, the island had always had "as able and honest representatives" and other local public officials "as . . . any [British] colony could afford."[85]

To some extent, this affirmative self-image was mitigated by a continuing awareness that Barbados was still one of the "remote Parts of the *British* Dominions," an essentially "dull Part of the World" where there were such limited opportunities to excel that fame could but rarely acquire "the power of conferring dignity, or of sounding her golden trumpet." But if, for Barbadians, the theater of "GLORY, VIRTUE, [and] FAME" remained in Britain, they more and more after 1750 began to depict Barbados as a rural Arcadia, "a second Paradise" whose "Happy inhabitants" lived retired lives in "peace and harmony," affluence, and "social joy," without either the fickle prospects of fame or the "Debauch[ery], lewd riot, and disorder" to be found in Britain. Never before had Barbadians revealed so "warm and Partial an attachment" to "*this dear little Spot of our Nativity.*" Not since the very first generations had they manifested such a fulsome appreciation of their island's beauty, which, they emphasized, was a combination of art as well as nature. If Barbados had initially been nature's "darling spot," its polite and industrious proprietors had managed, by art, to turn it into a cultivated garden. Comparable to certain "celebrated" places in the Mediterranean, they announced, it presented the traveler with "most inviting prospect[s]," in which "the Plantations[, themselves] . . . amazingly beautiful, [were] interspersed at little distances from each other, and adorned with Fruits of various Colours; some [being] spread out in fine and open Lawns, in others the waving Canes bowed gently to the Wind from hanging Mountains; while the continual motion of the Sugar-Mills dispersed in every part, and working as it were in Concert, enlivened the engaging scene." An island thus abounding "in culture, in people and [in] riches" and characterized by such extraordinary "stability and surety," Barbadians asserted proudly, certainly had to be "a Likeness of what *Eden* was." In the process of turning

---

[85] [Keimer], *Caribbeana*, 2:93; *American Husbandry*, p. 451; [Robertson], *Detection*, pp. 53–54; Hughes, *Natural History*, p. 9; [Frere], *Short History*, p. 86; *Universal History*, 41:201.

Barbados into "another Paradise," the "lovely Eden of the western isles," its generous and polite proprietors had also boosted it to "the first rank among the best regulated colonies" and made it "a model for" Britain's "other islands."[86]

In thus depicting Barbados as a cultivated British overseas society and as a place of blissful retirement, Barbadians largely glossed over the fact that from two-thirds to fourth-fifths of their society was composed of black slaves. Indeed, perhaps because Barbadian whites were far more numerous, they, in pointed contrast to their counterparts in Jamaica, displayed in their literature comparatively little interest in the black population of their island. Griffith Hughes, who provided the most systematic and sympathetic account of "the Manners and Customs of these Negroes," even apologized to his readers for the "Digression." But the spread of antislavery sentiment in Britain after 1750 forced white Barbadians to realize that a "state of slavery naturally" filled "an European mind with ideas of pity and detestation" and provided "a plausible objection against those countries that[, like Barbados,] admit it." Contending that "the notions which generally prevail in *Europe*" about slaves were "very erroneous," they asserted, in what would become a conventional proslavery argument, that the institution actually represented "a redemption of them" from a far more barbaric form of slavery "in their own country" to "a milder and more comfortable state of life" in America. "Regularly" fed, clothed, housed, doctored, and allowed time and space to cultivate their own fruits and vegetables and raise their own small animals, slaves in Barbados, according to their masters, not only lived with less care and "in much less indigence" than "the poor inhabitants of many European countries," including even Ireland, but also were able to acccumulate some property of their own.

At the same time, apologists for Barbadian slavery suggested that labor discipline among slaves was "not . . . so severe" as that exerted over British seamen and soldiers and that the slaves' ignorance of European ideas of liberty "in a great measure" both alleviated "their unhappiness" and added "to their content." One measure of the mildness of Barbadian slavery, they thought, was in the wide latitude enjoyed by slaves in the continued practice of African religion and culture. Although Barbadian whites admitted that the early settlers had opposed Quaker efforts to Christianize the slaves,

---

[86] [Keimer], *Caribbeana*, 1:62, 346, 2:94, 199; Samuel Martin, *An Essay on Plantership*, 6th ed. (Antigua, 1767), pp. vi–vii; Wynne, *General History*, 2:505; Weekes, *Barbadoes*, pp. 13–14, 21, 55, 59, 61, 63; Singleton, *General Description*, pp. 16–18, 123–29; Hughes, *Natural History*, pp. 1, 23; Richard Gardiner, *An Account of the Expedition to the West Indies . . .* (London, 1759), p. 9; Jeffreys, *West-India Atlas*, p. 20; *Universal History*, 41:201–211; [Orderson], Extracts from *Barbados Mercury*, p. 79.

they argued that by the mid-eighteenth century baptism was available to all those who wanted it. That more slaves had not converted, they explained, was attributable to their continued attachment to their own religion, an attachment that was so strong that some thought "it would be impossible [ever] to convert them." Indeed, as Hughes pointed out, they were so "tenaciously addicted" not just to the religion but to all "the Rites, Ceremonies, and Superstitions of their own Countries, particularly in their Plays, Dances, Music, Marriages, and Burials" that even creole slaves could not "be intirely weaned from these Customs."[87]

Notwithstanding the persistence of such Africanisms among slaves, a further argument of white Barbadians was that over time their slaves had become far better adjusted to slavery. Already by 1740, nearly two-thirds of the slaves were creoles and "as much *Barbadians* as the Descendants of the first Planters." "Now . . . habituated to the intercourse of Europeans," white Barbadians suggested, slaves no longer "need[ed] such a strict Hand to be held over them as their Ancestors did." That Barbados was "not so subject now, as formerly, to the insurrections of negroes" could only be explained by the fact that so "many of them" had been "born upon the island, and [were, therefore,] entirely reconciled to their state." One observer in 1755 even thought that in the event of enemy "invasion[,] 10 to 12,000 able negroes" could be safely armed and would willingly join in the defense of the colony. Already all of the drummers and trumpeters in the militia, numbering one hundred in all, were blacks. Hughes even suggested that as a result of prolonged contact the whites were developing a greater appreciation for the capacities of blacks, many of the most able of whom had been elevated to positions as artisans or domestic servants, and were recognizing that the blacks' alleged lack of aptitude in some areas was the result not of a "Want of natural Ability" but of a "Depression of their Spirits by Slavery" itself.[88]

Ultimately, however, Barbadians could not deny that even in Barbados slavery often tended to brutalize human nature. This was all the more obvious because, as Hughes remarked, the "great Lenity" extended to slaves by those masters who were "influenced by the Principles of Humanity, and the Fear of God," soon wore "the Edge of Savageness away" and rendered the lives of slaves more bearable and the slaves themselves more docile. But Hughes had to admit that too many masters were so "unpolished in their

---

[87] Hughes, *Natural History*, pp. 15, 17; [Frere], *Short History*, pp. 31, 124–25; *Universal History*, 41:207, 209; Samuel Martin, *A Short Treatise on the Slavery of Negroes, in the British Colonies* (Antigua, 1775), pp. 3–8.

[88] Oldmixon, *British Empire*, 2d ed., 2:12; Hughes, *Natural History*, pp. 8, 14–16; [Frere], *Short History*, p. 11; *Universal History*, 41:207; Hall, *General Account*, pp. 23–24; [Alleyne], *Remarks upon a Book*, pp. 52–53.

Manners, and insatiable for Riches" as to make the lot of their slaves extremely onerous. Indeed, as he affirmed, "hard Labour, and often the Want of Necessaries" annually "destroy[ed] a greater Number" of slaves than were "bred up" in the island, an outcome that Edmund Burke denounced as an "annual murder of several thousands." Too many masters, as Burke complained, still thought of their slaves as "a sort of beasts, and without souls." To improve the lot of slaves and their own reputation as a people, several Barbadians exhorted all masters to pattern themselves after those benign patriarchs among them who always treated their slaves with "Justice, temperance, patience, and fortitude."[89]

The contention that slavery in Barbados was becoming an ever more benign and acceptable institution was, of course, at once both a plea for exemption from the moral reproach inherent in the emerging antislavery movement and an expression of the uneasy hope that the island no longer had reason to fear destruction at the hands of its slaves. These hopes to the contrary notwithstanding, however, the numerical predominance of blacks over whites and the continuing degradations of slavery prevented Barbadians from ever putting entirely to rest their longstanding fears of servile revolt, and those fears became strikingly obvious whenever the colony's white proprietors felt exposed. Slavery might have been one of the primary sources of economic power and prosperity in Barbados and other British sugar colonies; as Burke pointed out, however, the exaggerated alarms precipitated by the "news of any petty armament in the West Indies" was "demonstrative proof" that it also made those colonies unusually weak. In the case of Barbados, this weakness deeply affected its relationship with Britain. During the 1760s and 1770s, when they first began to fear that the metropolitan government might respond to the growing antislavery movement by abolishing slavery in the colonies, Barbadians were outraged at the very thought of a course of action that was so heedless of their property and safety. But their resentment was mitigated by an acute awareness of their dependence upon the metropolis for protection against their own slaves. Through the middle decades of the eighteenth century this growing sense of dependence found an outlet in profuse professions of loyalty that emphasized the extent to which Barbadians had "always preserved a uniform and steady attachment to Great Britain."[90]

Whether its vaunted loyalty was merely a cloak for passivity and weak-

[89] Hughes, *Natural History*, pp. 14, 16–18; Burke, *Account of European Settlements*, 2:148–49, 152–54; Weekes, *Barbadoes*, pp. 33, 56–58; Hall, *General Account*, pp. 64–65; Singleton, *General Description*, pp. 153–54; Martin, *Essay on Plantership*, pp. xv–xvi.

[90] Burke, *Account of European Settlements*, 2:155–57; [Frere], *Short History*, pp. iv, 35, 124–25; Weekes, *Barbadoes*, p. 16; Hughes, *Natural History*, p. 9; [Orderson], Extracts from the *Barbados Mercury*, pp. 5, 10, 97; Martin, *Short Treatise*, pp. 10–12.

ness was a question that, much to the island's embarrassment, was powerfully raised by its behavior during the crisis over the Stamp Act in 1765–
1766. While almost all of the other colonies were actively resisting that
measure, the Barbadian Assembly, alone among the legislatures of the
older British American colonies, contented itself with entering a "dutiful
representation" against the act in a letter from its committee of correspondence to the island's agent in London. Although the committee complained
of the act as a "deprivation of our *old and valuable rights*," it emphasized that
the island had "submitted, with all obedience, to the act of Parliament" out
of "a *principle of loyalty* to our King and Mother Country," condemned the
"violent spirit raised in the North American colonies against this act," and
characterized North American behavior as "*REBELLIOUS opposition . . . to*
authority." Although the committee subsequently decided to omit the word
rebellious from the version that was actually sent to London, the initial
draft found its way to North America, where reaction was swift and negative. In *An Address to the Committee of Correspondence of Barbados*, the
Pennsylvania lawyer John Dickinson both denounced Barbadians for having at once "cast a most high and unprovoked censure on a gallant, generous, loyal people" and raised questions about the legitimacy of Barbadian
claims to an identity as men and Englishmen. By submitting to the detestable Stamp Act, Dickinson charged, the Barbadians had reduced themselves "to the miserable dilemma of making a choice between two of the
meanest characters—of those who *would be slaves* from *inclination*, tho they
pretend to love liberty—and of those who *are dutiful* from fear, tho they pretend to love submission." Refusing to believe that any people would actually choose to be slaves, Dickinson concluded that Barbadians were "*loyal*
and obedient, as you call yourselves, *because you apprehend you can't safely be*
otherwise." By suggesting that this preference for safety over liberty could
only be the product of frightened "dreams of submission," Dickinson associated Barbadian behavior with that which was conventionally regarded as
more appropriate to women than to men. Such "unmanly timidity," he
declared, belonged "not to *Britons*, or [to] their true sons."[91]

For "Gentlemen, and the Descendants of Britons" to be thus "painted as
Slaves prostrate in the Dirt" was unbearable, and Barbadian leaders rushed
to defend themselves in three separate pamphlets, including one written by
the Speaker of the Assembly, John Gay Alleyne. Though one of the authors criticized the committee for the "doubting, pausing, and hesitating"

[91] "A Letter from the Committee of Correspondence in Barbados, to their Agent in London" [April 1766], in *The Writings of John Dickinson*, ed. Paul Leicester Ford (Philadelphia,
1895), pp. 254–56; Dickinson, *An Address to the Committee of Correspondence in Barbados*
(Philadelphia, 1766), in ibid., pp. 259, 265–68, 275–76.

tone of its protest and admitted that Dickinson had to some extent written with "the Voice of Truth," the contention of these works was that the Barbadian response to the Stamp Act by no means deserved to be "branded . . . as slavish and detestable." Indeed, so far from constituting "a *voluntary and timid Submission to Slavery*," it had, according to Alleyne, been "founded on the wisest Policy, without being in the least open to any Kind of Censure for an unmanly Fear." Yet Alleyne admitted that the character of the Barbadian response had been determined by the island's weakness. Whereas "North America, boundless in its Extent of Territory, and formidable in its Numbers," had sufficient "Resources of Empire within itself" to be "*fearless* of the Consequences of Resistance," Barbados was only "a small Island, containing only a Handful of [free] Men." In "struggling for the Liberties she demanded," the former "might possibly have arrived at a State of Independence." But Barbados, "a well cleared . . . little Spot" with "no Woods, no Back-Settlements to retreat to," Alleyne declared, "could only . . . have *suffered* by a Revolt." Highly vulnerable to naval attack and dependent on the outside world for supplies of food, clothing, and the slave labor necessary to produce its principal export, Barbados "could not so much as exist without the constant Protection and Support of some superior State." Thus condemned "ever to be dependant," Barbadians could expect nothing from a more spirited resistance than the loss of the liberties they already enjoyed and "the Horror of an *unavoidable Subjection*." Though Alleyne hinted darkly at "other Considerations . . . arising out of Circumstances of Distress and Hazard from within" that tempered Barbadian opposition, he left it to the Reverend Kenneth Morrison, rector of St. James Parish, to make an explicit connection between the moderate character of that opposition and the Barbadians' longstanding fears of servile revolt.[92]

"To resist *one* Evil, with not only the Hazard, but the Certainty, of bringing down *more* and *greater* Evils on our Heads," Barbados's defenders thus argued, was "both absurd and frantick." They agreed that the Stamp Act was oppressive. But they could not, they insisted, permit oppression to rob them "of their Senses, because if it had, *that* must have exposed them to be robbed of every Thing else." "Too weak to succeed by any Thing but pacific Arguments," Barbadians in resisting the Stamp Act thus had to eschew "an *active Courage*" and gain "by *Policy* what we wanted in *Strength*." For "a small and helpless Colony" to express its objections "with some Reserve

<hr />

[92] [John Gay Alleyne], *A Letter to the North American, on Occasion of his Address to the Committee of Correspondence in Barbados* (Barbados, 1766), pp. 9–12, 15, 23, 27, 39, 46; A Native of Barbados, *Candid Observations on Two Pamphlets lately published . . .* (Barbados, 1766), pp. 6, 11; [Kenneth Morrison], *An Essay Towards the Vindication of the Committee of Correspondence in Barbados* (Barbados, 1766), pp. 4, 10, 18.

and Modesty" was only a testimony to the "*good Sense* and *just Discernment*" of its representatives. If such measures had failed, Alleyne assured his readers, "some other Means should then have been resolved upon for our Relief." But he insisted that "those Means would have had nothing of *Violence* in them." "Rash, fool-hardy" conduct was no longer consistent with the Barbadian character. "Common *prudence*" and persuasion, not violence, was the Barbadian way. Contending that the "English Nation" had "long been celebrated" not only for its "Love of Justice, and . . . Love of Liberty" but also for its "Moderation" and insisting that the "Sons of the Parent have a Right to imitate [*all*] her Virtues," the defenders of Barbados denied that "a dutiful Submission to lawful Authority" could ever be "thought . . . to indicate any Inclination to Slavery." In direct challenge to Dickinson's suggestion that they had become slavish through fear, they praised themselves as exhibiting "two of the most *virtuous* Characters, — of those who are unwilling to part with any of their civil Rights, though they will not easily be prevailed upon to throw off their Allegiance, — and of those who can shew themselves to be dutiful on Principle, though they will not yield, without a proper Remonstrance, to Oppression."[93]

By thus turning their defenses of Barbadian behavior during the Stamp Act crisis from an apology for their own timidity to a celebration of their own prudence and realism, Barbadians adroitly used this episode both to sharpen and to reinforce the deepening image of themselves as a people among whom moderation was "the Prevailing Principle." Disdaining "the Rashness of the Mob, and all unlawful Opposition to legal Authority," they told themselves that, in marked contrast to colonists on the American continent, they understood that genuine British liberty, like true virtue, was "found as far from an unbridled Freedom, as from downright Slavery" and interpreted their steady attachment to Britain as an example of this middle way. Indeed, in retrospect their wisdom in contenting themselves with "remonstrating against" the Stamp Act while "trusting to the equity of the British legislature" to repeal it as soon as "its pernicious tendency" had been pointed out seemed both obvious and appropriate. Yet some Barbadians found it difficult to accept this reading of the incident. Pointing out that even the smaller Leeward Islands, who were in no better "Condition to resist" than Barbados, had "sent home spirited Remonstrances" against the Stamp Act, they felt ashamed that "Barbados alone bore the Tyranny with Patience, and Resignation, and without Complaint" and that when its legislature finally did object it did so in an "abject whining Letter to the

<hr />

[93] [Alleyne], *Letter to the North American*, pp. 10–11, 13, 22, 27, 30–31, 41–42; [Morrison], *Essay Towards the Vindication*, pp. 9, 18, 20, 26; *Candid Observations*, p. 36.

Agent" rather than in a "manly and becoming Remonstrance" to the king.[94]

During the 1770s, Barbadians continued to explain their failure to follow the lead of the rebellious North American colonies in terms of their prudence, a prudence arising both out of a recognition of their weakness and dependence upon Britain and out of their acceptance of their obligation to "submit without Contention to every legal Ordinance of our Mother Country." Precisely because they had to be thus "content to look tamely on" while patriots elsewhere had "gloriously struggled for and saved the Liberty of America," Barbadians, from the Stamp Act crisis through the end of the American Revolution, remained peculiarly sensitive to any suggestion that they were less than fully devoted to British liberty. In view of their claims to be true sons of Britain, they could scarcely have done otherwise. Thus, in the late 1760s when Henry Frere, a member of the Barbados Council, seemed in his *Short History* to be seizing every opportunity to throw "cold Water . . . upon the bright Flame of . . . [Barbadian] Patriotism" by denigrating "every effort of Liberty" by the "Representatives of the People" against the colony's many "*venal, arbitrary, and oppressive*" governors, John Gay Alleyne felt compelled to denounce his work as an inaccurate and misleading effort to associate Barbadians with "a Doctrine of the most abject and undistinguishing Submission to our Governors" and as a rank "Apology" for power. In his own counterhistory, Alleyne gave special attention to those many "great Patriot[s]" in Barbados history epitomized by Speaker Samuel Farmer, who during the Restoration had suffered imprisonment in both Barbados and London for "no other" than urging "the Rights of an Englishman in his Country's Cause." If they could not follow the lead of the continental colonies in the late 1770s and early 1780s, however, Barbadians could—and did—engage in a spirited resistance to what they took to be a series of efforts by metropolitan officials to abridge the island's long traditions of self-government, and this renewal of the contention that had characterized the island for virtually all of the first half of the eighteenth century helped to assure its inhabitants that they could still mount a "manly" defense of liberty.[95]

"Little England"

During its first eight decades, Barbados had acquired fame as a colony that in proportion to its size exceeded all others in terms of its population,

[94] *Candid Observations*, p. 36; [Alleyne], *Letter to the North American*, pp. 32, 47; [Frere], *Short History*, pp. 75–76; [Orderson], *Extracts from the Barbados Mercury*, pp. 49, 65–66, 90.
[95] [Orderson], *Extracts from the Barbados Mercury*, pp. 49, 78–79; [Alleyne], *Remarks upon a Book*, pp. 7, 8–10, 15, 17, 76; S.H.H. Carrington, "West Indian Opposition to British Policy: Barbadian Politics, 1774–82," *Journal of Caribbean History* 17 (1982):26–49.

sugar production, and wealth. Despite a malignant disease environment, the harshness of its servile labor system, and the frequency of slave revolts, its inhabitants, many of whom derived from established English families, acquired a reputation for being a civilized, generous, and tranquil people who gloried in the status of Barbados as England's most valuable colony and wanted nothing more than metropolitan recognition of their own English-ness. After 1710, as the Barbadian economy became less robust in compar-ison with those of newer sugar colonies and the island had to endure a series of what it regarded as rapacious royal governors and other officials, its in-habitants developed a reputation as a passionate and contentious people who, incapable of adjusting to the new economic realities in which they found themselves, continued to live in idle luxury and extravagance heed-less of both their own and their island's welfare.

By 1740, however, this negative identity had already begun to improve. Increasingly, between 1740 and 1780, Barbados came to be seen as a settled society whose members, whites and blacks, had come to terms with them-selves and their environment with extremely positive results. No longer ex-travagant and idle, whites had retained their good-natured sociability and liberality at the same time that they had also learned to become more fru-gal, industrious, and moderate in their behavior, while the black popula-tion, heavily creole, reportedly had become both far less restless and more acculturated to white society. With both population groups enjoying better health, Barbados contrasted sharply and favorably with Britain's other Car-ibbean colonies in terms of its proportionately greater white population, the comparative mildness of its slave system, and, increasingly after 1750, the tranquility of its public life. Proud of their own civilized life style and the cultivated beauty of their social landscape, white Barbadians both cel-ebrated their strong attachment to Britain and exhibited a deeper appreci-ation for the society they and their ancestors had created in this "Eternal Summer Country." Alone among Britain's Caribbean colonies, Barbados seemed to be overcoming the dehumanizing and deanglicizing effects of the tropics. To be sure, the rise of antislavery in England, with its prescriptive denigration of all slave societies as unEnglish and the colony's passive re-sponse to the Stamp Act, raised profound questions about the Barbadians' devotion to liberty, that essential attribute of true sons of Britain. At the same time, however, those developments also pushed Barbadians to focus more and more upon moderation as their principal defining characteristic as a people.[96]

[96] Joshua Steele to Mr. More, May 24, 1785, in D.G.C. Allan, "Joshua Steele and the Royal Society of Arts," *Jo. Barbados Mus. and Hist. Soc.* 22 (1955):95.

In the decades after 1780, Barbados entered a new era that pushed its inhabitants ever farther in these same directions. The diminution of contact with the continental colonies in the wake of their independence and the intensification of antislavery in Britain further emphasized Barbadian vulnerability and dependence upon the metropolis and drove the colony to an ever greater emphasis upon moderation as the central ingredient of its identity. Not that Barbadians, like other Britons, could not be "high-spirited" in defense of liberty whenever such behavior was required. But Barbadians took greatest pride in their cautious and disciplined moderation. Some Britons, for whom Barbados represented their first encounter with the Caribbean, were impressed by the disheveled appearance of the island, the indolence, profligacy, and provinciality of its inhabitants, and the looseness of its society, and as the end of slavery approached, Barbadians themselves worried about the sudden decline in the size of the island's white population, which during the first three decades of the nineteenth century began to fall substantially for the first time since the late seventeenth century.

In their favor, however, Barbadians had long since adjusted to their less abundant economic circumstances. If other, larger, and more recently settled sugar colonies were "more prolific," they alone could emphasize their island's standing as the "most ancient" British Caribbean colony, in the words of the British traveler George Pinckard, "the venerable and decrepit parent of the race." From the antiquity of Barbados, Pinckard reported, Barbadians "assume[d] a consequence," a "sense of distinction," that was "strongly manifested in the sentiment conveyed by the vulgar expression so common in the island—'neither Charib, nor Creole, but true Barbadian.' " That sentiment, according to Pinckard, was shared "even by the slaves, who proudly arrogate a superiority above the negroes of the other islands! Ask one of them if he was imported, or is a Creole, and he immediately replies—'*Me neder Chrab, nor Creole, Massa!—me troo Barbadian born.*' "

The positive sense of being a Barbadian implied in this expression derived from the feeling that, in comparison with other British Caribbean colonies, Barbados was a place of settled regularity and its inhabitants a people distinguished by "the natural mildness and benignity of their tempers." This last quality was said by contemporaries to be manifest in many areas of Barbadian behavior: in the growing gentleness of Barbadian society and the perpetuation of the liberal hospitality and easy sociability of Barbadians of all races, in the relative lenity of the Barbadian slave system, and in the continuing warmth of the Barbadian attachment to Great Britain. "Adorned with many" people "of worth and humanity," Barbados seemed to be remarkable both for its gardenlike appearance and its "general confidence between the whites and the blacks." Extolling the status of their island as "the most ancient, humane and polished West Indian colony ever possessed by the freest nation upon earth," Barbadians had begun by the first years of the nineteenth century to refer to the colony as "Little England." The use of this particular phrase as the one that best encapsulated the identity Barbadians had achieved after almost two centuries of colonization would have been enormously pleasing to all generations of white Barbadians that had gone before.[97]

[97] John Poyer, *the History of Barbados* . . . (London, 1808), pp. 136, 216; William Dickson, *Letters on Slavery* . . . (London, 1789), pp. v, 93, 145, and *Mitigation of Slavery in two Parts* (London, 1814), p. 441; Daniel McKinnen, *A Tour through the British West Indies, in the Years 1802 and 1803* . . . (London, 1804), p. 23; Henry Nelson Coleridge, *Six Months in the West Indies in 1825* (London, 1826), p. 135; George Pinckard, *Notes on the West Indies* . . . , 3 vols. (London, 1806), 2:75–76. McKinnen seems to have been the first person to report the use of the phrase "Little England" to refer to Barbados.

8 ❧ Afterword: From Identity to Independence

Anthony Pagden and Nicholas Canny

THE MEANS by which the settler communities of the Atlantic world came to form, fabricate, or shape their identities were, as the essays in this volume make clear, highly individual ones. The contrast between the experiences of the English and the Spaniards and of the French and the Portugese may indeed seem more stark than any of the more obvious similarities. The parallels that do emerge often seem to owe more to the settlers' share in a common European culture than to any similarity in their experience of colonization. There is, of course, no reason to suppose that there was in the Atlantic, or had ever been in any other place, a single or typical colonial venture, for as Volney (perhaps still the most acute observer of the colonial process) recognized in the 1780s, it would be a "fanciful mistake . . . to describe as a new and virgin people a gathering of inhabitants of old Europe."[1] But if there was no common venture, the essays in this volume have clearly demonstrated that there was a set of broadly similar attitudes and a number of similar local conditions. Here we shall examine some of these attitudes and suggest what implications they might have for the history of the independence movements of the nineteenth and twentieth centuries.

In the first place, for all the colonists, there was the inescapable fact of their exile. All were compelled, sooner or later, to come to terms with their continuing absence from a land that they often persisted, even into the third or fourth generation, in regarding as their true "home," their "mother country." The illusion of proximity that such names as New Spain, New England, and New France afforded, the implicit claim that it was possible to export to other places not only the outward manifestations of a culture but an entire political community—a belief still fostered by the French government's insistence that Martinique and Guadeloupe are but *departements* of metropolitan France—was ultimately only an illusion. Even the settlers in Ireland, who were geographically far closer to Europe and often preferred to call Britain their "Sister Kingdom," came to recognize that—at least in the early-modern world—where you were very largely determined who you were. The famous outburst of William Molyneux against the idea that Ireland might be a colony ("of all the objections raised against us I take this to

WE WOULD like to thank Geoffrey Hawthorn for his comments on an earlier draft of this paper.
   [1] Constantin-François de Chaseboeuf, comte de Volney, *Tableau du climat et du sol des Etats-Unis* (Paris, 1883), preface.

be the most extravagant; it seems not to have the least foundation or colour from reason or record") was founded only on an administrative distinction. "Do they," he asked of the English monarchs, "use the title of Kings of Virginia, New England or Maryland?" They did not, or at least not consistently, but such distinctions, although not without significance, could do little to establish the status of a territory or its inhabitants.[2] In the end, the fact that all these settler groups had voluntarily abandoned their home countries demanded from them a response more radical than the insistence that the consequence of this move could be offset by building European-style houses in the tropics or wearing breeches in a rain forest. The attempt that all the first colonists made to preserve Old World traditions required a very high degree of imaginative innovation, if only because those traditions were already under serious threat in the metropolitan culture and could not easily survive—and in most cases could not survive at all—in the absence of the institutions and the normative structures that had traditionally sustained them and that *only* the metropolitan culture could provide. "Traditional ends," as Michael Zuckerman puts it, "had . . . to be achieved under novel circumstances by novel means."

Many colonists were conscious that the task in which they were engaged simply had no parallel in Europe's recent past, for they were all, with the exception of the Barbadians, compelled to come to terms with an indigenous population that they had committed themselves, in some degree, to "civilizing"; and they were all, without exception, bound by the prospect of creating a new world in an inhospitable environment. The language of "improvement" might be borrowed from contemporary European discussions on agronomy and accounts of the civilizing process derived from Greco-Roman social theory. But these models could at best offer only a limited purchase on a world that had to be created *ex nihilo* as the kind of place in which *they* could live and yet was not, as Jack Greene rightly insists, in any sense the *tabula rasa* described by so many contemporary observers. Some, like the Quaker William Loddington cited by Greene, made the point that "*England* was once as rugged as *America* and the Inhabitants as blind and barbarous as the *Indians*." But this analogy between the colonists and the founding fathers of their own mother countries had only a limited appeal, since it was difficult for the colonists to cast themselves with any degree of conviction in the role of ancient Romans, if only because, as Greene points out a propos the Barbadians, they relied too heavily upon

---

[2] *The Case of Ireland's Being Bound by Acts of Parliament . . .* (Dublin, 1698), p. 148, quoted by M. I. Finley "Colonies—An Attempt at a Typology," *Transactions of the Royal Historical Society* 26 (1976):187. Finley also cites the perhaps less problematical case of French Algeria which, although indubitably a colony, was also a fully integrated *departement* of France.

"their old country for the standards of what a civilized, improved, society should be." Whatever kind of cultural, social and political world theirs might ultimately turn out to be, it had become clear to all by the second generation that it could not be an accurate image of the world the colonists had left behind. That fact had to be accounted for, and the strategies the colonists used to account for it constituted, at least to begin with, their identity, their perception of who they were.

The processes by which such identities were created were not, however, self-conscious ones. No colonists set out with the *intention* of creating an identity for themselves. Such an ambition would have required the concept of a nation or at least a belief in the possibility of creating new communities based on political, religious, or cultural preferences, and even those who had gone to America in the hope of being able to pursue such preferences rarely saw that hope as constituting their identity.

The possession of an identity also presupposes the existence of a shared set of cultural or social values; and all of these were initially imported from the metropolitan cultures. The history of the formation of identities that are specific to colonial societies is, therefore, the history not of the creation but of the transformation of values. This transformation often took place under duress, for in every case—in New Spain and Brazil, in Ireland and British North America, in New France and in Barbados—self-perception and self-assertion, the recognition of separateness, was initially protective, a device with which the colonists defended themselves from metropolitan contempt. This meant that those identities were very uneven, always incomplete, and at times perilously fragile. In every case it is possible to find both colonists who stressed the difference between their values and those of their mother country and colonists who insisted on the similarities. In a society where the prevailing norms had to be detached from those of another, there could never be any binding consensus on what those norms should be.

Some groups, too, were always more self-aware, more ready to see themselves as independent communities, than others. The most self-aware may indeed have been, as Stuart Schwartz suggests, the blacks and the children of miscegenation, those for whom the colony was the only "mother country." As early as the 1560s a group of mestizos in Peru, claiming that they constituted a separate and truly "American" nation, rebelled against the white government.[3] But with the exception of the mestizo historians mentioned by Anthony Pagden, few such groups were able to give any articulate

[3] H. López Martínez, "Un motín de mestizos en el Perú 1567," *Revista de Indias* 24 (1964):367–81.

expression to their sense of identity until the rebellions of the eighteenth and nineteenth centuries. Like the poor of Europe, we can only know how they perceived themselves through the necessarily incomplete and partial accounts of others, and then only on those infrequent occasions when they succeeded in making their voices heard. No culture, no nation or society possesses or—except perhaps at the level of the extended family or phratry—has ever possessed a single and comprehensive identity. It would be as vain to look for it in contemporary France, Italy, or Germany. The essays in this volume have concentrated almost entirely upon the elites because it is only these that have left a clear record of their perceptions of themselves and the societies in which they lived. An identity—the understanding of what, culturally, one is—like an ideology, is frequently something imposed.

But, of course, no one group, however eloquent, can plausibly claim to speak for an entire community; and when in the eighteenth and nineteenth centuries the elites of these colonies came to create independent nations, they were, of necessity, imposing upon a large number of their people an identity and a political culture many of them did not share. In Mexico, for instance, there existed at least two distinct cultures: that of the criollos and their descendants, and that of the Indians and mestizos, whose aspirations first emerged in the Hidalgo-Morelos revolt of 1810 and then again, with more lasting results, in the revolution a hundred years later. In Canada, as Gilles Paquet and Jean-Pierre Wallot have shown, the awareness of the presence of distinct and discontinuous identities, even among the elite, prevented the emergence of anything resembling a "Canadian" identity until well into the nineteenth century, if indeed then.

II

No matter how limited, discontinuous, or inchoate the colonists' self-awareness might have been, all of the societies described here did emerge as distinct communities with some recognizable identity. They all came to know, culturally if not always politically, what values they stood for. The Atlantic colonies also have one other feature in common: they all, though in radically different ways and at very different periods in their histories, became independent states. The essays in this volume are explicitly *not* about the origins of independence. It was not our immediate assumption that self-perception or the acquisition of a cultural identity, however conceived, is necessarily part of the process by which colonies make themselves into nations. But the questions of the relationship, necessary or contingent, between identity and independence cannot easily be avoided.

The history of the origin of the independence movements in the Atlantic colonies is a history of the changing, and in most cases deteriorating, relationship between the colonies and their mother countries. So too, of course, are the histories of the emergence of colonial identities. But although these histories are sometimes coterminous and sometimes even identical, there are other times at which they are quite clearly unrelated. A separate identity was not only not a necessary cause for revolt; it was, in most cases, not a cause at all. The growth of an awareness of the difference that separated the colonists from the political and moral values of their metropolitan cultures made it possible for them to create what Benedict Anderson has called "imagined communities," that is, communities that exist not as perceived realities but as part of the individual's cultural or political imagination, if only because "the members of even the smallest nation will never know most of their fellow-members, meet them, or even hear of them, yet in the mind of each lives the image of their community."[4] All the essays in this volume have been attempts to describe the emergence of such images.

This kind of imaginative creation, does not necessarily result in a wish for political self-determination. Most modern nationalist movements, however, have worked with the assumption that a community can only acquire a true identity through *political* control over its own affairs and that by implication, at least, no nation is complete before it possesses both cultural and political autonomy. This explains the great emphasis placed upon the political role of culture in most of the New States in Africa and Asia and in such postrevolutionary societies as the Soviet Union. By the middle of the nineteenth century the nation-state had become the only acceptable frame of reference for the ambitions of colonized peoples, whatever origins those ambitions might have had. Self-perception had become a question of nationhood and of very little else. Cultural, political, religious, and even racial (or at least tribal) characteristics were all perceived in national terms. Because of this insistence on the primacy of the nation-state, it has often been assumed that earlier independence movements must have followed more or less the same pattern. There are, it is true, some similarities between the African and Asian revolts and the ones in the Atlantic world. Clifford Geertz's description of the formative stage of nationalism as consisting "essentially of confronting the dense assemblage of cultural, racial, local, linguistic categories of self-identification and social loyalties that centuries of uninstructed history had produced with a simple abstract, deliberately constructed, and almost painfully self-conscious concept of polit-

---

[4] B. Anderson, *Imagined Communities: Reflections on the Origin and Spread of Nationalism* (London, 1983), p. 15.

ical enthnicity" will do, *mutatis mutandis*, to describe any of the initial phases in the independence movements in most of the Atlantic colonies.[5] But modern states make far greater cultural demands on their citizens than the monarchies discussed in this volume did. At no time before the nineteenth century was there any clear relationship between self-perception and political independence that was thought to be sufficiently compelling to persuade people to give up their lives for it.

There are also two crucial distinctions between modern nationalist movements in Africa and Asia and those in the Atlantic world in the eighteenth century. The first is obvious: that the colonists who instigated those movements shared a common, if often remote, ancestry with their rulers. They were divided from them by culture, sometimes even by religion and political belief, but never by race. In some cases—for instance, that given by Schwartz of the white Brazilian speaking of his (white) king as "colored like us" or the Mexican criollos' muted claim to be racially descended from the Aztec kings—a language of race may be used to assert the colonist's identification with the land, but that identification remains cultural. When, as with the Hidalgo-Morelos uprising in Mexico, race did become an issue, the effect was to drive the majority of the colonists back into the arms of the metropolitan government. Three of the societies discussed above, Ireland, Canada, and Barbados, did not sever their relationship with their respective mother countries at the turn of eighteenth century precisely because the colonists feared racial conflict far more than they desired independence. In Ireland the prospect of independence, which had seemed appealing in the abstract, was recognized as a dangerous illusion once it became clear that it would be associated with claims to political rights by a seemingly unregenerate Catholic population who vastly outnumbered the settler community in every province except Ulster. This realization explains why the previously restive settler groups acquiesced in the Act of Union in 1801 and why their attachment to this act and to the assertions of Britishness that were associated with it became all the stronger in the second half of the nineteenth century, when the Catholic population began to aspire to independence of their own fashioning. Similarly, the Barbadians remained loyal in 1776, despite continual pressure to join the Revolution, because they were, as Jack Greene has shown, simply too fearful of revolt by the slave population of the island to do anything else. When independence did come to Barbados in 1966 it was, of course, of a kind that would have been unthinkable to the settler community of the

---

[5] "After the Revolution: The Fate of Nationalism in the New States," in Clifford Geertz, *The Interpretation of Cultures* (London, 1975), p. 239.

eighteenth century, not least because it constituted, in effect, the creation of a new and multiracial state. Canada was (if we set aside the brief Dutch presence in Brazil) the only area under discussion to have been colonized by two European powers. For the French, as for the English in Canada, independence might have meant not the creation of a new political community but annexation by a foreign state.

The second factor that distinguished the revolts in the Atlantic world from the nationalist revolutions in Africa and America turns on the revolutionaries' very different concepts of what constituted their political allegiance to the metropolitan power. Nationalism is, in Ernest Gellner's definition, "a theory of political legitimacy which requires that ethnic boundaries should not cut across political ones, and in particular that ethnic boundaries within a given state . . . should not separate the power holders from the rest."[6] This general principle that all people should be ruled by members of their own race and culture has come to be seen as an inalienable political right since the disintegration of the European empires. But of course it too is an appeal to the belief that the nation-state is the only legitimate political community and very close to being the only "natural" one, too. No such concept existed before the nineteenth century, and even if it had it is unlikely that the Atlantic colonists could have been able to make much use of it. Since they were all, if not usurpers, at least quite obviously not autochthonous, they could only make their demands in terms either of claims to some set of political traditions that they shared with the metropolitan culture or, as most were ultimately to do, of claims to a body of natural rights shared by all men everywhere. In early-modern Europe, political authority rested almost exclusively (except where nominally unoccupied territories were involved)[7] upon dynastic claims and such claims rarely took account of culture, national, or linguistic differences. The sovereignty of kings depended upon rights of succession and not upon their affinities with the people over whom they ruled. In a world where individuals were more likely to identify themselves with their village, town, or county and recognize direct allegiance only to their local feudal suzerain, it was perfectly possible for people with long histories of cultural independence and even political self-government—the Catalans, the Bretons, the Milanese, the Neapolitans—to accept the rule of a "foreign" power without complaint.

[6] Ernest Gellner, *Nations and Nationalism* (Oxford, 1983), p. 1.

[7] Spanish and English claims to property rights in America often rested on precisely the assertion that the Americas had, before the arrival of the Europeans, been unoccupied; but these claims were never, of course, employed in the struggle for political independence. See Anthony Pagden, "Dispossessing the Barbarian: The Language of Thomism and the Debate over the Property Rights of the American Indians," in *The Languages of Political Theory in Early-Modern Europe*, ed. Anthony Pagden (Cambridge, 1987).

The colonies in the Atlantic world also developed their identities over a period when their respective mother countries—with the possible exception of England—were in the process of acquiring *their* identities as nations. As Schwartz points out, the patriotism of most Spanish and Portuguese Americans closely resembles Iberian localism. The claim that one was a Mexican or a Brazilian might not, at least before the eighteenth century, have seemed so very different from the claim that one was an Extremaduran or an Alentejan or, more significantly, since Spain itself was divided into several culturally independent and politically semiautonomous kingdoms, an Aragonese or a Navarrese. The complex of attitudes and ideas, modes of behavior, codes of conduct, and styles of living that developed quite rapidly in the colonies came to be seen as the distinguishing features of a *patria* or an autonomous community. The ensuing conflict between the obvious need to explain and defend the differences between this community and the societies of their respective "mother countries" at the moment when those societies were creating their own identities often seemed to the metropolitan governments to be merely further instances of recalcitrant localism.

The defining feature of the new European nation-states was, of course, precisely the monarchs' ambition to reduce regional autonomy and to make loyalty to themselves more binding. The consolidation of the great centralizing absolutist states in France, Spain, Portugal, and, to a more restricted degree, England was, however, far less effective in the colonies than in the provinces. The distances that royal commands had to carry were obviously far greater; the local elites, though hardly more intractable than the European provincial nobility, were, because of their recent creation and obscure social origins, largely inaccessible through the older networks of kin and feudal obligations.

Because of their effective isolation from most of the changes that were taking place in their mother countries and the fact that so many of them had gone to the colonies in the first place to escape from changes that threatened their livelihoods, ambitions, or moral convictions, most colonists clung fiercely to the standards and traditions of their ancestors. The ideal of military service, for instance, which in the more developed areas of western Europe was beginning, even by the end of the sixteenth century, to seem a dangerous anachronism, persisted in Spanish America and Brazil well into the eighteenth century—and military service has been esteemed in the Irish Protestant community into the twentieth century. The fact, noted by Greene, that Barbadians could speak of their island as "a dull part of the world" and claim that "the theatre of Glory, Virtue and Fame" remained in Britain suggests that archaic social attitudes that placed undue stress upon the heroic survived in the Caribbean, even among a people whose wealth derived from commercialized agriculture, in a period when most articulate Europeans and progressive Englishmen in particular were seeking to replace such notions by a belief in the civilizing virtues of commerce and industry. The struggle between Brazilian settlers and Portuguese merchants or between Mexican and Peruvian criollos and seemingly intransigent *peninsulares*, which became one of the triggers of the insurgent movements of the nineteenth century, was not only the clash between the economic concerns of a landed class and a merchant one; it was also a struggle within a society between the self-conscious bearers of ancient traditions and those who held "modern" views concerning the power of the crown, the dignity of commerce, and the nobility of acquired wealth. As late as 1797 Volney wrote of his journey through North America that the continent was largely inhabited by "Frenchmen of the age of Louis XIV who have become half-Indian and . . . Englishmen of the last century."[8]

This is not to say that the Atlantic colonial cultures were only the repositories of seemingly outdated convictions and failed aspirations. They did, of course, change—the essays in this volume are, in part, histories of such changes—but they often did so in ways that were very different from those followed by the metropolitan cultures.

It was the colonists' very inability or unwillingness to register the changes that had taken place in their mother countries that, at the end of the eighteenth century, made so many of them into revolutionaries. The traditional values of one culture, or one generation, may become the revolutionary ideologies of another. When at last the metropolitan governments of England, Spain, and Portugal finally attempted to impose upon their colonies the same degree of central control to which the provinces had long been subjected, it seemed to the colonists that, far from being given what Charles III of Spain called "equality" and "unity" with the mother country, they were, in fact, being deprived of ancient liberties that they possessed by natural right. Like the European provincial nobility, the colonial elites adhered to older contractual principles that had been created precisely to check the ambitions of kings. The American rebels' claims to rights and liberties, although couched "in the restricted language of the rational century," can only be understood, as Bernard Bailyn has demonstrated, "in terms of a continuing belief in original sin and the need for grace," because it was only on those terms that the contract could be under-

---

[8] Quoted in Gilbert Chinard, *Volney et l'Amérique d'apres des documents inedits* (Paris and Baltimore, 1923), pp. 63–66.

stood.[9] For the rebels, the language of contractualism was morally the only valid one, and that language was based upon Magna Carta, English common law, and the Lockean notion that a ruler who had resorted to a "State of War" against his subjects by violating their traditional rights and privileges had reverted to the condition of a beast and might, indeed must, therefore be destroyed "like any other animal."[10] To the English crown, however, such claims seemed only to resuscitate ancient struggles over the nature of sovereignty that, in its own view at least, the crown had long since won. Not, of course, that the ideologues of the American Revolution were wholly wedded to the politics of providentialism. The Enlightenment, and in particular Montesquieu, had given the older languages of liberties and rights a new emphasis. But in the writings of the American revolutionaries, Magna Carta, Coke, Locke, and Montesquieu are all used to substantiate the same argument, that it was the British government that, in its thirst for power, had violated the natural rights of the English in America and had undermined the ancient liberties of the kingdom. A similar set of claims grounded upon an appeal to ancient traditions of the citizen may be found in the declaration of the Spanish American insurgents; only here it is Suárez instead of Locke and the *Siete partidas* in place of Magna Carta.[11]

In such a world the loyalties that bound subject to sovereign were often tenuous affairs—which is why their violation was always treated with such ferocity—and they could without difficulty be reduced, particularly in remote areas, to ceremonial acts of obeisance and simple affirmations of intent. The king's subjects might kill the king's agents and defy his armies while still insisting on their loyalty to his royal, if not his natural, person. The persistent belief that the king's sovereignty did not oblige the citizen to obey the monarch's commands if those seemed to conflict with the interests of the community—that, in the Spanish phrase, the subject must obey but need not necessarily comply—as well as the belief that sovereignty resided uniquely in the person of the king meant, in effect, that loyalty to Spain or France or Portugal or England involved only the surrender of a limited number of political rights to a single institution, the crown, and to the person who, quite literally, embodied it. Sometimes such loyalty could be detached even from this minimal notion, retaining only a residual concept of adherence to the political ideas that an individual monarchy was

[9] Bernard Bailyn, *The Ideological Origins of the American Revolution* (Cambridge, Mass., 1967), p. viii, and on the range of authorities used by the revolutionaries, see pp. 22–54. See also the same author's "Political Experience and Enlightenment Ideas in Eighteenth-Century America," *American Historical Review* 67 (1961–62):339–51.

[10] John Dunn, *The Political Thought of John Locke, an Historical Account of the Argument of the "Two Treatises of Government"* (Cambridge, 1969), pp. 178–79.

[11] See David Brading, *Prophecy and Myth in Mexican History* (Cambridge, 1984), pp. 37–53.

believed to embody. Thus Hidalgo, while vigorously trying to put an end to Spanish rule in Mexico, could still claim to be loyal to Ferdinand; the Canadians were until recently loyal to the British Crown; and Ulster Protestant Loyalists can still see themselves as "Queen's Rebels."[12] Rebellion then was not, or at least not always, the casting off of *foreign* rule. It was the assertion that the rebels had either, as in the case of the Cortés revolt, been released from their natural allegiance by the unnatural behavior of their king or, as in the case of the American Revolution, that they were upholding natural rights and liberties that the metropolitan government had betrayed.

Rebellion against such an authority, even a rebellion aimed at the creation of a new independent society was not, then, so very difficult to imagine. It clearly did not necessitate, as any revolt against a nation state would seem to require, any sense of independent identity on the part of the rebels. Although criollo "patriotism" played a far larger role in the ideologies of the Mexican and to a lesser degree the Peruvian insurgents than it did in that of the English Americans, an identity was certainly not among the social goods demanded by any of the rebels in the American colonies.

But the fact of rebellion and the existence of a set of political and moral convictions that seem to make that rebellion legitimate is too often confused with the usually quite separate activities required in the creation of a new society. Although it might be possible to conceive of legitimate rebellion without possessing any sense of belonging to a separate political culture, it is surely not possible to think in terms of building a new society on radical political lines without doing so. Rebels against any society may begin their revolt in the conviction that, since they are only acting in the interests of preserving traditional and hallowed values, they alone are loyal to that society. But any act of rebellion will eventually alienate rebels from the political culture to which they belong; and when that happens they will, in effect, have acquired an independent identity, if only an identity *as* rebels. Those who support rebellion—certainly those who supported the independence movements in the American colonies—are acutely aware of this fact. The ideology of the American Revolution was a highly complex affair; it could hardly have been foisted upon a society that had no sense that the espousal of such values would make it a political community quite unlike that of the "mother country." The American revolutionaries may have begun by thinking of themselves as Englishmen betrayed by their crown, or at least as American Englishmen—there is every reason to suppose that they did—but they ended their rebellion as Americans. The Eng-

---

[12] David W. Miller, *Queen's Rebels: Ulster Loyalism in Historical Perspective* (Dublin, 1978).

lish in America, the first to rebel, may not, as Zuckerman says, have sought "any larger conception of themselves as an encompassing community," but it is clear that the lineaments of that community existed long before 1776 and that the revolution brought it into being.

This is surely one of the reasons why all the peoples discussed here who rebelled in the eighteenth century attempted to create their new nations as republics. Quite apart from the contemporary conviction that republicanism—however defined—offered the only political society in which it was possible for the individual to lead a truly virtuous life, it was, ultimately at least, impossible for the colonists to imagine reconstructing a European political order in America. By the eighteenth century they had come to recognize that they possessed none of the traditions of that order, nor shared enough of its values, to wish to do so. The exceptions merely had the effect of confirming that distance between the old political world and the new. Dom Pedro I's kingdom in Brazil was made possible only by the translation of the Portuguese crown—and with it a somewhat depleted Portuguese court—to America, and it could not long survive the Portuguese attempt after 1821 to return to the colonial status quo. The short-lived attempts by Augustín de Iturbide in 1822 and in 1864 by the French to create empires in Mexico were similarly only tragic interludes in a process that Bolivar and those like him had seen as the struggle to establish independent republics in place of the old Spanish vice-royalties. For all of these societies Greene's sets of variables, the social and economic goals, the "standards of what a civilized society should be and how its members should behave," and the sense of history, had radically changed. All the Atlantic communities now had different goals, a different understanding of how a civilized society is constituted; and they now had a sense of their own histories as independent communities. This did not mean that an attempted break with the mother country came to be seen as either inevitable or even desirable; but the colonists' ability to perceive themselves as a separate community with a separate culture was one of the factors that gave them the confidence to make the bid for freedom whenever political circumstances dictated that it was in their interest to do so. In this limited sense, the emergence of an identity was a precondition of revolution in the Atlantic colonial world.

❧ Index

CPSIA information can be obtained at www.ICGtesting.com
Printed in the USA
LVOW06s0522100414

381037LV00001B/60/P